Winning with CASE

Managing Modern Software Development

McGraw-Hill, Inc.
New York St. Louis San Francisco Auckland Bogotá Caracas
Lisbon London Madrid Mexico Milan Montreal New Delhi
Paris San Juan São Paulo Singapore Sydney Tokyo Toronto

Winning with CASE

Managing Modern
Software Development

Robert L. Dixon

McGraw-Hill

Notices

Apple® **Macintosh**® **HyperCard**™	Apple Computer, Inc.
IBM® **OS/2**™	International Business Machines Corporation
Simscript®	CACI Inc.
Pro∗Kit™	McDonnell Douglas
IEF™	Texas Instruments, Inc.
Xerox®	Xerox Corporation
Easel™	Interactive Images, Inc.

FIRST EDITION
FIRST PRINTING

© 1992 by **Robert L. Dixon**.
Published by **McGraw-Hill, Inc.**

Printed in the United States of America. All rights reserved. The publisher takes no responsibility for the use of any of the materials or methods described in this book, nor for the products thereof.

Library of Congress Cataloging-in-Publication Data

Dixon, Robert L. (Robert Lee), 1960-
    Winning with CASE : managing modern software development / by Robert L. Dixon.
      p.   cm.
    Includes index.
    ISBN 0-8306-2558-5 (h)
    1. Computer-aided software engineering.   2. Computer software-
-Development—Management.   I. Title.
QA76.758.D58   1991
005.1—dc20   91-20618
                                                                         CIP

For information about other McGraw-Hill materials, call 1-800-2-MCGRAW in the U.S. In other countries call your nearest McGraw-Hill office.

Vice President and Editorial Director: Larry Hager
Book Editor: Marie Bongiovanni
Production: Katherine G. Brown
Book Design: Jaclyn J. Boone   TPR4

To K., who will think she doesn't deserve it.

Contents

Introduction ix
CASE confusion x
Chapter summary xii

1 The CASE arms race 1
CASE for competitive advantage 2
Software changes everything 2
Software in the driver's seat 4
Duty now for the future 6
Wallflowers don't dance 8
Organized competition 9
CASE makes sense today 14

2 The faceless acronym 15
Push-button software machines 18
A spectrum of functionality 21
Automated software development 22
Repository services 37
Methodology support 41
Project management 45
Where CASE ends 46

3 Waiting for the revolution 49
A suite of challenges 50
Strategic business impact 52
Management support 53
Quality 57
Productivity 62
Weeds among the flowers 69

4 Forging an alliance — 73
Beyond hardware   73
Integration's competitive advantage   79
Barriers to integration   83
Integration strategies   86
How to proceed   92

5 Diving into the method pool — 95
Method in the madness   96
Married to the methodology   97
The quality directive   98
Roping the wild methodology   98
The importance of technique   106
Diving into the method pool   109
Pool service   112
Summary   116

6 Living in the neutral zone — 119
The broad face of change   119
Political skill changes   121
Seven developer nightmares   122
Triggering transition   125
Change is not enough   127
Develop a shared vision   130
Make change personally beneficial   134
Breaking the news   138
Transition central   141
Making change a way of life   142
Summary   148

7 Planning for the software factory — 157
Anarchy's cure   152
A plan for the planners   155
The IS architecture   159
Goals of strategic planning   165

8 Designing an IS architecture — 177
Choosing a planning method   178
An IS planning case study   180
Working the plan   210

9 Reengineering the development process — 211
Why analyze?   211
CASE for process reengineering   212
An analysis methodology   214

10	**Retooling the software factory**	**229**
	Cooperative CASE tool selection 230	
	A CASE evaluation methodology 231	
11	**Shaping the method pool**	**267**
	Building the method pool 268	
12	**Measuring the splash**	**291**
	Poolside metrics 292	
13	**Stacking the deck**	**305**
	Don't burn the house down 306	
	Deciding where to fly 309	
	Making everyone a winner 311	
	Project management for everyone 312	
14	**Spreading the word**	**331**
	Develop a training program 331	
	Informal training 334	
	Organize for CASE and cooperative development 335	
	Roll out new tools and methods 338	
	Evaluate the IS architecture and transition plan 346	

Appendices

A	**Method pool management system**	**349**
B	**CASE evaluation criteria**	**357**
C	**CASE product directories**	**373**

Notes	**375**
Index	**385**

Introduction

People still search for "the method," the one true path to software development enlightenment. Many an author, drawing on great thought and untold experience, presents a new methodology or development tool as the best and only way to create software. They find flaws with all other approaches, with naught but praise for their own.

More than one conference speaker has stated, in almost as many words, "Everything you're doing today is wrong." Yet if it is—if we really are incompetent, out-of-date, or shudderingly afraid of change—why do we still have jobs? Why can most of us, those who read the books and listen to the speakers and try to make the technologies work, still excel at software development?

Clearly not everything is wrong. There's a lot of good software written today. I'm amazed at the PC packages you can buy: tightly programmed arcade games, for instance, that break new ground in human-computer interfaces, outdo every business package for ease of use and technical wizardry, and list for $25 and under.

Still, no single approach does it all. Advances in software technology make older methods obsolete. Try writing a neural network in COBOL. It can be done, but it isn't pretty. It's time we realize that "the method" won't show up anytime soon. Fred Brooks knew this when he wrote "No Silver Bullet."[1] However, most methodology and CASE [Computer-Aided Software Engineering] tool vendors can't admit it. Their marketing edge depends on their ability to convince the public that they've found "the way."

In fact, there are many ways and many vehicles to move you along them. Instead of junking old methods for the new, we need to think about synthesizing them. We talk a lot about reusing software; now let's think about reusing software development methods. Instead of riding herd on unruly projects, software development managers coordinate many groups that follow various development paths from abstract ideas to solid, functioning systems. They become the information system's (IS) equivalent of an air traffic controller.

---

[1] Fred Brooks, "No Silver Bullet: Essence and Accidents of Software Engineering, "*IEEE Computer*, April 1987. (*Note:* References cited in rest of book appear on pp. 375–383, Notes.)

This book promotes a philosophy of synthesis: success lies in selecting the best methods for each particular job. And you know better than I which methods make you most successful.

Just as there is no universal way to develop software nor to plan and create a software development environment, I don't expect anyone to read this book cover to cover and follow each and every step. I present it as a sourcebook, an idea book, with concrete suggestions for getting a few things done. I hope it provokes some thought. I hope some of my suggestions work within your environment as they have for me. Most of all I hope the book acts as a lever, raising the conversation about CASE to a higher level.

There is no one way, no one tool, but there is one final arbiter of the way systems will be developed. You, the manager or software developer, have the power to shape the future of software development. The best techniques and tools are those that make your job better—not those that are theoretically correct or that use the flashiest user interface.

In my software engineering career, I've worked with many different CASE tools. I've mentored systems from their strategic planning infancy to full code generation and implementation, speeding the process with CASE tools every step of the way. I've observed that:

- some tools slow you down, while others are surprisingly good
- some companies plan the CASE implementation, while others throw tools at people and expect them to use them
- there is very little knowledge-sharing among CASE practitioners

Good information about CASE tools is hard to come by. Since CASE is a strategic technology for many firms, they talk about it only reluctantly. In addition, no CASE implementation is free of rough spots; even the best are fraught with mass resistance and managerial doubt. People don't like to talk about failures, or incomplete successes.

CASE confusion

CASE might be the most promising concept in modern software development, but it is also the most misunderstood. CASE has been a popular industry buzzword for years. Yet only a few of the companies who could benefit from CASE technology use it on a continuing basis. More than 80% of all IS organizations have experimented with some type of CASE tool, but a much smaller percentage now use these tools to create working systems. Many companies have sunk millions into the technology and have yet to see the much-hyped benefits emerge. Interest is high and money is ready, but few know how to make CASE investments pay off.

Paralyzed by conflicting signals from industry leaders and overzealous hype from the press, most firms haven't fully embraced CASE tools or methods. IBM's announcement of its Application Development Cycle (AD/Cycle) strategy has sown further confusion, causing many companies to adopt a "wait and see" attitude. But CASE technology has already arrived; many firms are writing success stories now, and those who wait too long may be swiftly left behind.

Currently the CASE industry still has a product, not service, focus. Consulting firms have taken up some of the slack, offering the support CASE manufacturers seldom provide. Yet these firms generally only work (or are affordable) on a very large scale. Since CASE manufacturers won't help us plan or solve business problems, we need to gain our own expertise. That's what this book is for.

Many books have tried to define CASE or present its theoretical foundations. They explain the technology and marvel at its potential. Their CASE tool information is based upon information supplied by the vendors, rather than by independent observation.

This book takes a different approach. CASE has been around for years, and most IS professionals are familiar with it in some form. But few companies have forged CASE tools and techniques into practical software development environments, and few books share the knowledge of how these companies made it happen.

This book examines the business and organizational aspects of CASE, and offers ideas for making CASE work. It focuses on currently available tools and techniques, and how firms have used them to improve software quality and productivity.

Using CASE is much more than installing new software or workstations. This book attempts to describe the things you should consider when selecting, installing, and using CASE tools. I consider this a second-generation CASE book. It speaks to those who know something about the technology, but are struggling to make it effective.

After a pragmatic definition of what CASE means today, the book tackles both technical and nontechnical issues, including:

- using CASE to improve your company's competitive position
- knowing which CASE tools will be most beneficial to your organization
- balancing CASE's costs and benefits, both quantifiable and intangible
- marshaling management support for software engineering
- aligning CASE usage with corporate business plans and strategic IS plans
- selecting and internalizing effective software development methodologies
- evaluating the myriad of commercial CASE tools
- preparing for the cultural and organizational changes CASE might force upon your organization
- understanding the benefits of applications integration, and steps you can take to make it happen
- using strategic planning methods to select applications projects based on business need, not IS politics
- framing small yet effective development projects which minimize time-to-delivery
- breathing life into ancient software by reverse engineering

I'll try to provide concise, realistic advice for the manager risking his or her career on CASE, or for the project leader trapped between management commitment and employee resistance. I will also be very candid about the relative merits of the tools. CASE tools have lots of flaws. Some that claim to automate methodologies really just pay lip service to them. Others can be labeled as specialized drawing tools that don't directly contribute to software creation. The wide variations in tool quality can be bewildering. I hope to help you separate the wheat from the chaff.

Throughout the book I mention many specific CASE tools and methodologies, to ground important concepts or to highlight resources for further exploration. I'm not here to promote any specific software product or vendor, though I do offer opinions about which tools are best suited for particular tasks and environments.

Chapter summary

As you can see, this book covers a lot of ground. Chapters 1 through 3 discuss understanding CASE concepts, tools, and benefits. Chapters 4 through 6 present three of the major issues affecting CASE tool implementations: systems integration, methodologies, and organizational change. Chapters 7 through 10 discuss planning for CASE, determining your requirements, and selecting the right tools. Finally, chapters 11 through 14 discuss ways of using CASE to create effective, maintainable applications.

The chapters proceed as follows:

1. **The CASE arms race** Computer-Aided Systems Engineering (CASE) is a competitive requirement. CASE helps develop strategic systems. Plus a dozen other reasons why CASE makes sense today.
2. **The faceless acronym** CASE needs a new, practical definition. This chapter presents a CASE tool taxonomy, with examples. It lists features of many of the CASE tools available on the market today.
3. **Waiting for the revolution** Think hard about the benefits you want from CASE. Most CASE vendors' claims are deceptive. CASE's greatest advantages are better software quality and management support, not just higher productivity. In fact, productivity might be the last thing CASE brings.
4. **Forging an alliance** Systems integration is an important priority for many firms. CASE tools greatly simplify integration tasks. They can support decision support systems and coordinated application releases as well as more traditional systems development.
5. **Diving into the method pool** This chapter explains why methodology is more important than the tools that automate it. It also shows that one standard methodology will never be enough. You need to develop flexible, customized methods that support technological change.
6. **Living in the neutral zone** CASE radically alters the IS working environment, causing stress among software developers. Prepare the organization before you install the tools. This chapter suggests numerous techniques for smoothing the assimilation of CASE into the organization.
7. **Planning for the software factory** CASE is only one facet of the IS environment. Plan for it all before you buy any tools. You might discover better solutions than CASE tools.
8. **Designing an IS architecture** This chapter steps through a process for planning your software development environment.

9. **Reengineering the development process** Take a hard look at your software development process before you look for CASE tools. Think beyond yesterday's assumptions, and design an environment to serve you well into the future.
10. **Retooling the software factory** How to select the tools you really need, based on the requirements and methodologies you've already defined. Presents examples of economic cost/benefit analysis of tool alternatives.
11. **Shaping the method pool** This chapter steps through how to create and maintain a modular "method pool," a flexible methodology that promotes continuous improvement of the development process.
12. **Measuring the splash** If you don't assess your performance, there's no way to know what CASE is bringing you. You can set up measurement programs that are simple and self-managing, using CASE tools to help with data collection.
13. **Stacking the deck** Simple steps to ensure CASE project success. This chapter starts by discussing CASE pilot projects, and suggests techniques for making every project successful.
14. **Spreading the word** Running a pilot project is a piece of cake compared to a company-wide CASE rollout. This chapter discusses how to plan the CASE tool installations, how to set up a training program, how to prioritize CASE projects, and how to manage the resulting morass of software engineering models and repositories. Strategic IS planning is an important technique for governing the CASE rollout, especially if you're moving toward integrated business applications.

I hope this book is both informative and practical. I personally welcome every new source of pertinent information about CASE and how to apply it. I trust you'll consider this book a useful source, and that it will generate ideas for making CASE work in your environment. There's potential for great gains; it's time to start exploiting it.

1
The CASE arms race

In the early 1950s, the United States, perceiving a threat to its relative military and economic power, embarked upon a period of massive defense spending. In response the Soviet Union matched and eventually surpassed the United States' military spending levels. And in the 1960s, China's defense expenditures increased rapidly as well.

Thus began an arms race unparalleled in history. During this time the country that acquired the most weapons was generally assumed the strongest, despite its ability to deploy or use them.

In the late 1980s, a similar pattern began forming in the world of software development. Responding to predictions of unmanageable software backlogs and shortages of qualified programmers, CASE tool acquisition began in earnest. Vendors promised magical gains in productivity, and companies rushed to purchase their tools.

This triggered fears that competitors might exploit CASE technology to gain competitive advantage. Not unlike the cold war's "missile gap," experts began citing a "CASE tool gap." Companies scrambled for technological cover.

Most started by funding multiple, often competing "rearmament" programs, letting various groups within the company purchase and develop CASE tools and methods. To spread cost and minimize risk, these tools were acquired one by one, infiltrating the company from the ground up. It was the scatter method—at least one of the missiles had to hit the target.

Though some scatter efforts succeed, most fail dismally. Without a coherent plan for exploiting the successes, the technology stalls. Years after the first CASE tools are introduced, many companies are still looking for the widespread productivity gains they thought they were buying.

In an arms race, owning the weapons is more important than using them (or so we all hope). But CASE tools have little value as shelfware. They can't increase business competitiveness unless they are tightly managed and strategically applied.

CASE for competitive advantage

In the 1990s, more companies will use CASE to achieve competitive advantage. In 1990, 84% of IS managers in Fortune 1000 companies reported using CASE tools in their organizations.[1]

The fraction of companies regularly using CASE is much lower. Most purchased CASE in an ad hoc manner, and usage of the tools was neither planned nor coordinated. Because of employee resistance, insufficient training, and other factors, most CASE tools gather dust on shelves.

Estimates of ongoing CASE usage ranged from 25 to 30% of IS organizations in 1989 and 1990.[2] A separate 1990 survey found that only 57% of developers planned to use some productivity tool—a category that included both CASE and non-CASE productivity tools—within the next year.[3] It seems that IS managers are more optimistic than the actual systems developers.

Most firms have purchased some form of CASE tool and are using it sparingly. Only a handful make the tools work company-wide, but many are in the midst of planned campaigns to milk CASE for all it's worth. Most companies using CASE believe the technology will bring benefits. A sampling of Fortune 1000 management information systems managers showed that 71% were convinced that CASE will improve productivity. Only 2 to 4% of CASE users have tried and subsequently rejected the technology.[4]

CASE is not a technological quick fix for the software crisis, but over time it brings strategic benefits that cannot be ignored. Companies that don't start using CASE technology, and using it well, will find themselves at a distinct competitive disadvantage by the year 2000. There are five compelling reasons why:

1. Software changes everything, and great gains in software productivity can affect all facets of a company's business.
2. Strategic systems are hard to come by, and just as tough to defend against. Firms using CASE have a much better chance of recognizing and developing strategic systems.
3. CASE will be the basis for the development environments of the future. The sooner a firm starts with CASE, the better poised it is to take advantage of future technologies.
4. The best software developers want the new challenges of CASE tools and advanced development techniques. To keep your best people, you need to provide these challenges.
5. Government-sponsored consortiums in Europe and Japan are coordinating CASE development and training for large numbers of client organizations. Other commercial consortiums are making similar efforts in the United States. Companies who don't belong to these consortiums should get involved with CASE soon, or else will be left behind.

Software changes everything

Perceptions of a software crisis have been with us since the term first emerged at a 1968 NATO Software Engineering Conference. The crisis centers on the inability of developers to meet the increasing demand for quality software systems. The extensive backlog of unfulfilled system requests characterizes the software crisis in most companies. A recent survey found that in an average U.S. corporation, new systems requests take 29 months before bearing fruit.

CASE has the potential to cut a large chunk out of the backlog. CASE-developed systems are generally completed much faster than systems built using more traditional methods. CASE can drastically reduce the number of system defects, leading to impressive quality gains.

For many years these benefits were the stuff of theory. Until recently, few IS managers believed that CASE's supposed benefits were more than just vendors marketing propaganda. As recently as 1987, only 54% of IS managers believed that CASE technology could help increase programmer productivity.[5]

However, several pioneering firms have racked up impressive productivity gains using CASE. For example:

- DuPont Corporation has used CASE tools with a standard development methodology since 1985. Since then they have created over 400 programs, all failure-free, experiencing over 6:1 productivity gains. Software maintenance costs on these systems have decreased by roughly 80% since the advent of CASE.
- BDM International, a subsidiary of Ford Aerospace and Communications Corp., credits CASE tools for helping save $5 million over three years, chiefly through improved system quality and development productivity. Error rates have dropped from 8 errors per thousand lines of code in 1986 to 1.2 errors per thousand lines in 1989. While reorganizing to support CASE, BDM trimmed its development staff from 280 to 180, without reducing the company's product line.[6]
- In Japan, NRI & NCC Company, an information services subsidiary of Nomura Securities, has used CASE for structured design and system construction for more than seven years. They cite productivity increases of more than 200% over this period.[7]

Having already established a CASE infrastructure, these companies will continue to realize sharp productivity and quality gains in the future. These gains can directly affect the IS organization's bottom line, and their indirect effects might be even more powerful.

Unless a firm's industry is software, software is just a means to an end. Software is an enabling technology; it is a way of achieving business goals, but not a goal in itself. These days software is so entrenched that most critical processes within a company are automated in some way.

Yet old software programs often limit rather than enable. Most systems were built to support specific operational needs; they were based upon old, inflexible procedures. When the procedures change, the software must change too. Sweeping process changes force complete software rewrites. Such rewrites take at least two years in most companies, far longer than it normally takes to change the physical process itself.

CASE brings a possibility for much faster software response. This can break apart the software bottleneck that limits many firms' responsiveness. In addition, CASE-developed systems are usually much higher quality than their traditional counterparts.

The effects of successful CASE usage can ripple dramatically throughout an entire organization. Companies with faultless systems will improve production numbers by minimizing system downtime. Companies with quick systems development cycles will improve time-to-market for new production strategies or marketing programs. Companies that establish shared databases with perfect information will discover new patterns and trends faster, and make more timely business decisions.

By making CASE work, a well-run company can improve its competitive position with a few years. At the very least it will trim months off the time it needs to adapt to environmental changes.

Software in the driver's seat

Software development has traditionally played a reactive role, responding to systems requests from operational managers. Some exceptional companies have succeeded in reversing this relationship, to great effect. By getting IS involved up front in planning business strategy, these companies developed strategic systems that gave them extended competitive advantages.

The following list of strategic systems is now familiar to most students of modern management techniques:

- American Airlines' famous SABRE system gave the company strategic alliances with travel agencies and an advantageous position in the competition for flight bookings.
- Levi Strauss & Co. instituted its LeviLink systems, providing suites of services to suppliers and customers alike, and significantly reducing product delivery times.
- Harley-Davidson Company built a system to automate a reengineered and simplified manufacturing process, resulting in productivity gains, cost savings, and continued competitiveness for the firm.
- Benetton stormed to retail success by developing a strategic information systems architecture centered on a powerful network for sharing data among point-of-sale locations, manufacturing sites, distribution centers, and management offices.

Each of these systems helped the company establish new links to customers, or redesign outdated business processes, in ways that their competitors couldn't quickly imitate.

True strategic systems like the ones listed above are very rare. But without participation of IS managers in business strategy planning, opportunities for strategic systems may never be discovered. Structured planning approaches supported by many CASE tools provide excellent frameworks for cooperative strategic planning.

By synthesizing the knowledge of managers from every facet of a company, structured information strategy planning (ISP) can help pinpoint three main strategic systems benefits:

1. Opportunities for strategic systems that advantageously alter the company's relationships with customers or suppliers
2. Opportunities to fundamentally redesign business processes for marked productivity and quality gains
3. Articulation of and planning for a company-wide information architecture that will provide a flexible basis for future business planning and decision-making

Strategic systems

The classic strategic system uses information technology to forge powerful new relationships with customers and suppliers. American Airlines' SABRE and Levi Strauss' LeviLink systems both enabled new relationships that improved each company's competitive position.

Strategic systems are rare, but for each firm that develops one, many more react. American Airlines struck gold again in the late 1970s when it developed its frequent flier system, American Advantage. This system's success in drawing new business to the firm forever changed the dynamics of the passenger airline business. To stay competitive many airlines launched costly efforts to develop similar systems. Other airlines formed alliances with competitors that already had such systems. Today almost every airline offers some form of frequent flier program.

Strategic planning techniques that encourage attention to environmental forces can help uncover opportunities for strategic systems. Many CASE tools automate these strategic planning methods, simplifying otherwise overwhelming efforts.

Process redesign

Systems that support redesigned processes can have almost as much impact as those that redefine business relationships. Process redesign involves radically reengineering internal activities to greatly cut costs or improve service. This is a popular pastime among the top U.S. MIS shops. Of the top 100 MIS companies selected by *Computerworld* Magazine, 84 said they have redesigned internal processes for strategic advantage.[8] Opportunities for these types of strategic systems can be recognized more easily using CASE technology.

Information architectures

In the future, as more and more companies become fully competent in IS development, strategic systems will become even harder to develop. Strategic gain will be had not from single, centralized software applications, but from a powerful network of business information that enables quick, informed decision-making. As Max Hopper, former director of American Airlines' SABRE system mentions, IS managers "will focus less on developing stand-alone applications than on building electronic platforms that can transform their organizational structures and support new ways of making decisions." He predicts that "companies will be technology architects rather than systems builders, even for their most critical applications."[9]

Using architectures to effectively deploy and manage technology can provide significant competitive benefits. For example, it can drive up the costs of entry for new competitors. By setting an ambitious technology standard, you can force other firms to keep pace.

Information architecture involves high-level planning of business processes, business data, and information technology. Technology architecture will plan the complex interaction of hardware, including workstations, central computers, communications networks, and software applications—both centralized and localized.

Creating such sweeping architectures without CASE support will be almost impossible. To position your company for the future of IS, you need to embrace CASE.

Duty now for the future

CASE helps thrust a company toward the future in many ways. It can help you design the blueprints for future technologies and information-based organizational structures. To capitalize in either area, CASE is almost a prerequisite.

Future software technology

The future of software development will be CASE. There can be no question. Since the first programs were hardwired into the early machines, programming language has gradually grown more like true human language. Cryptic machine and assembly codes led to friendlier languages, like BASIC and COBOL, that used actual English words, albeit in limited structured syntax. More recently, fourth-generation languages boasting English-like syntax were developed, and artificial intelligence technology has led to database query packages that comprehend colloquial English (and other languages).

Now CASE is popularizing graphical ways of talking to computers. Early efforts included flowcharting programs that generated code shells and simulation packages that allowed graphical components to be moved, connected, and described. Most CASE packages today make extensive use of graphics and diagrams to communicate business and technical knowledge. The graphics become systems specifications, and eventually translate (with various degrees of augmentation and tweaking) into running computer programs. Some development packages are now completely graphical.

Graphical representations make the business model more presentable to users. In the hands of the right CASE tools, they also can greatly simplify the development process.

Ultimately, the goal of the systems development process is to represent business knowledge in the way the user finds easiest to understand. Some people glean more from pictures and resist long blasts of text. Others prefer structured text to pictures because it can be more detailed. Most people prefer to see words or pictures in their native language.

Systems developers should not be forced to learn arcane terminology and syntax—business knowledge should allow them to understand the business information system. A business representation should be automatically translatable into working computer systems, with limited hand-holding by developers or technicians. Short of letting the computers define business policies and program systems themselves, this vision brings the ultimate productivity gains.

The marriage of graphical knowledge representation and natural language interfaces will enable anyone with a grasp of a business problem to quickly model and develop a computer application to solve it.

Information-based organizations

The information-based organization, as described by management theorist Peter Drucker, is a model for the truly dynamic firm of the future. Information-based organizations are characterized by flat organizational structures, with a few professional managers aiding communications among many skilled, semiautonomous specialists. Workers are self-disciplined business experts, accountable to peers and customers as well as managers. Most operational work will be done by interdisciplinary task forces or project teams that work together until a specific objective is achieved. Communication becomes the crucial link between teams, specialists, and management.

Drucker believes many companies will be forced to shift toward this new model:

> Large organizations will have little choice but to become information-based. Demographics, for one, demands the shift. The workforce is moving away from manual and clerical workers, toward "knowledge workers." These workers resist the command-and-control model that business took from the military one hundred years ago. Economics also dictates change, especially the need for large business to innovate and to be entrepreneurs. But above all, information technology demands the shift.[10]

Social scientist Shoshana Zuboff recognizes a similar need for organizational change. She believes we haven't fully acknowledged the power of information technology to change the nature of work. Successful change to new work patterns, she says, "requires a comprehensive vision based on an understanding of the unique capacities of intelligent technology and the opportunity of the organization to liberate those capacities.... It means forging a new logic of technological deployment based upon that vision."[11]

Both Drucker and Zuboff say the organization must change to support new information technology; yet the new technology must first be mastered and directed toward strategic goals. The need to gain strategic advantage through information technology will drive the shift toward the information-based organization.

CASE-based methods and technologies will enable many companies to build information-based organizations. Knowledge workers must understand exactly what information they require, and what information others require of them. CASE techniques let users identify their information needs, and help build systems to meet these needs. CASE also supports the building of integrated corporate applications designed to give all workers access to the information they need, no matter who created that information. Already the move toward applications integration is forcing flatter organization structures in some companies.[12]

CASE itself will enable software developers to become true knowledge workers. CASE repositories provide a common source for shared software engineering information, and CASE techniques encourage new lines of communication between developers and business experts.

Information-based organizations also depend on clearly articulated, unifying goals. Only pervasive, shared goals can keep large groups of semiautonomous workers moving in the same direction. Top-down CASE techniques mobilize senior management to create strategic goal models, and to rationalize all future development projects accordingly.

It goes too far to say that CASE will usher in the age of the information-based firm, but CASE will enable the systems that let this model take hold.

The time is now

Information systems departments that can't cope with technological change might find their very existence challenged. Many companies are farming out work to systems integration consultants and outsourcing firms. These service firms generally come armed with effective methodologies and CASE tools. On paper, they often have better track records than the IS department, in terms of delivering results on time, within budget. A strong sales pitch by a systems integration firm at a moment of weakness might sound the death knell for in-house systems development.

CASE can help stave off the reaper, but unfortunately CASE is not simple to use. The principles it represents are often difficult to describe, and the learning curve for most CASE tools and methodologies is long and steep. You cannot expect to buy a tool today and have people using it productively tomorrow, or even three months from now.

Though future tools will be easier to use and understand, changing from traditional software development methods always involves a significant learning curve. If you haven't started this learning curve yet, you should soon. Begin gradual absorption of CASE within your company, perhaps starting with an isolated project or department. Once your competitors use CASE to great advantage and economic pressure forces you to follow suit, a quick catch-up strategy may not be available.

Even with future generations of tools, playing catch-up may be too disruptive. CASE forces cultural changes upon an IS organization. Those who try to force-feed such changes to their developers may face a serious backlash. Even with less-than-optimal tools, the lessons that CASE teaches managers and development staff will be valuable in the future. It will prepare your organization for the utopian tools and organizations yet to come.

Wallflowers don't dance

The people you need to make future software development work are the ones excited by the potential of CASE.

Much of the literature recounts the resistance of traditional developers raised on COBOL or C to newfangled CASE technology. Many authors believe that those who resist CASE are afraid of change. In the rapidly changing business environment, resistance can slow a firm's responsiveness. Yet most resistance is to the way CASE is introduced in the firm, not to the technology itself.

Many developers are excited by CASE's promise, and relish the opportunity to test out the new technology. These people look forward to new challenges and seek ways to improve their own productivity. They are prime candidates for Drucker's future "information worker." They are the ones whom IS organizations need to attract and inspire.

A company with no plans to explore new software development methods—such as CASE, object-oriented languages, or artificial intelligence techniques—will find it hard to keep a motivated staff. Most software professionals learn about these techniques from colleagues or the industry press. Many take time to educate themselves about new tools and methods. Most college graduates in computer-related fields are well aware of these techniques, and want to work for companies that use them.

Currently, developers familiar with CASE and structured development techniques are hard to find. The reason is simple: most of them already have challenging, satisfying jobs making CASE work. Backed by management commitment and trained in CASE methods and tools, developers can become highly motivated, productive, and more comfortable with business change.

A company that sticks to traditional development methods also limits the size of its potential information-worker base. By dealing with systems requirements in a way understandable to most business experts, CASE allows nonprogrammers to contribute greatly to systems development. Many systems analysts in CASE-based IS organizations come from nontechnical business backgrounds. A commitment to CASE will mean less dependence in the future on the dwindling supply of trained programmers.

Roles for traditional programmers and technicians will continue to exist for many years. But CASE provides a productive outlet for those who seek new challenges. It brings more than just a framework for systems development; CASE can help attract and hold the qualified information workers you'll need in the future.

Organized competition

There is some comfort in the fact that, though some companies have made great inroads, most companies are still struggling to make CASE effective. But some sweeping movements are afoot that might benefit many pioneering firms. Because the high costs of software R&D prohibit most companies from developing their own development platforms or CASE tools, many have joined forces in research consortiums. These consortiums are jointly funded by member corporations, sometimes with extensive government aid. In return for funding and personnel contributions, the member companies share the R&D spoils.

Most consortium research is directed toward defining utopian software development environments and powerful single-task CASE tools. Few consortium projects have produced commercial products, though many early technical breakthroughs are promising. Should any of these consortiums strike gold, their member companies will prosper.

The two largest consortiums, ESPRIT in Europe and SIGMA in Japan, are both government-sponsored. In the U.S., the Department of Defense (DoD) has carried out influential research into software development environments. The privately-funded Microelectronics and Computer Technology Corporation (MCC) carries out similar software engineering research on a somewhat smaller scale.

Europe's ESPRIT projects

In 1983 the Commission of European Communities (CEC) formed an incredibly ambitious research consortium to push the barriers of information technology. The European

Strategic Programme for Research in Information Technology (ESPRIT) was jointly funded by the CEC and numerous member companies. ESPRIT Phase One ended in late 1989. Phase One comprised 220 separate research projects involving more than three thousand researchers, at a total cost of roughly $1.6 billion.

ESPRIT projects divide into five research groups:

1. Microelectronics, including advanced chip design and interconnection
2. Software technology, focusing on software engineering methods and tools
3. Advanced information processing, including artificial intelligence, parallel computing, and signal processing.
4. Computer-integrated manufacturing (CIM), concentrating on CIM information processing standards
5. Office and business systems, concerned with hardware and software improvements for the workplace

Projects in the software engineering domain worked to develop an Integrated Project Support Environment (IPSE). An IPSE gathers multiple CASE and programmer tools into a common framework, supplementing them with project management and methodology support.

One ESPRIT project produced the Portable Common Tools Environment (PCTE), a CASE tool interface standard. PCTE is the glue that binds the tools developed by other projects into an IPSE framework. It contains a sophisticated object management system for storing and sharing the software engineering data captured by each tool. Subsequent projects are adding extra layers of CASE tools standards on top of PCTE, including user interface guidelines and hooks into common tool services. Though many competing sets of CASE tool interfaces have been proposed worldwide, PCTE is the most comprehensive.

In the advanced information processing domain, one ESPRIT project developed a novel Expert System Builder that might do for expert systems what today's code generators do for COBOL applications.

ESPRIT Phase Two, which began in 1989, will build upon the findings of first phase projects. Phase Two focuses on smoothly integrating all the tools into a commercially practical environment. Projects will explore new development methodologies, code reusability, development tools for parallel computers, and management-support interfaces for project control.

Few of ESPRIT's first phase projects have made it to the marketplace. Early projects like PCTE lay impressive groundwork for future research. Many ESPRIT research teams are forging agreements with private interests to commercialize their findings. Should future ESPRIT projects successfully unite the many products, the resulting framework will be the most powerful development environment ever made.

ESPRIT has also transformed the European research community into a directed and driven force. It provides an unprecedented forum for technology transfer and advancement. Through government and industry cooperation on a grand scale, ESPRIT could propel European firms into the technological forefront.

Japan's SIGMA projects

Japan, long considered a secondary player in the software market, is also betting that centralized, government-sponsored research can launch its companies into software preeminence.

In 1985, Japan's Ministry of International Trade and Industry (MITI) predicted that, by the year 2000, Japanese industry will need a million more programmers than it will have. In response MITI established the five-year, $200 million Software Industrial Generalization and Maintenance Aids (SIGMA) project, which ran from 1985 to 1990. One hundred eighty-nine private companies provided money and researchers to fuel SIGMA subprojects.

SIGMA applied production automation techniques to software engineering, attempting to do for software what earlier research efforts did for Japanese manufacturing. SIGMA strove to produce a comprehensive architecture for software development, including a standardized set of data structures, system services, hardware interconnections, and programming interfaces.[13] The creation of CASE tool components fell to private companies, who built the tools to fit SIGMA's standard. All 189 Japanese companies involved could then adopt this common architecture.

SIGMA was completed in 1990 to mixed reviews. The project successfully articulated a complex and thorough architecture, with associated standards. However, SIGMA limited itself, by choice, to working only with commercially proven technologies. As a result, some of its standards now appear out-of-date. SIGMA's software engineering database was limited to project management and "lower-CASE" design and construction data. It did not leave room for strategic planning and analysis information. In addition, fewer SIGMA-compatible CASE tools were produced by private companies than anticipated.

In 1989, a subsequent project, dubbed SuperSIGMA, began to address enhancements requested by early users of SIGMA prototypes. With Japan's Ministry of Labor, MITI also began setting up regional centers to retrain qualified citizens as software engineers. The goal is to retrain some 200,000 engineers by 1999, while simultaneously promoting the SIGMA standards and architecture.

According to a 1989 report by ADAPSO, the computer software and service industry association, large-scale success of the SIGMA project could do more than merely boost Japan's competitive position in the software industry. Says the report, "Their position will be strengthened in all of the industries that produce associated hardware (computers, telecommunications, factory automation systems)."[14] In addition, better software applications will likely boost manufacturing and service productivity countrywide.

However, Japanese firms will still need to manage the implementation of SIGMA architectures and handle the severe organizational change it engenders. The Super SIGMA project must open the architecture further, to include more abstract business knowledge and to accommodate new systems development paradigms. Yet the broad scope of CASE adoption and standardization in Japan lends the movement a unique momentum. Supported by mass retraining and information sharing efforts, Japanese software factories may soon match the renowned performance of Japanese manufacturers.

U.S. Department of Defense

In the U.S., most long-term research into large-scale software development environments occurs under military auspices. In 1979, DoD published the seminal Stoneman report, which stated the need for integrated development environments. It also specified requirements for an Ada Programming Support Environment (APSE), comprised of tools for project management, code generation, interactive debugging, and standard Ada language editors and compilers. Since then, DoD has specified a standard tool interface (CAIS) that allows new tools to be "plugged in" to existing APSE environments.

Though DoD gave the IPSE idea its first big push, subsequent research has all been Ada-related. Unfortunately, Ada is not a widely used programming language (though it is starting to penetrate scientific markets). DoD research findings will not have direct impacts upon much of the integrated CASE marketplace.

Microelectronics and Computer Technology Corporation

The largest consortium for cooperative technological research in the U.S. is the Microelectronics and Computer Technology Corporation. Formed in 1983 to provide a forum for leveraging applied technology research, MCC now boasts a membership of over 50 U.S. Corporations.

MCC struggled through its early years, shrugging off skepticism about the prospects for cooperative research in the U.S. As results emerge from consortium projects, and transfer to member companies, doubts about the group's viability are dissipating.

Like ESPRIT, MCC divides its research programs into five separate domains:

1. Advanced computing technologies, including artificial intelligence, human-computer interfaces, and object oriented databases
2. Software technology, focusing on tools for developing large-scale distributed software systems
3. Packaging/interconnect, including chip design and hardware architecture
4. Computer-aided design (CAD), concentrating on standards for CAD tool interfaces
5. Computer physics, covering superconductivity and data storage technologies

Many findings from MCC projects are not publicized because of their competitive value to member companies. However, some interesting projects have made it into the limelight:

- The cryptically-labeled CYC project is attempting to build a massive general knowledge rule base that will bring "common sense" to future expert systems.
- The Design Journal project uses hypertext technology in a distributed environment to capture and present software design specifications and issues.

Though MCC's scale doesn't approach that of ESPRIT or SIGMA (TABLE 1-1), its findings will significantly improve its member's technological competitiveness. Nonmembers with large R&D budgets should investigate the benefits of MCC partnership.

Table 1-1. Comparison of Software Engineering Research Consortiums

	ESPRIT	Eureka Software Factory	SIGMA	U.S. Department of Defense	MCC
Governments	13	5	1	1	0
Companies		13	189	0	52
Researchers	Phase I: 3,000 Phase II: 2,000	—	—	—	400
Year begun	Phase I: 1983 Phase II: 1988	1983	Phase I: 1985 Phase II: 1989	1979	1983
Year complete	Phase I: 1989 Phase II: 1993	1993	Phase I: 1990 Phase II: 1995	Ongoing	Ongoing
Software engineering objectives	Comprehensive IPSE, including full life cycle tools, project management, intelligent development support	In conjunction with ESPRIT, standard public CASE tool interfaces and prototypes of intelligent IPSEs	Architecture for computer-aided software design, generation, and reuse	Integrated project support platform for large-scale Ada programming efforts	Tool interface standards, tools for distributed software design, breakthroughs in expert systems capabilities

Smaller companies might need to wait until MCC research is applied in CASE tools from member companies like Texas Instruments or Andersen Consulting.

Will the wolf survive?

As enterprises band together in research alliances, the future of lone-wolf companies seems bleak. But by no means does membership in a consortium guarantee a better software development environment. Most consortium work concentrates on creating new tools, not enabling the organizational change needed to adopt these tools. MITI's SIGMA project is the lone exception, since it encompasses a comprehensive education program.

It will be a few years before most products of consortium research are commercially available. Of the consortiums, ESPRIT has the best chance of developing a commercial IPSE within the next decade. While SIGMA limited itself to technologies that were commercially available in the mid-1980s, ESPRIT and MCC looked forward to emerging technologies.

While member companies will initially benefit from these new products, they will also sell advanced CASE products to nonmember companies in order to recoup their research investments. Still, member companies will certainly streamline their software development methods because of their participation. They have recognized the need for better tools and methods, and opened their organizations to resultant changes.

To keep pace with these firms, independent companies should start researching new ways to develop software, if they haven't already. When the new technologies arrive, only the prepared can grab them and run. Companies that don't plan ahead will still be lone wolves, but wolves without a forest, lost in a cold metal world they no longer understand.

CASE makes sense today

Imagine that you have conscious control of your own nervous system. You can monitor the signals that flow to your brain, intercepting them ahead of time, reacting more quickly, gaining more time to make the right response. You can see ahead of time when a painful signal starts, and snuff it out before any real damage is done.

Information is the nervous system of today's corporation, and a well-planned IS architecture can give you this kind of control. It gives you the luxury of the big picture: an understanding of the depth and breadth of your business information.

CASE simplifies the creation of information architectures and recognition of strategic system opportunities. It is a stepping stone to future software technologies, and a magnet for motivated software professionals. Deployed with care and used to its fullest, CASE can augment almost any firm's competitiveness.

Yet CASE technology alone won't improve a company's position. CASE is a means, not an end. Software today is an integral part of day-to-day business. Good software enables business change, and CASE enables software change. CASE is merely technology, and technology is only a small part of the solution to current software woes.

2

The faceless acronym

Though variations exist, most people agree that CASE stands for computer-aided software engineering. Putting words to the letters is easy, as shown in TABLE 2-1, but putting meaning to the words is more arduous.

Table 2-1. The Meanings of CASE

C	A	S	E
Computer	Aided, Assisted, Automated	Software, Systems	Engineering

CASE is a malleable concept. To some CASE embodies the philosophy that software is merely a model of life, and that modeling can usually be automated. Many software engineers see CASE as simple automation of the tasks they do each day. Other equate CASE with simple programmer tools, like code analyzers or cross-reference utilities. Unfortunately, development tool vendors see in CASE a catchy buzzword they can attach to any product in order to boost sales, or at least pique interest.

Not even the experts agree on what CASE means, as evidenced by the following definitions:

- "The disciplined and structured engineering approach to software and systems development."[1]
- "Individual tools to aid the software developer or project manager during one or more phases of software development (or maintenance)."[2]
- "A combination of software tools and structured development methodologies."[3]

The lack of consensus about the meaning of CASE slows the technology's acceptance rate. Some vendors avoid the word CASE, saying the buzzword can now cause a backlash. Some customers shy away from CASE tools because previous tools with similar labels failed to uphold the hyped-up vendor claims. Because the acronym is neither consistently defined nor applied, it has lost its usefulness.

In its broadest sense, CASE covers everything that helps developers create software, including the simplest programming language editors and compilers. Since the *A* in CASE stands for *aided* or *assisted*, it can apply to tools that add no value to the software itself, but merely enable standard development practices. When the *A* stands for *automated*, however, it gives CASE a slightly new meaning.

Automation implies self-action or independent motion. The most valuable CASE tools are those that contribute information to the development process. A tool that transforms process models into application source code contributes far more than an editor that allows programmers to write code manually. CASE should stand for Computer-Automated Software Engineering and be applied only to tools that automate software development. Tools to help programmers using traditional type-and-compile methods can be labeled Computer-Aided Programming (CAP) tools.

The *S* in CASE can stand for either *software* or *systems*. In either case, this letter represents the true goal of all honest CASE tools: the creation or improvement of computer-based systems. When the *S* stands for *systems*, though, the scope widens. Systems are comprised of both hardware and software. This meaning will apply to future tools that design and manage hardware configurations and communications networks in conjunction with software programs.

Sometimes people are so awed by new tools that they forget what they wanted them for in the first place. Ironically most CASE tools are more visually exciting than the systems they help produce. CASE tools are just implements for systems creation. You are developing software, not just information models or data-flow diagrams. Modeling for its own sake is not useful, except as it documents a working system. The latest, sexiest CASE tools do no good unless they help propel you at least one step forward toward the goal of new and better systems.

E is for *engineering*, which brings rigor and precision to software development. Engineering requires executing a set of repeatable steps to produce a given result. This is a far cry from traditional hacking, or programming-on-the-fly. Many programmers start the program creation process by sitting at a terminal or PC and typing code. Some prepare first by doing sketchy flowcharts or shorthand logic on paper. The hacker's approach succeeds when the problem domain is small. A simple solution can be simply written. When systems become large and complex, however, the hacker's approach is inadequate. Teams of people working on the same system require common methods and structure, so each can understand what the other is doing.

A set of related methods is called a methodology. Software development methodologies outline the tasks and techniques needed to transform nebulous user requirements into working systems. Methodologies formalize software engineering principles. The most effective CASE tools support methodologies, and derive their engineering focus from them.

Construction without forethought or discipline is not engineering. Tools that don't add or enforce rigor, through methodology support, automatic transformations, or consistency checking, aren't truly engineering tools.

Many programmers lament the passing of the hacker's approach to programming. They fear that creativity will be stifled, and that the fun will drop out of software development. For some this will happen: modern software development requires lots of interpersonal contact, and those who feel most secure coding solo won't enjoy discussing systems requirements with users. However, creativity will still flourish. Ideally, CASE tools will take over mundane development tasks, leaving developers more time to create elegant solutions to business problems. Programmers will become designers; the difference between the two jobs akin to that between carpenters and furniture designers.

Figure 2-1 illustrates the need for design before construction. It shows desk chairs created with various degrees of design effort. When no design work is done up front, the result can be awkward and not at all what the customer had in mind. Basic design produces a functional result: all chair legs the same length, the back perpendicular.

Fig. 2-1. The importance of design

The functional solution meets most of the customer's original specifications, but doesn't anticipate new requirements, or consider possible omissions in the original specifications. A superior design is usually arrived at through multiple consultations with the customer. In this case, the designer discovered that the customer would like a mobile chair, and added wheels to the design.

Design quality is a subjective measure. CASE tools can automate mechanical development tasks, and some can even infer limited design decisions, but none can make developers into good designers. Still, by decreasing the effort developers expend on repetitive tasks, CASE can give them more time to practice elegant design.

The current definition of CASE is too broad to be useful. For the purpose of this book a new, narrower definition of CASE is in order. A CASE tool should:

- be computer-based
- help automate the development process, adding value of its own

- directly contribute to the production of implementable systems
- add or enforce rigorous engineering practices

Only the most effective and ambitious CASE tools will fit this description. By definition, they are the ones that will most benefit software developers.

Push-button software machines

A few years ago NEC Corporation hired actor Dom DeLuise to talk on television about how easy it is to use NEC PCs. One scene showed a close-up of the PC as DeLuise's finger pressed a key marked "Draw." A bar chart blossomed onto the PC monitor. "See," said DeLuise, "it draws graphs at the press of a button!" No data entry or chart design seemed to be needed. A single key-press and the computer read your mind, drawing the chart you wished to see.

Many people believe that CASE tools are push-button software machines. You put some user requirements into them, and out pops a new application. CASE vendors do little to dispel this notion. The hard truth is that today's CASE still requires a great deal of data entry, analysis, data manipulation, and systems design. Some tools bring major productivity gains, but they still require plenty of input.

CASE brings automation to software production much like machines brought factory automation. They started by automating manufacturing tasks using the same motions and techniques used by craftsmen.

Early industrial machines had a single-task focus. They performed single operations on items that were then taken manually and moved to the next station in the production line. Many CASE tools have this same focus. They automate one task, like data flow diagramming, and produce some output, like a graphic diagram or an export file. These outputs must then be transformed into formats the next CASE tools in line can understand.

Single-task automation certainly increases productivity, but only incrementally. Production technology currently favors Computer Integrated Manufacturing (CIM), which automates the production line from start to finish, efficiently passing items from one station to the next. CASE tools are heading in a similar direction. Many experts envision a completely automated software development environment that supports every stage of software development, from strategic planning to code generation, implementation, and maintenance. This concept has been labeled, not surprisingly, the software factory. Software factories require extensive, seamless integration between multiple CASE tools—a feature rarely found in today's CASE marketplace.

The number of CASE tools currently on the market is overwhelming. Most CASE tools fulfill a single function. Some provide limited integration through one-way data communications or file transfers. Only a few can be called integrated tools, using the same data in different ways to perform various analytical functions.

Some tools are functionally limited to automating certain tasks, while others combine multiple functions into tightly- or loosely-coupled toolsets. Many different labels have been given to integrated CASE toolsets, varying according to the scope of the tools and the data sharing method. TABLE 2-2 shows the classifications used in this book. At the bottom of the integration ladder is the single CASE tool, which automates

Table 2-2. CASE Tool Classifications

Type of Toolset	Features
Toolkit	• Common user interface • Common data interface, or database
Integrated CASE toolset (ICASE)	• Common user interface • Common data repository • Allows methodology compliance
Integrated project support environment (IPSE)	• Common user interface • Allows methodology compliance • Common data repository • Project management functions • Standard programming services • Reuse libraries
Integrated computing environment	• Standard programming services • Reuse libraries • Standard operating services
Programmer workbench	• Standard programming services

a single or tightly related group of methods. A tool that does nothing but draw entity-relationship diagrams fits into this category. A CASE toolkit provides multiple functions with cursory data sharing among them. Most toolkits automate structured analysis and design tasks. A product that combines entity-relationship diagramming, data dictionary management, and data flow diagramming qualifies as a toolkit.

Each tool within a toolkit normally presents a common user interface. Toolkits also allow their separate components to access the same data, usually stored in a local database. Some toolkits force data file transfers between separate components. Many single CASE tools provide similar one-way interfaces to other vendors' tools, allowing you to mix and match CASE tools into custom toolkits. However this transfer method only provides one-way integration at discrete time intervals. Backtracking to change something using the first tool requires retransferring the full set of data, and losing work you have already done with the second tool.

At the next integration level are Integrated CASE (ICASE) tools. Two things distinguish ICASE tools from toolkits: data sharing is handled by a repository; and progression through separate tools can follow one or a number of accepted software development methodologies.

A repository differs from most toolkit databases since it stores the meaning of object in addition to graphical information about the placement of objects on diagrams. The same entity type created with the entity-relationship diagramming tool, for example, can be used unchanged by the data flow diagramming tool, or within process pseudocode. The repository allows other tools to access information about the entity type, no matter which tool created it.

Integrated CASE tools provide opportunities for automating standard software methodologies. Many ICASE tools were built with specific methodologies in mind. Others try to be flexible, automating multiple techniques at a time. The best ICASE tools allow you to step through proven methodologies from start to finish, finally generating a working software system. The ICASE tool manages all of the software engineering information you create along the way.

Integrated Project Support Environments (IPSEs) extend ICASE tools by adding services for project management, systems implementation, and maintenance. IPSEs attempt to automate every aspect of software development, centrally storing information for any tool to use.

Table 2-3. General Features of CASE Tool Classifications

Feature Set	CASE Toolkit	Integrated CASE Tool	Integrated Project Support Environment	Programmer Workbench
Automated software engineering	• Strategic planning • Analysis • Design • Simulation • Construction • Reverse engineering • Automated testing	• Strategic planning • Analysis • Design • Simulation • Construction • Reverse engineering • Automated testing	• Strategic planning • Analysis • Design • Simulation • Construction • Reverse engineering • Automated testing • Common programming interfaces	• Construction • Reverse engineering • Automated testing • Common programming interfaces
Repository services		• Security • Version control • Metamodel access	• Security • Version control • Metamodel access	• Version control
Methodology support		• Methodology advice	• Methodology advice • Methodology selection	
Project management support			• Task scheduling • Process measurement	

Two other categories of integrated tools deserve mention. Programmer Workbenches contain tools that automate standard development tasks like code structuring, test data management, or code compilation. The data kept by these workbenches is in the form of source or object code.

Integrated Computing Environments (ICEs) are similar to programmer workbenches, but they also provide common operating services for functions like data communications, graphical presentation, or database access. Rather than rewriting common functions for each program that needs them, programmers can reuse code from the ICEs code library. These services can also free programmers from the vagaries of multiple operating systems and distributed systems architectures. The same function can be used on every potential delivery platform. The programmer's task becomes one of picking out the right items from the ICEs library, not rewriting the functions from scratch.

A spectrum of functionality

The number of packages promoted as CASE tools has blossomed in the past few years. The tools now number in the hundreds. While efforts are underway to derive a complete taxonomy of CASE tools and their capabilities, most tools still defy common classification.

CASE tools span a wide spectrum of techniques and methods. Functionality ranges from managing projects to planning business strategies to reverse-engineering existing programs. As shown in FIG. 2-2, CASE functionality falls into four basic categories:

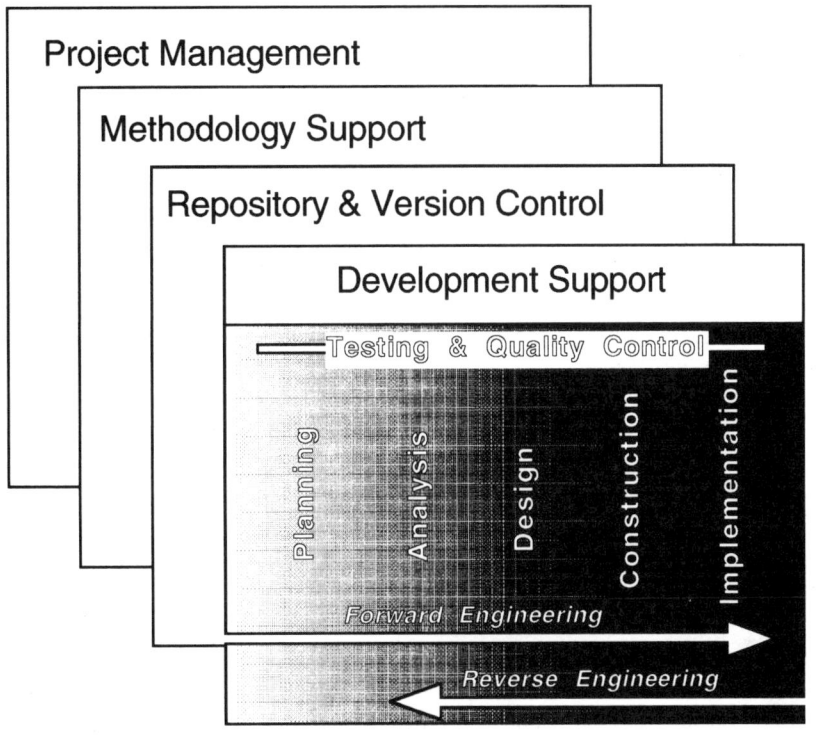

Fig. 2-2. A model of CASE functionality

- automated software development
- repository services
- methodology support
- project management

Automated software development includes all steps in what is normally known as the software development life cycle. The life cycle charts the growth of a system from initial planning and capture of user requirements through construction, testing, and implementation. The actual steps in the life cycle differ considerably depending on the methodology in use. Comprehensive life cycles include phases for:

- business or strategic systems planning
- requirements analysis
- system design
- system construction
- system implementation
- system maintenance

Testing and quality control can be applied within any phase, using different methods depending on the types of information being manipulated. Quality control functions can measure and evaluate metrics about the software systems being created, or help manage large quantities of test data.

Development of new systems usually entails progressing through each phase from planning through implementation, either linearly or in an iterative, back-and-forth fashion. Reverse engineering tracks backward through these same phases, disassembling implemented code or databases and transforming the pieces into structured design or analysis information.

Data created during these phases are stored as objects in the CASE tool repository. The repository manages the sharing of this information, keeping track of which users are interested in each object it stores. Some repositories also provide version control functions that track the history of these objects over time.

An integrated CASE tool's methodology support layer exists to guide developers through the life cycle. It holds knowledge about development methodologies, and can capture productivity measurements of specific steps and techniques.

Finally, the project management layer provides tools for managers to set up and track the progress of software development projects. Linked to the methodology component enables new insights into project achievements and team performance.

The CASE tool market spans a full spectrum of functions, but no single CASE product offers you them all. Each tool blends its own set of functions, some tightly integrated, others connected loosely. The next sections explore how CASE tools implement the functions listed above.

Automated software development

Progression through the many phases of the software development cycle can be seen as flowing top-down, from initial planning to final system construction and maintenance. Each successive phase involves making specifications more detailed and concrete. Concepts outlined in planning are tied to business practices in analysis, given specific incarnation in design, and grounded to a hardware and software platform in construction.

This process is like a community project to paint a mural on the side of a town building (FIG. 2-3). The initial concept development, the separation of the job into multiple projects, and the selection of personnel and supplies are all done during strategic planning. During analysis each team examines the requirements for their section of the

Automated software development   **23**

Planning

Community mural project
objectives:
- Brighten main street district
- Bring feeling of great
  outdoors to downtown

Four areas:
1. Coastal scene (Steve)
2. Desert scene (Kala)
3. Farmland scene (Paulo)
4. Mountain scene (Janet)

Analysis

| Ocean scene | Desert | Farmland | Mountain scene |

→ Very rough outlines of individual scenes

Design

→ Detailed sketches all the "interfaces" match up

Construction

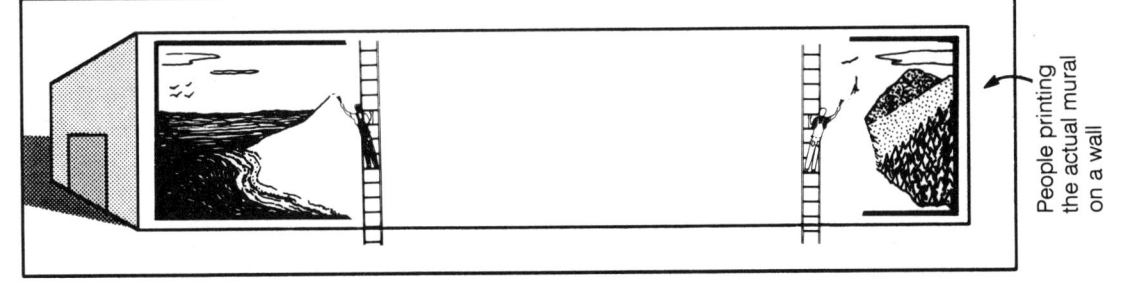

→ People printing the actual mural on a wall

Fig. 2-3. Growth of detail during top-down development

mural in more detail, sketching the fundamental requirements. The design phase has each team drawing detailed renditions on paper, and perhaps dividing the actual painting work among team members. The act of painting on the wall represents the construction phase, as paper design is translated into a finished, tangible work.

Top-down development projects proceed in the same manner. Requirements go from the general to the specific, and the domain is progressively narrowed for each successive project, allowing them to provide deeper detail. By narrowing the scope for each successive phase, project sizes remain manageable at every level.

Figure 2-4 illustrates this progression for an entire organization. The pyramid represents the sum of all software engineering information for the firm. Initially, the top triangle is filled with strategic planning information for the business as a whole. Four analysis areas, A1 through A4, are scoped from this broad model. An analysis project is funded for Area A2, judged to be most in need of immediate attention. The analysis project then scopes and prioritizes three design projects, D1, D2, and D3, which represent potential business systems. A design project for D2 is staffed and funded. The project identifies two construction modules, C1 and C2, which can be built and installed separately, thereby keeping module size manageable and reducing time-to-delivery.

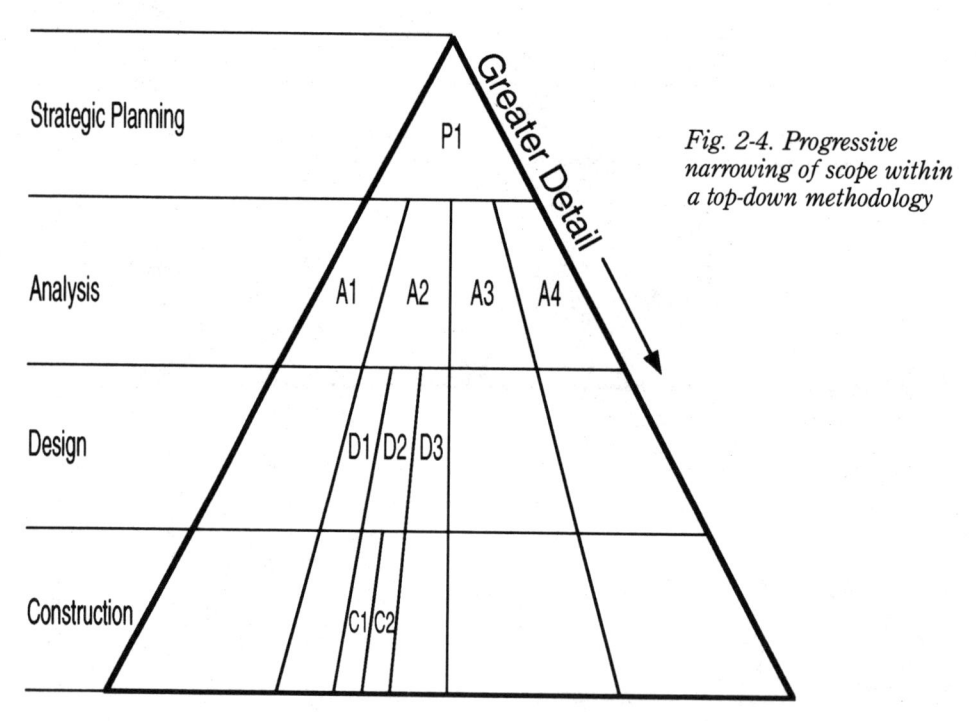

Fig. 2-4. Progressive narrowing of scope within a top-down methodology

Other structured methodologies are more linear, retaining the same scope from initial project planning all the way through construction. Project scope is defined by user system requests or forces within the IS organization. Instead of corporate-wide strategic systems planning, projects undergo proposal submission, feasibility analysis, and project resource planning tasks. Once approved, structured analysis begins.

Structured design is a direct follow-up to analysis, and normally retains the same functional boundaries.

Strategic systems planning

Strategic planning is nothing new for most companies. Some form of goal-setting and strategy formation occurs at every level of most organizations. Strategic planning for information systems is less prevalent and newer on the scene.

Strategic systems planning lays the foundation for future IS applications. Current systems development projects are often driven by the needs of a single division or department, without the welfare of the entire company in mind. Strategic planning is an opportunity to assess the entire applications portfolio, and to prioritize new projects based on relative contribution to the entire corporation.

Many different methods exist for planning systems and information resources, ranging from the simple to the Byzantine. Some of these methods are based on the tried-and-true business planning methods taught in every business school. Other methods designed specifically for systems planning require a wider planning scope and more rigorous analysis.

Strategic planning methods for information systems fall into three main categories:

1. Strategic business planning concentrates on modeling business goals, functions, and information needs, uses these to drive later project formation.
2. Information resource planning mainly assesses IS project feasibilities in terms of availability of human and technological resources.
3. IS project planning usually specifies some form of comparative feasibility study or cost/benefit analysis of potential development projects.

Many tools support traditional business planning methods. By definition, CASE tools only concern themselves with business planning applied to information systems. Many companies are finding that the more rigorous strategic systems planning methodologies can be used to produce more robust strategic business plans too.

Strategic systems planning methods capture information about:

- business goals and objectives
- critical success factors
- market factors
- business strategies
- business functions
- groupings of business data
- current information systems portfolios
- information systems resources

After capturing this data in structured form, you build relationships between the data and analyze patterns that emerge. By relating the firm's prioritized goals to its business functions, for example, you can form a picture showing which functions should be automated first for maximum gain.

The following tools are often used to support the strategic planning process:

- goal decomposition diagrams, to show how tactical goals support higher level strategic ones
- function decomposition diagrams, to show the full scope of all business activities
- association matrices, to show relationships between various types of information
- data models, to show how data areas interrelate

Though most strategic planning tools stand alone, some are offered as part of integrated CASE tools. Integration allows consequent requirements analysis effort to build directly upon the finding of the strategic planning phase.

Traditional business planning methods seem simple compared to some of the more modern information systems planning methods. Because business planning is done at high organizational levels by only a few people, the techniques need to be kept simple to keep the data manageable. Newer methods require a wider scope of information, and more rigorous methods of relating and comparing the data. Done manually, this type of planning is harrowing and demanding. CASE makes the strategic planning process faster and more palatable to managers.

Strategic systems planning results in the creation and prioritization of development projects. The results of the planning process reside in the software engineering repository, and they can directly influence subsequent systems development. Unlike the more general strategy statements that result from periodic business planning, the goals identified in an Information Strategy Plan (ISP) become "live goals." They will live productively, inspiring and justifying the systems that will be developed.

Strategic planning results in a coherent company-wide framework for developing information systems. Participants in the strategic planning process are encouraged to be visionary in their goals and estimates of future needs. Visionaries will discover new ways to work; pragmatists will seek conservative ways to automate current procedures. With the right participants, strategic planning sessions will produce suggestions for restructuring business processes to cut costs and time-to-market. Strategic planning can also help unearth opportunities for new strategic systems.

Requirements analysis

During requirements analysis, developers examine a specific area of the business in detail, capturing user requirements for eventual systems. Using a top-down or telescopic methodology like Information Engineering, the scope of each business area is defined during the strategic planning process.

A business area is a tightly grouped collection of business activities and things of interest to the company. A marketing business area, for example, might include the functions market research, selling, and advertising, and the data areas customers, customer orders, and demographics. Each business area is the topic of a separately staffed analysis project. When the analysis tasks are complete, a number of system design projects are identified and prioritized. Each design project has an even narrower scope. Linear methodologies, on the other hand, maintain a constant business scope across all development phases.

Whether the methodology is telescopic or linear in nature, requirements analysis captures the same types of information about the business. Analysts break down general business functions into more detailed processes, and outline the steps that occur to execute these processes. Data areas break down into constituent entities—objects that are of interest to the business. For instance, the customer data area identified in planning is found during analysis to contain specific entities: customer, customer address, and customer contact.

In most methodologies, analysis attempts to capture fundamental business knowledge rather than details about specific systems. It deals with what the business does, rather than how specific procedures work. For example, analysis might capture the basic steps needed to accept a new customer order as a list of essential processes:

1. Receive order.
2. Retrieve customer information.
3. Check customer credit.
4. Match order against available inventory.
5. Fill order.

The specific behavior of each process can be described in many ways, using graphic diagrams or structured English pseudocode.

In contrast, a procedural description might start: "Fill out form M-195 with customer and order information. Enter the order into the ORDENT system using screen TC4550. Hit the key F1 to add a new order, or key F2 to change an existing open order . . ."

This information is very specific to an implemented operating environment, and normally such details are left to the subsequent structured design tasks. The procedural description is so tied to a specific environment that it can't be generalized and applied to other situations. Essential processes, on the other hand, carry fundamental descriptions that can be transformed in design to fit any number of possible implementation environments. By doing fundamental analysis before design, you leave your design options open. You also gain the ability to easily design and implement the same business processes across multiple delivery platforms.

Most analysis methods rely on graphics to represent business knowledge. Structured analysis techniques were used by many companies before CASE tools became available. The biggest complaint about manual structured analysis was the labor-intensivity of drawing diagrams by hand. CASE tools make analysis techniques practical by automating the drawing process, and retaining graphics information to speed later changes.

Analysis diagrams include:

- entity-relationship diagrams
- process decomposition diagrams
- process dependency diagrams
- data flow diagrams
- data navigation diagrams

- state-transition diagrams
- action diagrams or pseudocode

Most CASE tools for structured analysis handle a number of diagram types. The set of diagrams offered by a tool depends on which methodologies the tool supports and which types of systems the tool understands.

Structured analysis methodologies date back to the mid-1970s, when Ed Yourdon, Tom DeMarco and others developed graphical techniques for representing systems functions. Complementary data analysis methodologies were developed around the same time by E.R. Chen and Charlie Bachman. During the 1980s, other experts augmented these early methods, adding new information to diagrams for special purposes, or combining multiple methods into "full life-cycle" methodologies. The number of methodologies today is overwhelming: Warnier-Orr, Ward-Mellor, Hatley-Pirbhai, Gane-Sarson, and information engineering, to name a few. Each methodology requires different sets of graphic diagrams, and often different conventions for each graphic.

Many methodologies draw a distinct line between data analysis and process analysis. Initially, data models and process models are created separately. The results of these independent efforts are then merged using data flow, data navigation, state-transition, or process action diagrams. Newer methodologies, especially those based on object-oriented analysis methods, attempt to bridge the crevasse between process and data by considering both in the early stages of analysis. Booch and Buhr diagrams have gained popularity for object modeling.

Methodologies also differ according to the types of systems that will eventually be created. Analysis of real-time or embedded systems—involving direct interaction with instruments or hardware systems—require specialized diagrams and analysis techniques. Fundamental analysis will be a smaller part of real-time system development efforts because these systems are highly dependent on detailed hardware information, to be captured during the design phase. Similarly, business areas ripe for expert system or neural network solutions might need different graphic or textual representations.

TABLE 2-4 shows a sampling of available CASE tools which support structured analysis diagrams and techniques.

Business system design

Analysis defines what needs to happen, and business system design describes exactly how those things will occur. Design describes specific ways of implementing the business requirements outlined during analysis.

During the design phase, developers specify the user interface behavior and internal structure of the system using a variety of diagrams and structured test formats. Many of these specifications build directly upon the result of analysis tasks. Conceptual data models are transformed into relational or hierarchical data structures. Fundamental business processes become program modules or submodules. Designers surround these descendents from analysis with screens, reports, and program structures, wrapping them like gifts for systems users.

*Table 2-4. Structured Analysis
Capabilities of Integrated CASE Tools*

Structured Analysis Tool -Vendor	Diagrams Supported	Methodologies Supported
Information Engineering Facility -Texas Instruments	• Entity decomposition • Entity-relationship diagram • Process decomposition • Process dependency diagram • Process action diagram	• Information engineering*
Application Development Workbench -Knowledgeware	• Entity-relationship diagram • Process decomposition • Process action diagram • Data flow diagram	• Information engineering • Gane-Sarson
Foundation: PLAN/1 -Andersen Consulting	• Entity-relationship diagram • Process decomposition • Data flow diagram	• METHOD/1*
Pro*Kit -McDonnell Douglas	• Entity-relationship diagram • Process decomposition • Data flow diagram	• Gane-Sarson*

*Indicates tightly coupled methodology support.

Products of the design phase include:

- screen layouts
- report formats
- data flow diagrams
- module structure charts
- module flow charts
- Booch and Buhr diagrams for object-oriented design
- Petri net diagrams
- action diagrams or pseudocode
- user interface specifications
- dialog flow diagrams
- data structure diagrams

Design diagrams provide graphic illustrations of overall systems structure and user interface components. Most tools still require the detailed program logic to be textual, written using traditional programming languages, or structured, high-level dialects which resemble fourth-generation languages. Other tools ignore internal module logic completely, focusing instead on user interfaces and systems structure. These tools force detailed processing logic to be done as program code during the construction phase.

As in analysis, design tasks differ radically according to the type of system being built. If the system will run on a parallel-processing computer, for example, you will need special design tools for viewing simultaneous processing paths. Designs for real-time embedded systems need ways to show hardware interaction and simulate signal throughput.

Almost all of the earliest CASE tools automated design tasks. Many still support systems design exclusively, ignoring planning and analysis. The most effective design tools are those which generate working systems from the design specifications.

Three categories of design tools deserve further description: prototyping tools, interface generators, and simulators.

Prototyping tools Prototyping is a form of accelerated systems design. Prototypes are mock-ups of design products like screens or report layouts. After cursory analysis, developers create prototypes and review them with potential systems users. The users critique the screens or reports, and help the developers align the prototype with business requirements. Some CASE tools can convert the final, user-approved prototypes into working systems, but many just produce skeletal specifications from the prototypes for later embellishment.

Prototyping brings three major benefits:

1. early verification of design feasibility
2. opportunities to quickly consider alternative designs
3. a dynamic, exploratory development cycle for gradual refinement of nebulous requirements

Skilled prototype developers can often create working business systems in a fraction of the normal development time. Systems users participate closely in systems development, so they normally accept the resulting system with few reservations. But prototyping alone is not an answer to the software crisis.

Since prototyping methods tend to skip fundamental analysis tasks, the resulting system is usually very implementation-specific. Prototypes are defined for specific delivery platforms, and aren't easily translated to fit other operating environments. For instance, a prototype that makes use of a mouse, windows, and pull-down menus can be easily built to run on an Apple, Macintosh or an IBM PC running OS/2. Yet porting it to an IBM mainframe requires a major conversion effort, since mice, windows, and pull-down menus are unavailable.

In addition, prototyping does not address systems integration issues. Integrated applications require solid, shared data structures and reusable processes. Prototyping without analysis makes both goals much harder to achieve. Prototypes reflect the views of a small group of users, not a broad spectrum of business experts. Since prototypes are built for systems with predefined scope, user requirements are limited to that view. Developers ask users, "What do you want to see on this screen?" rather than "What do you do to meet your goals?" The former question elicits responses about field sizes and screen colors, while the latter gets answers which illuminate the company's business practices.

Prototyping techniques can be more effective as immediate follow-ons to analysis. They allow users to quickly apply the results of analysis to their real world of screens and reports. Prototyping is most valuable when used for:

- small, self-contained systems
- building on top of structured analysis objects
- temporary capture of user requirements for subsequent design

Interface generators In the days before online transaction processing, few people worried about software's user interface. Since online systems brought terminals to computer novices, interface issues have escalated. Study of man-machine interfaces is now a complex discipline, and the interfaces themselves are just as complex. It takes more code, when written from scratch, to handle function keys, a mouse, multiple windows, and pull-down menus—the staples of modern user interfaces—than it does to write the core logic of most business applications.

Enter interface generators: tools to accelerate interface design. In the CASE perspective, they allow systems designers to rapidly design user interfaces which will be directly used for the creation of a working system. These tools can double as prototyping tools, though they are most often used to create small stand-alone applications which access central databases.

This category does not include code libraries or other inventories of interface objects, since these provide none of the automation of a CASE tool.

A screen "painter" is a simple example of an interface generator. After specifying which data items will be used for a screen, the designer drags each item to its proper place on the screen using cursor keys or a mouse. The resulting screen picture will then be automatically transformed into a screen "map" or embedded in program code during the construction phase.

Other generators create more sophisticated interfaces which make use of windows and pull-down menus. Many interface generators stand alone, producing skeletal program code for a programmer to flesh out afterwards. Others, like HyperCard, for the Apple, Macintosh or Easel, for OS/2, combine sophisticated interface features with rudimentary programming languages. When hooked up with an underlying database management system, these tools provide powerful means for creating database applications.

As with prototyping tools, interface generators do little to further systems integration. Frequently these tools are used by business people to create localized systems; they aren't used to build integrated applications.

Simulators Prototyping accelerates development by providing early user validation of systems requirements. Simulation offers another path to early quality-checking.

A simulator steps through the design model, mimicking the behavior of the finished system, before any code has been generated. It helps find algorithmic problems and performance bottlenecks in real-time and distributed transaction-based system models.

Most simulation tools exist independent of CASE tools. Some programming languages, such as Simula and Simscript, are dedicated simulation languages. If you seek an integrated CASE tool for real-time system development, though, you will be better off purchasing one with built-in simulation capability. Stand-alone simulators force duplication of effort—you specify the design once in the CASE tool, and again for simulation purposes. Built-in simulators let you "prototype" all aspects of your design, not just the user interface, with little extra effort.

Systems construction

Construction involves transforming design specifications into working systems. This phase ties the design model to a specific hardware and software environment. Construction tools can provide automatic generation of program source code and databases.

Code generators transform design specifications into compilable program source code and supporting files. They pull together information about program structure, module logic, and user interfaces, mixing them into coherent, compilable programs.

Many code generators produce skeletal source code which must be augmented by skilled programmers, though a few can produce complete programs. Complete generation is far superior to partial generation, since it means that all maintenance can be limited to the analysis and design specifications. When design requirements change, a new, modified program can be swiftly generated. Partial generation forces redundant maintenance of source code and design specifications.

Some recent CASE tools forego the compilation step, producing object code directly. Others boast "executable specs," meaning that the diagrams and pseudocode created in the CASE tool can be run directly as a working program, usually in an interpreted mode.

Early code generators were beset by complaints that their generated programs ran slowly. Many vendors have fixed this problem, some by embedding expert systems into their products, so that many generated programs now outperform comparable ones created manually by skilled programmers.

Full code generation can provide the biggest productivity boost of any CASE tool. When based on solid structured analysis and design, generated programs usually show few defects. Complete code generation eliminates the errors of translation and typography that often plague programmers.

Most code generators can deal with a limited range of program types. Some can only create online screen-based programs; some generate batch programs and nothing else; others are limited to real-time embedded systems. Only a few can handle multiple program types. Similarly, few CASE tools provide multi-lingual code generation. Often you are limited to one target programming language and database platform.

Many CASE tools also generate database structures directly from data models developed in the design phase. Frequently these structures are created in the form of data definition language (DDL) statements which are transferred to the target platform and fed to a database creation utility. Some database generators only generate skeletal statements which need manual rework. As with code generators, this weakness might force duplicated maintenance effort in the future.

TABLE 2-5 lists the features of a sampling of integrated CASE tool code generators.

Table 2-5. Sampling of Integrated CASE Tool Code Generators

Code Generator —Vendor	Output System Types	Target Environment			Features
		Language	Other Hardware/OS	DBMS	
Information Engineering Facility —Texas Instruments	• online • batch • database • JCL	COBOL	IBM Mainframe: MVS, CICS, TSO, IMS, VM	DB2	• debug at spec level • generates screen navigation logic • generates SQL data access statements
		COBOL, C	DEC VAX: VMS	RDB, Oracle	
		COBOL, C	IBM PC: OS/2	DBM	
		COBOL, C	Tandem: NonStop	NonStop SQL	
		COBOL, C	TI 1500, Fujitsu: UNIX	Oracle	
Application Development Workbench —Knowledgeware	• online • batch	COBOL	IBM Mainframe: MVS, CICS	DB2	
		COBOL	IBM PC: OS/2	DBM	
Foundation INSTALL/1 —Andersen Consulting	• online • batch • database	COBOL	IBM Mainframe: MVS, CICS	DB2	• manages test data • supports windows on VAX • generates screen navigation logic
		COBOL	DEC VAX: VMS	RDB, RMS	
		COBOL	BULL: GCOS7, GCOS8		
		COBOL	IBM PC	ORACLE	

Testing and quality control

Testing is frequently seen as a distinct development phase that follows systems construction. It is far more useful to treat testing as a continuous set of quality control tasks that touch every software development phase.

Structured analysis and design techniques intend to trap and correct requirements errors very early in the development cycle. Error correction costs less early on; once you've written program code, bugs become more difficult to hunt down and kill. Yet most shops see testing as the final phase of development, not an ongoing development activity.

CASE tools are starting to provide testing features which make continuous quality control more practical. CASE tools can help:

- check consistency of analysis and design specifications
- automatically test programs and specifications
- develop test plans
- manage test data

One big reason for testing's spot at the end of the line is the difficulty of testing anything other than detailed program logic. Information gathered in the planning and analysis phase is intentionally less precise than program source code, and thus more difficult to evaluate.

Some CASE tools can help evaluate the models built during planning, analysis, and design. Using rule-based knowledge about supported development methodologies, some tools will check the consistency of these models, bringing potential errors to the developer's attention. Currently the types of errors caught are the most blatant ones: referencing entities or processes which haven't been defined, for example, or building a looped dependency chain (also known as the "chicken-or-the-egg" syndrome). As the underlying artificial intelligence techniques mature, more subtle errors will become identifiable. A few tools can now catch things like stylistic errors in diagrams. Some allow users to alter the rule base, letting the tool check against locally developed modeling standards.

Some integrated tools also use a software engineering knowledge base to ensure consistency of automatically generated information. Under certain circumstances, for example, a change to a design data structure can be propagated back to analysis, causing a matching change to the conceptual data model. Similarly, a change to a program module's list of input data might be tracked back to the analysis model, causing an alteration to the data flow diagram of the module's ancestor.

Systems testing has two main objectives: to ensure that systems' behavior matches the users' requirements, and to verify the systems' technical and structural integrity. Consistency-checking only verifies the internal integrity of software designs. It can't validate external behavior.

Ideally, you want a bank of users to spend days in front of terminals running new systems through their paces. Systems users are the ultimate validators, but their time is usually limited. Often user requirements can be stated in the form of business scenarios, a sequential set of actions within the business environment. They can be transformed into detailed test plans, which specify systems inputs, expected actions, and expected results.

Some CASE tools can generate skeletal test plans directly from objects in the repository. These test plans focus on the structural integrity of systems, though; they don't generate business scenarios. Generated test plans can help determine the scope of data you need to fully test the systems. However, more complete test plans, based on business scenarios, are needed for comprehensive validation.

Thorough testing—especially using regression techniques—can require overwhelming volumes of test data. Given basic parameters, some tools will also generate batches of test data, removing the need for mindless data entry.

Many CASE tools provide services to help bring these volumes of data under control. Test data managers keep track of reusable sets of test data, and tie these data to specific program modules and testing objectives. The tester specifies the part of the system to be tested and testing objectives, and a suite of test data is either retrieved or prepared.

Some tools will automatically apply test data to actual programs. This greatly simplifies the testing of online screens; the testing tool simulates a system's user, exercising the online system at breakneck speed.

System implementation

In large organizations, deploying applications systems can be as complicated as developing them. Among the many tasks required to smoothly "roll out" new systems, implementors must:

- schedule system installations
- announce the rollout strategy
- install database components
- convert existing data to new formats
- install applications
- install data exchange "bridges" to existing systems
- run new and existing systems in parallel and compare results
- train users how to use new applications
- set up mechanisms for user evaluation and feedback

Rollouts of integrated applications require tight coordination of all tasks listed above, often involving multiple project teams and different groups of affected users.

Sadly, CASE tools do little to help the implementation effort. Some tools can be used tactically: project management tools for scheduling and tracking of tasks; and automated testing tools for parallel system tests and other validations. Data conversion modules and interface bridges to existing systems can be built using standard CASE methods and tools, leveraging off of the CASE repository and code generation capability. Yet no tools are now available to help plan application rollout or coordinate simultaneous installation of integrated applications.

Maintenance

Unlike most products, software systems rarely become "finished goods." Software is constantly changed, enhanced, and reinstalled. Commercial software follows the same pattern: new features are sold as upgrades for nominal fees. Imagine if other manufacturers had the same upgrade policies as software houses: after a year with your 1991 Mercedes 300SL you could upgrade to the 1992 version for an extra $2000.

New systems development is expensive, and maintenance is often a cheaper alternative. The tendency is never to retire old systems, but to constantly change and improve them over time.

A 1986 study found that 67% of the costs incurred during the life of traditionally developed software systems go to maintenance.[4] Experts estimate that between $22 billion and $30 billion are spent on software maintenance each year, worldwide.[5]

When software is built using CASE, maintenance costs drop radically. At DuPont, for example, CASE developers experienced maintenance cost reductions of 75%.[6] Integrated CASE tools with code generators offer features that dramatically simplify maintenance:

- repository-based cross-referencing of data and program components
- detailed documentation that traces implemented code back to its original specifications

- version control to track maintenance history
- automated management of software components needed to regenerate changed applications (configuration management)
- debugging and testing at the specification level

Code generation also speeds the maintenance effort by accelerating the change-compile-test cycle.

Unfortunately, pre-CASE applications can't benefit from these features. And older systems are the ones that need the most help. Developers have two alternatives to slash maintenance costs for these applications: user better tools for manually maintaining traditional code; or transform existing code into components that the CASE repository can understand, and use CASE techniques to rebuild and maintain the application in the future.

The former alternative cries out for a programmer workbench composed of tools for analyzing and restructuring program code. The latter alternative, reverse engineering, will be discussed in detail in the next section.

Maintenance programmers find that locating the source of problems in existing code, and identifying where new enhancement code should be placed are the most time-consuming tasks. Most automated maintenance tools, therefore, help the developer understand program structure or isolate potential danger areas. Maintenance tools include:

- code reformatters, which improve readability
- code restructurers, which provide logical reorganization
- cross-reference utilities, to index occurrences of data items or code segments
- program analyzers, which highlight potential logic problems or performance bottlenecks
- cross-compilers and language translators, for transporting code to new hardware or software platforms
- configuration management tools, to control selective regeneration of program components
- code libraries, to store source code and catalogue reusable routines

Maintenance professionals find all of these tools valuable, though most of the tools do not qualify as CASE tools. CASE tools automate engineering techniques, and add value as they transform information. Tools like code reformatters and cross-reference utilities simply document software internals. Configuration managers and code libraries just keep track of software components. These are programmer productivity tools, not CASE tools. Even so, a powerful suite of programmer utilities can do wonders for maintenance productivity.

Most maintenance tools are sold as stand-alone utilities. Very few integrated programmer workbenches are sold commercially. Because of this void, some IS organizations elect to build their own workbenches by combining multiple tools.

Reverse engineering

Reverse engineering is the process of dissecting existing systems and rebuilding them using superior techniques and development tools. Deconstruction tracks backward through the sequence of development tasks, gleaning design knowledge and diagrams from existing code, and then converting this information into analysis specifications. These objects can be pulled forward again through the development cycle, with varying degrees of transformation (FIG. 2-5).

Beware of merging reverse-engineered system information into the corporate development repository. System integration requires visionary top-down planning, but information drawn from current systems is heavy with the weight of old routine. Most existing systems were built with little vision and little communication with business experts. As a result, they reflect old, often distorted business practices. Bringing old information into the repository can cause severe integration problems, and even prevent new procedures from taking hold.

In other contexts, reverse engineering is often useful, especially when:

- restructuring or redesign will strengthen the program for future maintenance work
- the program needs to be transferred from a dying technical platform

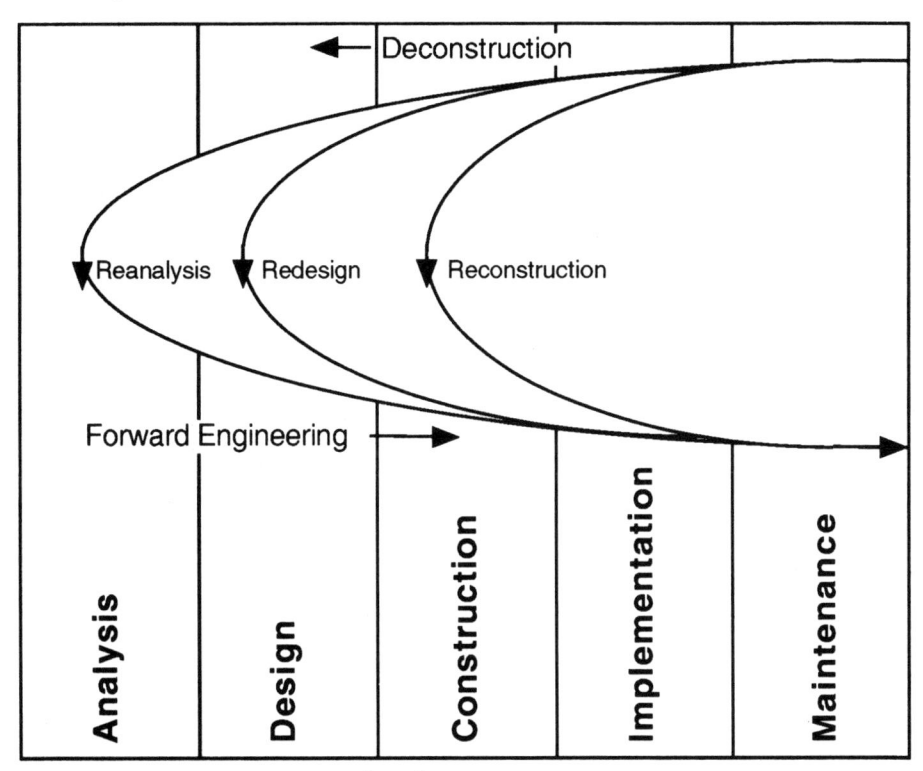

Fig. 2-5. The flow of reverse engineering

- transferring to new platforms
- building bridges to existing systems

Reverse engineering tools can distill design information from existing code, and allow you to rebuild and maintain the application using CASE tools. This can greatly reduce future maintenance costs; the integrated CASE tool effectively obviates the need for a programmer workbench of code maintenance tools. Once in the repository, the application can be documented, redesigned, or restructured using CASE techniques. It can then be rebuilt for any platform supported by the code generator.

By pulling information about existing data structures—databases or flat files—into the CASE repository, you can easily build data conversion programs to integrate new applications into your current application environment.

Repository services

Though companies can tactically apply single-function CASE tools to good advantage, they need integrated tools to really get the most out of CASE. Integrated tools automate the full software development life cycle, and minimize the costly management of tool-to-tool interfaces. They make it far easier for teams of engineers to share data during large-scale development efforts.

Large systems are plagued with a number of problems:

- Increased system complexity. The new need for global systems is one of many influences on system complexity.
- Diverse development and production environments. Portions of a system might be developed in different ways, using different techniques and languages, and then patched together to create the final system. Similarly, parts of the system might be spread across a number of different delivery platforms. For instance, the user interface portion might run on a personal computer, while the database access and storage part executes on a mainframe or minicomputer.
- Coordination of large teams of developers. Increased complexity of the business and systems development make communication between users, managers, and developers critical.
- Construction of centralized, data-sharing applications. Application integration is almost impossible without development tool integration.

In order to combat these and other problems, a more comprehensive approach to CASE is in order. CASE tools must be integrated, the data created by one directly usable by others.

The central repository provides this mechanism for sharing data. The repository is the backbone of an integrated CASE tool. It holds the information created during the software development process, and acts as the clearinghouse for transferring consistent information among multiple CASE users.

The repository is more than a simple database or data dictionary. It stores information about how all software engineering objects relate to each other—which corporate goals a certain system supports, for example, or which programs all share certain common code components.

Many repositories contain only basic software design information. A more robust repository also stores information about:

- business goals and strategies
- organizational structure
- functional business models
- business data models
- development methodologies
- diagrams and graphics
- reusable code modules
- computer hardware, networks, and distribution capabilities

A repository is really a complex database, founded on a model (called a metamodel) of the data and processes that make up software engineering. This model specifies the types of data that will be captured and manipulated by the integrated CASE tools.

Repositories evolved from early data dictionaries, which organized descriptions of corporate data items into easily usable form. TABLE 2-6 shows the range of dictionaries and repositories that underlay CASE tools.

Table 2-6. Types of CASE Databases

Database Type	Description
Data dictionary	A database or flat file used to store information about data elements or software components.
Active data dictionary	A data dictionary that is an integral part of the database system it documents.
Dedicated repository	A complex database, founded on a software engineering metamodel, that centrally manages information for a vendor-specific set of CASE tools.
Open repository	A repository, based on a generalized metamodel, that allows CASE tools from different vendors to share common software engineering information.
Intelligent repository	A dedicated or open repository that contains knowledge about software development methodologies

Many integrated CASE tools come with a dedicated repository. Each tool in the integrated set creates or changes certain repository objects. The flexibility of a tool's repository dictates whether other tools can share information with it.

To facilitate sharing of data among various CASE tools, a number of vendors now offer "open" repository tools designed to manage information created by many different CASE tools. These tools provide generalized metamodels and sets of services for analyzing and reporting about repository information. They seek to unite many different tools under one flag. Open repositories have arisen in two ways: attempts by a hardware or software company to set a de facto standard that guarantees future sales, or research consortium efforts to standardize tool interfaces for the common gain of member companies.

The lack of CASE tool interface standards has thwarted widespread CASE acceptance for many years. Despite the hundreds of CASE tools on the market, customers find it difficult to mix their favorite products into integrated toolsets. Rarely does one vendor's suite of tools fit a customer's style exactly. Often CASE tools must be dragged reluctantly into productive use.

Some companies have developed their own repositories, which either supplant or work in conjunction with the repositories of the CASE tools. Custom-built repositories normally arose in response to poorly integrated CASE tools, as vehicles for better company-wide data sharing. They have the advantage of capturing all kinds of business and software engineering data, not just the subset of data defined by the CASE tool's metamodel.

Open repositories

Unfortunately, the current level of CASE tool integration is poor, and the cost of designing and building a custom repository is prohibitive for many companies. Currently a number of CASE tool standards are being proposed, but few of these standards have made impacts in the marketplace. It will take widespread acceptance of an open repository product to establish true CASE tool standards.

Though a number of companies and research organizations offer open repository products, the two with the most potential for common acceptance are Pact, from the European ESPRIT effort, and IBM's AD/Cycle Repository. Both of these efforts attempt to define common frameworks for mixing and matching CASE tools into integrated development environments.

Acknowledging the barrier imposed by nonstandard tool interfaces, an ESPRIT project developed the Portable Common Tool Environment (PCTE), a shareable tool interface standard, in 1986. Since then, additional ESPRIT and privately-funded projects have extended this standard, leading now to Pact, a set of specifications for integrated software engineering tools. Pact and PCTE are public tool specifications, not actual products, but they are serving as the basis for many emerging integrated CASE products. Some commercial development environments based on these standards are now available, though all still lack a a rich set of automation tools for the entire development cycle.

On the same grand scale is IBM's AD/Cycle framework. AD/Cycle is a conceptual framework for uniting multiple CASE tools into an integrated development environment. Its cornerstone is a product called simply the Repository. IBM has contracted with a number of CASE vendors—among them Knowledgeware, Synon, and Intersolve—to provide tools that will plug into the AD/Cycle repository. Mixed with their own tools like Cross-System Product (CSP) and DevelopMate, IBM plans to forge a coherent integrated CASE environment.

Though the AD/Cycle framework is not nearly as conceptually thorough or elegant as PCTE and Pact standards, IBM's clout give AD/Cycle an advantage in the marketplace. The need to conform to the AD/Cycle repository's metamodel and interface with other AD/Cycle tools might force *de facto* standards upon CASE vendors.

A lack of tool interface standards hasn't stopped other vendors from delivering open repository products today. For example, ManagerView by Manager Software Products lets users define their own interfaces between development tools and the central repository. ManagerView handles the translation of development information to fit a customizable metamodel.

Many CASE vendors supply repository products as foundations for their integrated products. These repositories act as a clearinghouse for information shared between product components.

In addition to basic storage and reporting of software engineering information, repositories can provide other useful features like version control, security control, and metamodel access.

Version control

Version control tools manage systems evolution and track changes made to each part of a software system. For integrated CASE development, version control should take hold at the object level. Each change to a software development object—a data item, an entity type, a process—should be recorded, and previous versions of the object stored. Versioning serves two purposes: as an archive of inactive objects, and complete system snapshots that allow changes to be made to one version while another continues to run in production.

Some integrated tools provide sophisticated version control; others force the user to manage versions as manual backup copies of repository data. Repositories with no version control capabilities will make it difficult to manage large volumes of software engineering information in the long run.

Security control

Repositories allow many users to access the same software engineering data. This greatly improves communication among developers, and provides for data consistency across the organization. However, uncontrolled access to this information can cause enormous problems. CASE repositories ensure the integrity of the data they contain in two ways: by preventing data access by unauthorized users, and by avoiding conflicts among related data.

User security is an important issue for a repository. Repositories can hold more than just technical software information—used for strategic planning, they can contain sensitive data about corporate goals and plans for strategic information systems. Repositories should enforce user security at the object level. For instance, a database administrator user might be allowed access to entity type objects and data structure objects, but denied access to strategic goal objects.

Security also plays an important role in keeping data consistent. Reusability of software components means that many different developers will change an object over its lifetime. The repository must ensure that two developers don't make conflicting changes to the same object. This is usually handled by granting users specific types of control over objects. A process designer might be given "update" access to all the processes within his project's scope, but granted "read only" access to another project's processes.

User capabilities kick in when objects are transferred between developer workstations and the central repository. Normally a check-out scheme assigns objects to a developer when they are drawn from the repository, and prevents other developers from changing these same objects until they are returned. Some repositories allow many developers to simultaneously work on the same objects. Each time a copy of the object is checked in by a developer, the others are notified of the change. This simultaneous-change scheme is less secure and more prone to conflicting data and lost work.

Metamodel access

The software engineering metamodel harbors knowledge about the types of objects manipulated during software development. Many CASE tool vendors keep tight control of their tools' underlying metamodels, treating them as strategic assets. Open repositories must publicize their metamodels, to encourage third-party vendors to develop tools that conform to them.

Access to the metamodel allows shrewd repository users to develop their own utilities for repository reporting or extending the model to include new types of information. Homegrown utilities can compensate for shortcomings of a CASE tool's repository services. Some of the tools that CASE users have built include:

- reports of entities and data items, sorted, indexed, and cross-referenced
- tools to calculate quality and complexity metrics
- database extensions to manage analysis issues; task and project information; annual business planning and budgeting information
- bridges to third-party code generators and database platforms
- interfaces to graphics tools for improved documentation
- database extensions to support object-oriented and rule-based systems

To build any of these, you need in-depth knowledge of the repository's database structure. The metamodel represents this structure and its inherent rules and constraints at a conceptual level.

Homegrown utilities don't come cheaply, though, and they carry the extra price of maintenance. When the CASE tool structure changes, so must the utilities. If your company is a prized customer, you might convince the vendor to provide some utilities for you. Most vendors look to customers for ideas about new features, especially if the features are applicable (and easily sold) across their entire customer base.

Though most large-scale integrated CASE tools maintain the central repository on a mainframe or minicomputer, some newer products manage repositories on a LAN server. The best of these tools allow true multi-user access. That is, many developers can work simultaneously with the same model. This can greatly improve work group productivity, since it eliminates the file transfer steps most other tools require. Learmonth & Burchett Management Systems, Inc.'s (LBMS) Systems Engineer boasts a multi-user LAN-based repository.

Host repository tools typically cost the most of any CASE component. Prices range from $20,000 from LAN-based models, to close to $1 million for larger-scale mainframe offerings. TABLE 2-7 shows samples of available integrated CASE tool repositories.

Table 2-7. Integrated CASE Tool Repositories

Repository —Vendor	Category	Features
Repository manager —IBM	Open repository	• Security control • Metamodel access
Application Development Workbench —Knowledgeware	Dedicated repository	• Version control • Security control
Information Engineering Facility —Texas Instruments	Dedicated repository	• Version control • Security control • Check-in/check-out • Metamodel access
Foundation —Andersen Consulting	Dedicated repository	• Security control • Check-in/check-out
ManagerView —Manager Software Products	Open repository	• Security control • Version control • Check-in/check-out • Metamodel access • Metamodel extensibility
PACBASE repository —CGI Systems, Inc.	Dedicated repository	• Security control • Version control • Check-in/check-out • Metamodel access • Metamodel extensibility

Methodology support

The most effective CASE tools automate proven software development methods. Methodologies formalize software engineering principles by listing distinct, repeatable steps for developers to follow. Methodology is more important, in the long run, than the CASE tool that automates it.

Many CASE tools supposedly automate popular software engineering methodologies, but very few do a good job of it. Most structured methodologies were developed before the advent of CASE tools, and they never specified tasks to the level of detail that computers require. For instance, early structured analysis texts suggest building data flow diagrams first, then organizing a data dictionary (the precursor of the CASE repository) later.[7] This sequence can work if you're doing everything with pencil and paper, but most CASE tools require you to define data elements before you reference them from process diagrams.

Many CASE tools try to be all things to all people. Some vendors claim their tools support more than a dozen methodologies. These claims aren't false, but they can be misleading. Most CASE tools support a methodology by allowing you to draw the right diagrams, but they don't help you figure out which diagrams to draw, or in what sequence each one should be done. Nor do they suggest which of the dozen methodologies is the best one for your particular project. Flexibility shifts the burden of defining a methodology from the CASE tool vendor to the customer.

Some integrated tools now offer true methodology support, in the form of methodology advisors and methodology selectors. These tools help direct attention to the development process itself, and encourage continuous process evaluation and improvement.

Methodology advisors

Many tools provide passive methodology support, also known as method companionship,[8] by enabling most of the tasks needed to follow a specific methodology. In order to use these tools effectively, especially in a large organization, you need to establish detailed methodologies of your own. Methodologies must be specific in order to foster the standards needed for easier communication among developers.

Methodologies must also be adapted to the organization. None will be sufficient in their initial form. Every organization has a unique style and mix of skills and tools, and methodology must account for this. Even using tools that are tightly coupled to specific methodologies (and often unjustly criticized for being "inflexible"), companies will spend significant effort refining and documenting detailed development methods.

After struggling initially to use Knowledgeware's Application Development Workbench (ADW) tool, Levi Strauss & Co. embarked on a year-long project to write their own internalized methodology. ADW supports the information engineering methodology, but the developers at Levi's found that neither the tool nor the texts on information engineering gave enough methodology guidance. Now in place, the new methodology helps synchronize multiple development efforts and indicates when and how CASE tools should be used.

Some CASE tools go beyond passive methodology support to offer active advice to developers about techniques and tool usage. The tools sport knowledge-based advisor modules, sometimes called methodology drivers, that prompt developers each step of the way. Upon completing a data flow model of an instrument control system, for example, the designer might ask the methodology advisor which step to perform next. The advisor responds with two options: test the system using the CASE tool's simulation module, or proceed to code generation. It might recommend the testing step, but still let the developer generate code if she so chooses. If the data flow model were incomplete in some way, the advisor would identify the missing pieces and suggest they be filled in next.

Methodology selectors

Standard methodologies provide continuity across multiple projects. However IS organizations won't find a single methodology that meets every development need. Wide varieties of systems thrive in most companies: transaction-based mainframe systems, expert systems for specialized problem-solving, real-time systems to run manufacturing lines, local PC databases and spreadsheets for small applications. Each type of systems must be developed in a different way.

The official methodology in a company generally supports only one development paradigm—usually the one developers find most comfortable. When other types of systems are required, the developer either uses renegade techniques, or struggles to chart a new path through the current methodology.

To solve this problem, you need to recognize the need for multiple methods, depending on the type of system you're building. Separate methodologies must be used for developing:

- large-scale transaction-based mainframe systems
- small team tactical applications development
- object-oriented systems
- expert systems or neural networks for specialized problem-solving
- real-time systems to run manufacturing lines or control other hardware
- end-user development of database query systems, reporting systems, or spreadsheets

Each type of systems development can require different skills, methods, and tools. Matching the right tools to the job at hand is a large part of any engineer's skill, yet software developers do a poor job of it. Because software development tools are deep and complex, software professionals prefer the few they already know. This often leads to awkward systems solutions. As they say, when all you have is a hammer, everything looks like a nail (or, as an object-oriented friend of mine once paraphrased, "When all you have is COBOL, everything looks like a procedure").

The process of selecting appropriate methodologies deserves to be centralized. Because most developers don't know about alternative methods, they tend never to consider them. A central group or system with knowledge of multiple methods and tools can help developers make better choices.

Very few CASE products offer this kind of help. Method selection transcends most tools, considering the entire set of tools and skills available to the organization. A detailed solution to this problem is suggested in chapter 5.

Project management

Project management involves estimating project completion dates, scheduling and estimating development tasks, and capturing measurements about task and project performance. Project management gives managers firsthand views of development progress and status.

Structured methodologies and dependable tools bring consistency to software development, simplifying the job of the project manager. Project durations become more predictable, and progress becomes more easily tracked.

Tools with methodology knowledge take the first step to automating project management. Add facilities to create specific projects, indicate who will work on them, and track the time taken and quality of the results, and you have full project management support.

A number of integrated CASE products now include project management features. Unfortunately most of them are very tightly coupled to the specific CASE tool; they can't be generalized for use on other types of projects. During the early months of

CASE introduction, only a small percentage of development projects will use the CASE tool, so the tool's project management support won't have great impact.

CASE project management tools have some strong advantages over general scheduling tools, including tight coupling with the methodology and the ability to draw measurements from the CASE repository. Yet many companies already have standard tools in place for managing projects, consistently reporting hours worked and task completion dates. If you run CASE projects with special project management tools while still managing most projects using standard tools, you might introduce confusion and inconsistency into the project evaluation process. If there are no common project management practices, though, the CASE tool's capabilities will be a boon.

Project management consists of two major functions: task scheduling and process measurement. Task selection and scheduling should be tied to the methodology. The scheduling tool can present a boilerplate work breakdown structure for project managers to edit and assign resources to. As tasks are completed, the project manager (or the developer themselves) record the amount of effort and time taken, and the results of the task.

CASE tools that know about development methodology can help you improve it. The standard methods you choose will affect all future development efforts, so you need to know which methods work well and which need polishing. By gathering task information, especially using standard measurements of time, effort, and quality, you can assess the effectiveness of various development tools and approaches.

Where CASE ends

CASE is not the only new technology that promises to eliminate problems of software development productivity. Object-oriented languages, artificial intelligence tools, and other newly popular development tools can also help you achieve this goal. These aren't one-for-one alternatives to CASE, though. They are complementary technologies.

In fact, CASE might soon become the pivot around which all these technologies turn. With its emphasis on centralized business and systems knowledge, CASE is poised to be the foundation technology for multiparadigm development approaches. Once we know that a data item or a business process has certain meaning to the business, does it matter whether we express this as lines of COBOL, or objects that pass messages, or a structured set of loosely linked rules?

CASE transcends programming languages. It is a tool framework, while languages are the material the tools operate upon. To draw a workshop metaphor, CASE is your toolbench, holding saws and drills and hammers; programming languages (and graphic diagramming languages, for that matter) are the wood from which you carve your model.

Many firms already have systems built with fourth-generation, object-oriented, or logic programming languages already in place. Will CASE force them to abandon other investments in nonstandard development tools? Directions in the development tool market will dictate the answer to this question. CASE tools can potentially automate any kind of software development. They can be tailored to fit almost any existing development environment. However, only a few environments are popular enough to ensure substantial sales of CASE products.

Currently, many CASE products are only loosely coupled to methodologies, and can be coerced into supporting techniques they weren't designed for.[9] As long as you don't want full code generation, tools can be found to support planning, analysis, and design for almost any type of system. However, fully integrated project support environments will only support limited types of systems in the near future. To get the most out of integrated CASE for the next few years, you will need to target fairly standard system types and development platforms.

For now, given the cornucopia of available CASE tools and methods, you can certainly find some that fit your development style. You can implement them as you want, starting slow with a single tool or two, or buying wholesale into the tools and concepts. The next chapters discuss ways to make either CASE strategy succeed.

3

Waiting for the revolution

The business environment changes rapidly; yet most IS organizations try to adapt using outmoded development techniques and organizational structures. Some 85% of all IS organizations still rely on traditional third-generation programming languages for the bulk of their systems development. The typical IS organization still follows the hierarchical command-and-control model first formalized by the military, and widely adopted by industrial companies after the Second World War. In other words, most companies still react to the changes of the '90s with development techniques of the '60s and organization of the '50s.

Many companies have experimented with new techniques and organizations, but few have fully adopted them. Matrix organizational structures were in vogue during the 1970s, but few remain. Task forces and project teams often surface in many companies, but only for small operational segments of the business.

Many IS organizations have adopted new development tools, including fourth-generation languages and PC-based development packages. Yet the fundamental development process remains unchanged; it has merely been translated into different languages.

Successful implementation of CASE tools and techniques can help bring about the changes that many firms need to stay successful. By helping to align systems to business goals, CASE encourages robust applications which are more easily adaptable to changing business conditions. In addition, CASE provides an impetus for flattening the IS organizational structure, by allowing shared access to consistent business and development information, and simplifying the task of project management.

None of these changes come cheaply, however. Introduction of new technology causes social and organizational turbulence; organizational changes trigger similar upheavals. Proactive management of the problems of organizational change can sharply reduce the costs of such change. Still, there has never been a revolution without pain. And to deal with the new business environment, we truly need a software development revolution.

A suite of challenges

Rapid changes in the business environment make new demands upon the IS organization:

- Faster environmental changes require faster systems turnaround.
- System complexity increases due to distributed technology, sophisticated user interfaces, and a need for applications integration.
- One strategic system by a computer requires one by you in response.
- Users now want decision support and small-systems development capabilities.

Unfortunately, the IS organization must respond to these demands while fighting some perennial problems:

- constant backlog (estimated at 29 months, on average[1]) for new and enhanced systems
- IS's often shaky systems-delivery track record
- organizational distance between IS and other functional departments
- inflexible systems base requiring constant upkeep
- reduced availability of skilled personnel

This suite of challenges won't be addressed by any one solution. However, CASE technology, embedded in an effective development organization, can provide benefits that address every point listed above.

Software professionals have often heard glowing praise sprinkled over CASE by tool vendors and an eager press. The benefits of CASE have been so zealously publicized that many people now discount every new tale they hear. Such disbelief isn't completely unjustified.

Many early CASE implementations got their names in the industry papers by claiming spectacular gains in system quality and productivity due to the use of CASE technology. Of course firms which struggled to implement CASE are predisposed to find great productivity gains; they've invested lots of money and time, so the technology better work. In most cases, successful CASE adoption probably resulted in improved productivity. However, the figures quoted by CASE implementors—productivity gains of 20 to 500% for software development and maintenance efforts—are usually ballpark estimates that aren't founded on quantifiable measurements.

Most companies have no productivity baseline against which to compare CASE productivity measures. Traditional methods resist consistent measurement, and most companies have not instituted standardized measurement programs, before or after CASE. Many CASE productivity estimates, then, are based solely on the personal experiences of the estimator. A manager whose last project produced 10 programs in six months will say there was a 100% productivity gain if a CASE project does 10 programs in half the time. Factors like program complexity, quality of supporting documentation, and agreeability of systems users don't enter into these estimates, because there is no provision made for measuring them.

Even without exact measurement, though, it is clear that CASE brings wide-ranging benefits. Surveys of CASE users consistently show improvements in systems quality and development productivity. A University of Houston survey of twelve CASE-using companies found average time savings of 20% during system development, and 35% during system maintenance.[2] In an additional survey, 2000 IS managers credited CASE with providing a 28% increase in overall productivity.[3]

Productivity is the most-cited CASE benefit, but it isn't the most important. Advantages gained by tying systems development to business strategy, or by reining in previously unmanageable software projects will be more valuable than simple productivity gains in the long run.

There are four major categories of CASE benefits: quality, productivity, strategic business impact, and management control. Frequently these benefits build upon each other (FIG. 3-1). The strategic business impact of established, shared goals improves management control, since workers tend to move in the same direction with less management supervision. Common methods improve project control and also increase systems quality. Repeatable processes give consistent results, and can include specific validation and verification techniques.

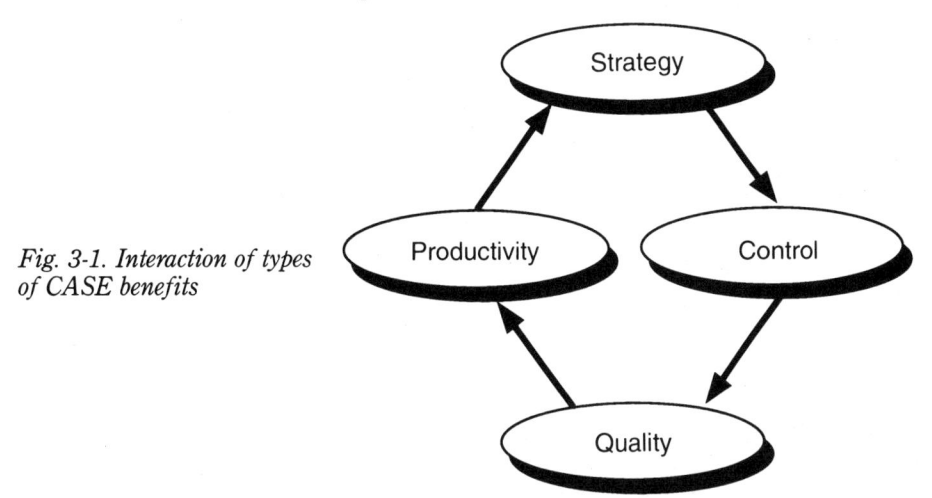

Fig. 3-1. Interaction of types of CASE benefits

Quality improvements—fewer defects and better system documentation—lead in turn to greater productivity, especially during systems maintenance. CASE also raises developer efficiency by automating tedious manual processes. Finally, widespread software productivity gains can translate into similar improvements throughout a company, augmenting CASE's positive business impact.

Successful company-wide CASE usage can boost performance in all these categories. By tactically applying CASE tools for productivity or quality improvement, you can get incremental improvements. But revolutionary gains require revolutionary strategies. To really revamp the development process and prepare for accelerated business change, you need to launch sweeping changes of your own.

Change for the sake of change is energy wasted. Part of any expert's skill is knowing which tool to use for each job. While exceptionally promising, CASE won't solve everyone's development problems. The next sections describe many of the benefits that CASE can bring, and also the problems it has been known to create. By weighing the good against the bad, you can decide if CASE is right for your organization.

Strategic business impact

The combination of CASE and structured planning techniques, fueled by solid support from senior management, can generate significant strategic benefits. These benefits include:

- ability to gain a gestalt or holistic view of the business, and the systems architecture
- clearly articulated goals and strategies used to rationalize development projects and guide employees
- potential to use information systems for competitive advantage

Gestalt visualization

Top-down software engineering begins with a high-level view of the business, capturing information about internal dynamics and the external environment. Most companies have operated for years with only one model of the business: a chart of the organizational structure. The strategic information planning model is far superior, since it captures the essence of the functions each organization performs, and describes the information needed to fulfill these functions.

The strategic model collects the knowledge of many business experts—who often have no other forum for sharing this knowledge—into a single coherent picture of the business and its environment. CASE technology allows workers throughout the company to view this model, increasing everyone's comprehension of the business and its goals. Structured techniques emphasize thoroughness, and the resulting model should reflect complete consideration of internal and external forces.

The planning process transforms this high-level business model into a cohesive information systems architecture, which provides a conceptual map of current and future information systems. And as they say, unless you have a map, how do you know you're going in the right direction?

Clear rationales

Part of the strategic business model is an articulation of the company's overriding goals. These goals rationalize the business, and functions exist solely to achieve these goals.

When you map these goals to the information systems architecture, clear rationales emerge for every systems decision. Each system will help achieve stated business goals, or it will not be developed. Development priorities are influenced by the importance of goals each resultant system will support.

Throughout the development process, the strategic direction stays visible, influencing tactical decisions along the way.

Competitive advantage

In chapter 1, I asserted that CASE can better a firm's competitive position because:

- Firms using CASE have a much better chance of recognizing and developing strategic systems.
- Great gains in software productivity can improve performance throughout the company.
- CASE will be a stepping stone to the development environments of the future.
- Advanced development techniques attract the best software developers.

Most of these are indirect CASE benefits. They arise once CASE has been successfully installed and applied on a large scale. However, some methods for identifying strategic systems have direct CASE tool support.

Despite the intangible nature of some of CASE's strategic benefits, their importance cannot be overlooked. Shared understanding of the business, common goals, and opportunities for competitive advantage all have pervasive effects. In concert they can align business and IS efforts to an unprecedented degree.

Management support

Software development projects are traditionally difficult to control. Most business managers complain that IS organizations cannot deliver quality systems on time and within budget. Software quality expert T. Capers Jones has noted that up to 25% of large software projects are cancelled before completion.

A number of factors contribute to software developers' project management problems:

- Project managers are often drawn from the ranks of programmers and seldom trained in management techniques before inheriting the reins of a new project.
- Professional managers don't feel they have the technical skill to manage programming teams.
- Technical project managers are often called upon to contribute to project deliverables, like a player-coach in baseball or basketball.
- Traditional development methods are susceptible to unexpected changes in user requirements, which might cause long project delays.
- Systems integration problems are often unanticipated.

When software projects go out of control, they often begin a vicious cycle. Rather than addressing problems inherent in the process, management institutes additional reviews and controls. This adds to development time and antagonizes developers. As a result, the next set of projects slip just as far behind schedule.

On-time delivery follows from visible, disciplined processes done by teams with the freedom to do their best work with a minimum of interference. To gain control of systems projects, address the development process and lines of communication between managers and developers.

While CASE certainly can't restructure your organization, it can help streamline the development process, and provide avenues for improved management support of development. CASE encourages:

- sharing of consistent software engineering data
- clear project boundaries manageability of systems
- knowledge and control of the development process
- better tools for project planning and management

Centralized software engineering data

Integrated CASE repositories provide a central source for all software engineering data. Most CASE tools also enforce consistency among this data. For example, an entity called "customer" will have the same definition and the same attributes, no matter which development project chooses to use it. This means that all developers and business experts will see and use consistent information. This hasn't always been so. Many of the integration problems IS groups now face arise from inconsistent definitions of data and processes.

At one large company I worked with, a problem with data consistency provided the impetus for large-scale CASE implementation. A vice president requested from a corporate IS group a list of the company's top ten customers, measured in sales volume, across all divisions and product lines. After six months, the IS group manager admitted to the VP that they couldn't fulfill the request. Every division kept track of its own customers and had different definitions of what a customer was. They all stored different customer information in different data formats. Conversions from one format to another were difficult, and once converted, the data was often unreliable.

Integrated CASE encourages common definitions and formats for business information. It stores the data centrally in the repository, and allows multiple users to access it in various ways. A manager can see a summary of the company's functions using a planning tool; a developer can see a detailed data flow diagram of the components of one of these functions using an analysis tool. Both choose which view they want to see—different views of consistent information.

The information management functions of a repository help developers manage an overwhelming volume of details. The source of all software information in most organizations (except the military, due to their strict documentation requirements) used to be the source code itself. This provided a detailed sequential view of the system, easily understandable only by the author. The repository lets different developers mold data into meaningful shapes. A database administrator examines a system's database structures; a program designer sees structural representations of the code modules and the data structures they exchange; a systems operations manager looks at projected data and transaction volumes for these structures, to plan future system capacity. Each person concentrates on the details that concern them most, and no one is burdened with the full complexity of the system at a detail level.

The integrated CASE tool ensures the reliability of information in many ways. It can check the consistency of information as it enters the repository. This prevents one developer from creating the customer entity type a second time, with a new format or definition, without the approval of other interested developers. Most repository tools also protect the data through security functions. Many have object-level security, which prevents unauthorized users from accessing specific types of information. Power to change database structures may be given only to database administrators, for example.

Clear project boundaries

Projects often get out of control when their boundaries shift. A new interface becomes necessary; business changes necessitates new system features; developers' assumptions about the project scope turn out to be much different from the project sponsor's. Communication breakdowns exacerbate these problems, but current project planning methods are also to blame.

Even among those who use structured analysis and design techniques, an initial project requirements statement often reads more like a features list for a new car than a statement of purpose for a new capital investment (which it is). Many years ago, as a rookie project manager, I was handed an approved proposal for a new system to be developed. The systems scope was defined by a brief statement of purpose and the following list of features:

- multiple invoice formats
- dual currency billing
- automatic tax calculation
- function-key support
- electronic data interchange (EDI) capability
- cost accounting interface
- sales system interface

The rest of the proposal was devoted to cost estimates and impacts upon other development efforts.

While the proposal process at many companies is far more elaborate, very often the "list of features" handed the project manager is just as sketchy. Certainly the authors of the proposal assume that the details of the system will be fleshed out by the project team. Yet the above list is very ambiguous. The rationale for each feature is conspicuously absent. Why must there be a sales system interface? Who requires function keys? Does this mean point-and-click mouse support is out of the question?

The project team's first step is to get more specific requirements from the eventual systems users, causing the first drastic boundary shift. Users might not care about EDI, but they really want shipment packing lists to print along with the invoices. Perhaps the French sales office just bought some new laser printers they would like the system to support. The users' set of desired features might be much different from the proposed features, upon which all cost estimates and project schedules were based. Schedules stretch and costs rise.

A strategic IS architecture minimizes these problems. It places each project in a business context, tied to specific corporate goals: the invoicing system must speed the collection of monies due the company, while providing summarized data for use by managers, and tailorable invoice formats for improved customer service. It outlines the technological path the company plans to follow by stating, for example, that all sales offices will have laser printers for invoicing by 1993. Bounded by the functions it must support and the technologies available to do so, the project team can now discern, by consulting business experts, the most appropriate system features.

Boundary shifts will still occur as business requirements change, but they won't be nearly as radical as what most projects experience today.

Process control

Project control also follows process control. Without CASE, the software development process is rarely consistent. In smaller IS organizations, developers are often free to pursue any course they wish, as long as the system is delivered. Many larger companies have adopted standardized Software Development Life Cycle (SDLC) methodologies, which describe required project deliverables. Yet rarely do SDLC methodologies describe how to create these deliverables, or how each set of deliverables relates to the products of later development phases. An SDLC document might describe the format of an External Systems Specification, but it won't tell how to convert this specification into equivalent COBOL code. This part of the task is left to the programmer, who attacks it in his own inimitable style.

Unfortunately, differences in coding style lead to confusion during systems maintenance, as one programmer must familiarize herself with inner workings of another's mind. Many shops address problems of alien coding style by publishing coding standards. These standards documents suggest formats for comments within code, or guidelines for high-level program structures. But again this does little to address the real problem: an inconsistent process which breeds inconsistent results.

Structured analysis and design methodologies tighten up the development process. They rely on graphical languages which can be easy to grasp, while enforcing rigorous analysis. They provide consistent sets of tasks as well as standardized deliverables. CASE tools encourage conformance to these methodologies by only accepting information in appropriate formats. Some tools advise developers about the methodology, suggesting the next task to be performed, or pointing out steps that were missed.

Once standard techniques are widely used, projects will begin to show comparable results. The effectiveness of techniques can be measured and compared across all projects. Future project estimations can be based on solid measurements of past results. Measurements can be used to identify which processes work well, and which should be replaced. This enables continuous process improvement—a logical search for the most efficient techniques.

Projects that follow standard methodologies are more easily controlled than maverick projects. Consistent development processes improve estimation capability and set a benchmark for better processes in the future.

Better project management

The three benefits listed above—centralized software engineering data, clear project boundaries, and standard development processes—all simplify the project manager's job.

Centralized data provide consistent definitions, encourage common understanding of complex concepts, and build links between project details and the strategic directions they further. Clearer project boundaries ward off unanticipated requirements changes. Standard methods lead to better estimation of project costs, schedules, and resource requirements.

Project management tools within some CASE environments make these advantages concrete. Project scopes can be identified in terms of the software engineering objects they govern. Schedules can be tied to official methodology tasks, and first-cut estimation can be done automatically by the tool. Progress can be measured against baseline schedules, and new estimates automatically generated if task dates slip.

Many of these can be found in stand-alone project management software packages. The advantages of CASE project management tools include the potential for tight coupling with the development methodology, and the ability to tie quality and complexity measurements to the tasks and results.

Quality

Though improved management control is laudable, CASE's biggest impact is upon software quality. By automating structured methodologies, CASE tools provide unprecedented consistency of analysis. Tools with the ability to check the consistency of analysis and design models enable developers to trap errors before they become costly. Simulation and prototyping tools can put a system through its paces before any code is generated.

Integrated CASE tools can monitor systems quality throughout the development cycle; yet many developers shun integrated CASE tools, saying the methodologies they support are too restrictive. This reaction stems from a belief that methodology, since it requires discipline, also smothers creativity.

Creativity is a strong concept in the realm of software development, a basic principle of the hacker ethic. Programming folklore is ripe with stories of individual inspiration and midnight oil-burning. Where is the romance in following a prescribed set of steps to the letter?

In fact, a good methodology doesn't squash creativity. It encourages directed creativity. Analysts and designers need inspired solutions to business problems and creative ways to sidestep technological constraints. By providing frameworks for software development, methodologies allow analysts and designers to concentrate on the important business of solving real-world problems.

To illustrate, compare a methodology to a programming language. Each requires a certain structure and sequences of items. You can write an innovative new COBOL routine to sort a list of numbers, for instance. But it won't do any good if you decide, for aesthetic reasons, to replace the word PERFORM with the word UNDERTAKE. COBOL doesn't understand the word UNDERTAKE. The program will never compile, and the creative sorting solution will be lost. Your creativity is limited to solving the problem; you can't use it to change conventions of the language.

Methodology is the programming language of business analysis and project management. It provides the rigorous framework from which we carve our solutions. Greg

Boone of CASE Research Corporation likens the alleged dichotomy between discipline and creativity to the quality versus productivity controversy in manufacturing. Japanese manufacturers have shown that when quality is made paramount, productivity suffers little, and improves over time. Likewise, says Boone, "Rigor and creativity are not mutually exclusive. Each represents a highly desirable goal."[4] Creativity follows from rigor. If software development is based on engineering discipline, creativity within that discipline will flourish.

Traditionally there is assumed to be a zero-sum trade-off between software quality (in terms of software defects, and adherence to user specifications) and productivity (the rate at which software can be produced). As shown in FIG. 3-2, when CASE tools are introduced, the trade-off curve shifts upward. CASE tools increase productivity by automating design transformations at the same time they improve software quality by automatically flagging potential defects. An IS organization performing at point A on the original curve can shift to point B with CASE, making gains in both quality and productivity.

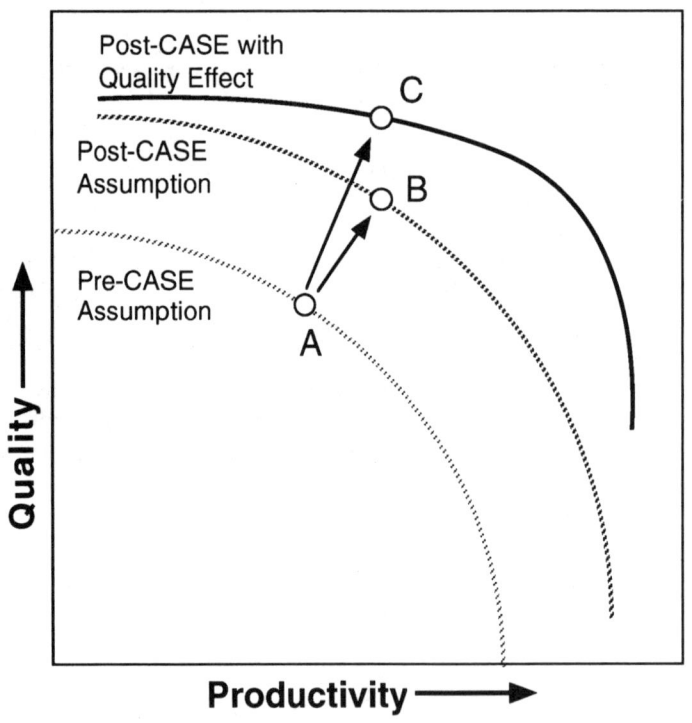

Fig. 3-2. Effect of CASE's quality emphasis on productivity

As many manufacturing companies have shown, though, productivity doesn't necessarily suffer when quality is improved. This drastically changes the slope of the curve: CASE's very high quality levels can be achieved along with sharp productivity gains. A successful CASE implementation can shift the firm to point C on the new curve. Significant trade-offs don't occur until the company stretches for excessive levels of performance—adding new tasks in a fanatic effort to catch the last 2% of software bugs, for example, would greatly decrease productivity.

Integrated CASE tools can improve software quality in a number of ways, both direct and indirect, by:

- improving communication between developers and business experts
- identifying and removing software defects
- encouraging standard systems structures and interfaces
- providing comprehensive systems documentation

Improved communication

Many IS organizations are viewed by the rest of the company as a closed society, a special priesthood with its own language and rituals. Most software developers did little to dispel this myth. They dazzled the uninitiated with weird jargon and behavior. Isolated in their workshops, they transformed mere user requirements into Brobdingnagian constructs, through some strange science. They rarely met project deadlines or cost estimates—but then who could understand their mysterious methods? No one else in the company could perform the same feats.

Truly, wizardry does abound in the IS world. Technology swirls around us in accelerated, awe-inspiring patterns. Part of an IS organization's mission is to harness these forces for the firm's benefit. Yet an IS priesthood distances software developers from the rest of the company, hampering business communications and leading to inappropriate systems.

Is it any wonder that outsourcing of software development projects has become so popular? Contracted firms will often guarantee delivery within a certain timeframe and establish costs ahead of time. This relieves many of the headaches that management has with IS. But outsourcing is not a strategic solution. Requirements can't change in the middle of the project, as they are apt to, since most contractors won't allow this. You also don't want to trust true strategic systems to outsourced firms. You can't copyright an idea, after all.

New techniques, many of them arising from CASE efforts, are demystifying the priesthood. It's not unlike the brightening of the Dark Ages, when the church lost much of its control over individual lives. End-user computing, for one, has put power into the hands of users, but few have felt the inspiration to use it. CASE and structured techniques are enlightening the priests, and forcing them to listen to their congregations.

In the past, most interaction between users and developers occurred at the start of a project, when the initial requirements were gathered, and at the end when the user inspected the system and decided whether to accept it. Before users had veto power only; if they didn't like a system they could refuse it, or request enhancements to make it acceptable. Usually even if a system didn't meet their requirements they would accept it—to get some benefit from it now—rather than kick the project team back for another extended development effort.

The new techniques let users positively influence systems throughout the development process. Studies consistently show that structured techniques, supported by CASE, improve communications between technical and business personnel.[5] CASE techniques emphasize user involvement from the earliest stages of planning and analysis. Some techniques, like prototyping, require constant user participation. This leads to validation of the system's requirements at very early development stages. Once these requirements are fully understood, further transformations of design and construction will simply fill out these requirements. No surprises should slip in unannounced.

The rigorous nature of structured techniques also encourages objectivity on the parts of both developers and business experts. Each participant's role is firmly defined: developers control the development process, users define the business needs. This takes some of the politics out of systems development. Business experts will still haggle over policy decisions, and developers can still try to steer them toward the most efficient technical solutions (in fact, analysts sometimes tend to steer business experts toward elegant model structures at the expense of business sense). But data and process modeling techniques are dispassionate by nature. They allow little room for ambiguities, forcing all participants to be very clear about their requirements. Developers will find it harder to justify unresearched assumptions about business policy than they have in the past, when such assumptions were often hidden in program source code.

Fewer defects

Software quality depends on two different measures: how few errors exist in the resulting systems, and how well the result matches the user's requirements. CASE techniques address the latter concern by emphasizing validation of user requirements during early stages of development. In planning and analysis stages, the business model is still in a form that's easily understood by business experts. The cost of changing the business model at these stages is relatively low compared to the cost of fixing errors in the resultant software system.

CASE helps reduce software errors in a number of ways:

- Automatic transformation of objects reduces typographical and other minor errors which often creep in during manual transformations.
- Errors in analysis and design models can be automatically flagged and sometimes automatically removed.
- Simulation tools allow simple testing of design models before the system is generated.
- Many CASE tools provide trails for tracing systems problems back to the requirements that spawned them.
- Automated testing tools help manage test data and ensure that every piece of a program or design model is thoroughly examined.
- Methodology advice and coaching that some tools provide steers developers clear of glaring development gaffes.

Naturally some CASE tools provide more of these features than others.

Despite the best efforts of CASE tools, true quality assurance comes only from the people and the organization. No tool will catch or fix every error that a developer can introduce. Nothing can protect you from users who got the requirements wrong from the start.

CASE tools alone can improve software quality through automatic transformations and consistency-checking. Extended quality gains require a good measurement and quality enhancement program. Despite CASE's testing aids, there is still no good substitute for a walk-through of systems components with peers and business experts. Solid metrics are also needed to pinpoint areas for quality improvement, and to determine the acceptability of delivered systems.

Comprehensive documentation

CASE also adds to systems quality by improving systems documentation quality. In many companies, especially those that write software for the U.S. Department of Defense, documentation is as important as the resulting systems. Producing large volumes of documents that meet strict government standards can take a large fraction of a project's time.

Unfortunately, most CASE tools give documentation a low priority. All can send output files to a printer, but not many let you alter or embellish output reports or diagrams. Only a few CASE tools directly interface with desktop publishing or document processing software, giving you complete control over the final output.

Still, there is no question that the documentation generated from CASE tools is far more thorough and poignant than that created to support older software systems. Traditional development projects created two types of documents: systems specifications and user manuals. The systems specifications, in most shops, were chiefly used for management control. Developers referred to the specifications initially while programming the system, but once a technical constraint forced a change to the program structure, the specifications fell out of sync with the actual system. Very few IS groups, even when commanded, kept systems specifications up-to-date. Later changes to the system were documented in separate "change logs" which captured basic technical information about the changes, but little of the business rationale behind them.

User manuals were sometimes kept more current because the users demanded it. In many environments, though, plagued by slow response from IS, users developed their own informal systems of recording software quirks and changes. Many user stations hold terminals framed in little yellow stick-on notes that describe new or undocumented system features. Other users compose tables of frequently used system codes, or common screen commands.

CASE tools with code generation make it easier to keep documentation up-to-date. Since changes can be made to specifications instead of code, the specifications will always be in sync with the system. If the central repository is available to all, the most recent documentation is available upon demand.

Developers and users alike find that documentation created by CASE tools is easier to understand. Prior to CASE and structured techniques, most systems documents were purely textual in nature. CASE relies heavily upon graphic representations of business and systems models. Graphic presentation allows readers to more easily grasp complex concepts and relationships among objects.

Once CASE is widely used, graphics become a common language for developers, managers, and business experts. After a short time in a data analysis meeting, I've seen business experts with no training in structured techniques jump up and start drawing data models for group discussion. The graphic language can be intuitive enough for nontechnical users to grasp quickly, and use productively themselves.

One of the main benefits of quality documentation is transferability of expertise. The author alone understands an undocumented system, and frequently no one but the author can easily maintain it. Once a system's structure and rationale is visible, maintenance—or even construction—can be handed to different contributors. Before code generation was common, one of my clients used CASE tools to create structured analysis and design specifications which they sent to a contract programming firm in Taiwan for final construction. Good documentation opens up new avenues for distribution of development work, and enhances communications throughout the development process.

Productivity

In industrial engineering terms, productivity measures how efficiently development resources are used to produce desired products. There are two sides to productivity: efficiency, the rate at which products are produced, and effectiveness, the ratio of quality products to total products created.

Quality, as described in the previous section, goes far beyond software logic defects and program failures. New definitions of quality affect how productivity is judged. Says software consultant Tom Gilb:

> Productivity should be measured in terms of net real effects on high-level management goals of a business or institution. Any attempt to quantify productivity by many common, but more partial measures such as "volume of work produced," is a great deal less useful.[6]

Since the previous section discussed system quality and effectiveness, this section will concentrate on software production efficiency. CASE can drastically enhance production efficiency. Despite the availability of CASE and other enabling technology, some analysts claim that software productivity today is less than it was in 1950.[7] Management reluctance to establish standards for methodology and code reuse hinders the achievement of large-scale productivity gains.

Most IS organizations seem to be waiting for irrefutable proof that CASE painlessly boosts production efficiency. Because most companies struggle to implement CASE, the evidence of productivity gain appears tainted. "Sure," says the IS manager, "I can boost productivity by 20%. But I need to invest a million dollars and retrain my entire staff." Many managers plan to wait for the next generation of CASE tools, hoping for that elusive technological fix. Yet technological solutions aren't enough. The impact of technology upon the organization must be managed, or productivity improvements will never materialize.

A study of software projects reported by Capers Jones shows how other technological factors can influence CASE productivity gains.[8] TABLE 3-1 shows an excerpt of Jones' findings, in terms of function points per staff month. Function points measure the size and complexity of a software system, independent of the programming lan-

Table 3-1. Productivity Effects of Combined Changes to the Software Development Environment

Software Technology Factors	Function points per staff month		
	Lowest	Median	Highest
Without CASE tools			
• Inexperienced staff • Unstructured methods • Low-level languages (COBOL, C, FORTRAN, Assembler)	0.25	2.5	5.0
With CASE tools			
• Inexperienced staff • Unstructured methods • Low-level languages	0.3	3.5	6.0
CASE tools plus single technology changes			
• Inexperienced staff • Structured methods • Low-level languages	1.5	6.0	10.0
• Inexperienced staff • Unstructured methods • High-level languages (4GLs)	2.0	7.0	12.0
• Experienced staff • Unstructured methods • Low-level languages	3.0	8.0	12.5
CASE tools plus double technology changes			
• Experienced staff • Structured methods • Low-level languages	6.0	12.0	20.0
• Inexperienced staff • Structured methods • High-level languages	6.5	14.0	25.0
• Experienced staff • Unstructured methods • High-level languages	7.0	18.0	30.0
CASE tools plus triple technology changes			
• Experienced staff • Structured methods • High-level languages	20.0	40.0	100.0

Source: Capers Jones*

guage the system is written in. One function point is roughly equivalent to one hundred lines of COBOL source code.

These numbers illustrate that CASE tools alone will not bring major productivity benefits. With ad hoc methods, an inexperienced staff, and standard low-level languages, the best you can expect is a 40% productivity gain, and often no gain at all. However, when all factors change positively, the increase can be dramatic: up to twenty times current productivity levels.

Of course the more changes you introduce at once, the greater the organizational impact. Organizational change delays productivity benefits of CASE. Sweeping changes in the development process and organizational roles usually follow CASE implementation. In addition, most structured methodologies alter the amount of time spent performing various development tasks.

CASE pulls effort farther forward in the development cycle. In the past, most time was spent in the construction and testing phases. Code generators and automated testing tools slash the time needed to actually build the system. Structured analysis methods focus efforts on the building of business and systems models. This promotes early detection of errors and validation by business experts, clearing the way for relatively smooth systems design and construction.

Figure 3-3 shows how the distribution of effort changes under CASE. The maintenance category only includes effort needed to correct system errors—ongoing enhancement is not considered. The base figures are drawn from a survey by the University of Houston, which polled 40 developers in twelve companies. Most of these developers used stand-alone or loosely integrated CASE tools. Overlaid on this graph are metrics taken from three projects that used the Information Engineering Facility (IEF) from Texas Instruments. The shift toward planning, analysis, and design is more prominent with the IEF projects, reflecting the construction and maintenance time savings that fully integrated tools can bring.

This redistribution of effort means that dramatic productivity gains won't emerge until the later phases. First-time CASE implementors get very anxious when they first experience this. They spend most of their time analyzing and documenting in the early stages, not hacking code like they are accustomed to. Managers must constantly assure first-time developers that they don't need to have the programs written tomorrow. Planning and analysis focus on business requirements and early user validation. Production efficiency won't increase dramatically during code generation and later maintenance cycles.

Because of the early emphasis on validated requirements, CASE-created systems have fewer defects and better documentation than traditionally developed systems. In contrast, most maintenance programmers today must spend days wading through undocumented source code looking for clues about a program's logic, structure, and intent. Integrated CASE tools allow you to maintain analysis and design specifications rather than source code. Unlike the code patches which riddle most aged programs, fixes made to specifications become tightly meshed within the resulting generated code. Old techniques threw a patch over each hole; CASE lets you reweave new requirements into the very fabric of the system.

Prototyping and object-oriented programming methods alter the traditional life cycle even more. The evolutionary nature of these techniques blurs the lines between analysis, design, and construction tasks. Productivity measures can only be taken at a project level for these techniques, since task-by-task comparisons with traditional methods are impossible.

Fig. 3-3. Redistribution of effort with CASE

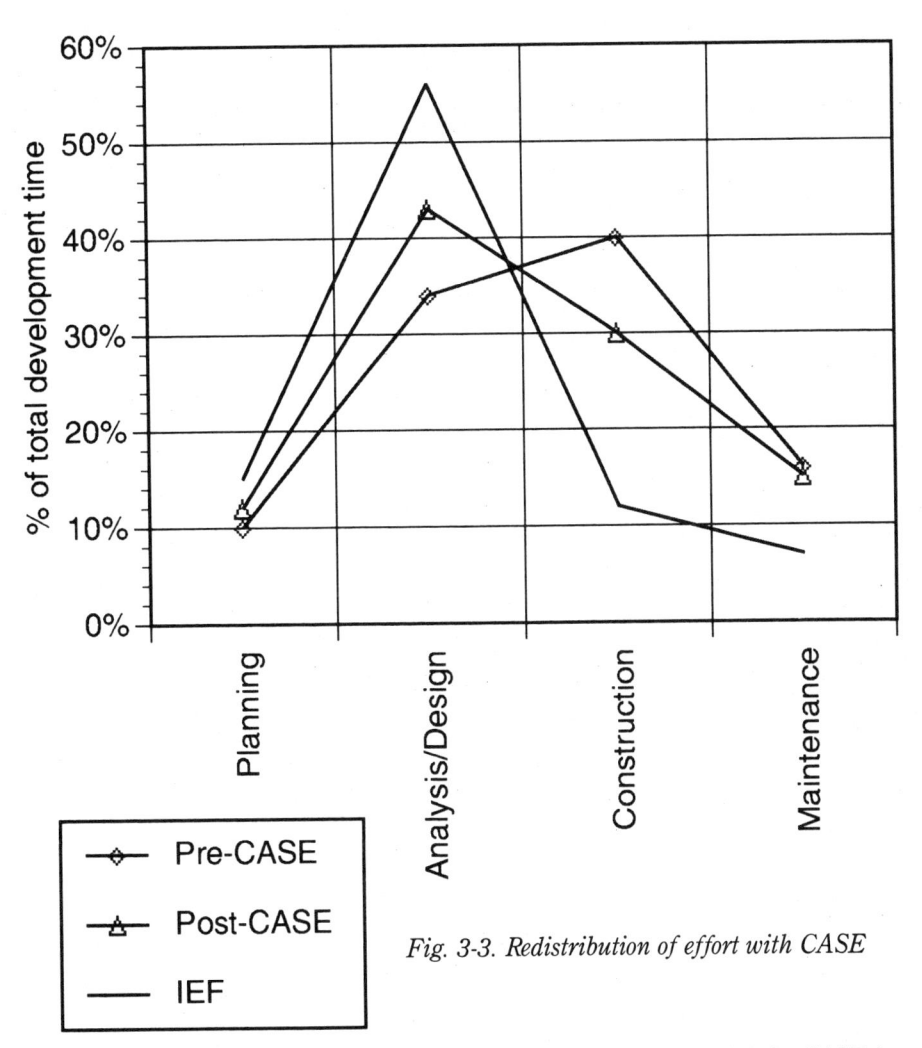

On early projects, production efficiency might only increase slightly. CASE is not an easy animal to tame, and it's hard to run a race astride an uncooperative beast. It takes time and a coordinated effort to marshal development forces to use CASE to its fullest, because:

- The initial learning curve for CASE tools and structured techniques can be steep.
- Reusable software libraries need time to gather useful stock.
- Unless a standard automatable methodology is in place, one must be developed and implemented.
- CASE causes cultural change, which doesn't happen quickly.
- Cautious use of multiple stand-alone CASE tools slows the process of gaining consensus about methodologies and integrated tools.

Initially, only a controlled pilot project will show the expected returns in development efficiency. It will take at least a year before most companies achieve a consistent rise in production efficiency on all CASE projects.

CASE directly improves production efficiency through:

- automated transformations
- software reusability
- cross-platform system generation
- system specification at high levels of abstraction

In addition, successful CASE implementation can indirectly boost the quantity of software the IS organization can produce by providing an increased developer base and more employee motivation.

Automated transformations

Automatic transformations, of which code generation is the prime example, are what most people think of when they talk about software automation. Other transformations result in generated screens and databases, system design models translated from more abstract business models, test plans generated from design specifications, and formatted documentation built directly from objects in the CASE repository.

Integrated tools bring greater productivity gains because they perform automatic transformations throughout the entire development cycle. Stand-alone tools can only provide incremental productivity gains. The savings of automation are diluted by the time it takes to import and export data to the tool. Integrated tools exchange objects with the central data repository, and impose little import/export penalty.

Software reusability

Improved productivity also arises from shrewd borrowing of previously designed software components. Why rebuild new software from scratch when such a large body of software already exists? Most programmers already espouse this principle. Few COBOL programmers have ever written every line of a new program; most instinctively grab an existing source code file and rip out its guts, leaving a skeletal template as a starting point for the new code.

Software reuse can dramatically affect productivity by reducing the development workload. Many companies are reusing software to their advantage. Developers at Hartford Insurance apparently pull up to 40% of new system objects from their reuse library, resulting in strong productivity hikes.[9]

The challenge of code reuse is finding existing components that do just what you want. It is difficult to find a needed subroutine in a Sargasso Sea of undocumented code. Once you find it, you must usually spend more time changing it to fit your needs. Often the costs of searching and adapting outweigh the benefits of reuse.

Integrated CASE minimizes some of these costs. The CASE repository is an ideal storage mechanism for reusable analysis and design objects. These objects are normally well-defined and -documented, and they can be retrieved based on the data they interact with. Finding reusable components which fit your needs now requires database inquiries rather than manual searches through reams of source code.

CASE tool vendors are responding to the push for reusability in different ways. Some CASE tools now provide special searching and object management facilities that turn the repository into an effective reusable software library. Other vendors offer design templates—complete system designs which can be transformed into working systems, with or without customization.

Cross-platform system generation

The most powerful CASE tools combine the best facets of reusability and automated transformation. Together these two features can allow you to reuse entire system design models. Most CASE tools capture business requirements in language or pictures that aren't constrained by the features of a specific hardware or software delivery platform. From a generic design model, you should be able to generate nearly identical working systems on a variety of different platforms. In the future, if you decide to shift from one platform to another, you won't be forced to rewrite all your systems. As long as the new platform is supported by the CASE tool, you can just regenerate from existing specifications with a new destination in mind.

At this time, only a few CASE tools, including Andersen's Foundation, TI's IEF and IBM's CSP, are able to generate working code for multiple platforms. However, in the long run, any CASE vendor with a strong commitment to tool integration has an incentive to provide such capability. Each new delivery platform vastly augments a CASE vendor's potential market.

Most tools today target IBM mainframe platforms with a DB2 database system, and DEC VAX seems to be running a distant second. Generation of PC-based applications is also popular, though most tools which support this don't do it using structured analysis techniques. PC application generators usually have distinct methods of their own, involving screen painting or interface building in conjunction with flowchart or icon-based procedural specs. The first CASE vendors to enable code generation from analysis specifications onto an HP or Prime platform will make a killing. No integrated CASE tools currently generate code for these platforms.

Abstract specifications

The fewer details developers must handle, the faster their jobs will be. The most productive CASE tools insulate the developer from detailed "housekeeping" chores. For example, instead of writing a dozen lines of COBOL to locate a database file, set up memory buffers, and manipulate record pointers, the developer can write one statement: READ CUSTOMER WITH number = input_number. Like fourth-generation languages (4GLs), some CASE tools can generate complex software logic with minimal typing. Others let you specify logic graphically.

Unfortunately, the process logic most CASE tools manage is still at the third-generation language level. You must still allocate buffers and manipulate pointers—the tools just give you sophisticated ways to attach this source code to graphical models. These tools are still beneficial, since they provide excellent source code documentation. But they won't bring the great productivity boons of those tools that operate at high levels of abstraction.

Larger developer base

CASE can help increase the amount of software an organization produces by allowing more people to participate in the development process. Structured techniques raise analysis and design to nontechnical levels. As a result, analysts and designers don't need the detailed technical skills required of today's programmers. Analytical thinking and communication skills are indispensable; and comprehension of the technical architecture is desirable but not crucial. IS organizations therefore have a larger potential developer base to pull from.

Most IS organizations I've worked with have already set up new business analyst job functions. These workers act as liaisons between the business community and IS project teams. Business analysts usually use the analysis CASE tools directly, along with their generally more technical developer colleagues. Business experts, often previous system users, generally fill these jobs. Rarely do business analysts come from technical jobs—they will more likely be recently graduated psychology majors rather than computer programmers.

Powerful end-user computing tools can also transform employees with limited programming skills into systems developers. Interface generators like Easel™ or HyperCard™, and natural-language interfaces like Intellect™ from AICorp, let users build data access systems while becoming familiar with basic software development concepts. Users who develop their own applications request fewer systems from the IS organization. This can help lessen the applications backlog, and contribute to overall systems development productivity. However, management of end-user computing can be costly, and handled wrongly it can hinder corporate systems integration efforts.

More employee motivation

Another indirect productivity benefit is the enthusiasm that CASE often generates. CASE hype hasn't escaped the notice of most software developers. Many first-time CASE users are thrilled to be on the acknowledged cutting edge of their profession, and their excitement carries through to their work. I've known developers who don't get excited about traditional programming to work excitedly at a CASE workstation for hours straight.

Many developers don't react to CASE this way; they resist the introduction of new technology that threatens the way they currently work. Managers can lessen this resistance by publicizing their commitment to CASE and providing ample opportunities for training in CASE and structured techniques. It's a recognized phenomenon that the first six-figure investment ever applied to improving the development process will speed the acceptance of any new technique. Developers worry less when they see this investment applied to increase their own knowledge and career options.

Once developers believe in CASE, they commit themselves to making the technology work.

Weeds among the flowers

No CASE tool can give you all the benefits listed above. Each type of tool provides different general benefits (TABLE 3-2), and not even the most comprehensive integrated toolset contains all of these components.

Table 3-2. Main Benefit Categories of CASE Tool Types

Type of Tool	Main Benefits
Automated testing	• Quality • Productivity
CASE repository	• Management support
Code generator	• Productivity • Quality
Metamodel access	• Management support
Methodology support	• Management support • Quality
Project management	• Management support
Reuse library	• Productivity
Reverse engineering	• Productivity
Screen prototyper	• Quality • Productivity
Simulator	• Quality
Strategic planning	• Strategy
Structured analysis and design	• Quality

Many nontechnological factors can alter the paybacks you receive from CASE tools. Benefits vary according to levels of tool integration, degrees of management commitment, attention to human factors, and establishment of standard methods. For these reasons, CASE alone doesn't guarantee quick solutions to software development problems.

When CASE implementation is badly managed, the technology can backfire. CASE tools still have some blemishes that some IS organizations don't like:

- They can be very expensive.
- The techniques they automate can clash with established practices and corporate cultures.
- They require an extensive adjustment period and potential short-term productivity declines.
- Concrete CASE benefits take a while to materialize, and anxiety can mount until they do.

Expense

Entry costs for new CASE users can be prohibitive. The current cost of an integrated CASE toolset ranges from $7,500 to $50,000 per analyst workstation, not including hardware. Most IS organizations have already invested in workstations and personal computers, so new hardware costs might be minimal. However, many CASE tools require exceptional levels of main memory and hard disk storage capacity, good graphics display capabilities, and mouse support, so hardware upgrade costs are likely. Mainframe- or minicomputer-based repository products are also expensive, ranging from $50,000 to $500,000 per copy. Most companies can get by with one or two repositories, though larger firms might require more. The repositories of some integrated products run on workstations attached to local area networks (LANs). These generally cost less than their big-machine counterparts, though they support fewer satellite workstations.

During the first year or two of CASE usage, the cost of developer training can match or exceed the software investment. Developers usually need education about structured methodologies and communication techniques in addition to the expected software training.

You can see why IS organizations often shy away from full-scale investment in integrated CASE tools. To outfit a shop of twenty developers, the IS manager might expect to spend between $500,000 and $800,000 on CASE software and training. Ad hoc purchases of stand-alone CASE tools seem tame in comparison. Many integrated CASE tool vendors offer component tools for sale separately. For $2,000 you might purchase the analysis tool component of an integrated toolset that costs $10,000 as a package. Less ambitious tools for drawing structured analysis diagrams or doing screen prototypes are available for most personal computer platforms at the cost of a few hundred dollars.

While these stand-alone tools provide cost-effective ways to familiarize developers with CASE, they will only bring incremental benefits. However, when cost is a barrier, as it will be for many small firms, stand-alone tools might be the only alternative. If possible I suggest purchasing tools which can one day be combined into an integrated toolset.

Poor fit

In some companies, cost isn't the only barrier to CASE. Structured techniques tag along with CASE tools, often surprising the new owner. Many companies already use standard development methods which aren't well supported by existing CASE tools. Usually these companies can make a smooth transition to the new methods, since they are already committed to rigorous software engineering practices.

Firms that haven't standardized their development practices face a more problematic situation. Some corporate IS cultures value developer autonomy above all else. This sets a sometimes insurmountable hurdle for CASE adoption. While some of these developers might use CASE tools for their own purposes, few will be ready to accept the standardization of techniques that integrated CASE requires. These developers will feel more at home with tactical, stand-alone tools that automate familiar programming tasks. At most, an integrated programmer workbench can be installed, to allow some tool and data sharing. If the developers already use some form of structured analysis or design techniques, then a methodology-independent CASE toolkit might be in order.

The other dimension of CASE's "fit" in an organization is the level of communication that exists among managers, developers, and system users. Companies in which the isolated IS priesthood still thrives might derive only minor benefit from integrated CASE tools. Structured techniques rely on open communication channels and interpersonal negotiation. If developers aren't comfortable talking the language of the business expert, they may find CASE hard to swallow.

If your company doesn't seem immediately ready for CASE tools, don't try to force-fit them. Introduction of tools without warning, or training, can heighten resistance to CASE and other productivity tools you might introduce in the future. It can cause resistance among developers who feel their expertise being threatened. Work first to establish standard development practices and improve IS's communication channels. Then work with developers—the eventual users of the CASE tools—to determine when and how CASE should be introduced.

Impediments to progress

In the long run, returns from CASE investment can be dramatic. In the short term, things will not seem so rosy. Transition carries pain, and even the best managed changeover will cause work disruptions. Expect pilot projects and new projects that strictly follow the new techniques to produce encouraging results. Expect disappointing results from ongoing projects that switch to CASE halfway through.

Most CASE methods proceed top-down. Coherent business plans drive further analysis, each task examining the business and systems areas in increasing detail. Project teams that jump to CASE techniques in the analysis or design phase don't have the benefit of higher-level road maps. Their workload immediately doubles. They must continue to show forward progress while learning new techniques, and simultaneously back-fitting their project into the newly integrated top-down model. These "middle-out" projects invariable lag, showing drastic schedule slippage.

Training requirements will also cause work slowdowns. You can't send half of the development staff to three or four weeks of training classes and still expect the same work to get done.

While the introduction of CASE might take time away from current project schedules, you will certainly recoup this time in the long run. However, organizations that cannot afford any project delays should wait to implement CASE. Throwing new technologies into an already overloaded organization is like giving amphetamines to someone who's hypertensive. You've set them up for a breakdown.

Short-term uncertainty

The wait for CASE benefits to emerge can fray the nerves of the most steadfast IS manager. The eventual CASE paybacks are long-term and can be hard to quantify. If you don't have baseline productivity and quality metrics against which to compare, you may never know what CASE has done for you.

Everyone involved in the CASE rollout will repeatedly question the strategy. Expect lots of soul-searching and stress in the short term, especially for those who were instrumental in CASE's introduction. CASE hype can create overblown expectations that are hard to match.

After the first successful CASE project, most of these fears will fade away. When you, as an IS manager or developer, get that first comment from a user who is thrilled about the quality of the new system, and grateful for the chance to participate in its creation, you will know the anxiety was worthwhile.

4

Forging an alliance

Some developer colleagues and I were talking shop over cubicle walls when their manager stopped by. A vice president of marketing had asked him for a list of the firm's top ten customers. The firm planned to start a showcase account program for their star customers, the ones that racked up the highest sales from all company divisions combined. The IS manager had agreed to the request, and he now asked one of my colleagues to pull the information together.

A month later, no list was forthcoming. Each of the ten marketing divisions kept its own customer database, and my colleague was swamped trying to correlate the information. He asked for help, and his manager responded by creating a three person project team. The marketing VP was calling weekly to get the information, so all three people were given the task full-time.

Five months later, they still had no list. Not only were there separate divisional databases, but each one indexed customer data in a different way. Some divisions tracked large customers as single enterprises with multiple addresses; others treated each address as a different customer entirely. This simple request for information could not have been answered by the entire IS staff. The IS manager admitted this failure to the VP. Weeks later, a major push toward applications integration began.

Most IS managers can tell similar stories. They recognize the power of dense, expressive pools of referential data, but their current systems give them isolated puddles. Single application databases and files are exceptionally useful in their intended context, but can rarely extend beyond it. Now that information sharing spurs competitive advantage, many firms find that their old systems development methods promoted data separatism, not data integration.

Beyond hardware

When some people think about integrated systems, they picture a hulking mainframe stuffed with product codes and charts of accounts, under constant demand from crowds of system users. Yet integrated systems don't necessarily involve one giant corporate database.

Integration doesn't have to mean centralization. Integrated systems can be distributed across multiple locations, used by many different users, and developed by decentralized organizations. They are integrated around common business strategies and definitions, and common data and process architectures. This is virtual integration: a common interface layer over an intelligent "librarian" or server that knows where each bit of data is kept, and how to fetch it.

Most current systems integration efforts focus on providing basic connectivity between a company's various machines and software applications. Many computer, software, and consulting firms thrive on helping large clients "integrate" their old, stand-alone systems. This integration sometimes takes the form of one- or two-way bridges between applications. This is really systems interconnection, not systems integration. Each "bridge" between applications is itself a small application. The resulting web of connections, as shown in FIG. 4-1, can be hard to maintain.

To examine this impact, FIG. 4-1 shows the potential ripple effect of a change to one interconnected application. Say application A must expand the size of one of its data elements; every interface bridge must be modified to accommodate this change; and then the internal databases or files of each connected application must be changed.

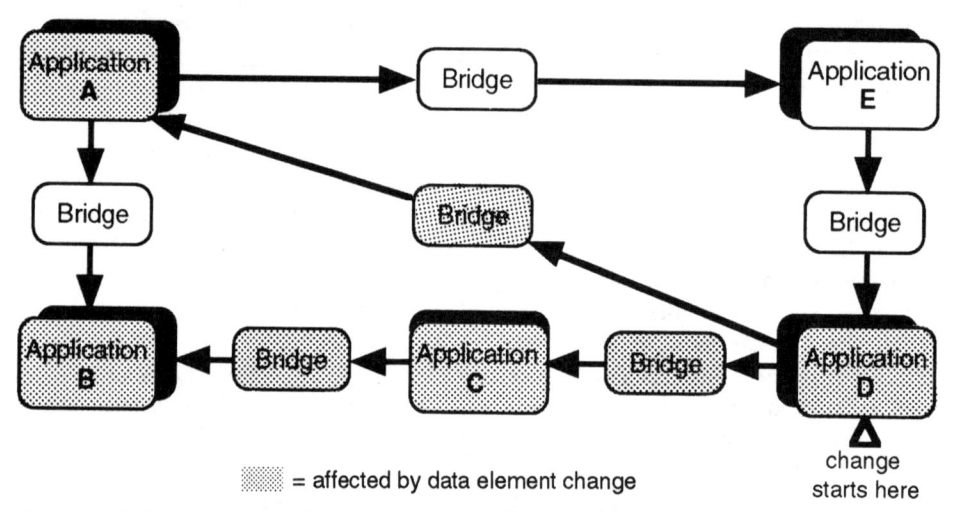

Fig. 4-1. Primitive systems integration: connectivity provided by bridge programs

Sometimes the systems integration effort relies upon a new, centralized decision support system (DSS) that summarizes data fed to it by many different applications. This DSS acts as an information clearing house, distilling raw operational data into palatable summaries for use by business managers. As shown in FIG. 4-2, this scenario doesn't lessen the interconnection complexity. All operational systems feed information to the DSS database. Yet most of the system interconnections must remain. Because of the loss of detail in the DSS, it can't be used to redirect information from one operational system to another.

The impact of a change in this scenario is more severe than in the last one. Some interconnections between systems have been removed, but new links to the DSS have

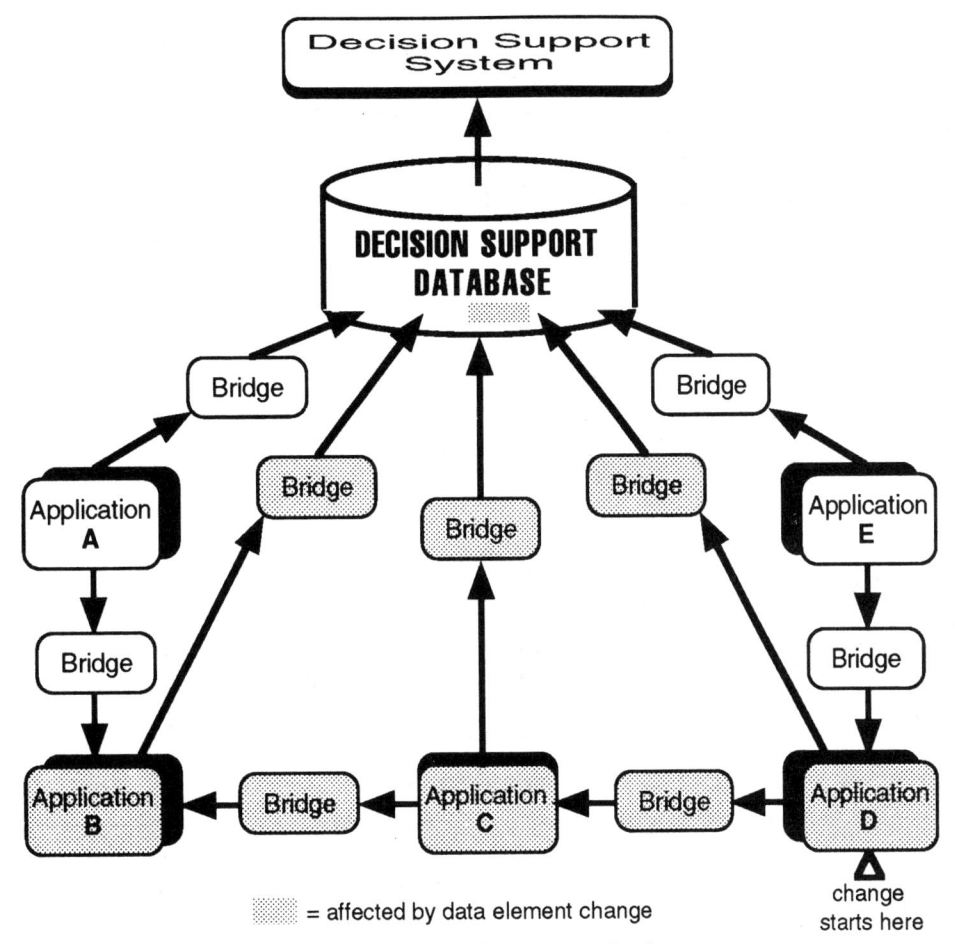

Fig. 4-2. Systems integration based on decision support database

▓ = affected by data element change

change starts here

been added. The DSS database must change whenever operational data definitions change.

Full data integration—shown in FIG. 4-3 as a simplified central database—minimizes system bridges. Each data item is defined once, and all applications accept this definition. No bridges are needed to convert data between applications, since all work directly with the central database. A change to one item still affects all of the applications that use it. Yet the cost is halved, compared to previous scenarios, since no bridges must be repaired.

Integration has marked advantages compared to bridged interfaces. As John Phipps and Ray Cotten of Microdynamics ask:

> What is wrong with an interfaced structure? First, interfaced automation is sequential in operation—sending data at fixed intervals and usually after the fact. An even greater problem is that such automation tends to be unidirectional, with data flowing only one way and from multiple databases.[1]

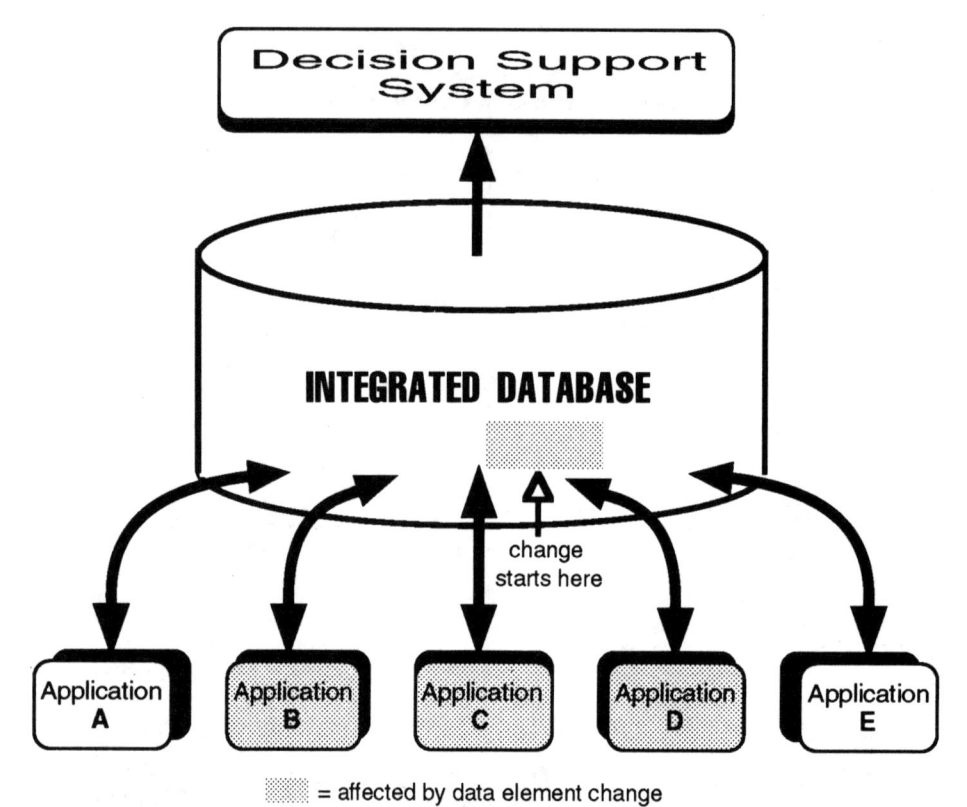

Fig. 4-3. Integration through a centrally defined database

These limitations mean that people can only use data once the sender has explicitly decided to distribute it. This decision is often arbitrary, or periodic, and not related to the time the information was collected. Integrated applications make data available immediately. Instead of being pushed out by the sender, data can be pulled in by the receivers, when they need it. As an analogy, consider how you might notify everyone of a department party. You can send out memos to everyone, incurring copying costs and clogging everyone's mail slots. Or you can post a notice on a central bulletin board. People can read the notice at their leisure, and make copies only if they need to.

The final integration layer involves commonly defined business processes. Everyone accepts integrated data as a good thing, and we have the CASE and database tools to make it a reality. However, integrated processes aren't as well-defined (except in the object-oriented world). Figure 4-4 shows how these processes form a common layer around the integrated database. These processes are available to many different applications. They are defined as the "official" processes for certain business activities—much like data definitions govern the use of items of information.

Common processes insulate applications from the effects of change. You can accommodate a change to a data item by modifying a few common processes, instead of a multitude of redundant processes embedded in applications.

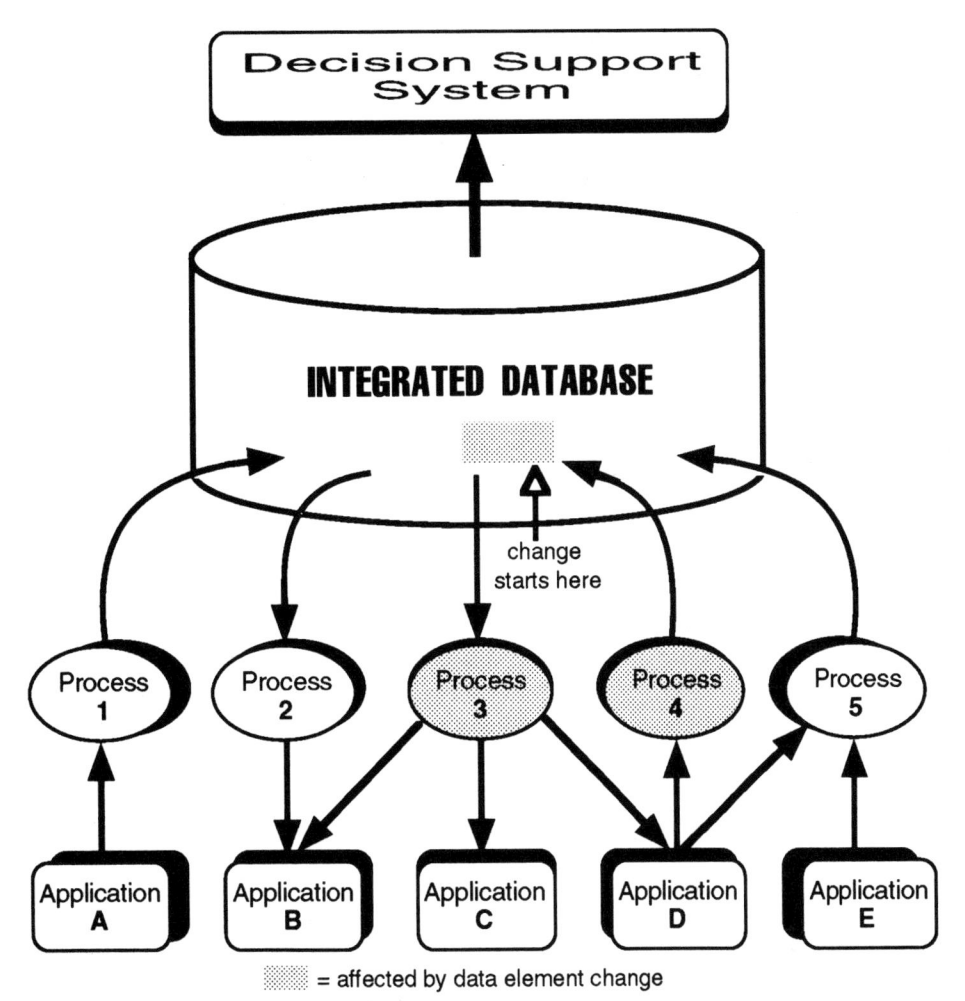

Fig. 4-4. Integration of data and processes

Levels of integration

To achieve these visions, systems integration must operate on several different levels:

- hardware connectivity
- operating system compatibility
- integrated business information
- common business processes
- integrated software development environments

Figure 4-5 shows the various levels of integration, proceeding from hardware connectivity to common data and processes.

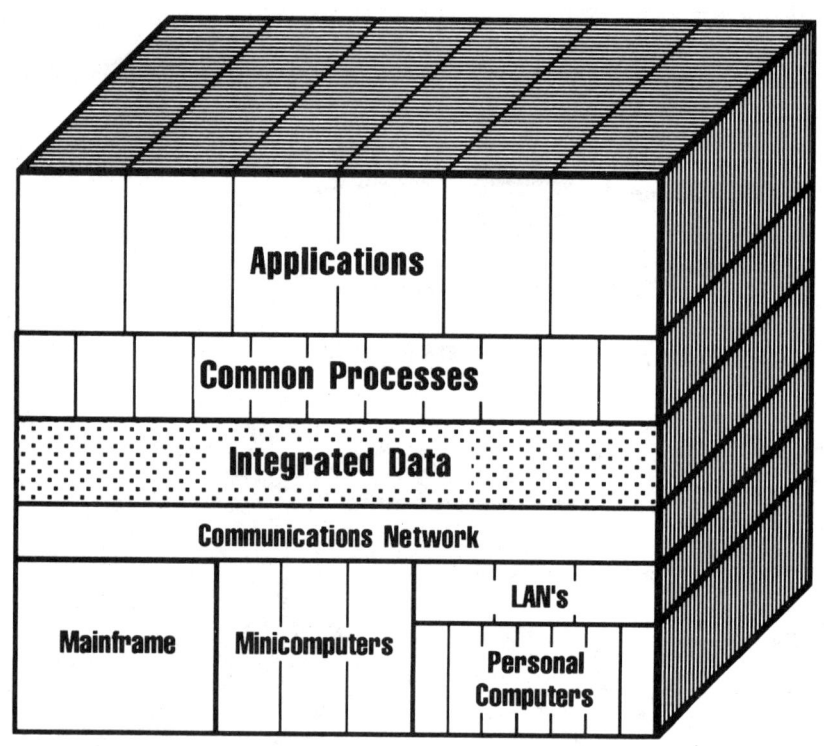

Fig. 4-5. Layers of integration

Basic connectivity is the main concern of hardware integration. Dumb terminals connected to mainframe computers aren't yet a thing of the past, but they are being rapidly replaced by client/server and cooperative processing architectures. The trend toward "open" computer systems should make hardware interconnectivity easy in the future. Computer and communications hardware, plus the operating system and communications software to run them, must be established before other levels of integration can take form.

Data integration forms the next layer. Entity-relationship modeling and other structured techniques help data designers catalog information needs. Acting as arbiters of corporate data definitions, data administrators can ensure consistency. Data administration groups are common in most large firms today.

Process integration requires common data definitions. In an object-oriented paradigm, data and process are inseparable, and integration operates through a common class hierarchy. Other structured development approaches tend to separate data and processes. These approaches work toward common data, but rarely toward common processes. Yet process integration can be just as valuable, as I'll explain later in this chapter.

Integrated applications need integrated CASE

High levels of software integration will be difficult to achieve without fully integrated development environments. You can't manage data element definitions for an entire company with pencil and paper. You can't handle common processes with a stand-alone data dictionary tool. You'll have a hard time building distributed databases from a common data model without an industrial-strength repository and database generator.

Integrated CASE tools form a backbone for software development and for the company as a whole. The development environment fills a slot in the company's integrated applications base. CASE tools are applications for software developers, but they also have value for business users. They can investigate the business models captured in the CASE repository. Imagine a new employee learning the firm's definition of a customer or supplier by exploring the repository. When accounting practices change, accountants can inquire about everyone in the firm who will be affected.

Systems integration not only needs integrated CASE, it includes it.

Integration's competitive advantage

Systems integration doesn't just apply to gigantic corporations. Small software companies must constantly check the compatibility of their product with others, whether the applications will exchange information or simply coexist on the same machine. Small businesses often operate with one or two custom-designed applications that interface with packaged accounting or payroll systems. Though scale differs, the need for integration is just as great.

Truly integrated systems create significant competitive advantages. These include:

- Product differentiation. Marketers can discover new ways to present information to potential customers. Merchandisers can widen the range of information they scan for new market trends and information about product cost and profitability. A U.S. sales representative might discover an Australian client using the product in a new way that might attract customers.
- Accelerated response to customers. Customer service representatives can answer unanticipated questions more easily. Everyone in a service organization can have swift access to customer histories and up-to-the-minute events.
- Streamlined work flow. Many jobs today involve gathering information from elsewhere in the company, analyzing it, and reformatting it for presentation. Many of the memos, forms, and documents that deluge most bureaucratic organizations can be eliminated when integrated information is available to all. Integrated systems support faster and better-informed decision-making.
- Empowered "knowledge workers." Flexible information-based organizations require integrated systems. Environmental changes are making centralized decision-making impractical.[2] Yet company goals and principles must be disseminated so that everyone is informed enough to make their own decisions. To enable distributed decision-making by empowered workers, we need integrated information systems.

Information is becoming a critical ingredient in company performance. It enhances product marketability, and enables swift response to rapid environmental changes.

These environmental forces push toward three major aspects of integrated systems:

1. flexible, cross-functional decision support
2. common data definitions
3. process and software reusability

Cross-functional decision support

Today's environmental changes cut horizontally across the breadth of a company. Quality affects every product and process. Every employee can enhance a firm's ability to provide customer service. Global thinking must become habit for every part of the organization.

Yet almost every firm is saddled with an entrenched, vertical organizational structure. This structure erects tall barriers to cross-functional decision-making: walls over which communications don't flow, and partitions that slice up the big picture.

Shared information helps dissolve these barriers. Each division can contribute to the same set of financial plans, for instance, instead of creating dozens of separate ones that must be reconciled later. Production information can be viewed daily by plant managers or inventory clerks, who might have waited days or weeks to receive formatted reports in the past.

Previously, much data traveled from operational workers up through the ranks to managers, who summarized and distributed it to other managers. These managers then let the information drip down through their own ranks to the operational folk who needed it. With integrated data, decision-making can be pushed to smaller organizational units without sacrificing quality or perspective. It means you don't have to sacrifice decision quality when you promote worker autonomy.

Systems integration ties in with the business trend toward cooperative goal- and value-setting. When common principles drive a company, they must be represented similarly in every system. When the bottom line is drawn at a company level, not a divisional or departmental one, then systems must exist at the same level. You can't pursue cooperative goals with xenophobic little systems.

Decision support systems To discover new opportunities, companies must constantly analyze themselves and their environment. Yet rapid changes generate enough data to swamp most firms. The challenge is to distill useful information from mounds of raw data without succumbing to information overload.[3]

The modern vehicle for meeting this challenge is the decision support system. There is no standard form of DSS, but all have a common basis: an integrated view of company-wide data. The DSS allows workers and managers to access this information in an ad hoc, flexible manner, to address a variety of business situations.

DSS's perform many of the summarization and dissemination functions previously done by middle managers. They gather meaningful information from operational systems, and store it in more useful form.

If data are raw facts, information is data with meaning. Classical information theory treats meaningless data as "noise." It used to be a middle manager's responsibility to transmit meaningful signals to upper managers, with as little noise as possible. Now this task can fall to a DSS.

Raw data input to the decision support database is selected according to its potential to be turned into information. Transmissions from the decision support system to its users should have a high signal-to-noise ratio.

Unlike operational databases, decision support databases must be flexible. They should let users form new relationships between data, to make new connections. In human thought, new connections lead to new ideas, strategies, and directions. The more closely integrated the data, the more flexibility the user has.

Common data

Uncoordinated software development created redundancy of both data and processes. As a result, most companies now have data duplicated or split across many separate databases or "master files." Most Fortune 1000 companies use over a million separate data elements in their systems portfolios, yet studies show that few companies require more than 5000 basic elements.[4]

This diffusion of company data frustrates high-level decision-makers. For example, scattered customer data can make it impossible to:

- count the total number of customers
- identify the top customers across all divisions
- link up each division's separate view of the same customers
- prevent duplicate statements or mailings from being sent to customers that do business with more than one division
- satisfy customers who want to place single, cross-division orders instead of separate orders for each type of product

The demands of fully centralized company data often outstrip the abilities of current database management systems. But common data definitions will enable information sharing even if the data must be stored in many different files and databases. Once everyone uses customer identification numbers of the same length and meaning, for example, systems can transfer customer information much more freely.

Process reusability

Information systems planning is normally a passive activity. Users generate systems requests response to recent business problems. IS tackles requests haphazardly, according to staffing limitations and funding constraints. With no incentive for cross-project cooperation, development groups constantly reinvent the wheel.

I once worked on a project to converge a large company's customer invoicing systems into one worldwide system. Over the past ten years, various international offices had developed more than forty separate invoicing systems—for only one niche within the company's many product offerings. Every time a new invoice format was proposed, programmers cloned and modified an existing invoicing program. The new program went into production alongside the old ones, adding to the morass. Yet every program took essentially the same information and threw it onto paper.

By consolidating the programs, the company's software maintenance burden declined drastically. Core invoicing functions were built as reusable software modules. Each office could activate or deactivate specific modules, or add one or two new ones, to create essentially customized applications. The code for each application was basically the same; it simply operated differently in each environment. Future changes could be made to one application instead of forty.

Most IS groups exploit some form of process reusability, be it common security subroutines or shared tax calculation modules. But few develop common processes into the valuable corporate assets they can become.

Reusability is essentially process integration. Many experts cite software reusability as the biggest factor influencing development productivity. Companies such as Raytheon and Hartford Insurance receive up to 50% productivity gains from using reusable code libraries, and NASA claims a four to one return on investment from its reusability program.[5]

Common processes also benefit the business. Business processes that are consistently done can be more easily improved. People can compare best practices, and improvements applied in one place will benefit everyone.

In addition, common processes encourage a consistent company image. Take, for example, a manufacturer organized into four marketing divisions: In the past, product lines, manufacturing lines, and information systems were all aligned by organizational boundaries. This forced customers who purchased from more than one division to submit multiple purchase orders. The respective invoices came back in different formats, annoying the financial clerks who had to consolidate them.

Common ordering and invoicing processes reduce this confusion. Even if the customer must still contact each division separately, they will know how to place an order and inquire about it. Common processes cut through procedural quirks to the essential steps needed to do good business.

Cooperation isn't free

Integrated systems aren't easily made. Consultants offering to integrate your business applications will not do so quickly or cheaply. It's a mammoth job, with little automated support available.

Even if you pursue a patchwork, bridge-based strategy to get immediate connectivity benefits, you should plan for fully integrated data and applications in the future. Webs of interfaced systems don't stand up well to business changes. You'll want full integration to prepare your firm for future challenges.

A push toward integrated systems forces changes throughout IS and other parts of the company. These changes include:

- A loss of developer independence. Software engineers must work together, regardless of their place in the IS organizational structure.
- New coordination tasks. Many developers get frustrated when forced to do

things other than write program code. Coordination tasks might also be perceived as nonproductive.
- New values. The IS culture must learn to value integrated data and reusable code, instead of simply rewarding people for delivering something on time.
- A need for common methods and tools. Most engineers will be forced to learn new tools and techniques, chosen for their ability to manage complex, cross-functional information.

Each of these changes carries significant costs, in either cash or personal adjustments forced upon developers. Many characteristics of current IS organizations make the push for systems integration doubly difficult.

Barriers to integration

Most successful systems integration efforts have been performed by external consulting firms. These firms bring manpower and experience, but their main selling point is their externality. This lets them cut through many of the political or organizational barriers that might otherwise slow the progress of integration.

The effects of integration will reverberate long after the first systems are patched together. External consultants and internal "integration commando" teams can conjure quick results, but they only sidestep organizational barriers; they don't remove them.

Some of the major integration barriers are:

- proprietary data ownership
- information greed
- software project funding practices
- end-user software development
- technological limitations

To create a lasting environment that both prizes and exploits integrated information, you should address all of these.

Data ownership

Information can be seen as a company's fourth major resource, along with money, equipment, and personnel. Personnel and funds move fluidly throughout a company. Most firms have centralized payroll and accounting organizations to manage these pervasive corporate assets. Information is the most fluid resource of all, yet it is rarely managed centrally.

As a resource, information approximates money. Everyone uses it. It can be pooled by all organizational units for the good of the company. Yet many groups want to own their data, locking it away in private databases for their use only. They usually justify this with calls for data security and integrity. But outside, very few tidbits of information are sensitive enough to cause important security risks. Security can be tight around the corporate periphery, to prevent competitors from stealing secrets. But internally, a free flow of information lets workers become far more productive and innovative.

Today, data ownership means power. The owner of the data can control how it is presented, and prevent others from challenging his or her conclusions. But this ownership erects barriers to free exchange of business data, like tollgates on a thoroughfare. In a modern organization, influence should flow from interpretation of data, not ownership of it. The person who draws the keenest conclusions from the sea of business data will rightfully gain power.

The problem of data ownership can be overcome with organizational incentives for sharing data. A systems integration effort can be a lever for coaxing information from data hoarders.

Information greed

The flip side of data ownership is information greed. Once people entertain the thought of freely available information, they start wanting every bit of data imaginable.

Often this is a result of not knowing ahead of time what data might be useful in the future. When software engineers ask business experts what information they need, they often get lengthy lists of unrealistic items. Without a clear idea, but afraid that they'll only get one chance to spout their requirements, users tend to ask for it all. Developers often assume that everything requested is necessary, and trudge off to start a two-year development project.

A common vision cited by top level managers is the all-powerful PC on the CEO's desk.[6] Many managers covet the power this would give them to control every detail of their subordinates' operations. But such detailed control can be both difficult and undesirable. It can cause turmoil throughout the chain of command, and even lead to poorly informed decision-making. Imagine the CEO reprimanding an assembly-line worker for poor performance, based on isolated facts about daily line production.

Shoshana Zuboff of Harvard University observed a plant manager who described this problem. "It is very hard," said he, "for a manager to have information and not want to do something about it. If you give me the data from that system, I will make more decisions."[7] I believe that few CEO's really want day-to-day operational details, and their requests for them should be evaluated carefully.

Integration should be accompanied by new principles of information economy. Outlandish requests for myriad data items only slow progress toward integrated systems. Information overload should be managed in concert with data acquisition.

Funding practices

Current funding practices thwart many systems integration efforts. When systems were made specifically for an organizational unit, the unit happily funded the full development effort. But who pays for a system jointly commissioned by the manufacturing and distribution organizations? What if the functionality is 80% manufacturing, and 20% distribution? What if it also includes some features desired by the marketing group, and some put in only for finance?

When systems development efforts are funded by specific functional organizations, there is little financial incentive to negotiate cross-functional solutions. Unfortunately, few good models exist today for accounting of cross-functional development efforts.

When you look at information as a resource, however, some easy parallels appear. IS can be set up as a separate organization on a par with personnel and finance. These other groups also manage pervasive resources, and are centrally funded by the company. This gives IS a company-wide focus. It is still at the service of its client organizations, but is no longer subject to uneven funding.

For many companies, this solution requires a major—and perhaps currently impossible—reorganization. Short of this, some other cooperative funding efforts have been tried, with varying levels of success, by companies pushing systems integration. These include cooperative funding of development projects according to:

- shares of system functionality
- percentages of installed base systems being replaced
- perceived urgency of the new system to each group

These options all apply to specific systems projects. They aren't too helpful for funding more general strategic planning or business analysis projects, which can't be tied directly to existing or future systems. Since integrated systems bring advantages to the entire company, centralized funding is the simplest and fairest way to support them.

End-user development

The rapid rise of end-user systems development can't be considered a problem. New tools have given users the power to create and manage their own information, sometimes bypassing an IS group that they consider unresponsive. The cost of this user autonomy, however, is a new set of uncoordinated stand-alone applications.

End-user developers are motivated by the need for speed and specificity. Their intent is normally to pull information from central sources and manipulate it for their own use. Yet many end-user systems create new information during these manipulations—information that could be useful elsewhere in the firm. No forum exists for sharing these end-user systems, or for developing them cooperatively in the first place, so the information languishes in spreadsheet files, or on printed reports in a file cabinet.

A side effect of end-user development is the growing technical sophistication of users. They have learned the state of the software art—most end-user tools are more technologically advanced than the systems provided by IS—and will be disappointed by future systems that don't aspire to it.

Integrated systems can provide end-users with unprecedented abilities to rearrange and analyze data. Instead of sending end-users off with application generators and best wishes, IS should educate them about the value of integrated information. If IS can provide flexible, integrated databases and tools for accessing them, then users will happily contribute to the effort.

Technological limitations

The final barrier to systems integration is the one most often cited. Only recently has information technology evolved to be able to support distributed databases, cooperative processing, and client/server architectures. Only recently have CASE tools emerged that can transform common data definitions into similar databases for a variety of physical platforms and DBMS packages.

Still many technological barriers to integration still persist. They can be put into two categories: limitations to developing integrated systems, and limitations to operating them.

Limitations to developing integrated systems Process-driven development methods have been perhaps the biggest barrier to data and process integration in the past. These methods treat most data as local appendages of single programs or subroutines. The most popular form of common data definition in the past was the copy book or copy library: files containing code segments that could be used by many different programs. These libraries were provided simply for programmer convenience, though, and did little to promote consistent data definitions across a company.

Data dictionaries and, more recently, CASE repositories have emerged to manage common data definitions. However, most of these tools still aren't capable of supporting large-scale data and process integration. Most don't capture information about how data elements will be distributed (on which physical systems they will be implemented), or support the cataloging and searching of reusable processes. And very few can handle the gigantic volumes of metadata large integrated systems require. Often the demands exceed the limits of the DBMS software upon which the repository rests.

If you plan to pursue fully integrated systems, make sure the CASE products you select can handle gigantic repositories. Some products will support hierarchical repository structures that provide centralized views of strategic information, and partitioned views of more detailed data.

Limitations to operating integrated systems Centralized corporate databases will test the character of any DBMS on the market. Most firms above a certain size must implement integrated databases in a distributed fashion. This calls for multiple machines, perhaps multiple DBMS's, and sophisticated networks and communications software. Until a few years ago, these demands made integrated systems infeasible for all but the most advanced firms.

An added drawback for decision support systems is the trade-off that often exists between flexible data structures and system response time. Users of DSS's often pay for the ability to freely manipulate data with tiresome intervals staring at inactive PC screens.

But at least the technical problems can be treated as trade-offs rather than showstoppers. Integrated systems are achievable with available technologies. The smart company will carefully balance the costs of technology against the benefits of integration, and choose its weapons carefully.

Integration strategies

Though the costs of integration are high, ample returns are almost guaranteed. If you keep developing stand-alone systems with one-way interfaces, you'll face mounting maintenance costs and difficulty responding to environmental change.

Patchwork systems integration is like using duct tape to stop a leak in the plumbing. It will work for a while, but eventually your problems will return.

IS must start thinking about integration before it builds new systems. It won't happen as a side effect of traditional development methods. Strategies for total systems integration include:

- strategic information systems planning
- coordinated application releases
- a separate data warehouse for decision support information
- data and process administration functions
- organizational incentives for integrating
- integrated CASE tools to develop and manage integrated data and applications

Strategic information systems planning

Most IS groups plan specific development projects in-depth, but don't give much thought to the bigger picture. Without a strategic plan, this is like starting four builders at each corner of a house, and telling them to match it up in the middle. Strategic IS planning creates an architectural outline for later projects to embellish.

Architecture is the answer to redundant data and systems. Strategic planning efforts are search-and-destroy missions for data and process redundancy. If an invoicing system is necessary, for instance, the strategic planning team might note the many groups with an interest in the subject, and commission a cross-functional team to investigate the area. This ensures that resulting systems will achieve common solutions that satisfy all parties.

Strategic data planning encourages a common data model acceptable to everyone in the firm. As appointed caretakers of this model, data administrators can coordinate data definitions across the company, ensuring common usage even if the data itself becomes distributed across separate machines.

Other components of a strategic IS plan are common goals and principles. These subtly push people toward integrated systems by giving them a common target to shoot for. If managers state that improvements in product quality are are more important than cost-cutting, for example, a quality assurance system will take precedence over one that tracks minute cost increments throughout a factory. Few people will develop systems that run counter to management goals when the goals are plainly stated.

Coordinated application releases

There's a psychological barrier to break when thinking about integrated systems. They provoke images of impossibly gigantic packages, far too large for mere mortals to comprehend, much less install in one piece. Taken together, a set of integrated applications, in their eventual form, might indeed be incredibly large and complex. However, you don't need to create or install them all at once.

After strategic information planning and close coordination throughout software analysis and design, coordinated implementation is a logical extension. When applications depend on common data structures, they must be installed at the same time that the databases change. Yet each release need not contain entire business systems.

The coordinated release concept combines principles of evolutionary system delivery with principles of integration. It takes the long established practices of commercial software houses and applies them to in-house applications.

Think of your operational systems as subprograms within a single integrated application. As with commercial software, enhancements to each component system are held pending a periodic release schedule. Then they are tested together and finally installed as a synthesized version of the larger corporate application.

Each coordinated release centers upon a new version of the corporate data model. With the model as an anchor, the system components that make up a release can be much smaller than most are used to. Today, when you ask most project managers to scale down the size of the system they plan to deliver, they say it can't be done. The system, they say, is too complex and interdependent to be broken into smaller pieces.

Integrated databases remove two of these dependencies. First, they eliminate the need for bridges to other systems. Second, they remove many dependencies between submodules of the same system. Instead of passing all data along real-time links to other components, these submodules can interact with the database directly. Other modules can then pull data as they need it.

A coordinated release then becomes a set of tightly scoped software modules organized around common data structures. Each module can be analyzed and designed relatively quickly, and then combined for testing and installation purposes.

Release planning can be handled using a timebox approach. A release date is set, and all project managers who think they can have modules ready by that date are invited to offer proposals. Each proposed module must meet basic qualification criteria. For instance, you might require that the module was scoped using structured analysis techniques, and was the subject of a thorough risk assessment procedure. The best candidates are then selected according to business goals and risk factors.

As the date nears, the likelihood that each module will be ready is reassessed. If a project team encounters delays, their module might be pulled from this release and targeted for the next one.

There are a number of advantages to the coordinated release approach:

- It reduces burden upon system users. They handle two to four periodic releases per year, instead of more frequent, uncoordinated ones. They can set up many different subsystems with one installation package, and do only one database update.
- It ensures data and process integration. Today, many projects pay lip service to integration throughout systems planning and analysis, but then abandon all pretenses when schedules get tight and software must be built and installed.
- It simplifies testing and verification. The difficulty of coordinating test environments for ad hoc systems development was a major factor in Levi Strauss and Company's push for coordinated system releases. Now full releases can regularly migrate from one test environment to the next, and on into production.
- It eases technical resource planning. Releases can be handled using timebox techniques, meaning that release dates will nearly always be met. Demands for support resources and peak computer performance can be scheduled with accuracy. Today, as most projects consistently miss deadlines, people assigned to sup-

port integration testing and system installation rarely know what they'll be doing next month.
- It breaks down old notions of big, unilateral projects. Instituting the release concept with timebox overtones makes rapid systems delivery a reality. It will force project managers to carve smaller systems, and get things out the door faster.

The release concept can't be instituted without management commitment and some changes to the organization. Specifically, some new roles are needed:

- steering committee to assess release candidates and adjudicate ongoing development issues
- release architect to define and communicate the overall release structure
- release manager to coordinate multiple project groups, and manage communications with the steering committee

Actual development can be handled either by separate project teams, or by focused release building, testing, and implementation teams. It helps when everyone working on a release develops a larger team identity.

Coordinated application releases will mobilize everyone involved to make integration a reality. They involve considerable effort, but so does patching stand-alone systems together with shaky "duct tape" interfaces.

Decision support warehouse

Integrated databases trigger performance concerns. How can such massive systems respond quickly to user inquiries, or operate real-time equipment? The key to ensuring efficient integrated databases is to partition them according to how people will access the data.

William Inmon and Michael Loper of American Management Systems write that past approaches to a single, company database "failed to accommodate the differences in the ways data is used within an organization."[8] Operational systems require split-second response time and rapid, repetitive transaction processing. Decision support systems, on the other hand, value flexible data relationships over performance or availability.

A single integrated database can't easily be tuned to support both operational and decision support functions. The solution is to create a separate integrated store for decision support data, sometimes called the data warehouse.

The warehouse serves two purposes. First, it removes a lot of overhead, historical data from the operational storage, lessening response time and demands upon the DBMS. Second, it adds value to detailed data, deriving summaries and calculated information during the collection process.

The data warehouse concept involves some basic principles:

- You don't need everything online 24 hours a day. Many users ask IS to keep years of operational data accessible at all times. After all, they say, you never know when they might need to look up an invoice from 1985. The larger the online volume of data, the slower the response time. As long as historical data is kept

somewhere, accessible within a reasonable amount of time, it doesn't need to reside in the operational database.
- Keep operational data close to the source. Some pioneers in client/server and cooperative processing get bitten when data gets distributed too far afield. You don't want mainframe problems in New York to shut down manufacturing plants throughout the U.S. and Mexico. By separating operational data and storing close to its source, users retain some autonomy and gain better response time.
- Make strategic data available everywhere. The philosophy of free information exchange is powerful, but it need not extend to every tiny data element in every file or database. Do sales people in Hong Kong really care about detailed payroll information from a Canadian subsidiary? The information that's valuable across the firm is a small subset of the data that's available operationally.

Design the warehouse structure with information economy in mind. Make it flexible, so that adding new tables or columns in the future won't be catastrophic. Then apply the nightclub selection process to inclusion requests: line them up outside the warehouse, and only let the most interesting ones come inside.

Warehouse design implies changes to popular data design methods. For instance, most data modelers are fanatics about data normalization: the techniques of removing data redundancy by breaking information into small, atomic bits. However, warehouses require summarized data, pithy extracts of the raw operational facts. A decision support data model won't be as normalized as data purists would like. In addition, data designers must capture new properties for entities and attributes: are they warehousable?

The data warehouse can act as a catalyst for common data definitions, if this path hasn't yet been followed. When selecting data for inclusion in the warehouse, don't accept every data element variation. Force people to negotiate and select the best of the alternatives. Why manage three different supplier code formats if you can decide upon one flexible format? If everyone shares the cost of conversion, no one loses.

CASE tools for integration

CASE makes the software side of systems integration much easier than it has been. For most large-scale integration efforts, CASE tools are a necessity. According to Clare Gillan of International Data Corp. in Framingham, Massachusetts, nearly 50% of the DSS's in current use were generated using advanced application development tools.[9]

Integrated CASE tools can support integration efforts in many ways:

- The centralized repository acts as a clearinghouse for multiple project efforts, helping ensure consistency among systems.
- Organizations sharing CASE tools must follow similar development methodologies. This leads to similar project deliverables and documentation, and more cooperative development. The methodology can include explicit integration tasks: checkpoints where findings are compared to those of other projects, or steps to combine disparate modules into coordinated software releases.
- Some integrated CASE tools let you set up common standards for user interfaces and program structures. This encourages integrated system components to have common interface characteristics.

- CASE tools can provide automated "group memory" during cross-functional planning and analysis sessions. The repository provides an objective source for all group deliverables.
- Some CASE tools allow designs to be generated into working applications for numerous physical delivery platforms. This enables two sets of users, working on separate computer systems supplied by different vendors, to effectively use the same software applications.
- User-centered CASE tools make distributed reporting and warehouse access a reality. Armed with models of the warehouse, users can use interface generators, 4GLs, and natural language tools to call up any kind of information they wish.
- Reverse engineering tools can simplify the bridge-building process. They can dissect installed applications and put the pieces into the common CASE repository. Then you can use CASE tools to build and manage interfaces between old and new systems.
- Data modeling tools can manage separate models for operational storage and the data warehouse. Programs to transfer data to the warehouse can be designed and generated with the CASE tool.
- Smaller project models can be combined into larger integrated models using central repository technology (and a bit of perspiration). This facilitates the creation of coordinated software releases from multiple module design efforts.

If you plan to integrate your systems, you need integrated CASE tools. It can be done without them, but the results are often inconsistent and short-lived. Integrated CASE tools let you manage and control large volumes of software engineering data. They are built to handle the complexities of integrated software.

Data and process administration

Most companies that will attempt data integration have already established a data administration function. Data administrators help plan and design enterprise data models, and then help software developers modify and conform to them. Data administrators are key personnel in the push toward integrated systems.

The concept of process administration, however, is not widely accepted. Somewhere between the database and the software that uses it is an invisible line that data administrators don't cross. Data formats are sacred, but software processes are fair game. This creates an environment that discourages software reusability.

Data administration groups have brought order to hordes of unruly data elements. Process or reuse administrators can do the same for reusable software components. As object-oriented pioneer Bertrand Meyer writes, "A database administrator's charter is to develop the organization's data investment and maintain its consistency; the reuse administrator does the same for the company's software investment."[10]

One reason for the dearth of process administrators is the inadequacy of accepted process modeling techniques. Functional decomposition, for example, a technique for breaking processes down into elementary components, has few adherents and many critics. The technique has presentation value, but little rigor, making it insufficient for encouraging software reuse.

Some newer tools and techniques support reusability more strongly. Object-oriented methods in particular encourage process abstraction, the generalization of processes into more widely useful components.

The responsibilities of process administrators include:

- educating people about the need for reusable software
- helping people design processes with reusability in mind
- inspecting new process definitions and suggesting changes to increase their potential for reusability
- helping people locate reusable components, including processes, program templates, and screen and report definitions

With data administrators tending to the integrated database, and process administrators managing reusable software libraries, you've stacked the deck in favor of lasting systems integration.

Organizational incentives

Though everyone might see that integration will benefit the company, few people will work for it if they are penalized for doing so. Current management practices tend to favor adherence to schedules and budgets over more altruistic integration goals. When programmers are rewarded for hacking out code within certain time limits, they aren't eager to take time out for "unproductive" integration meetings.

Integration incentives can be established at three levels:

1. well publicized integration goals and principles
2. changes to employee evaluation procedures for developers
3. recognition of those who further integration—for example, awards for people who contribute the most to the reusable software library

These tactics apply to every significant change affecting the IS organization, so I'll talk about them in a broader sense in chapter 6.

How to proceed

No one can afford to dump all of their current systems and start fresh with fully integrated developments. Every firm must do some patchwork interfacing to get basic systems connectivity in the short-term. However, the migration to fully integrated systems can begin at any time.

CASE tools and a centralized data model can drive this migration. You can inject data from stand-alone systems into the operational and decision support databases. When a stand-alone system is converted to use an integrated database directly, there will be little or no impact upon the readers of its information.

With reverse engineering tools, you can manage enhancements to older systems using the CASE repository that you use for new development. Once downloaded into the repository, these applications can be bridged to, and eventually replaced, a piece at a time.

Figure 4-6 lists some stages on the way to complete systems integration. Stage I involves managing redundant data and processes in the best way possible, plus laying the groundwork for future integration. Initial data modeling and coordination begins in Stage II. Stage III sees the assimilation of installed base software into the CASE repository, simplifying future maintenance and bridging. Process reusability gains importance in Stage IV, and Stage V culminates with a program to tightly coordinate application releases.

Stages of Integration

Stage I: Patchwork and Groundwork

- build bridges as immediate needs arise
- establish a data administration function, if one isn't already present
- increase cross-functional project participation; discourage large unilateral development projects
- begin formal strategic information systems planning
- acquire CASE tools to support strategic planning and large-scale data modeling

Stage II: Define Common Data

- start education about the need for data and process integration
- require conformance to common data definitions from all new software projects
- plan and design a decision support data warehouse

Stage III: Rework the Installed Base

- acquire CASE tools to support reverse engineering of installed systems
- load intalled base systems into CASE repository (but don't merge models with new development efforts)
- use CASE methods to maintain installed base systems, and build bridges to new ones

Stage IV: Push Process Reusability

- establish a process or object administration function, if one isn't already present
- acquire CASE tools capable of supporting integrated and reusable processes or objects
- institute incentives to promote process reusability

Stage V: Manage Application Releases

- launch a coordinated application release program

Fig. 4-6. Stages toward complete system integration.

5

Diving into the method pool

I recently spoke with the chief designer of a popular CASE product. I asked him what kind of methodology his product supports and his answer shut me up fast. "I don't go in for that methodology garbage," he said. "People just want to get things done. They don't have time to do all that busywork. I talk to a developer, see what he wants to do, and then add it to the tool. That way he gets something he can use."

He was echoing a popular opinion: methodology means extra time spent on impractical tasks. In other words, don't use a methodology if you want to get things done. Though dangerous, this opinion is often based on direct experience. Methodologies, designed to control software projects, rarely have practical impact. "Every organization has a software development methodology," says Watts Humphrey. "Many just don't know what it is."[1]

Few if any methodologies are strictly adhered to, and most require so many "optional" steps that their usefulness is limited. Methodologies that sound great in theory can fail grimly in practice. And the whole concept of methodology takes the blame.

Yet methodology is really an essential part of software development. To invalidate all methodologies when one fails is to overreact. You may as well say that when a country's government has fallen, the concept of government itself was at fault. This reasoning might be popular with an anarchist minority, but most people would attribute the failure to a specific governmental system. Another system would emerge and try a new path. Methodology is a necessary component, a prerequisite, for successful CASE tool use. CASE tools are only as effective as the methodologies they support. If a methodology isn't giving you what you want, reevaluate it and come up with one that meets your needs.

This chapter will discuss the need to develop a robust, thriving methodology as the basis for all CASE efforts. I'll describe some problems with current methodologies and life cycles, and suggest ways for tailoring popular methodologies to fit your own development environment. I'll also introduce the concept of the *method pool*, a multiple-methodology approach that addresses a critical concern: how to integrate multiple tools, approaches, and techniques currently used within most IS organizations. In this regard, the method pool is far superior to the single-threaded methodologies most developers follow today.

By the end of this chapter, you should have a better idea how to gain control of methodologies, instead of letting them control you.

Method in the madness

Every few weeks an article appears in the industry press about a company using CASE tools to gain a competitive advantage. CASE is used to quickly implement a new strategic system, or to crystallize business data that had lain about for years, unorganized and misunderstood. Yet recent surveys imply that these success stories are the exception rather than the rule. For example, consultant Paul Price of PTD Consulting in Plano, Texas, recently studied 16 companies who have used CASE tools to develop large-scale software projects for at least two years. All of these companies began their CASE efforts with enthusiasm and management support. Now only three of these companies label their CASE efforts a success. The others say that CASE hasn't delivered the expected gains in system quality or development productivity, despite massive investment in tools and training.[2]

The three successful companies all had one thing in common: a detailed structured methodology, applied with discipline throughout the organization. Clearly, structured methodology is an essential component of CASE success.

The benefits of a good methodology are easily explained. Adopted throughout an organization, a methodology can help:

- improve software quality
- guide developers along the shortest path to an effective production system
- foster standard means of communication throughout the organization
- define the optimum mix of skills required within the organization
- facilitate coordination of multiple projects and tasks
- improve project estimation and control
- form the basis for further process improvement

"Methodology" is often used to describe the groups of techniques offered by theorists like Finkelstein, Martin, Gane and Sarson, Yourdon and others. Hence the "Gane and Sarson methodology" refers to the set of techniques advocated by these authors. These "designer methodologies" are powerful. They provide rigorous foundations for software development; they put the engineering into CASE. However, most designer methodologies don't address all phases of the software development life cycle.[3] They don't cover the application of techniques in terms of resource requirements, substitute methods, or time estimates. In short, they only paint part of the picture.

The definition of methodology must be more attuned to the needs of practical software development:

> **Methodology**: a coordinated group of applicable techniques, tasks, and guidelines designed to fulfill a defined set of objectives.

Objectives will of course vary by organization. By adding the main objective for most IS organizations, the definition becomes:

Software development methodology: a coordinated group of applicable techniques, tasks, and guidelines designed to capture essential business and systems design information and translate this information into an effective computer-based system.

A methodology, then, is a plan that addresses the full systems life cycle. It must cover requirements gathering, analysis, systems design, systems construction, and testing. It easily can (and should) be extended to cover early planning phases and later systems implementation and maintenance.

Married to the methodology

Despite the claims of many vendors, CASE tools do not implement methodologies. Methodologies implement CASE tools. They identify where CASE tools can contribute to systems development, and govern the ways in which tools are used. The CASE tools themselves simply automate a subset of techniques within the broader life cycle.

CASE tools do not in fact provide methodologies. They help analysts perform and in some cases automate various methods. Most CASE tools require rigor of diagram notations, but not rigorous analysis across all deliverables. For instance, CASE tools can force analysts to use specific methods and notation while creating an entity-relationship diagram, but can't encourage analysts to review the diagram with business experts, or suggest the use of a facilitated session to gather data requirements.

Methodology and CASE are complementary. Methodology provides engineering discipline and quality improvements, while CASE contributes productivity and reusability benefits. A detailed structured methodology without a CASE tool will generate impeccable systems at a snail's pace. Structured techniques are generally slow and costly.[4] When the application of software engineering was limited to hand-drawn diagrams and matrices, few companies practiced it.

On the other hand, CASE without a supporting methodology can be dangerous.

The first CASE project I worked on was with a company new to the technology. They wanted to improve systems analysis by producing data flow diagrams and structure charts. They added these new deliverables to their existing Software Development Life Cycle (SDLC) requirements. Months later, they found themselves with an unhappy project team and a poorly designed system.

The programmer/analysts saw the new deliverables as extra tasks that only slowed them down. They produced the DFDs and structure charts as ordered. But then they filed them away and programmed the system as always: from memory, by trial and error. All revisions were made to the COBOL code, and none to the diagrams, so the final product didn't match the earlier analysis. The bad reputation of this project discredited CASE throughout the company.

Structured methodology prevents this outcome. It specifies how to produce the new deliverables, not just what to produce. It outlines the ways the deliverables and techniques build upon each other, not just the order in which they should be done. It is the glue that binds the techniques together into a viable whole.

The quality directive

Despite the benefits described above, many designers and analysts react to the word "methodology" with fear or disapproval. Another reason for disenchantment with methodology is that most of them have been poorly designed and badly applied.

Companies using a structured methodology usually developed it in one of two ways. They upgraded an existing SDLC to include some structured analysis techniques, or they bought wholesale into one of the designer methodologies (such as Yourdon's, Gane and Sarson's, or information engineering). The latter choice is often made because a purchased CASE tool automates specific designer methodology techniques. Unfortunately, neither approach tends to produce a strong development methodology.

SDLC-based methodologies tend to emphasize deliverables and management checkpoints. They rarely support the interdependencies of structured analysis and design techniques. Nor can they cope well with concurrent tasks, or iterative methods.

The SDLCs main advantages—well-defined activities, consistency across projects, and management checkpoints—improve project management, not software quality or productivity. SDLCs are a management tool, not a development tool. Albert F. Case makes a similar point: "The phases and activities (sometimes referred to as subphases) are essentially arbitrary, management-oriented segmentations of project work, designed to ease communications and statistical reporting about the project."[5]

Designer methodologies chart a better map of methods and deliverables, but rarely mention pragmatic concerns: who contributes to each task, when reviews should occur, or what substitute methods are possible.

To really streamline software development, you need a better methodology, tailored to your own way of working. You need one that:

- covers all stages of the software life cycle, from high-level planning through construction, implementation, and maintenance
- contains detailed descriptions of methods, including who should perform them, what inputs they need, and what deliverables they produce
- identifies the shortest path to the production of quality software systems
- optimizes the use of automated development tools
- blends in with the "corporate culture"
- leverages off of the strengths of development personnel

You need, in short, a homegrown methodology. Customized methods don't come in packages.

Roping the wild methodology

Getting a good methodology is in fact far more important than selecting a CASE tool. CASE tools simply automate certain practices. If these practices are the wrong ones for you, you'll just be messing up at a blistering pace. The methodology defines the scope of all software development. It really is essential to decide on the methodology before you get the CASE tool. Then pick a CASE tool that does the best job with the methods you've chosen.

Of course you shouldn't choose exotic techniques that can only be done with pencil and paper by computer science Ph.D.'s, even if they're touted as the analytical best. Select your techniques from the realm of the feasible, the set of techniques that have some sort of automated support.

Convinced of the importance of methodology, some people rush to grab the first one they can find. Yet it is not true that any methodology is better than none at all (though many vendors and consultants will tell you so). CASE and new methods bring organizational change, and you shouldn't force your company through such change for less than the best. An ill-fitting methodology can hurt morale and productivity, and perhaps discredit CASE altogether.

I said before that the methodology should do more than just describe methods or deliverables. It should explain all the following software development objects:

- objectives and subobjectives of the IS organization
- specific products that support these objectives
- evaluation criteria for each product
- specific methods and tasks to create the products
- inputs required for each task or method
- methods for validating the products
- contributors needed for each task
- automation opportunities
- estimation guidelines and other metrics
- past experiences of previous users of the methodology

I'll discuss each of these in more detail.

Objectives

The main objective, or mission, of software development is more than just "to write software." A better statement for many IS organizations might be "to deliver maintainable software systems that enhance the users' ability to perform their jobs." Every organization's mission will be different, of course. And underlying the mission are a series of subobjectives, outlining the small steps that make the mission achievable.

Regardless of your approach to methodology, publication of the organization's objectives is essential. It's one thing for a manager to send a memo saying that everyone must do data models before creating databases in the future. It's another thing to start basing analysts' performance evaluations on how well they model data. It's a far nobler thing to explain the actual business objectives that led management to conclude that data modeling is worthwhile.

In some cases, these objectives will be obvious. They can sometimes be pulled directly from the literature supporting certain analysis or design methods. However, the theoretical purposes of these methods will often be a subset of your own objectives for using them. For instance, data modeling serves many analysis purposes, chief of which is the achievement of nonredundant or normalized data. But one side-effect of data models is that they can often be a great medium for communicating with business experts. Data modeling, then, also serves the objective of fostering communication with business users.

Just publishing these objectives proves that someone really did think this through, that all this "new work" serves a purpose. Someone who understands why he or she is doing something is much more motivated to do it.

Objectives should be defined for the entire methodology and for each phase within the methodology. If the methodology you select doesn't rely on phases, then the high-level objectives should be broken into more concrete subgoals.

Objectives must be stated clearly and concisely. Some sample objectives are:

- to deliver completed software systems within six months of the initial requirements' acceptance date
- to fully test all software products
- to produce software systems that correspond to requirements of end-users

The breakdown of objectives into subobjectives can be easily shown using an indented list, outline format. For example:

3. To thoroughly document all implemented software systems.
    3.1. To provide readable and detailed user documentation.
        3.1.1. To provide detailed reference information for systems users.
        3.1.2. To provide basic information that allows users to quickly begin using the system.
    3.2. To thoroughly record internal analysis and design information.
        3.2.1. To collect structured information about the business, for better understanding and information strategy planning.
        3.2.2. To record detailed information about the system's internal design to support later systems maintenance and enhancement.

Fulfilling every subobjective implies that the parent objective has also been met. You can later tie every deliverable in the methodology to the objective(s) it supports. The hierarchy need not be as detailed as the one above, merely detailed enough to provide direction to developers. By chaining through this hierarchy, you can determine which sets of deliverables fulfill all of your basic objectives. Each project can choose from these possible sets according to its own skills, tools, and directions. This allows dynamic creation of work breakdown structures.

It's then very easy to justify each deliverable-producing task in terms of the objectives it supports. If you can't, then you've found a useless task that you can trim away.

Products

Products are the concrete deliverables that support the aforementioned objectives. For example, "documentation of the system's user interface" might be an objective of the design phase. This objective can be supported by a screen snapshot product, or alternatively by an interactive screen prototype product.

Products are also used as input to subsequent tasks or methods.

Describe products in excruciating detail. The description of a product defines its standard format and usage. It isn't enough to say you need to produce an entity-relationship diagram. Which conventions will the diagram follow (Bachman, Chen, or IDEF notation for data models?). How should the diagram be presented (on paper, or during a facilitated session?) and stored (paper files, PC files, or in the central repository?).

Don't overspecify to the point of ridicule. Saying it needs to be printed on white paper with 1/2-inch margins and the company logo in the left corner is going too far. Some products might not need to be formally presented. If it will only be used as an input to a later task, perhaps the product can be created and stored informally (pencil and paper aren't totally obsolete) for later use.

Deliverables are the things developers use to communicate. They are the currency of software projects. Like currency, they must be officially sanctioned and widely recognized before everyone will accept them.

Evaluation criteria

Too often quality is something enforced during a final testing phase. Robert Wallace and his colleagues submit: "Assessing quality is really an integral part of any methodology. Techniques must be available for assessing quality not only of the end product, the delivered system, but each product, document or model. . . ."[6]

Evaluation criteria aid quality assurance throughout the development process. They encourage quality to be internal to each task. When you rely on formal reviews for all checks, you're performing quality control. If something is amiss, you must back up and start the task again. When the evaluation criteria are plainly given at the start of the task, the people performing it can constantly test their own performance.

To produce quality products, people must know how quality is defined. You need to set a scale for judging deliverables. How does one know what makes a good product? The main criterion should be "does it support the objectives it was supposed to support?" The answer to this question is usually subjective, so more specific criteria are required.

If the deliverable is subject to certain software engineering rigor, many of the evaluation criteria can be pulled from textbooks. For example, data flow diagrams should normally obey rules of data conservation. An evaluation criterion for the DFD product might read: "All data leaving a process must have either been input to the process originally, or created during the process."

Many CASE tools help you enforce rules like this automatically. If using such a tool, the above statement might alter to read: "The diagram passes the CASE tool consistency checks with no errors."

Some criteria must be more fully defined according to parameters specific to certain projects or systems. For example, you can't specify exact performance criteria for a software module unless you know the type of system it's a part of. For a customer inquiry screen, wide response time variation might be acceptable; for an aircraft guidance system, such variation might prove deadly.

Though some evaluation can be automated, you will always add your own criteria, to encourage adherence to standards or to support additional objectives. The textbooks will tell you how to recognize "normalized" data, for example; but they won't talk about your in-house standards for naming attributes or presenting the finished diagram.

To illustrate, the evaluation criteria for an entity-relationship diagram product could include:

- entity names and definitions are precise, unambiguous, and meaningful in terms of the business vocabulary
- relationship names are indicative of business rules and constraints
- many-to-many relationships have been broken apart

Experienced data modelers will notice that few of these criteria apply universally. Naming standards for entities and relationships vary widely from site to site (and are never enforced by CASE tools). Many-to-many relationships are prohibited by some CASE tools and allowed by others. The above criteria consider the specifics of your environment: standards, policies, CASE tool features and limitations. No canned methodology will encourage deliverables that fit this well.

Methods and tasks

A method is a technique to transform input products into desired deliverables. A task is a low-level or elementary method. Each method must use at least one product to produce at least one product. Methods can be thought of as a collection of rules for transforming one set of products into another. Evaluation criteria, in comparison, are constraints that must be met by the outcome of this transformation.

Note that you can often create the same product using many different techniques. To record the basic logic (or *pseudocode*) of a business process, for example, you might interview someone who goes through the process every day. Or, if no such expert exists, you could instead produce the same pseudocode by reverse engineering, or digging into the code of an existing system.

A strong methodology would acknowledge both of these techniques for creating pseudocode. In this example, each technique requires different contributors (a business expert was required for the first one) and different inputs (existing system code for the second one). The second technique might be partially automatable, while the first one is not. We gain a lot of insight into your development process by listing multiple methods for each deliverable produced. Multiple methods reflect the real world.

Many CASE vendors try to remove methodology dependencies from their tools to appeal to a wider customer base. As a result, they view CASE repositories as neutral platforms able to store information generated using many different methodologies.[7] The advantage of this approach is flexibility. The tools enable multiple methods for producing similar results. The disadvantage is the burden this approach places upon the CASE customer. Flexibility means more work defining techniques, and selecting from among them.

Methods can be discrete or iterative. Discrete methods are performed once, while iterative ones follow a repetitive perform-review cycle. Screen prototyping is a good example of an iterative method. The analyst designs a screen, which is reviewed by business experts. These experts suggest changes to the screen, which are made by the analyst, and reviewed again by the experts. The iteration stops when the business experts officially accept the screen layout. Iterative methods play an important role in some of the rapid development paths currently in vogue.

Iteration can be handled in the method pool two ways. First, within a task work continues until the evaluation criteria are met. Something is produced, then evaluated, and if found lacking, more work is done. The task is repeated until the product meets the evaluation criteria. This type of iteration is assumed and need not be explicitly specified.

The second type of iteration crosses task boundaries. Take a task to perform integration testing upon a software system. The inputs are an integration test plan, and a group of software programs. Evaluation criteria specify the correctness and performance levels that must be met. What happens if the test fails? You can test the software a second time, but it won't improve the results. But if you mark a specific input product as the cause of the failure, you can then backtrack and redo the task that created it. In this case, the offending program would be marked, and someone would change the defective part of the program. Each task, then, can potentially iterate with preceding tasks, tied by the products that pass between them.

Inputs

As mentioned above, each method requires at least one input product. Input products are often deliverables of an earlier task, though they can also be products that existed before your current efforts began. For instance, defining business area objectives might depend upon the corporate mission statement and a three-year divisional strategy plan. Or the technique described above for creating process pseudocode by reverse engineering would depend upon inputs such as existing code listing and existing screen layout.

Inputs to a method can be required or optional. For instance, a division that hasn't yet done a three-year plan might still be able to define business area objectives, basing analysis solely on the knowledge of the participants.

Validation

The evaluation of criteria mentioned above helps determine the completeness and correctness within the realm of the specific task. It represents the quality assurance aspects embedded within each task. Validation checks the results of one task against another, to ensure traceability of business requirements and consistency across all facets of the software engineering model. Validation steps provide quality control.

Most products require validation of some sort, often provided by a separate method. The product being validated will usually be listed as an input to the validation method.

For instance, program code, a product created by the method called programming, can be validated by the method called unit testing. A process decomposition diagram in analysis can be validated by a method that produces process dependency diagrams. Review meetings can be set up as special methods for validating deliverables.

If the validation task discovers a problem with its inputs, a new iteration of the task that created the inputs should be launched.

Contributors

Somebody's got to do all this work. Each method requires the participation of at least one person. The involvement of additional people can be optional. This involvement should be defined in terms of roles rather than job titles, unless the two match. A list of contributors for a facilitated session method to define a data model might read:

> business expert   1 or more
> business analyst   1 or more
> data modeling specialist   1 or more
> session facilitator   1
> CASE tool operator   1 (optional)

Normally you will want to describe each contributor's responsibilities within the task. In the above example, the business expert provides knowledge about business information needs, and the CASE tool operator draws a data model using automated modeling tools.

Automation opportunities

If all your techniques could be automated and integrated, you wouldn't need much of a methodology. In fact, very few methods are automatable. To accelerate development, you need to recognize every opportunity to automate and save time and effort.

If a method can be automated in any way, you should say so. For example, take the method of transforming a logical data model into a layout for a relational data base. This method can be done manually, following certain steps to arrive at a perfectly valid data structure diagram. Or it can be done automatically by a CASE tool, a hundred times faster than the manual method.

Automated methods musts often be set up separately from their manual counterparts. The automated method often requires different inputs and fewer contributors.

Always specify the exact CASE tool to be used. If you own many tools that support the same technique, list them all, describing the pros and cons of each. Formal procedures do exist for deciding which tools to use for specific techniques,[8] but usually this is a judgment call. Test the value of using a tool against the value of doing it manually or with a different tool. Document the results using the methodology. In large organizations with multiple CASE tools, the methodology can be the guidebook to the practical use of these tools.

Estimation guidelines

Estimation of project or task time and effort is essential for good project management. Usually this estimation is left to a project manager, who derives ballpark figures based on previous experiences. However this is akin to predicting tomorrow's weather on today's: luck plays a big role in the outcome. When you change the methods and tools, estimating new projects based on old experiences is no longer possible (it's like predicting tomorrow's weather in Los Angeles based on today's weather in Helsinki).

The methodology is an excellent repository for estimation guidelines. Each method can carry suggestions for project managers. For example, the time needed to create analysis-level process pseudocode might be estimated at "two to three hours of effort per business process." You can specify whether more contributors will lessen the duration, and what other factors might enter the equation.

These guidelines can be general or specific as desired. If they are specific, standardized, and kept current, such guidelines can improve project scheduling in many ways:

- All projects will be estimated on the same basis, allowing for better schedule comparison.
- Task estimations will begin to reflect the experiences of many people on many projects (not just one project manager's limited experience).
- Competing methods can be evaluated by projected effort and duration, leading to shorter project schedules.

Estimation guidelines should be revised according to experience. Keep productivity metrics for each method, and use these to improve your ability to estimate in the future.

Organizations with process measurement programs in place can use the methodology to identify or capture additional metrics. The use of similar measures for competing methods provides a basis for comparing the effectiveness of each method.

Past experiences

The best way to learn about new techniques is from people who have done them. In fact, the most effective sources of practical development information are not always trainers or consultants. They are developers who have been down the path before.

You can use the methodology to share these actual experiences. A sophisticated method management system could use this information to maintain an ongoing project notebook. Ask each developer to do a post-mortem review of each method, answering questions like:

- What problems arose when following this method, and how were they surmounted?
- How did the products created by this method fare against the evaluation criteria?
- What changes would make this method more effective in the future?

As some studies have shown, a forum for proactively exchanging CASE hints and shortcuts can greatly compress the CASE learning curve[9].

Figure 5-1 shows how the methodology objects fit together. Objectives are defined for the methodology itself and each of its phases. Products are created to support each objective. Each product is described in detail, and criteria for evaluating its quality are established. Each product can be created by one or more available methods, and validated by separate methods. For each method, describe which inputs are needed, who should participate, and how it can be automated. You can also suggest algorithms for estimating how much time and effort each method takes. Ideally, you should be able to record the experiences of the contributors who actually use these methods.

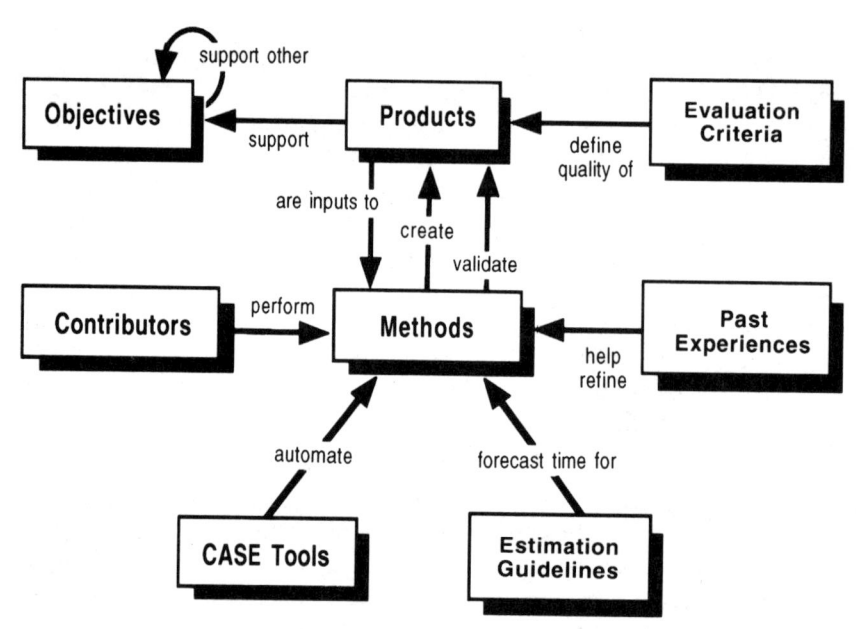

Fig. 5-1. Interaction of methodology components

The importance of technique

You've defined the components of an effective methodology. Now you need to build it.

Notice that I say build and not purchase or acquire. No canned methodology will fit exactly. No one has anticipated the mix of technologies and skills in your organization. Most methodologies you acquire—by buying a methodology package or CASE tool, or by adopting techniques of certain theorists—will describe only some of the components discussed above.

Canned methodologies are often great starting points, but you can't just adopt them unchanged. This is like forcing an athlete to use a certain style. Up until the 1940s, all high jumpers cleared the bar by rolling their bodies over it, one leg after the other, face forward. Richard Fosbury found a better way, a backwards "flop," that helped him win the Olympic high jump event in 1968. Fosbury was a good high jumper using the roll method, but he became a great one by defining his own.

If you were to set up Fosbury's technique in a method pool, it might look like this:

Objective: to get over the high-jump bar
Product: a jump
Evaluation criteria: must not touch the bar of its supports; must land in the pit
Validating method: judges' review

Method 1: "Western Roll." Get a running start, push off with one foot, throw the other one over the bar, roll face first, raise trailing foot, land on back.
Contributors: one high jumper

Inputs: one pair spiked shoes, official uniform
Automation: none available

Method 2: "Fosbury Flop." Get a running start, push off with one foot, throw head and shoulders up past bar, lean backwards over bar, kick feet up at apex, land on back.
Contributors: one high jumper
Inputs: one pair spiked shoes, official uniform
Automation: none available

The homegrown "Fosbury Flop" method is added as a competitor to the previously standard "Western Roll" method. Over time, athletes' experiences with both techniques would soon demonstrate the flop's advantages.

All methodologies normally describe input, methods, and products. These are the foundation for much of the rest, and are indispensable. Methodology packages (defined as a published methodology for sale by a vendor) will often consider review points, and contributors. CASE tool methodologies consider automation opportunities by definition. Acquired methodologies rarely address objectives and evaluation criteria.

Figure 5-2 illustrates the gaps often found in acquired methodologies. None of these methodologies contain all the components you want. In order to get them, you'll need to internalize and customize any methodology you acquire.

	Objectives	Products	Evaluation Criteria	Methods	Inputs	Validation Methods	Contributors	Automation Options	Estimation Guidelines	Record of Experiences
Packaged Methodology	○	●	○	●	●		●			
CASE Tool Methodology	○	●		●	●	○		●		
"Designer" Methodology	○	●		●	●	●				
Pre-CASE SDLC	○	●	○	○	○		●			
Optimal Methodology	●	●	●	●	●	●	●	●	●	●

Legend: ● = usually describes this feature   ○ = sometimes describes this feature

Fig. 5-2. Information covered by methodology types

A second reason for internalizing the methodology is even more compelling: you want it to evolve. The methodology must keep up with the rapid pace of change in development tools and methods. You've taken the first step by recognizing essential objectives, multiple competing methods, and automation opportunities. Next you need to give the methodology a life of its own.

Methodology is often considered sacred: the religious foundation for our actions. Adherents of various methods often speak with religious fervor, and disagreements among them sound like clashes between followers of different prophets: "James Martin says the DFDs aren't the best way!" "But Gane and Sarson tell us that DFDs, when leveled, bring true understanding of the whole!"

But methodology aspires to far less than religion. It doesn't describe a world view. It's designed to pinpoint quick paths to fairly concrete goals. Never fear changing the methodology, or improving it. Treat it as a repository of information about the development process. To improve the process, gather more information, analyze it, and be free to act on this analysis. Even religions have to change with their times in order to survive. A static methodology will soon lose all its followers.

You should not only revamp your current methodologies, you should continually reassess and improve them. Given the rapidly changing business climate and incredible pace of technological innovation, successful companies in the 1990s and beyond will be those who thrive on change and uncertainty. Already the call has gone out for a new corporate model: the "learning organization."[10] This model depends on constant training of employees and frequent process improvements. It requires looking on change as an opportunity, not an obstacle.

Methodology in the 1990s should parallel this model. You need a learning methodology, constantly revitalized by drawing in the best available methods and tools.

The Software Engineering Institute at Carnegie Mellon University has developed a *maturity framework* to help companies gauge the sophistication of their development process.[11] The framework consists of five levels:

1. Initial. No process definition or measurement of process effectiveness.
2. Repeatable. The development process is fairly stable, and includes rigorous management of project commitments, costs, and schedules.
3. Defined. The process is fully defined and handled the same way throughout the organization.
4. Managed. Additional quality and productivity metrics are captured about the development process, enabling incremental process improvements.
5. Optimizing. Process improvement happens continuously, based on consistent measurements across methods.

Organizations with higher maturity levels are better able to increase productivity and quality, and are more capable of adopting and exploiting new technologies.

A standardized methodology can boost the organization from the repeatable to the defined level. A methodology that helps capture metrics supports the higher managed level. To reach the optimizing level requires a cultural shift—a commitment to continuous process improvement—and a highly adaptable methodology.

Over time, development objectives stay fairly constant, while techniques and CASE tools continually improve. Incorporate new and promising techniques as they arise, even if they aren't fully proven within the company. The methodology is a communicator, and a good forum for recording new ideas.

In today's environment, new methods are usually advocated by a single project manager and sold to management. The project manager then purchases a specialized tool and tries it out. The company-wide result is a morass of incompatible tools and techniques, and an uneven distribution of knowledge across project teams.

When a new method is included in the methodology, everyone becomes aware of it. It can be marked "experimental" at first, if the first project team is piloting it. Once the method is successful, there will be very little lag time before the next team can take advantage of it. And if the first team's experiences with the methods have been recorded, the later teams will get an initial headstart.

The basic steps for reassessing methods are simple:

- incorporate new methods and tools as they become available
- keep quality and productivity metrics about each method
- record the experiences of those who have tried each method, including difficulties faced, suggestions for improvement, and hints or tips for future users
- constantly review methods for effectiveness
- remove methods that have proven consistently inferior

For example, a certain project might be delayed because business policy issues took forever to resolve. This problem is common to many projects, so a new method is established, to manage a text-based prioritized issues list for the project. This next project team finds this method useful, and suggests a database product for further automating the method. Future teams benefit from an improved method and are able to resolve policy issues relatively quickly.

Many people are uncomfortable with the concept of a changing methodology. They liken it to a roadway: how can you get anywhere if the road keeps shifting? My response: you're not redirecting the road. It still points you toward the goal of effective, quality systems. You're just repaving it, smoothing out the potholes. And when you can, you're letting the road transport you. Like a moving walkway in an airport, whisking passengers along.

Diving into the method pool

Part of changing a methodology is recognizing and incorporating new techniques as they become practical. Most organizations currently favor a single way of developing systems, but nearly all are experimenting with new methods that are superior for certain types of applications. For example, expert systems technology and object-oriented development methods have been proven effective for many types of applications. Few IS organizations limit themselves to one set of methods, though their methodologies rarely reflect this.

Adoption of new methods does not pollute your "pure" development process. How many have ever followed a published methodology to the letter, after all? Rather it makes the process more useful and robust.

IS organizations face rapid changes on two fronts: the business environment and the software development process. As information systems play more strategic business roles, the importance of improving the development process increases. As consultant Howard Rubin puts it, "Survival in the 1990s involves a skillful, intelligent blending of tools, concepts, and methods suited to the task at hand."[12] Developers can no longer keep the blinders on and say, "There's only one way to do systems here." They must learn to deftly juggle the available methods and apply them selectively when most effective.

The proliferation of new methods and tools suggests that a standardized single path methodology will never be followed exactly. A project manager faced with such a methodology starts by deciding which tasks will be done, and which will be skipped or replaced. Some tasks are excluded because they take too long, or because they produce an obsolete deliverable—the "nobody reads that document anyway" syndrome. Other tasks are replaced by new, improved methods like the ones described above. For certain projects, such as expert systems, the entire methodology might be junked in favor of a new set of tasks, designed on the fly by the project manager or outside consultants.

Some methodologies are built with these compromises in mind. Tasks are either required or optional, depending on the type of project. The required tasks produce the standard deliverables that make everyone feel comfortable. All other tasks are optional because someone, somewhere might not need to do them. The predictable result: a lot of corner-cutting when project deadlines approach, and a system that's delivered incomplete or underanalyzed. In addition, the methodology is seen as unrealistic and barely useful.

The root of this problem is that today's methodologies are linear: sequential series of tasks. Yet reality holds a vast pool of methods, with various levels of applicability. A good analogy is a highway system: from an origin to a destination we can choose many different routes. Each route might be more appropriate, depending on the type of trip being taken. A single-path methodology might express this as in TABLE 5-1. All trips must pass through San Francisco and Chicago on the way to New York. All other stops are optional. Since time is always important, it is likely that no one will ever stop in the other cities; they have no reason to do so.

Table 5-1. Single-path Methodology, with Options

Destination:	New York City from Los Angeles	
Deliverables:	San Francisco	(Required)
	Boise	(Optional)
	Denver	(Optional)
	Chicago	(Required)
	Indianapolis	(Optional)
	Philadelphia	(Optional)
	Washington, D.C.	(Optional)
	New York City	(Required)

Yet, depending on the purpose of the trip, the skeletal required route might not be sufficient. For example, Philadelphia and Washington, DC, would be required stops for someone on an historical tour of the United States. For someone on a camping tour, Denver and Indianapolis might be required because of their good camping facilities.

A better methodology sets it up as in TABLE 5-2. Now there are specific routes defined for each type of project, with limited optionality of deliverables. This gives each project manager (or bus driver) a clear and tested path to follow. However, it also assumes that you can predict ahead of time the nature of all potential projects.

Table 5-2. Multiple Single-path Methodologies

Objective:	U.S. Historical Tour	
Deliverables:	San Francisco	(Required)
	Denver	(Optional)
	Chicago	(Required)
	Philadelphia	(Required)
	Washington, D.C.	(Required)
	New York City	(Required)

Objective:	U.S. Camping Tour	
Deliverables:	San Francisco	(Required)
	Boise	(Required)
	Denver	(Required)
	Chicago	(Optional)
	Indianapolis	(Required)
	New York City	(Required)

To improve the methodology, you can categorize methods according to the objectives they support. Once each project team determines its specific set of objectives, they can then select the methods that best meet them. The deliverables would be presented as in TABLE 5-3.

Table 5-3.
Objective-based Method Information

Deliverable	Objectives supported
San Francisco	Camping, history, nightlife
Boise	Camping
Denver	Camping, nightlife
Chicago	History, nightlife
Indianapolis	Camping
Philadelphia	History
Washington, D.C.	History
New York City	History, nightlife

Once the objectives for a project are known, the appropriate deliverables fall into place. From this example, you could build a camping tour, a historical tour, or a historical tour that also considers the local night life.

To gain this level of flexibility, you need to stop thinking of your methods as a linear set and start treating them as a method pool. Method pool concepts have surfaced many times in the past few years, and prototype systems have been developed.[13] Some

IBM sites have used a method pool system called Programming Process Architecture since 1984.[14] A group at AT&T has developed a smaller-scale system called the Software Development Assistant.[15] A method pool has two main characteristics:

1. It includes all methods proven useful to developers within the organization.
2. It holds enough information about each method to allow informed selection of the best methods for specific projects and circumstances.

Given enough information about each method available, project members can choose which ones to perform. The full set of chosen methods becomes the method path for the project.

The method path is similar to a single-path methodology. Both are a collection of methods used to develop systems. Single-path methodologies are standard linear sequences of tasks. Method paths are specialized sequences of standard tasks, unique to a specific project. New method paths can be generated according to project characteristics, and effective ones can be reused by similar projects in the future. The method pool provides a framework for managing a myriad of methods, and assembling them in structured fashion upon demand.

Method pools also encourage process evolution. Since the methods are encapsulated and independent, new ones can be added at any time without affecting existing method paths. When those AI consultants you called in lay out the techniques for developing expert systems, take the new information and add it to the method pool. When someone on a project team writes a utility to reverse-engineer existing documentation files, describe it in the method pool. Future projects can then choose from an up-to-the-minute inventory of methods when forming their method paths.

Categorize methods by types of systems they support, or by specific situations in which they're most useful. For example, a technique to translate business knowledge into structured rule format is most appropriate for developing expert systems. A technique to convert current file formats to a first-cut data model is only appropriate in a reengineering situation. This categorization lets you narrow your first view of the method pool as you chart your method path. Instead of a blinding sea of methods, you'll view a calmer pool, showing only the best things for your circumstances.

Method pools add complexity to the current concept of methodology. The require maintenance and support far above what is normally supplied today. Yet they have compelling advantages. I've already described the power and flexibility that custom selection of method paths can bring. Perhaps better still: once a method pool is implemented, it might never need to be replaced. Current life cycles and methodologies become obsolete soon after they are published, and must be redone later at great cost. A method pool evolves over time, if supported, staying relevant and useful. Until you start "direct-brain" system development, or some other advance that wipes out programming entirely, the method pool concept will apply.

Pool service

Method pools are repositories of large amounts of information about software development. Publishing this information in a giant book, with no clues about how to select and use the various methods, is like consigning it all to limbo. The book will clutter offices, gather dust, and be opened only rarely. To make sure that this information is accessible, usable, and continually relevant you should sketch out a methodology support plan.

Methodology support involves three general areas: publication, training, and evolution.

Before you can publish the methodology, you must first gather and store all the information. This information is really no different from the other business data you deal with, and it can be managed in similar ways.

Methodology information is usually stored as text. Most existing life cycles were written as one book, with some general guidelines, a chapter for each phase, and techniques and review points described within. Text is still a viable format for storing the methodology, as long as attention is paid to a new imperative: the ability to continually capture new information and incorporate new methods. A central person or group can manage the methodology, accepting contributions from developers about new methods or experiences with existing ones.

One limitation of many text processors is their inability to display good graphics. If the graphic capabilities of the publishing format are below those of the methods you follow, then you won't be able to store examples of many important deliverables.

Publishing text-based methodologies can be difficult. You want everyone to have access to the full range of available methods, but you don't want to print a hundred copies of a five hundred page book every time something changes. Alternatives range from keeping a few current copies available centrally to keeping everything online and letting people print pages at will.

Newer technologies provide superior ways of storing and publishing methodologies. The methodology support team at the Library of Congress, for example, publishes its methodology in hypertext format, using HyperCard on an Apple Macintosh. This allows readers to explore the methodology in whatever level of detail is appropriate. It also gives readers a better sense of a methodology's flow, since their reading can parallel the progression of methods for a development project.

Perhaps the best way of storing methodology information is how we store the rest of our business data—in a database management system. The same graphics limitation applies here: many DBMS's cannot capture graphics. But storing the methodology in a DBMS allows you to build functionality that:

- supports decentralized updating of methods, metrics, and experiences
- prompts for information about a project and then suggests sets of methods that best fulfill objectives
- supports selection and printing of custom methods paths: road-maps of a specific project's chosen set of methods
- performs "shortest path" analysis to decide which methods provide fastest results

In short, a database system can fully automate the method pool. Of course such a system is another full-fledged application, with its own requirements for development, documentation, and training. Yet the benefits of an automated method pool can more than balance such costs. A well-designed method pool system brings flexibility, adaptability, and efficiency, qualities that rarely grace today's development process. The method pool, if fully supported, can grant these qualities to every future project.

An automated method pool can take many forms. Most simply, it manages information about methods and provides predefined method paths to tailor to specific needs. The use of distinct objectives and goals allows for more powerful analysis capabilities. Each technique creates products that support specific tactical objectives, that in turn support larger strategic objectives. And each technique can have quantifiable costs associated to it. By modeling the process as either a network flow or shortest path problem, or as a backward-chaining rule based system, you can determine the optimum set of methods to use, subject to cost constraints. An example of a method pool management system is presented in appendix A.

Some vendors offer packages to manage methodologies, though none contain all the features just described. The market for tools like these is still in its infancy. For example, LBMS provides Project Engineer, a module that creates and manages work breakdown structures for projects following systems engineering or SSADM (structured systems analysis and design methodology) methodologies. Project Engineer lets you tailor the tasks to match customized methods, and also provides some estimation support.

The second area of methodology support is training. Even with a road-map and descriptions of landmarks, people get lost touring through unfamiliar country. The best descriptions, guidelines, and hints can't ensure that developers will perform techniques well. Familiarity and hands-on experience are essential.

The story here is the same as with any new technology: you can't just bless people with experience. You can either grant experience through training, or by sharing the knowledge of your most experienced folks.

Methodology training is different from CASE tool training. Methodology training conveys the foundations and objectives for a set of methods, not just the application of the methods themselves. It covers how to apply the methodology to specific projects, and how to choose the best methods. CASE tool training is valuable for learning specific methods in depth.

Most CASE tool training is done by the vendors themselves, or by licensed partners. The picture presented is invariably rosy; the product's strong points are emphasized, its rough spots glossed over. Methodology training presents your own view of the big development picture. It shows where CASE tools work best, and how you can compensate when they don't.

Training requirements vary depending on the type of methodology you adopt, and how much its techniques differ from current ones. Even if you're not changing the current life cycle, some methodology training might be in order. Very often the life cycle manual exists as some arcane tome only to be read by the anointed (project managers). By trial and error they apply its teachings, but they are eventually forced by deadlines to follow the nefarious minimum-deliverables strategy. By training project managers to use the methodology to help estimate and plan projects, you can avoid lost time and disillusionment.

Personal experience can also be accelerated through mentorship or consulting. Though not the best way to convey general software engineering principles, it can be excellent for teaching the application of tools and techniques. I'll discuss two kinds of consultants: external and internal.

External consultants are those you hire from outside consulting or software firms. You usually bring such consultants in when facing the first CASE-based projects. These consultants are chosen because they are already experts with the CASE tools you just spent so much money on. But unless these same consultants helped you develop your in-house methodology, their advice will be less relevant. Most CASE consultants are unaccustomed to firms with a solid, internalized methodology. They are in the habit of bringing their own methodology with them, and teaching it along with the CASE techniques. They can confuse people and undermine the power of the internal methodology ("If it's so great, why don't the consultants do it that way?").

The problem is that most external firms still work with single-path methodologies. Many CASE tool vendors have developed the methodology along with their tool; many consulting firms have formalized the methodology as an internal standard. Unless you have adopted one of these as your methodology (or at least an approved method path), you should negotiate with consultants before they start work. Tell them you have a solid methodology already in place, and ask them to work within it. This will limit the scope of their advice to the application of specific tools and techniques, not the progression of the entire development process.

External consultants are most valuable when you are setting up the method pool in the first place. If your firm has no employees with CASE experience, consultants are almost necessary. They can give you a first-cut sequence of techniques that have worked for them. This might reflect the "party line" of the consulting organization, but that's all right. You're building a flexible, changeable methodology that can begin from any point. Your future experience will get rolled back into the methodology until it becomes distinctly yours.

Internal consultants can be more useful than external ones. Generally drawn from a central support group, internal consultants have a number of advantages:

- They understand the mission and objectives of your organization.
- They speak the "corporate language" and can communicate more easily.
- They are "one of us" and more easily accepted by project teams.
- They usually cost less than external consultants.

The sooner you build a corps of experienced internal consultants, the smoother the transition to company-wide CASE development.

Internal consultants are usually set up as a central group aligned only with the IS function (usually just one or two levels below the CIO). The group has a charter to aid every project, and is responsible for maintaining consistency and identifying commonality among them all. The internal consultants need expertise in three main areas: methodology, techniques, and CASE tools. It is usually helpful if they have had significant application development experience in the past.

One of the quickest ways to bring internal consultants up to speed is to pair them with external consultants early on. After one project observing the external consultant, the internal expert can usually fly solo.

An initial CASE "pilot project" can provide the bases for a future support group. Staff the pilot project (including the project manager) with three or four people who would make good internal consultants. Bring in an external expert or two to work with them.

Once the project is successful, the project team can become the core of an internal consulting group. This central group should also be responsible for the third area of methodology support, evolution. Internal consultants will be the only ones, aside from IS managers, who see the big cross-company picture. They can assess the affectiveness of existing techniques across many projects. They can document successful new techniques for the benefit of future project teams. Through periodic review, they can keep improving the methodology and help it keep pace with technological change.

Of course to really support process evolution, the corporate culture should encourage it. People who come up with new techniques or successfully apply a good one they read about in a magazine, should be rewarded for their efforts. We should foster an environment that supports experimentation without punishing failure. I'll talk more about a learning environment in chapter 6.

Summary

In summary, concentrated support of the methodology, in concert with CASE tool support, lets you build a streamlined, hard-hitting development process. The main facets of methodology support are:

- publication in a flexible, updatable format
- training in tools, techniques, and the methodology itself
- tactical use of external consultants
- establishment of a centralized internal consulting support group
- constant review and improvement of the development methodology

Taken together, these facets comprise a strong and flexible methodology (and CASE tool) support plan ready to propel the organization well into the future.

6
Living in the neutral zone

As many companies have failed with CASE as have succeeded. No one can point to a lone culprit for the failures. The reasons usually are many and varied. Yet every time I read accounts of unsuccessful CASE implementations, or talk to managers involved with them, one reason for failure is always mentioned: developers' resistance to change.

Envision ranks of developers squared off across a hallway. Managers stand facing them, pitching packages of CASE software into the crowd. The developers toss them right back, chant slogans, and lock arms against future barrages.

A milder version of this scenario must play over and over in the minds of some bewildered IS managers. They hand the developers a technology which, by all accounts, equates to what a chain saw is to a lumberjack, and the developers don't want it. They complain about the tool's technical capabilities, and make up stories about how it creates extra work for them. Either the tool is faulty, or the developers are blindly resisting. Managers usually formulate an answer that's a combination of both: the tool's "not ready yet," and the developers are "resistant to change."

These assumptions are firmly ingrained in the collective wisdom surrounding CASE. Many of the most influential authors describe developers as blindly resistant to anything new:

"Technical staff tend to resist change with a passion."[1]

—Roger S. Pressman

"Because information-systems managers often hesitate to learn something new, it's frequently difficult to alter the culture of a large IS organization."[2]

—James Martin

"In any organization there is a certain amount of inertia, or resistance to change, which must be overcome before any progress can be made."[3]

—Albert F. Case, Jr.

But no one really dislikes all changes. A raise in salary is a change; do people resist it? Even the most reactionary developer will start using CASE tools if you pay him an extra $50,000 to do so. People resist changes they don't understand, not changes they believe will make them better off. The key to avoiding resistance, then, is convincing those affected that the change will improve their lot.

Regardless of objective realities, acceptance of change will be determined by the perception of those affected. Perception defines truth. But you can't just monkey with developers' perceptions. When the complex value orientations of developers are summed up as "resistance to change," the process of managing transitions becomes a game. "If you use tactic x, you will reduce the resistance to change."

The point is, you don't want to reduce resistance to changes that aren't in the developers' best interests. You want to formulate changes that are. If you rush to redo the software environment without planning, chances are you'll be trying to force-fit solutions that don't make much sense for your organization. No matter what you say once the decision is made, you'll experience resistance to a poor solution. Worse still, many will see through the verbal tactics used to paint a rosy picture. Even a hint of dishonesty invalidates all the forces in favor of CASE. For CASE to be accepted smoothly, it must promise more than just long-term, intangible benefits. It must be shown to be in the developers' best interests almost immediately. This way you avoid most resistance instead of trying to overpower it.

Unfortunately, this is a major drawback of many CASE tools. They promise benefits that will only materialize after long stretches of time and truckloads of effort.

Of course the developers' interests alone aren't at stake. CASE will affect the roles and responsibilities of developers, managers, end-users, and other IS professionals. Few tools or methods will universally improve everyone's job. Somewhere in the organizational web, the tool will engender resistance. But through conscious planning for the changes CASE entails and the disorienting personal transitions these changes trigger, you can minimize the pain.

Industry analyst P. N. Le Quesne rightly notes that "social and organizational issues are more important than technological issues for IPSE success."[4] Yet most firms just address physical changes—new workstation and software rollouts—and basic training needs, while ignoring the impact CASE can have on people and organizations. Technical change doesn't occur in isolation, but most people plan for it as if it does.

CASE can trigger large-scale organizational changes. But the technology is really just a smaller wave in a larger flood of changes affecting the IS environment. How your firm responds to these challenges will determine its readiness for more rapid changes in the future. You can use the introduction of CASE as grease for the wheels of organizational improvement, or you can use it to further the command-and-control hierarchy of the past. Only the former will prepare you well for the future.

CASE can engender organizational change at three levels:

1. initial shifts in job roles, responsibilities, and task requirements
2. more widespread reorganization to support new methods and tools
3. shifts toward new change-oriented organizational forms, supported by CASE environments

This chapter attacks each of these levels in detail, starting with the most urgent—managing the transitions that CASE imposes on specific employees.

The broad face of change

Developers aren't the only ones whose roles change with a new development tool. Others affected include:

- IS managers. They must learn new ways of managing projects, determine new methods for measuring software quality and development progress, and learn to communicate benefits of the new development environment.
- Business managers and experts. They will need to develop familiarity with some of the new techniques, and figure out new patterns of communication with the IS group. They must also support the new strategic IS direction, especially if a planned application or two is delayed by the shift to CASE.
- Business analysts. Often new CASE methods encourage the creation of a new job role: the business analyst. This person investigates business processes and data needs, but doesn't necessarily translate these into final, working systems. Often this role falls to an ex-developer or an ex-systems user. Either person must gather a new set of skills, and learn to bridge the communications gap between the IS and user worlds.
- IS technical services. Large-scale changes to the development environment require large-scale support from the technical staff. Most CASE repositories reside in relational databases on host mainframe or minicomputer machines, and require frequent surveillance and support. Luckily these tasks aren't markedly different from the ones technical support teams perform today.
- Development support staff. Many companies will start a central IS development support group for the first time when they introduce CASE. This group will be responsible for spreading knowledge about CASE tools and techniques to the rest of development staff. On top of learning the tools and techniques themselves, this group must also learn new consulting and training skills, and become adept at communicating with developers and business experts alike.

TABLE 6-1 lists the changes felt by each group in more detail.

CASE is a big change by itself, but occurs in conjunction with other sweeping changes in the IS organization. Some of these, like applications integration and cooperative group software development, are closely tied to CASE. Many changes will arise whether or not you change the software development environment.

The biggest change of all attacks the very mission of the IS organization. Traditionally, software developers automated existing accounting and clerical processes. They didn't design new business processes; they recast the old ones in a new electronic medium. IS group recruited people skilled in this environment, people who preferred directed technical work to cooperative, interpersonal analysis.

But now strategic systems and "competing on information" are the clichés of the day. IS must drive business change, not slowly react to it. The mission of IS has changed, but the workers are still invested in the old directions. It's not that IS has the wrong people; it's that the mission they were hired to follow has changed.

At an individual level, implementation of integrated CASE causes three major types of changes:

Table 6-1. Changes Faced by Specific Job Roles

Job Title	Changes Faced
Developers	• New skill requirements • New measurements of developer performance • New reward structures • New development life cycles • New tools • More interaction with users and analysts • More interaction with other developers
IS managers	• New measurements of developer performance • New reward structures • New development life cycles • More interaction with business managers • Developers' resistance to new tools and methods • Less unilateral control over development sequence
Business managers	• More interaction with IS managers and developers • Less unilateral control over development sequence • Need to dedicate business organization resources to information systems development
Business analysts	• New job roles • New skill requirements • New measurements of analyst performance • New reward structures • New development life cycles
Technical services	• New technologies • New demands on time
Development support services	• New job roles • New skill requirements • New measurements of consultant and trainer performance • New development life cycles • Greater training demands • Greater consulting demands • Developers' and IS managers' resistance to new tools and methods

1. technical skill changes, driven by new tools and methods
2. interpersonal skill changes, driven by a need for cooperative development
3. political and organizational skill changes, driven by new tasks and task visibility

Technical skill changes

The most evident changes are those forced by the introduction of new development technologies. These include:

- knowing how to use new methods and development tools
- learning to select appropriate development techniques from the many available
- managing increased complexity of information systems

- understanding multiple hardware platforms, operating systems, and communications methods
- understanding new developments in hardware, software, and communications technologies

Most software professionals prepare themselves well to face these technological challenges. As a community, software professionals enjoy opportunities to learn and take advantage of new technologies. As Sheldon Laube, director of technology for Price Waterhouse says, "People program because they love the intellectual challenge."[5]

This propensity for learning makes the issue of "resistance to change" all the more puzzling. Apparently the changes new technologies force upon interpersonal and political skills have a greater impact than do the technological changes themselves.

Interpersonal skill changes

A common perception is that technology drives most of the changes IS groups face. Yet most software professionals resist changes to their interpersonal skills. I can't count how many times I've heard developer colleagues complain about time spent in meetings with users, or negotiating the resolution of systems integration issues with other development teams. Often these new communication demands surface before CASE is introduced. But cooperative CASE projects remove most of the avenues developers used to take to avoid these communications.

Changes to interpersonal skills include new needs for:

- understanding the business and its vocabulary (or, for business experts, a need to understand the software development process)
- gathering new business knowledge to keep pace with rapid environmental change
- developing strong presentation and negotiation skills
- learning facilitation skills to run Joint Application Development (JAD) sessions
- specialization or generalization of duties: programmers become information planners/analysts/designers, or specialize to handle only database administration duties
- sifting through growing volumes of information communicated by others

Most of these interpersonal demands remain project-specific at first. Developers negotiate with users at the start of a project to develop mutually acceptable system specifications, for example. But soon interpersonal skills become integral to all software development as the organization shifts to institutionalize cooperative development methods.

Political skill changes

Many firms find that the organizational structures they've relied on in the past inadequately handle the demands of rapidly changing technologies and business needs.

CASE accelerates this changeover to new organizational forms by forcing the entire company to rethink the software development process. This opens a previously closed subculture to scrutiny from outside. As the dirty laundry get aired, the organization restructures itself to prevent future soiling.

Everyone involved in software development must develop new political skills to cement their roles in the new structure. The political skill changes involve:

- recognizing that IS people need political skills in the first place
- coping with the "informating" power of CASE tools: the new visibility it provides about software development tasks and performance
- acknowledging that current hierarchical structures can't handle increasing volumes of information about the development process
- learning to support and expect free information exchange within the company

The political skills needed depend upon the company's organizational philosophy. In a rigid hierarchy, political skill requires bypassing the structural barriers to information exchange, without bringing down the wrath of management control watchdogs. In a flatter, change-oriented structure, good skills involve forging new communication paths and sifting useful information from seas of data.

Seven developer nightmares

Potential CASE users who realize the magnitude of the changes facing them tend to panic. When managers impose the CASE decision from the top, with little input from the people who will actually use the new technology, these people are immediately thrown on the defensive. Add to this the veiled threats that surprisingly often accompany the decision—threats that your career is at risk if you can't cope with the new direction—and you've got the makings of mass hysteria.

Though rarely verbalized, most developers imagine worst case scenarios caused by CASE.

Loss of identity

Many developers identify strongly with the myth of the programming wizard or hacker. This identity tightly intertwines with specific development tools and techniques. A hacker must spend long midnight hours navigating through oceans of cryptic source code and memory dumps. Hackers don't draw cute pictures of trucks and warehouses, or get online coaching from obnoxiously friendly development tool tutorials. Radically change a hacker's tools and you remove one of the most solid anchors of his or her personal identity.

Get them to use end-user development packages and you cut them off from their group identity as well. Before, they belonged to a privileged group of technological wizards. Now they're just another end-user with technological skills that don't count for much. I've noticed many programmers actually prefer obscure, detail-oriented CASE tools to those that simplify the development process. They recognize that these tools require more technological sophistication and will preserve their status as software gurus.

Formalized discomfort

Though it seems that few formal methods exist in the IS group, in reality a set of informal methods and mores are already entrenched. When CASE or formal methodologies are brought in, they don't fill a vacuum; they replace informal systems.

Cyrus Gibson and Richard Nolan note that, "On the whole, the stronger these informal controls and structures are (and the weaker the formal controls and structures, the stronger they will be), the more resistant the personnel will be to change and the more chaotic and traumatic the introduction of formal systems will be."[6]

For the developer, new ways of working will seem uncomfortable at first. The old informal systems, built up over years, no longer function. It seems like the new system, especially when touted as the "new direction" by management, will perpetuate this discomfort forever.

Loss of competence

Much of a software developer's skill centers upon methods and technology. They know complex programming language syntax rules, lists of calling parameters for reusable subroutines, long sequences of steps for editing, compiling, and linking code to create software applications. These are the skills that change with CASE. If the CASE tool doesn't offer markedly superior (and more marketable) techniques, the developers will be replacing valuable skills with temporary ones.

When managers imply that job success depends on learning these new techniques, fears of obsolescence take root. Since CASE promises incredible productivity gains, many fear they'll be replaced by the tools. In fact, most financial models that illustrate CASE cost savings derive the bulk of these savings by reducing IS staffing levels.[7] Even so, I have never heard of a programmer losing a job as a result of a CASE implementation. During the early implementation days, all IS resources will be in strong demand. And once CASE starts showing benefits, these resources are turned toward cutting through the monumental development backlog. Demand for software will keep developers' jobs secure for many years to come.

Developers aren't the only ones whose competence will be tested by new environments. Developers feel competent with current tools and methods; managers feel competent with current reporting relationships and managerial procedures. These relationships and procedures will change too, forcing managers to develop new skills. Past management practices were based on needs for control and stability. Future workers will know their jobs better than their managers do (many already do). They will need to function in flatter organizations with more limited supervision. They will be accountable for their own performance, and rely less on managers for day-to-day direction. And managers must develop new techniques for effectively coordinating this dynamic body of workers.

Turning men into machines

Traditional automation systems in factories and offices parceled work into specialized, repetitive tasks. This took much of the skill from the worker's job, reducing artisans to cogs in a production machine. The system stripped the most fulfilling aspects from these jobs. As James R. Johnson, director of Hallmark Cards' data center, says, "Specialization and separation of duties are barriers to individual recognition, achievement, and responsibility.[8]

Some developers fear CASE will force them into a new pattern of purely mechanical tool-jockeying, removing all creativity from their jobs. They might find themselves doing repetitive data entry instead of creative design tasks. Trends toward expert systems have led a similar anxiety—that knowledge and expertise will be siphoned into a "black box" software system, and the experts themselves will become expendable.

Despite these fears, most CASE approaches result in a broadening of job skills and responsibilities, not a reduction. Some poorly designed tools require meaningless, repetitive operations, known to prompt cries of "I am not a typist!" as Le Quense has noted.[9] But on the whole, new methods are injecting humanistic concerns into the development process, not siphoning them away.

"Big brother" project management

CASE doesn't just automate routine tasks. It also generates new and useful information about the development process. Sociologist Shoshana Zuboff coined the term *informate* to describe this phenomenon. "Information technology," she writes, "even when it is applied to automatically reproduce a finite activity, is not mute. . . . It both accomplishes tasks and transforms them into information."[10] For example, a system that lets brokers enter stock transactions can also track how well the brokers estimate daily prices, and report which brokers log the best daily performance. This system provides unprecedented visibility of the internal aspect of the brokers' jobs.

CASE similarly *informates* the process of software development. It not only automates specific development tasks, it opens a view onto the workings of each task and the performance of those who carry it out. This fact isn't lost on developers. When CASE is brought into a company to control unruly projects, the developers often see it as a first step toward "big brother" IS management. They view CASE as a tool for oppressive management, a vehicle for keeping developers in line.

Unfortunately this scenario sometimes rings true. Used as an instrument of control, CASE can work against the developers' best interests. Managers must question if it's in the company's best interests to do this.

Doomed to repeat history

CASE probably isn't the first big change your group has faced. IS groups are not strangers to reorganizations or to technological changes. The history of such changes in your company influences the attitude of people to future changes. A recurring pattern of unannounced equipment or software installations will put developers and technicians into a constant defensive stance. Sudden reorganizations will prompt cries of, "Why am I always the last to know?"

When change is imposed upon people, they become victims. They feel no love for the symbols of the new change, be they computer systems, software packages, or new bosses. Some will go so far as to sabotage new efforts that are imposed from above.

If your firm has a poor record of change and transition management, use the CASE implementation to prove new ways of managing change. Overcoming skepticism and cynicism won't be easy, but implemented correctly the results can pave the way for effective change management in the future.

Attack of the killer robots

Organizational issues are extremely hard to broach in some companies. Proposals that imply the organization might change stand a slim chance of succeeding. Many managers respond by ignoring the possibility of such impacts. Change becomes seen as an inevitable technological progression. The wheels of technology roll on, unfettered by the pretty concerns of humans. The robots draw the humans wailing in their wake.

Unfortunately, this belief discourages openness about technological change. Managers introduce new technologies with little advance discussion, and people must adapt or perish, in an organizational version of natural selection. Many a CASE user tells a story of the boss dropping the CASE package on the desk, saying, "Here, try this out."

Naturally, this scenario triggers sharp resistance from those forced to adapt. It's like playing a game with someone who keeps changing the rules. You soon lose interest in winning the game, and start trying to sabotage your opponent's chances.

Though technology can drive new business opportunities, people who feel that technology is in control need their windshields washed. People control technology, with varying degrees of skill, not the other way around. They use new tools to create their own opportunities. Some IS managers overlook this fundamental fact when they bring in CASE tools. They expect the technology to suddenly take control and force everyone to be productive and do high-quality work. This management dream and developer nightmare is a long way from coming true.

Triggering transition

Absurd as these scenarios seem, they're not baseless. CASE will change the way developers work, but its effects will rarely be as bad as people fear. Yet fear ignored swiftly turns to paranoia. There are ways to allay such fears once they arise, but it's far easier to remove most of the causes for fear before you start to implement big changes.

Figure 6-1 shows a simple change model. This model describes change as a process, not a split-second occurrence. Before the change is introduced, a solid "current" state exists. People feel a need for change, announce it, and begin "unfreezing" the current habits and practices. This thaw leads to a nebulous, uncertain "conversion" process. After a period of readjustment, things "refreeze" again to form a new solid "desired" state.[11]

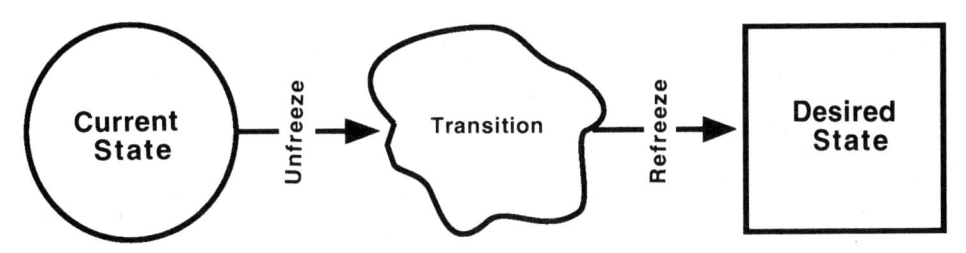

Fig. 6-1. Simple change model

William Bridges, author of numerous books about managing change, says to focus attention on the conversion process, which he calls "transition." Transition, he says, "is the gradual psychological process through which individuals and groups reorient themselves so that they can function and find meaning in a changed situation." Bridges also remarks that "resistance to change" really means "resistance to transition."[12] He highlights an important notion: transition is nine-tenths of change. Stating a new goal is easy compared to the steps you must take to achieve it.

In Bridges' model, the area between the end of the old and effective functioning of the new is called the "neutral zone." This is the land of transition, where neither the old nor new rules make sense, and people constantly search for meaning. Few companies plan for this kind of dislocation. They prepare thoroughly for the changes themselves, but neglect transitions altogether.

Fear, discomfort, and insecurity are all symptoms of someone in transition. The nightmares described above haunt the sleep of people in the neutral zone. To minimize the dislocation caused by change, you must acknowledge the costs of transition.

Out of alignment

Transition involves breaking down old alignments and creatively forming new ones. Professors Samuel A. Culbert and John J. McDonough describe how people set up the present state that's threatened by change. "Each time people enter a new work situation they engage in the implicit process of aligning personal values, interests, and skills with what they perceive to be the task requirements of their job. They seek an orientation that maximizes self-purpose and organizational contribution."[13]

Many developers have invested years aligning their jobs and their value systems. They aligned to a structure that valued patience, persistence, attention to detail, and arcane technical skill. But the IS environment of the future will emphasize business knowledge, communication, and ad hoc problem-solving skills. When these paradigms meet, they clash.

Studies show that, on average, software programmer/analysts have unusually high needs for personal growth and amazingly low needs for social interaction.[14] Compare these needs to the nature of the programming task. Pure programming offers constant, impartial results in the forms of working products (programs) or objective criticism (compiler error messages). Programmers tend to get more feedback from the machine and development tools than they do from their supervisors and coworkers. Most programmers find themselves in jobs they're well suited for, and well aligned to.

Changing task requirements force developers to reorient themselves and find a new alignment of values and tasks. Some find the newer tasks more to their liking. Perhaps they always wanted more contact with other humans, and less with computer screens. Others get disoriented in the new environment, and experience the nightmares described.

Cynics and careerists

Culbert and McDonough describe typical reactions of those who can't realign themselves: they become cynics or careerists.[15] Cynics subordinate the company's interests to their own. They view company policies as shackles that hold them back, and don't hesitate to make their grievances known. Careerists let company interests tread all over their own values. They secure their spot in the organization, doing what they think will keep them well positioned in the organization, but rarely risking changes to the status quo.

Neither cynics nor careerists adapt well to new changes. Cynics become doomsayers for the CASE effort, scoffing about the value of tools and techniques. Careerists attempt to follow the new direction, but don't develop creative ways of using the new technology. They flounder when forced to define their own procedures for using CASE. They scream for standards and policies before anyone knows enough to do a good job writing them.

How can you base the success of a change program on the ability of others to realign their personal and work values? There's no way to force people to alter their view of the world. The best you can do is give them opportunities to do work that they really want to do. New technology can open doors or close them. Managers can prop the doors open and turn on the lights, but workers must find their own way out of the neutral zone.

My prescriptions for reducing the organizational costs of CASE fall into six general statements:

1. Plan for transition, not just change.
2. Develop a shared vision of future software development.
3. Make the changes personally beneficial.
4. Openly state reasons for the change.
5. Monitor the transition plan.
6. Make change a way of life.

Change is not enough

Transition is a harder beast to tame than change. You can diagram the future CASE environment, list the tools you'll purchase, even outline the consulting and training needs for the organization. But you can't show personal disorientation on an organizational chart. Transition management is subjective at best, and a little too "touchy-feely" for many IS managers.

Still there are concrete steps you can take to minimize transition costs. For starters:

- Develop both change and transition plans.
- Publicly acknowledge the need for a time of transition.
- Plan symbolic activities to recognize progress toward the vision.
- Set a realistic pace for transitions (even if the pace of change itself is impossibly fast).
- Don't prey upon people's fears and insecurities.

Develop change and transition plans

Few people argue about the need to plan for large-scale technological changes. Managers draft architectural plans, financial cost/benefit models, new organization charts, training plans, and rollout schedules to ensure smooth introductions of new equipment and techniques. Much of this book discusses such planning for the introduction of CASE.

Planners often cover the "people aspects" of change with simple announcements of a new direction, and perhaps a training program to teach people about the new tools. However, the "people aspects" can make or break a new technology implementation. You can plan every detail and still fail if the users of the new technology, the targets of the change, don't want it to succeed.

There's no way to force people to like something. But you can give them every opportunity to decide for themselves that the new technology or technique is in their own best interest. Transition planning describes an environment that makes it easy for people to align their values and beliefs with those the change implies. For example, transition planners identify ways to:

- Get employees involved in up-front change planning.
- Identify training needs for nontechnical skills required for a successful change.
- Establish new channels of communication.
- Create special incentives for people to support the change.
- Hold symbolic activities to acknowledge progress.
- Set up employee groups to monitor effects of the change.

Transition planning should be integrated with change planning, not reactive to it. Changes determine the nature of transition, and transitions determine the success of the changes. Transition costs should be estimated before you finalize the change plan. Why choose a course that you know will throw most employees into a downward spiral of despair?

Many IS groups standardize upon a CASE tool, and a methodology, before really testing it out or adapting it to the environment. One large company I worked with established a popular CASE tool as its official standard before anyone in the company had even tried the tool. It turned out a senior manager had gotten a great price break for 250 copies, and he had to force the standard so he could distribute them.

Remember that CASE affects more than just your software; it will change the way developers, users, and managers interact. It can provide impetus for altering organization structures or reengineering business processes. Never commit to a substantial investment in CASE tools or methods until you've gauged some of these impacts.

Most planning methods include an assessment of project risk. Transition risk is rarely considered. One risk assessment method I've seen handles transition with a single question:

How likely are the developers to resist the new techniques?
(0) Not likely. (1) Somewhat likely. (2) Very likely.

It's hard to put a lot of thought into a question like that. Preferably you should ask questions like:

- Whose task responsibilities will change? Remember that managers and support staff will be affected too.
- What are the main principles underlying the new environment, and how do they differ from earlier assumptions? For example, structured analysis assumes that you should catch errors early in the development cycle. The old culture might have valued "quick and dirty" development: give me a few weeks and I'll give you something that works.
- How much continuity is there between the old methods and the new? Radical changes will be more disorienting. However, they also have more symbolic significance.
- What old tasks and tools are being replaced? Who has strong attachments to them? For example, throwing away a compiler leaves the gurus of that old language adrift.

You want to identify who must change and how severe the disorientation will be. It's a glorified process of putting yourself in their shoes. The answers to these questions will help you plan communication channels, and tailor communications to specific concerns.

You'll get better results of transition planning if you make it a formal process, or at least an official part of the change plan itself. This implies that the change program itself doesn't end once the physical changes take place. Change happens quickly while transition lingers. The plan should provide for transition support for a while after the change occurs. For example, don't try to snap back to business-as-usual the day after a CASE tool's installed. Plan for continued employee support. Take transition seriously and you'll greatly improve the chances that change will succeed.

Grassroots change The simplest way to minimize transition costs is to narrow the distance between the old and new. Top managers can't know everyone's value alignments; only those who must change can say which course is easiest to change to. This principle explains why most top-down, directed change programs don't get results.

In an article called "Why Change Programs Don't Produce Change," Michael Beer, Russell A. Eisenstadt and Bert Spector describe the "fallacy of programmatic change." "The greatest obstacle to revitalization," they write, "is the idea that it comes about through companywide change programs."[16] Their studies show that nondirective, buttom-up change, supported by senior management, is far more effective. They suggest a process of "task alignment" that lets employees help define problems, suggest solutions, and align their own roles and responsibilities to fit.

In my experience, every successful CASE effort requires an element of grassroots change. Only through doing can developers and managers learn the best ways to use CASE. They must have the power to define new roles, write new procedures, and even seek out new tools. Too many IS managers buy CASE tools and force their people to use them unquestioningly. Let the pioneer CASE users puzzle out the best practices, then let them help spread the new behaviors. Don't formalize things until you know what you're doing.

Beer and his colleagues suggest a six step process for directed grassroots change:

1. Jointly diagnose business problems. Visions and architectures are only valuable if they promise relief from specific pain. When everyone understands the problems, everyone will see the need for solutions.
2. Develop a shared vision of how to organize and manage for competitiveness. Top management sets a climate for change, but doesn't directly try to alter actual behavior. Cooperative vision ensures future commitment.
3. Foster consensus for the new vision, competence to enact it, and cohesion to move it along. Make the vision real by communicating it and providing resources to support the direction chosen by the task forces. Now is the time for leadership and political savvy.
4. Spread revitalization to all departments without pushing it from the top. You want to light a fire under people, but let them find the best way to harness the energy. There's no simple way to enforce the changes company-wide. Each group must reorient itself in its own way.
5. Institutionalize revitalization through formal policies, systems, and structures. Wait until successes have arisen before changing organization structures and building systems around them. Don't incur widespread transition costs until the changes prove beneficial on a small scale. Let the pioneers refine specific roles and responsibilities, and formalize such roles only when they are comfortable.
6. Monitor and adjust strategies. Plenty of things will go wrong during the transition stages. If the organization can learn from its mistakes, it won't be wiped out by them.

In short, management must first set up a climate for change, then let other managers and workers discover the best ways to proceed. Seek effective behaviors first—find a workable approach to a real business problem—and only then formalize things.

With CASE, then, the approach must be to first jointly decide whether the technology addresses pressing business problems. Form a vision of your future environment and principles to govern your march towards it. Then form groups to select methods and tools, to use them and learn from them. When something works well, spread the word. Draft standards, provide education, and roll out the tools.

Develop a shared vision

A shared vision of the future is the most essential ingredient of successful change. To develop a shared vision:

- let everyone help decide how to change
- develop principles and a vision of the future
- set ambitious goals, but move toward them incrementally

Let everyone help decide how to change

You hear a lot about the importance of management commitment. Yet you really need commitment from everyone involved. A command from management carriers far less weight than a cooperative decision to change. Developers resist CASE, says James R. Johnson, "because another group . . . is telling them how good this is for them. Then they've got to sit down at a tube and enter things that are history to them."[17]

When employees help determine the future course, they will give their all to make it happen. As Le Quesne finds, "When CASE is the developers' choice, they are much happier with it."[18] Get participation from the targets of change before you start firing.

These targets should be encouraged to:

- help evaluate current problems and their solution
- help develop guiding principles of behavior in the new environment
- choose which roles they want in the new order of things
- change course toward the new vision as they see fit

Evaluate current problems The quickest way to mobilize support for a change is to openly air the problems being faced. Managers often try to enforce changes before the problems are clear to most people.

For instance, managers might see an outrageous systems backlog that's not apparent to specific systems developers. Developers might complain among themselves about inefficient compilers and debuggers, but never air their complaints at a higher level. Senior managers might try to encourage high-quality software, while project managers grade their teams on how quickly they can create programs. You need to get consensus about the scope of the problems, and the changes they might entail.

Department meetings and task forces provide excellent forums for discussing the burning issues, and deciding which ones are hottest. By the end of the meeting, participants emerge asking, "What can we do?" If management clearly gives them the power to explore solutions and propose changes, the answer will be, "A lot!"

Develop guiding principles Guiding principles express the values of the IS organization. Principles aren't policy statements; they don't dictate courses of action. They set boundaries for behavior and enable distributed decision-making. They also indicate the types of tools and methods that the organization will easily accept.

Studying the influence of personal values upon the development environment, Kuldeep Kumar and Neils Bjorn-Andersen state, "If a methodology overtly espouses values which are alien to the values of . . . the designated users of the methodology, the methodology will not be accepted."[19] For example, developers who believe in project cost control prefer CASE tools that help measure development costs. Developers who believe strongly in personal autonomy and task responsibility will rebel against tools or methods that narrowly limit their choice of activities.

Principles statements make hidden values explicit. They "provide a way to talk about . . . difficult trade-offs inside the company,"[20] according to Bob Haas, CEO of Levi Strauss & Co. For many years, Levi's has maintained a set of aspirations, statements about the behavioral values emphasized by the firm.

Principles are often stated as trade-offs between competing goals. For example, "customer service is more important than cutting costs." These statements must be more than nice-sounding platitudes. They must have a ring of honesty and clarity. Unbelievable aims breed cynicism.

Principles can be grouped into categories. Organization, technology, information, and business system categories work well for IS organizations. TABLE 6-2 lists some sample principles statements for IS.

Table 6-2. Sample Principles Statements for IS, by Category

Area	Statement of Principle
Business systems	• It is the right of developers to select the best ways to work, within funding limits, provided they measure the costs and benefits of the approaches they try. • Development projects should attempt to reengineer business processes, not just automate current steps. • Information systems will be used to encourage a common face to customer, suppliers, and other external agents from every unit within the company. • Applications should be analyzed, designed, and delivered so that users can expect useful results within 12 months from the start of development efforts. • Software quality is paramount. Cost control and speed of development are secondary.
Information	• Information belongs to the company, not to any specific employee or organizational unit. • Integrated information is more valuable than isolated islands of data. • Every employee must be able to access all of the information he or she needs to do their job effectively and completely. • Business experts should have access to tools and technical support that let them access and analyze warehoused data.
Organization	• Developers and business experts alike should be personally accountable for the quality, timeliness, and performance of systems products and services. They should raise the visibility of barriers to their progress, and attempt to find ways of breaking through them, instead of working around them. • Developers must try to learn about the business and speak with managers and users in business, not technical, terms. • System users can expect honest and complete estimates of project costs and durations. • Both system users and developers can expect full visibility of development issues—full disclosure from both sides.
Technology	• We will manage a multi-vendor technical environment, with an emphasis on information connectivity. • We will limit the number of different technologies we use, to allow effective technical support. • Business effectiveness is more important than cost-cutting or technical efficiency.

Let people choose their roles Success depends on whether workers can align their values and self-interests with new job tasks. Since you can't easily change their values and interests, you should let them choose which tasks work best for them. Let people choose which roles they'd like to play in the new order of things.

Don't just force all programmers to become business analysts. Counsel them about the roles that will exist, and find out which ones appeal. Let them learn the new skills they want to pursue. They'll see that the changes don't lock them into horrible new tasks, but open up new opportunities.

Freedom to change course Managers must trust their charges to make decisions that help the firm as well as themselves. Yet with a common destination and principles to steer by, the direction should never be in doubt.

Once transition begins—when the tools are in, and projects underway—analysts and developers will start learning the best ways to use them. Their knowledge won't come from user manuals or training classes. Few of these adequately prepare people to get results from CASE tools. They'll learn by applying the tools. This puts them in the best position to suggest changes to the current directions.

Give those affected some power to shape the nature of future changes. The closer those changes are to their own visions of the future, the easier transition will be. With a clear idea of the strategic direction and some first steps mapped out, the people using the new tools will know best which next steps to take.

Workers must have the freedom to alter the process when they know it will improve the outcome. This encourages constant process improvement. CASE users should be able to:

- alter "standard" methods for bigger payback
- criticize the methods and tools they use now, in light of common development goals
- try new methods and tools
- seek new ways to communicate among managers, developers, and business experts

This approach encourages experimentation and frequent improvement of the development process.

Big plans, baby steps

Fear of transition costs is why most companies prefer limited, tactical CASE tools to integrated ones. However, you should match transition costs against the true goals driving the change. As Bridges says, "Nothing is more disruptive than throwing everyone into transition, and then having to do it all over again because the first change wasn't fundamental enough."[21] In other words, effect the changes you need without compromise. But rather than deluging people with a hundred changes at once, plan to dole them out in small doses. Develop an ambitious vision, but let people take baby steps toward it. If the steps represent a choreographed movement toward a greater vision, you'll simplify the transition costs at each step. Tom Peters and Nancy Austin note that "the literature on resistance to change (in both individuals and in groups) suggest that the best way to overcome it is taking tiny steps, and, moreover working on the positive ('we can do something right'), rather than trying to confront negative feelings directly. . . ."[22]

IS groups should develop an ambitious plan for a future development environment, and then move toward it a step at a time. Don't rule out comprehensive CASE solutions. Many full-cycle products can be implemented piece by piece. You can install the whole product, but only ask people to learn part of it for now. Or purchase a single component now, and buy others only when you need them. Just make sure that the pieces you use first don't force you to build bridges and interfaces to other tools.

Evolutionary development doesn't just apply to application systems. It can be a good philosophy for CASE implementation too.

Make change personally beneficial

While common goals create plenty of commitment, this commitment will waver unless personal benefits emerge. Changes should be calculated to provide short-term benefits as well as loftier returns.

This doesn't mean productivity must jump fifty percent the day you install new tools. Personal benefits might seem like side-effects to change planners, but they're very real to the people they affect.

To gauge direct impact upon developers, ask yourself:

- Do the new tasks replace any tedious old ones people will be happy to do without?
- Will system quality or productivity visibly improve within a few months?
- Will new skills make the employee more valuable in the job market?
- Will employees gain broader business experience and find it easier to move laterally within the company?
- Might new career paths open up?

If you can't answer yes to any of these, the course you're planning might be difficult to sell. There are some specific steps you can take to make the change to CASE directly beneficial:

- Choose tools that bring quick results.
- Don't use CASE to punish people.
- Help people learn new skills.
- Provide incentives for adapting to the new situation.

Choose tools that bring quick results

Managers support CASE because they believe it will improve their jobs and solve project management problems. Developers only see how it will affect their day-to-day job performance. Says Le Quesne, "Initial judgment [of CASE tools] is in terms of an individual support system."[23]

Tools that automate familiar practices will get a better reception than those that introduce alien concepts and methods. For example, a better source code debugging tool won't cause severe transitional pain. It just improves an already common practice.

Shifts to fully integrated environments can happen quickly as long as the new tools help developers quickly produce working systems. Full code generation or executable models impress developers far more than prettier requirements specs do. Texas Instruments' Information Engineering Facility (IEF) consultants routinely run two week pilot projects with client teams, creating working applications within that time frame. After the pilot project, the developers thrill to the prospect of doing that new two year project in six months or less. They'll work hard to make it happen.

The moral is that: no matter what the long term vision is, start by bringing in tools that improve the jobs people do every day. For most companies, this means starting with "back end" tools such as code restructurers or documentation aids. Design and prototyping tools, supplemented with code generators, can also improve system quality while easing the programmer's job. If you want full-cycle tools, choose those that drive seamlessly integrated code generators. When developers see quick results from their efforts, they become enamored with the tools.

Bear in mind that developers expect technically awesome tools. Today's PC-based editor, compiler, and debugger tools are slick and hard to compete with. Developers used to graphical window-based packages show contempt for text-based CASE tools. Select tools that directly help developers (and seem like a technological advance) and chances for acceptance improve dramatically.

Don't make CASE a punishment

CASE tempts managers with a promise of impersonal control: a nice, sterile technical solution to the development backlog. But as I've already said, there's no simple way to avoid the costs of transition.

Many CASE features enhance management's ability to control the development process:

- availability of reliable metrics about the number of software objects produced
- more detailed understanding of project progress, through use of a common methodology
- controlled sharing of software components

Yet introducing CASE as a means of controlling software developers is one of the biggest mistakes a manager can make. It's an easy script to follow. Software development is characterized by missed deadlines and poor coordination. What the developers need is some discipline. Hence, bring CASE in to enforce discipline among the developers.

This thinking mirrors trends in other types of automation. Zuboff observes how factory managers want to use computer-based systems to "rigidify the production process and increase central control."[24] Other studies show similar trends: instead of using information systems to remove barriers to data access, many employ them to consolidate management control over business information.[25]

A purely disciplinary motive for CASE causes problems in most organizations.[26] Using CASE as an implement of control triggers certain resentment. Developers traditionally shun extensive management control, thinking of themselves as artisans, masters of craft. Sociologist David J. Osborne reports research that shows software developers "are more interested in problems and problem-solving activities, and tend to dislike 'regimentation.'"[27]

The problem of professionalism Most software developers consider themselves professionals. But introducing tools to control how people work runs counter to notions of professionalism. Critics say that software developers have the freedom of professionals, without the performance standards.

Professional freedom developed from years of lax development standards, and the fact that developers generally knew more about the development process and tools than their managers did. "Without specific directives for project development or new hardware acquisition . . . computer personnel developed expectations of a loose work environment."[28]

Cost and schedule overruns are legacies of this environment. But clamping down on developers won't force a turnaround. A tight work environment won't force productivity; it will just increase the costs of transition. When the clamps come down, the message developers hear is, "You're not smart or disciplined enough to control your own costs, so we've brought this tool in to do it for you." Given no further discretion, they'll withdraw, sulk, or leave. Few will strive to make the tool a success.

Managers realize the problem of professionalism (since most are from the same background) and waffle around it. This makes it harder for them to commit to CASE.

If wide professional latitude doesn't exist, then control-driven CASE can be a good fit. Again, it's only automating established practices. Most IS employees enjoy some professional latitude, though, and rebel against tightened control.

Don't make management control your sole reason for introducing CASE. Quality and productivity motives cause far less turmoil. Treat the added information CASE gives you about the development process as a supplemental benefit. Encourage the developers to use this information themselves, to better estimate future tasks, or to pinpoint bottlenecks in the process. In the future, CASE will enable new IS structures: confederations of empowered professionals. As Tom Peters says, " 'In control' by the old standards is 'out of control' (fast slipping behind) by the new standards"[29]

Smooth the way to new skills

Every new technology requires new skills. CASE often arrives hand-in-hand with other changes, such as systems integration or closer business ties, so training needs are often broad.

To minimize transition costs, you should provide all the training opportunities that people can handle. It should be easy for them to learn new skills, and apply them immediately. To build a good training portfolio you should:

- take inventory of current skills
- define new skill requirements
- define formal training for the most crucial skills
- set up informal knowledge sharing forums
- provide informed career counseling

Training programs Most CASE courses tell you how to use the tools, but not how to develop software. In the previous chapter, I discussed the need for education about development techniques and methodologies. Other skills can be taught either formally or informally:

- project management skills for CASE
- how to use the software engineering DSS
- Joint Application Design (JAD) facilitation skills
- working with business experts
- consulting skills for CASE support teams

To determine which courses are most important, start with an inventory of the skills people already have. Compare this to the new skills that CASE and cooperative development will require. As the CASE campaign progresses, let people suggest new areas for training as well.

As I discussed in chapter 5, the more you customize the training classes, the better. Often outside teachers and consultants espouse techniques different from the ones you adopted. Information engineering taught by a consulting firm might be nothing like the information engineering you've adopted. If you have the resources to develop your own courses, do so. Otherwise make sure an experienced person audits each course, and comments when the teacher's material conflicts with your own direction. Though many development methods are similar, even minor differences can confuse novices.

Informal knowledge sharing Most of the good information on CASE hasn't made it into formal training classes yet. The best learning comes from doing, which is why the most effective courses involve hands-on CASE tool exercises.

To shorten the learning curve for new CASE users, you should provide opportunities for informal information sharing. In a recent study of CASE implementation, professor Ronald J. Norman and colleagues state that "a proactive stance on spreading the 'tricks' and shortcuts will almost certainly shorten the learning curve as the collective experience grows."[30]

A company-wide CASE users' group provides an excellent forum for spreading informal knowledge. Set up and run by developers, it can help them air otherwise unstated concerns. Some users' groups I've worked with also bring in outside speakers, to share other companies' CASE practices.

Some other ways of sharing knowledge include:

- a CASE newsletter, with sections for hints, discussions of new tools and techniques, and stories of successful (and unsuccessful) CASE projects
- a bulletin board on the company's electronic mail system, where people can ask questions about the tools, or share experiences
- an evolving CASE users' handbook that includes information about tool standards as well as compiled hints, tricks, and shortcuts

In addition to accelerating the spread of knowledge, these forums also show developers that they're not in this new situation alone.

Career counseling Personnel departments are often the last to know about the decision to bring in new tools. Career counselors must know about the new skills required for CASE, and the opportunities they mean for employees. They should point employees to the training courses and other skill-building activities they'll need.

Once CASE becomes widely used, new positions will spring up. You might have business analysts, integration specialists, JAD facilitators, release architects, or methodologists. Informed career counselors can help people pick their way through a maze of new skills and titles, speeding the realignment process. Make sure the personnel department stays up-to-date once CASE starts moving in.

Provide incentives

Today developers have little incentive to do anything but deliver systems on time and under budget. Performance evaluations rate how well the developer stuck to her schedule, but not how thoroughly she discussed issues with system's users, or how elegant her module designs were.

However, CASE tools won't immediately improve developers' productivity. As they take time to learn the tool, their productivity might drop. Many will blame the CASE tool for this, whether their managers are going easy on them for awhile or not. Software developers are accomplishment-oriented. They get satisfaction from their working applications, not from going through the motions.

Praise developers for being effective with the tools, not just for test-driving them. CASE will help improve system quality almost automatically. Evaluate on the basis of the common goals of the organization, not by how quickly they jump when managers say "CASE." Though one CASE tool works for you now, you want to be free to jump to a better one in the future. Don't lock your reward structures into a specific technology (as I've seen some companies do).

Start rewarding developers on how well they move the firm toward the shared vision. Do they support business users' information needs, improve the flow of information through the company, or contribute to the company's competitive edge? Do they take time to integrate processes and data across applications, instead of pushing blindly ahead to meet deadlines? Productivity and quality are secondary, supporting results. Schedule adherence and document "sign-offs" should be played down.

Reward people for improving the process. This includes finding out how to make the new tools work. People who pioneer a new methodology or discover ways to measure CASE productivity should be given quality awards. Most companies give these out, but rarely to software developers. It's time to recognize that quality resides in the process as well as the product.

Breaking the news

Sometimes the decision to buy CASE tools is announced only by the thud a box of software makes when it's thrown onto a desk. The best planning for change won't help you unless you communicate the thoughts that have led to the change.

How you announce the decision is just as important as what you say. Culbert and McDonough present three components of successful change communication:[31]

1. highly principled logic
2. linked to specific, practical outcomes
3. backed up by legitimate authority

CASE often fails in the second category.

Highly principled logic If you've developed a shared vision and principles, this component is already complete. You merely need to convey the problems faced, and the goals and principles that address them.

Whether common goals are set or not, it's not hard to build a logical argument for CASE. The development backlog and high rates of software defects point directly to a need for new methods and tools. Articulate the lofty long-term goals, even if you can't map out the whole strategy yet.

Provide detailed information about the need for changes, especially if your company is performing well overall. Unless the need is felt at all levels, change will be hard to effect.

Specific, practical outcomes CASE's practical benefits can be the hardest to convey. There are two kinds of practical outcomes of CASE: better software for the company and better environments for software developers. You should state what the firm expects to get from CASE in the short term. The actual deliverables may be few; even with CASE it can take six months or a year to develop a working software application. Yet the company should gain other benefits, such as:

- assessment of an important new technology
- better communications between systems developers and business experts
- documented development methods
- greater change-readiness

I've already alluded to some of the personal benefits developers get from a CASE environment:

- replacement of tedious old tasks, like lengthy code-compile-link-debug loops or the typing of data structure descriptions
- ability to quickly create systems they can be proud of
- broader business experience that makes it easier to move laterally within the company
- marketability of the new skills they'll be learning, as evidenced by employment ads or newspaper articles
- chance to be a technology leader within the company

Some of these advantages will compel people more than others. Depending on the audience you're addressing, stress certain benefits over others. For example, some programmers might be more impressed with the chance to use advanced technology than with the need to learn a business language. Tailor your communications to the interests of the audience.

Don't cover up difficult issues Be careful not to paint too rosy a picture. Be forthright about the costs of change. Nothing hurts credibility more than a failure to acknowledge reality.

Manage expectations of what CASE will and will not do. They can't solve interpersonal, political, or organizational problems. They can't make people manage better. They're not push-button software machines.

Admit that new development methods might also:

- increase workloads until the new technology settles in
- require developers to take on more responsibility (and perhaps gain more autonomy), as they experiment to make CASE work
- alter how managers do project scheduling and approval tasks
- eventually require new performance review criteria
- change job roles and the organizational structure

Many of these costs won't be incurred until after the initial pioneers determine the best ways to use CASE. Yet increased workloads and responsibility begin at once.

Acknowledge transition You should also acknowledge that these changes might affect people on a personal level. People will experience turbulence whether you tell them this or not. By recognizing this up front, though, you defuse some explosive objections.

Without acknowledgment of pain to come, you'll hear comments like, "How do they expect us to do our job if they take away our tools?" By publicly recognizing the transition process, you start people thinking about how the changes will affect them. You remove the taboo that stifles discussions of personal adjustment. You also give people breathing room, time to plan their own path from the present to the future.

Reduce the perceived threat No matter how well you communicate the issues, developer nightmares will still surface. You can reduce the perceived threat by assuring them that CASE is here to help them in their day-to-day jobs, not to police them, or destroy their freedom.

Don't position CASE as the cure to developers' poor performance. Developers alone aren't to blame for today's software woes. Such a position provokes resentment and makes smooth transition far more difficult.

Avoid preying upon the fears and insecurities of developers during a time of transition. Some consultants suggest you motivate developers to use CASE tools by threatening their job security. They tell you to state that people who can't learn the new tools won't have a place in the new organization.

Threats only increase the disorientation people feel in the neutral zone. People who are nervous or afraid rarely perform well, and seldom feel committed to making a change successful. Instead, try to focus upon positive aspects of the change, and why people will be better off with it than they are today. Dispel job security fears immediately. No one is likely to get fired because of CASE.

Discuss contingency plans You should emphasize that the current decision is not irrevocable. Discuss contingency plans. Evolutionary CASE implementation is seldom irreversible. A single failed project won't throw the whole company into turmoil. Others in the IS organization can continue working as they are today.

Contingency plans reduce the perceived risk of the change. Leave room for a graceful retreat, if necessary, and you won't jeopardize your chance for further changes.

Backed by legitimate authority No organizational change will become real without top management's support. Occasionally you can get local successes by bringing in CASE for specific projects. But lasting change requires support and commitment from the very top.

You can supplement sponsorship from senior IS managers with advocacy from middle managers. A charismatic CASE "champion" can help sell ideas.

Management support and advocacy must be visible and unwavering. To start things right, the managers themselves should help announce the change.

There are three main factors affecting an announcement of a large-scale change: time, place, and style of the presentation.

Communicate before you install (time)   Start by communicating the reasons for change and developing an overall software development architecture. Don't wait for the yearly division meeting. The earlier you communicate the reasons for change, the more time you give people to reorient themselves to the new realities.

Choose the right forum (place)   Some companies use staff meetings as the main channel for communication. The senior IS manager tells department managers to use CASE, and they tell project managers, and so on. The final message usually ends up as: "Use CASE because your manager says to." Even if the decision to use CASE wasn't cooperative, the reasons behind the decision should be clearly communicated.

Pick a planned group or department meeting, if the timing's right. Otherwise plan a meeting specifically to announce the change. Make sure you set it up to allow direct feedback from the audience.

Plan symbolic activities (style)   The world's leaders have long known the power of symbolism and ritual. Silly though they seem, symbolic activities can be effective ways to push people from thinking about change to actually doing something about it.

You can make a symbolic statement the first time the change is announced. If the change was a cooperative decision, let some of the developers who contributed tell their peers about the new plans. This will be more effective than a management dog-and-pony-show.

Symbolism gives people a concrete handle on the unfocused issues they face. You can plan rituals to celebrate different phases of the change, to mark the end of the old or the beginning of the new. Publicly award people who make change happen. Throw a wake for the old software tools. As transition progresses, look for opportunities to make symbolic statements, ways to make each step more concrete.

Transition central

It would be nice if, having firmly launched the ship, it would continue to steer a strong, straight course. It can't though, without periodic guidance. You should monitor the transition as it progresses, with an eye toward facilitating problems, and improving the process of managing change.

Dealing with transitional problems

Big changes don't happen quickly. Problems will inevitably spring up along the way. If you've simply announced a change, and then left everyone on their own, these problems can grow into change-killers.

"In many organizations," writes Bridges, "deep and lasting change is aborted simply because the people involved could not bear the chaos and uncertainty about what was emerging long enough to let it take shape."[32] He suggests the creation of a transition monitoring team, made up of workers and managers alike. Often this can be the same body that planned the changes. The team can watch for trends that jeopardize successful change, and propose adjustments to the change and transition plans. They can be the first refuge of those having problems with transition.

Deal gently with resistance to the change, through this team or individually. Hard-line measures only aggravate transitional pain. You want to encourage new ideas while diverting cynicism. Change and transition should progress in a spirit of informed opportunism. Let everyone know that no action is irreversible, that all ideas for improvement are encouraged, and that transitional pain is expected.

Improve the change management process

Today's CASE tools aren't the ultimate software solution. In the next few years, you'll introduce many similar new technologies. Now is the time to pay attention to how you manage change and transition. Keep track of the tactics that work and those that fail. Note which goals are met, and which were too optimistic.

During periodic review meetings, ask questions about the change management process:

- How do they feel the changes were handled?
- Are the goals of change apparent?
- Were training plans adequate?
- Are people comfortable with their new responsibilities?
- How could the change management be improved?

The only future constant will be change. Learn to manage it now.

Making change a way of life

If you can convince people to see change as an opportunity instead of a threat, you'll be better able to take advantage of it. Some of the imperatives for an organization that thrives on change include:

- staying liquid and ready for change
- fostering empowered developers
- encouraging a free flow of information
- becoming a learning organization
- actively researching new technologies
- emphasizing work teams and task forces

Staying liquid

The simple model in FIG. 6-1 shows transition as a temporary process on the way to a new stable state. Staying liquid means avoiding the "thawing" and "freezing" processes of this model. In the future, change will happen so fast that no one will have time to refreeze anything. All groups must be liquid, pliable, ready to exploit environmental shifts. Everyone must learn to live in the neutral zone.

You need to foster enthusiasm for constant, incremental change. Let people know they can suggest new steps and new directions to bring the group closer to its shared vision. Let them share in the planning for change and transition, and build an organization that thrives on improvement. As Tom Peters says, "The most efficient and effective road to bold change is the participation of everyone, every day, in incremental change."[33]

The learning organization

A learning organization makes incremental change a way of life. Learning can't be seen as a separate activity. It becomes an integral part of every job and task. New learning should be rewarded, not gotten out of the way so you can come back to your real work.

Informating is a necessary prerequisite for the learning organization. It provides data for understanding and measuring the IS organization's events, assets, and processes.

CASE informates the development process, enabling future improvement. Based on this information, you can dedicate some IS resources to identifying, documenting, and managing development methods. You should also encourage constant research into new tools and methods.

Encourage cross-training of developers and business experts. A consulting manager tells me, "Our best consultants are the ones who know the entire life cycle covered by the CASE tool. They need to understand the entire process, from determining business strategies to generating the eventual application system." A change-oriented company has multitalented people who can grow into new tasks and responsibilities.

Empowerment

Traditional organizations are built for control, consistency, and predictability. Managers assumed this emphasis would minimize costs, and often they do. But when customer service is the great differentiator, cost-cutting becomes secondary. If you accept that most advanced Western societies now contain service-based economies, you must also acknowledge that current organizational structures, formed to support product manufacturing, must change. New organizations need to change paradigms toward empowerment.

Empowerment means trusting workers to do what's best for the company. It means delegating authority and responsibility to those closest to the basic work, those who can respond quickly to external changes. For an IS organization, it means giving developers more discretion over tools, methods, and project management. It means forging a common vision of the future, setting principles for behavior, and trusting people to do their best within these limits.

Skeptical managers ask, "How can I be sure they'll do what I want them to?" You can't. In fact, you can be certain that they'll do a lot of things you never would have suggested; things you never thought of; things that work better, for them, than the things they did before.

Empowerment requires two major organizational shifts: new roles for middle managers and new definitions of success.

New roles for middle managers Department and project managers must become coordinators and troubleshooters, not cost controllers and disciplinarians. Continued emphasis on cost accounting ignores the IS organization's increasing service role.

Empowerment can imply flatter organizational structures, which mean less managerial performance feedback. But CASE systems can trap data about development processes: metrics, audit trails, narrative histories. Informating systems like CASE can supply objective feedback about quality and performance.

CASE can also aid empowered developers by promoting software quality. As the quality assurance features of CASE tools improve, IS can shrink the number of design inspections and code walk-throughs, streamlining the process. Developers will become personally responsible for the quality of the components they create.

New definitions of success Projects can no longer succeed just by delivering something. The quality of the product and its impact upon the business should define success. You should try to measure IS success according to business success. The degree to which teams improve old methods must also be considered.

Systems quality, flexibility, reusability, and developer responsiveness to systems users will become more important than costs and schedules. Until performance evaluations consider these factors, cost-cutting will continue to undermine system and service quality.

When cost and time drive developers, the chances that CASE will be easily accepted diminish. In the short-term, CASE increases quality much more than it reduces cost.

Free flow of information

For years, managers have employed information, or rather the restriction of information flow, for organizational control. Empowerment will force us to kick this habit. People held accountable for their performance can't be spoon-fed. They need free access to information. As Peter F. Drucker suggests, "Everyone in the information-based organization needs constantly to be thinking through what information he or she requires to do the job and make a contribution."[34] Then they must be able to get it: query the database, print the report, call up someone who knows.

This leads to a principle Drucker calls "information responsibility." When developing information systems, this responsibility cuts two ways:

- Developers are responsible for soliciting business information from business experts, and faithfully transforming this into useful applications.
- Business experts are accountable for providing timely, relevant knowledge about the business, and making sure that developers represent it correctly.

In all but the most sensitive areas, the burden of proof should shift from those who want information to those who want to restrict it. Most firms routinely lock up all files and databases, and then dole out security codes and passwords like feudal favors.

Instead, everything should start out with universal read-only access. Those who want to protect their data must justify their requests, and prove that free access to their data isn't the best course for the firm.

This principle should apply directly to software development. Integrated data and reusable software require cooperative development techniques, multiple development teams sharing information. In the past, teams worked with users up front and then retreated to hack out systems in a vacuum. Toward the end of a project, interfaces from one system to another would be thrown together in time for installation.

New development methods won't work unless all the teams go public with their information. They should openly air business issues, design decisions, plans, and schedules. The software engineering repository should be accessible by any employee, even from outside of IS. It should be offered as a company resource, available to anyone who can use it.

CASE encourages information exchange in many ways:

- It augments Joint Application Design and requirements-gathering sessions, and break down information barriers. Issues that might take weeks to resolve through memos and hallway discussions can be tackled in one or two group meetings.
- It facilitates the management and distribution of essential business information. The repository doesn't just hold software data. It contains some of the best business information in the company—models of business strategies, processes, and information flow.
- It establishes a common modeling language for communicating among groups. For the first time, people can use the same formats for sharing goals and information needs.

Like other new technologies, CASE can help cut through information barriers and improve your ability to quickly respond to change.

Active research

Most IS shops take a conservative approach to new technologies. If IBM hasn't endorsed it, or most Fortune 500 companies aren't using it, then it's probably not a practical technology.

Unfortunately, if everyone else is already using it, they can use it against you. Safe technologies don't create competitive advantage, risky ones do.

Active research means finding out what the universities, research consortiums, and high-tech start-up companies are up to. It means gathering information about all promising new technologies, even if they don't seem immediately practical. It means watching the technologies your competitors acquire, and speculating what they want them for.

All the technologies that will create competitive advantage five years from now exist in some form today. You should be on the lookout for them now. Once they're "proven," it will take years to develop in-house expertise. You should start up the learning curve much sooner.

Most large companies have established research and development departments, but, except in software or computer firms, these R&D groups rarely consider software development technology. Larger IS organizations can establish an information technology R&D group. But even small firms can afford to do some basic research. Technology fanatics abound in IS organizations. Many programmers keep PCs at home so they can play with technologies too "advanced" for their workplace. Let the technology hounds do your R&D work for you:

- Send them to classes and conferences occasionally to scout out advanced subjects that might one day be applicable in your environment.
- Make the price of these excursions a brief report on the subjects and how they might be harnessed for the future gain of IS.
- If something looks promising, let them follow up by calling vendors or contacting researchers.
- If you bring in a trial product as a result, let your scout be involved in the pilot effort.
- Occasionally adopt one of the new technologies.

Through this process you get enthusiastic developers, advance notice about new technologies, and sometimes an excellent way to develop software.

Without some research, the fast pace of change will switch you to constant catch-up mode. Don't blindly adopt every sensational new technology—that can be damaging. But complacency is worse.

Task forces

The organizational structure can be change's biggest obstacle. It is the symbol of the organizational status quo, and the refuge of those who fight transition.

Many IS groups mirror the functional hierarchy of the firm. Another popular structure places IS units within functional areas. However, today's challenges are all cross-functional. Imperatives like "time to market," "total customer service," and "systems integration" cut horizontally across the breadth of a company. They require workers who can bridge organizational boundaries.

The natural construct for bridging these gaps is the task force. Most companies use task forces as emergency measures; when a company-wide problem emerges, they form a task force. However, most ad hoc teams don't produce much. They are often seen as a stalling tactic (Don't have the answer? Set up a task force!).

Companies that use ad hoc teams well also handle change well. Tom Peters and Robert Waterman describe this phenomenon in their book, *In Search of Excellence*: "The task force is an exciting, fluid, ad hoc device in the excellent companies. It is virtually the way of solving and managing thorny problems, and an unparalleled spur to practical action."[35]

Effective ad hoc teams can react swiftly to changes that petrify the standard hierarchy. A directed task force with the power to enact its suggestions is the most effective change agent.

IS is an area ripe for "adhocracy:" team-based management that works across organizational lines. The organizational barriers that IS must bridge include those:

- between IS and the business experts
- among functional organizations, such as finance or human resources
- among functionally-aligned IS groups, for example, sales systems or logistics systems

Gaining cooperation between IS groups can be the most difficult of all. Functional areas like finance and human resources habitually work together to solve business issues. But functionally aligned IS groups rarely interact. Their systems were developed separately and maintained separately, and only connect, if at all, through obscure data interfaces.

Applications integration, as a result, requires team-based development. For example, Shoshana Zuboff presents evidence that data integration requires a more "team-centered, problem-solving orientation." She cites a group of managers who now

> faced a broad array of data that integrated disparate production, business, and organizational processes. Their capacity to deal adequately with such data seemed to require interactive discussion and analysis . . . as well as a new interdependence among the various business and operations functions.[36]

But integration isn't the only change that calls for development task forces. Others include:

- reengineering of business processes
- business requirements gathering
- process and data structure reusability
- prototyping and interface design
- software release management
- change and transition planning
- transfer of CASE skills

The switch to CASE, especially when accompanied by new development methods, calls for new team structures. Often a CASE expert must team with other developers and business experts throughout the development cycle. The CASE expert works to reduce the others' learning curve for the new tools and techniques.

CASE can simplify cooperative development approaches. A skilled CASE "scribe" can capture live meeting information in structured formats, and print and distribute the definitions and diagrams at the end of a session. Integrated CASE tools with central repositories ease the sharing of software information among team members.

The task force is clearly superior to old back room coding approaches. Consultant Tom Gilb cites evidence that "cooperative teams" accomplish the same development objectives with fewer tasks, fewer lines of code, and fewer errors than do standard development staffs.[37]

Team-based development isn't new for IS. Gerald Weinberg introduced the concept of self-managing "egoless" programming teams back in 1971.[38] The JAD concept has been around for years. Yet JAD sessions are often one- or two-shot "get the requirements and run" meetings. Development steering committees can be set up to maintain this joint participation for a more extended period. The steering committee is a representative group of managers and business experts. It follows development efforts from initial strategic planning through design and implementation. It can be a dynamic body, spinning off working subcommittees or adding and subtracting members as required.

If task forces were used as a "cop out" in the past, you might want to revamp their image. Give them new, dynamic names such as "action team" or "working team." Charter them to solve specific goals. Give them the power to change things. Make sure their recommendations are put into action.

Make sure that important people don't dodge task force participation. Management commitment to the team is essential, and it should be demonstrated in person. Since corporate reward structures don't often help team members, management visibility (and a learning experience) is all they can hope for.

Over time you can create incentives for task force participation. Require everyone to participate on at least two task forces per year. Let people's performance evaluations hinge, in part, upon how well the teams they served on met their goals.

Team-based development can be used to pilot potential IS reorganization. Task forces are temporary by nature. But if one works well, why not keep it going? For example, the JAD concept can be extended to all aspects of software development. Many firms have created special positions for JAD facilitators. Some formalize the concept, creating joint application teams of developers, business experts, and technical specialists that follow a software product throughout the entire development cycle.

Some argue that adhocracy must become the foundation of tomorrow's company. Others favor frequent reorganization, every six months or so. Either way the message is the same: make the organizational structure much more flexible than it is today. Otherwise it will sit there, a monolithic Berlin Wall, thwarting enlightenment and smothering change.

Summary

This chapter presents numerous suggestions for minimizing the cultural costs of the switch to CASE. Taken together, they seem daunting. But even a few of them, cleverly applied, can cut down the pain of change.

This chapter started with discussion of the large number of changes facing IS today, and the fact that software developers are only one of many groups who will be affected. Yet I've tried to show that change itself is not the problem. Change is good—it's the only way your company will stay competitive. But even the best planned changes are costly. Physical change might be easy, but the mental and social reorientation costs—the costs of transition—are always difficult. People in transition get disoriented, they think up strange worst-case nightmares and dig in their feet to stop change from taking place.

Such resistance to change is never blind. Resistance occurs when people think a change works against their best interests. Make sure that change is personally beneficial, and resistance dissipates.

I suggest the following ways of pouring oil on the troubled transition period:

- Plan for transition as well as change.
- Develop a shared vision of the future, and move toward it a step at a time.

- Make the change personally beneficial.
- Communicate all facets of the change, and the reasons behind it.
- Monitor the ongoing effects of the change, and improve the change management process as a result.

Suggested principles for improving the change-readiness of your organization include:

- Stay "liquid," fostering a culture that values constant, incremental change.
- Make learning an integral part of everyone's job.
- Form a confederation of empowered professionals, putting decision-making power closest to the customer.
- Remove all internal barriers to information about the business and its information systems.
- Actively research new development technologies, even unproven ones.
- Make the task force or cooperative team the foundation of future development work.

With some of these principles in effect, you'll be in a position to quickly exploit future changes, instead of just reacting to them.

Finally, I suggest a number of new task roles to support CASE tools and new development methods. My position isn't biased toward centralization or decentralization of IS. As long as you recognize the need for new roles, and build the skills to support them, you can locate people anywhere and give them whatever titles they want.

7
Planning for the software factory

Most CASE products are bought by IS department or project managers who want to apply them on a limited scale, to one or a group of ongoing development projects. The purchase is made at a departmental level, so fully integrated solutions are unaffordable. The managers buy a specialized tool that gives them a few immediate benefits. The tool is probably cheaper than more complete solutions, and therefore seems less risky. Since the benefits of CASE are hard to quantify, cost alone tips the scale. After a few years, various IS groups and departments find themselves with different "partial solutions," which together don't seem to make a full one.

Because of the support resources and the cultural and educational changes CASE requires, it rarely succeeds in a corporation without coordinated planning and support. Departmental purchasing leads to CASE tool anarchy, each department owns a combination of CASE tools, and struggles with a growing pool of accepted techniques and practices. Upper management is less familiar with CASE concepts, so purchase decisions are based on the political clout of the requesting manager, or budgetary considerations alone. Information sharing across departments becomes difficult. It's like teaching one person French and another person Chinese, then asking them to get together and compare notes. When people do communicate, they'll despair at the lack of common ground. "Wouldn't it be nice if we could all use the same methodology?" ask developers of their colleagues. The scenario can continue on to undesirable conclusions:

- CASE tools are "proven" useless, since few of their supposed benefits have emerged. Management postpones further investment in the technology until someone (preferably IBM) finally comes up with a better mousetrap. The CASE concept is discredited, and with a sigh of relief, the programmers start typing program code again at their terminals. Applications integration, leap-frog productivity, and minimal-defect software remain insubstantial buzzwords.
- A need for a common development environment is eventually recognized. But achieving this goal means throwing out three-fourths of the CASE tools that

have already been purchased. The tool that follows the best methodology and has the best integration potential emerges as the winner. The departments currently using this tool gain prestige, while others face new costs and learning curves. Many developers remain pessimistic about the technology, since the last tools they used didn't do much for them.

To combat anarchy without causing resentment among the people, you must lay down guiding laws and principles to which everyone can agree. IS management must forge such principles, expressing them as plans that address the growing complexity of software development, and the environment within which it operates.

The complexity of the IS environment has increased steadily for years, and lately this growth has been exponential. For years, computer hardware and business application systems, and the people and money needed to manage them, were the chief resources managed by IS. Since the adoption of third-generation programming languages like FORTRAN, COBOL, and C, most software development platforms stayed relatively stable. The biggest problem many firms faced was installing a new compiler version, or converting old source code to new language standards. This first resource level was simple to manage.

The introduction of centralized databases and decision support systems added a second tier of IS resources. Data, which once seemed an incidental byproduct of application programs, now must be inventoried like other company resources, and managed by IS. The right data items must be in stock when the information customer wants them, and information storage capacities must be carefully managed.

The advent of CASE, expert systems, intelligent workstations, and other advances focused attention on a critical third resource tier: the development environment. CASE tools and methodologies are the equipment developers use to build the systems that created the information resource. This represents vertical integration of a sort unmatched by most other functional groups in the firm. It's akin to the manufacturing division managing the heavy machinery and processes for creating the equipment that is used to manufacture the product. And teaching the workers how to do it all, too. Is it any wonder IS managers feel overworked?

Improvements in development tools now enable many business users to develop their own information systems. The advent of end-user computing adds heavily to the demands upon the IS organization. Today's end-user computing arsenal ranges from spreadsheet macro languages, database languages, and 4GLs to interface generators and full-fledged CASE tools.

As industry analysts Boynton and Zmud remark, IS organizations must now "simultaneously provide centralized direction and coordination while recognizing the value of increased discretion regarding [IS] decision-making on the part of managers throughout the organization."[1] This challenge will never be met by random applications of information technology.

Anarchy's cure

Organizations that use information systems for competitive advantage didn't gain these systems by accident. Boynton and Zmud point out that the ability to consistently and effectively apply information technology is "developed over periods of time in which technology has been tightly integrated into the organization's core business activities and strategic planning."[2] Concerted planning efforts help ensure that the application of technology will bring desired results.

Planning is rapidly becoming an imperative for most IS organizations. As shown in TABLE 7-1, "IS Strategic Planning" placed fifth out of all concerns in a 1990 survey of IS executives by Index Group.[3] Nearly all of the other concerns on this list can only be tackled once strategic IS planning has occurred.

Table 7-1. Top Concerns of IS Executives

Rank	Concern
1	Reshaping business processes through information technology
2	Educating senior management on information systems
3	Instituting cross-functionalal IS
4	Aligning IS and corporate goals
5	IS strategic planning
6	Boosting software development productivity
7	Utilizing data
8	Using IS for competitive breakthroughs
9	Developing an information architecture
10	Cutting IS costs

Source: Index Group, Inc.

The cure for development tool anarchy is apparent: before buying tools, thoroughly plan and prepare for them, on a company-wide basis if possible, considering all of the information resources at your disposal.

Planning for CASE implementation is nothing new. Most books about CASE discuss the need to plan before you buy. Suggested planning steps usually follow a sequence such as:

1. Assess the current state of your software development environment.
2. Establish repeatable development methods.
3. Train developers in the new methods.
4. Evaluate and select CASE tools which support these methods.
5. Conduct a pilot project.
6. Assess the CASE tool's effectiveness.
7. Roll out CASE to the entire organization.[4]

With some additions, the message usually reads: plan for CASE as you would for any large-scale hardware or software purchase. This advice is not wrong, but it's usually given in the wrong context. It's based on the uncertain assumption that you need CASE tools in the first place.

CASE has many benefits, but it might not be exactly what you require. When you set out to plan a CASE tool implementation, you presuppose that CASE is the solution.

When you limit your vision to the purchase and use of a new tool, you also restrict the benefits you can earn. You let a CASE tool vendor limit what you can achieve.

The planning approach outlined above addresses important concerns for CASE implementation, but it presents them in a narrow context. The decision to use CASE affects more than the IS organization and its developers. Business concerns should drive the decision, and its impacts should be evaluated for the entire company.

First understand the strategic direction for the IS organization, and then plan for CASE as another piece in the information resource puzzle. You can't rationalize massive investments in this new technology without looking at the IS organization as a whole. CASE implies many other things besides new software tools: training, organizational change, hardware purchases, resource shifts. To mobilize the resources needed to successfully use CASE, you must examine the entire IS infrastructure.

Operations management textbooks present a hierarchical view of the planning process, as shown in FIG. 7-1. The strategic level involves policy and business strategy. The tactical level addresses action plans and resource usage. The operational level represents day-to-day execution of business plans.

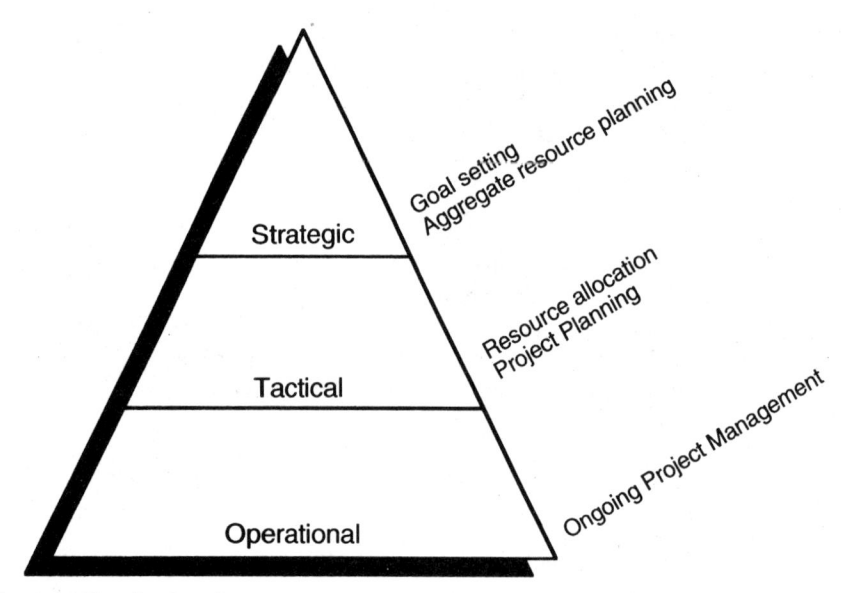

Fig. 7-1. Classic planning structure

Traditionally, planning for development tools has been managed at the operational level. Project managers acquire tools to boost productivity for a specific project or set of tasks. When IS managers plan for development tool implementation, they do so at the tactical level. They bring in CASE to boost productivity and quality for the whole organization, and consider constraints on money, people, and time.

Now that information systems are becoming strategic in nature, planning for the resources to create them should escalate to the strategic level. Just as functional plans should consider information systems support, IS plans should be based on business strategies. IS planning must become a visible subset of overall corporate planning.

The degree of strategic planning for CASE increases when companies perceive strategic benefits from the technology. Since information systems now influence the ways companies operate, IS planning can influence corporate goals, rather than just react to them. When information systems start affecting business strategy, as they are today, business strategy must acknowledge information systems.

Many firms have already adopted strategic planning for their business application portfolios. CASE should be seen as part of this portfolio, an application for IS. It should be planned for along with other applications, or at least in the same manner. Having forced their users to undergo rigorous planning for business applications, IS groups should start doing some strategic planning of their own.

A plan for the planners

Strategic planning for IS will point your CASE efforts in the right direction. It is the first step of many in a larger plan to streamline the software development process. The entire effort will involve large amounts of time, money, and resources, and should be managed with the same care given to other large projects.

This effort unites a number of subprojects. The major steps include:

1. Develop a change plan.
2. Plan a strategic software development architecture.
3. Reengineer the software development process.
4. Evaluate and select CASE tools.
5. Refine specific development method paths (build a method pool).
6. Start gathering baseline metrics.
7. Run a full-cycle CASE pilot project.
8. Plan the CASE rollout.
9. Develop a training program for new methods and tools.
10. Organize for CASE and cooperative development.
11. Roll out new methods and CASE tools.
12. Evaluate and refine the IS architecture, change plan, and transition plan.

Use these steps to outline a change plan for the superproject. This change plan provides an overview of the tasks involved in implementing CASE throughout an organization. It can include:

- rough schedule and resource plan
- high-level budget
- initial personnel transition plan
- risk management plan

Schedules

Figure 7-2 shows a sample schedule for the superproject in PERT chart format. Because most of the steps within this plan represent subprojects, your time and resource estimates cannot be too detailed right now.

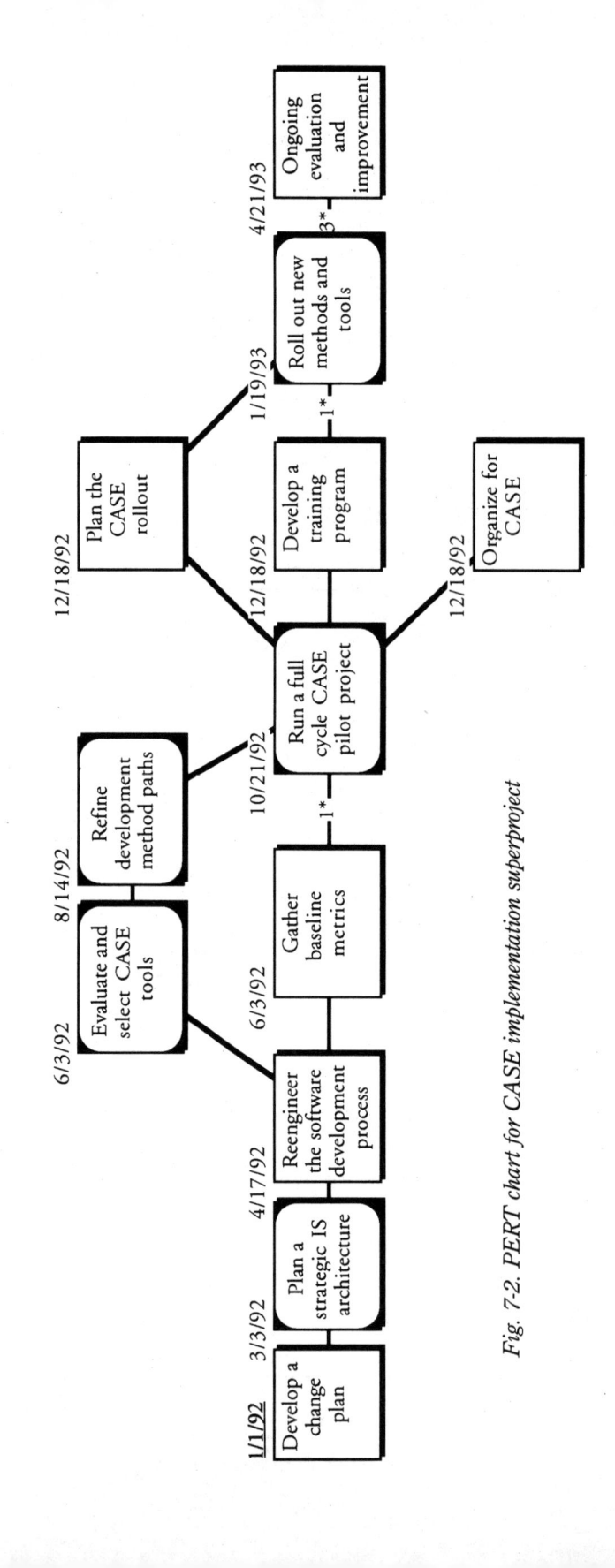

Fig. 7-2. PERT chart for CASE implementation superproject

Budgets

Your budget planning will necessarily be sketchy. The costs of this effort extend beyond the purchase costs of the CASE tools. You'll require substantial time commitments from a few of the best managers and developers. You'll spend money researching CASE tools, and taking preliminary training courses. The main reason for budgeting this effort is to determine what your financial constraints are. The best way to find this out is to present an estimate, and then ask for feedback. If you can't get senior managers to spend money on strategic plans, methodology development, or CASE tool evaluation projects, your chances of getting the right CASE tools are slim.

Risk management plan

Few things are as uncertain as the likelihood of successful CASE implementation. Risks abound, and many companies have fallen prey to them. Yet risks can be managed, and techniques exist for doing so. The simplest is the creation of a risk management plan.

Decide and document the most likely risks. Then brainstorm ways for reducing or controlling them. Periodically revisit the plan. Document new risks as they arise, and cross off the ones that have disappeared. Once you know what risks you face, you can take steps to eliminate them before they become problems. Without this knowledge you'll be frequently surprised, the victim of innumerable crises.

TABLE 7-2 lists some potential CASE implementation risks, and ideas for thwarting them. All of these ideas will be described in detail throughout this book.

Transition plan

The risk that people can't adjust to the new methods or tools might be the most probable of all. An initial transition plan should be formed in conjunction with the overall change plan. Personal transitions and realignment will begin once the first rumors about CASE get out.

A transition plan is another form of risk management plan, listing the various ways that changes might disrupt the work environment and impede personal realignment. TABLE 7-3 lists some of these transition risks, and ideas for managing them.

Communicating the need for change

The simplest way to ease transition is to freely communicate the need for change. Whether your company is small or large, a department or division meeting is the best way to start communications. Some of the best things to discuss up front are:

- reasons why changes are being considered
- general principles for managing the change, including commitments to widespread education and support
- reassurances that everyone's voice will be heard throughout the change process

Once everyone knows the general direction, you've primed them to participate. When the decision to use CASE is kept hidden until the last moment, it meets with resis-

Table 7-2. Major Risks of CASE Implementation Projects

Risk	Risk Limiting Techniques
The IS organization isn't ready for CASE	• Strategically plan for the IS organization. Consider needs in all areas, not just software creation. • Bolster fundamental skills, in areas like project management and communication with business experts, before rolling out CASE.
Resistant or cynical developers	• Involve everyone in the decision-making process. • Initially select tools that improve day-to-day work of software developers. • Create transition plans and transition monitoring groups to help people raise and resolve problems caused by new approaches.
Acquisition of inappropriate or ineffective CASE tools	• Identify software development goals and requirements before purchasing tools. Let these requirements determine how you evaluate candidate CASE products. • Develop software development methods in conjunction with tools.
Unrealistic CASE implementation schedules and budgets	• Build implementation schedules from the ground up, estimating time and costs for lower-level tasks and summing them to get total estimates. • Extrapolate all implementation costs, not just purchase costs.
Inability to justify the new techniques to management	• Measure current development performance in all areas (including measures of quality and business impact, not just efficiency). • Measure CASE efforts and compare against current baseline.
Trying to change too much at once	• Limit yourself to a few incremental changes at once, or reengineer the entire process while providing extensive training and support. • Involve everyone in the decision-making process.
The tools or techniques don't improve things	• Pilot everything as quickly and cheaply as you can. • Review your performance every step of the way. Foster an atmosphere for continuous improvement. • Use the method pool as a framework for evaluating tool and technique effectiveness.
Results are minimal, because the tools only automate a narrow range of IS functions	• Use a modular method pool to document and improve both CASE and non-automated techniques. • Train people to be better project managers, information gatherers, and information sharers.
The need for integrated systems cancels out CASE productivity	• Introduce the concepts of evolutionary delivery, and coordinated application releases. • Select CASE tools that support development of large-scale, integrated systems.

tance. When it's discussed openly, the results will be more amenable to everyone involved.

As each of the subprojects gets done, you will need to revisit the overall change plan. Though CASE implementation seems like a unique effort, it's not. You will have the chance to introduce new development tools and methods many times in the future.

Table 7-3. Detailed Transition Risks of CASE Implementation

Risk	Risk Limiting Techniques
People feel CASE is imposed upon them	• Involve everyone in the decision-making process. Discuss reasons why change is needed. • Create transition plans and transition monitoring groups to help people raise and resolve problems caused by the new approaches.
No perceived personal gain from CASE	• Initially select tools that improve day-to-day work of software developers. • Communicate marketability of CASE skills. • Encourage cross-training for everyone.
Developers can't learn new skills	• Develop a comprehensive CASE training program. • Make time for people to attend training courses.
Classroom training can't prepare people for real-world CASE	• Set up forums for informally sharing CASE knowledge. • Begin post-project evaluations to discuss lessons learned, and gauge effectiveness of tools and techniques.
Perception that CASE makes software delivery harder	• Run an initial pilot project to assess CASE effectiveness. • Make sure everyone gets training before they start using the tools. Delivery *is* harder if you must learn as you work.
Panic and finger-pointing if a CASE project isn't remarkably better than a traditional one	• Manage expectations. Early projects must deal with learning curves and setting up the infrastructure. • Develop contingency plans. This usually means falling back upon today's methods.

By forming an official plan, and improving it as you progress, you'll learn things you can apply to future technology introductions.

The IS architecture

Take your first step toward CASE by discussing strategies for the IS organization as a whole. The strategic IS plan is also known as the IS architecture. Like a blueprint for a house, the IS architecture says how the applications and development environment will be built. It lays plans for builders to follow.

The need for architecture didn't emerge until construction technology became complex. When all people had were mud, rocks, and sticks, building design was pretty simple. Primitive builders consigned simple design techniques to memory, then used them over and over to build house after similar house. No one had to say "Make the west wall out of mud bricks." Mud bricks were all they had. When the development environment is simple, architecture seems superfluous. When all you have is a COBOL compiler, chances are you'll end up writing similar programs over and over. More advanced tools, materials, and designs make the concept of architecture more relevant.

In fact, the concept of architecture has been applied to IS planning now for many years. A seminal article by John Zachman of IBM outlined a comprehensive architectural framework for information systems, and has been widely quoted.[5] Other writers have discussed information resource architectures, referring to organizational and technological infrastructures that support the applications plan.[6] James Martin has used the house-building metaphor extensively in most of his books on information engineering.

Unfortunately, the metaphor breaks down at a certain level when applied to information systems planning. For architects and housing contractors, the constructed house is the end product, the final goal. For most companies, though, software applications are an intermediate deliverable. The true product is information, and the applications are the equipment used to manufacture and process it.

To make the metaphor more robust, we need to alter it slightly. Rather than designing a house, we're designing a factory—a complex manufacturing concern devoted to the production and maintenance of information.

The information factory

IS is really a microcosm of an entire manufacturing company. It manages the procurement of raw materials (raw data), the transformation of these materials into useful products (meaningful information), and the summary distribution of the products (online inquiries, reports). IS is vertically integrated, building the equipment, (integrated development environments) used to create the equipment (applications) which manage information.

The manufacturing metaphor is powerful because it focuses attention on the true product: information, not applications. Most IS organizations live to churn out applications software. Many are so schedule-driven that they will trim system functionality in order to deliver the system on time. Removing system features isn't a good way to please systems users.

A retail customer who wants a racketball won't accept a football-making machine instead. An information customer shouldn't care about getting applications-information-making machines—on time. She wants the right information, not tools to manage different data. Most users today clamor for large applications systems because IS has conditioned them to do so. But few users care about the systems themselves. They want the information these systems produce. Witness the prevalence of user-developed spreadsheet applications, "underground" systems that provide data the users can't get from the standard applications. Rather than complain to IS and hope for a new or changed mainstream application, many users go vigilante, rounding up data from application files and feeding them to spreadsheets.

When information, rather than applications, becomes the true currency of IS, the role of IS within the company shifts. Rather than continue with a strategy built around large-scale system projects, in which various functional groups commission specialized applications for their own use, IS must take a broader view.

Information can be seen as a company's fourth major resource, along with capital, equipment, and human resources. Top management should look at software development costs as investments rather than expenses. Applications—the equipment used to create the company's information resource—should be managed as assets themselves.

Most companies plan extensively for other assets; strategic IS plans cover planning for information resources. IS planning should mesh with other types of resource planning and occur at the same strategic level. The IS architecture must consider these other company assets, as well as the goals and strategies of the functional groups that manage them.

Information management can be viewed as a high-level business function on a par with others like marketing, manufacturing, financial management, or human resources management. Just as these functions require applications support, in the form of sales or payroll systems, the information management function requires applications of its own. CASE tools can be seen as applications that support the software development portion of the information management function.

CASE implementation then becomes just another software development project. A CASE tool is a computer system that transforms data from one state into another. The metadata that describe software can be managed like business data about products, customers, or currencies. CASE is an application supporting the business function of information systems development.

The same steps apply to CASE implementation as to applications development projects:

1. Gather requirements of end-users (developers).
2. Analyze data needs.
3. Determine the technology platform.
4. Evaluate alternative system solutions (some companies develop their own CASE tools).
5. Consider training and ongoing support requirements.

Rather than treat CASE implementation as a large-scale hardware or software purchase, as many consultants prescribe, you should treat it as a software development project.

A CASE system might not be the only application you need to support IS functions. All the functions related to applications development—including planning, consulting, training, and metrics management—should be supported in the IS infrastructure.

IS architecture characteristics

The IS architecture should include an applications architecture for the information management function. Figure 7-3 shows where the IS architecture fits in the context of company-wide strategic planning, and the planning of other functional areas. At the top level, the mission and goals of the entire company must be established and advertised. Each functional area then builds its own strategic plans or architectures based on these high-level directions. Out of each architecture come projects designed to accomplish the goals set out for each group. One of the IS projects might be CASE implementation; another could be a methodology development project, or a measurement program.

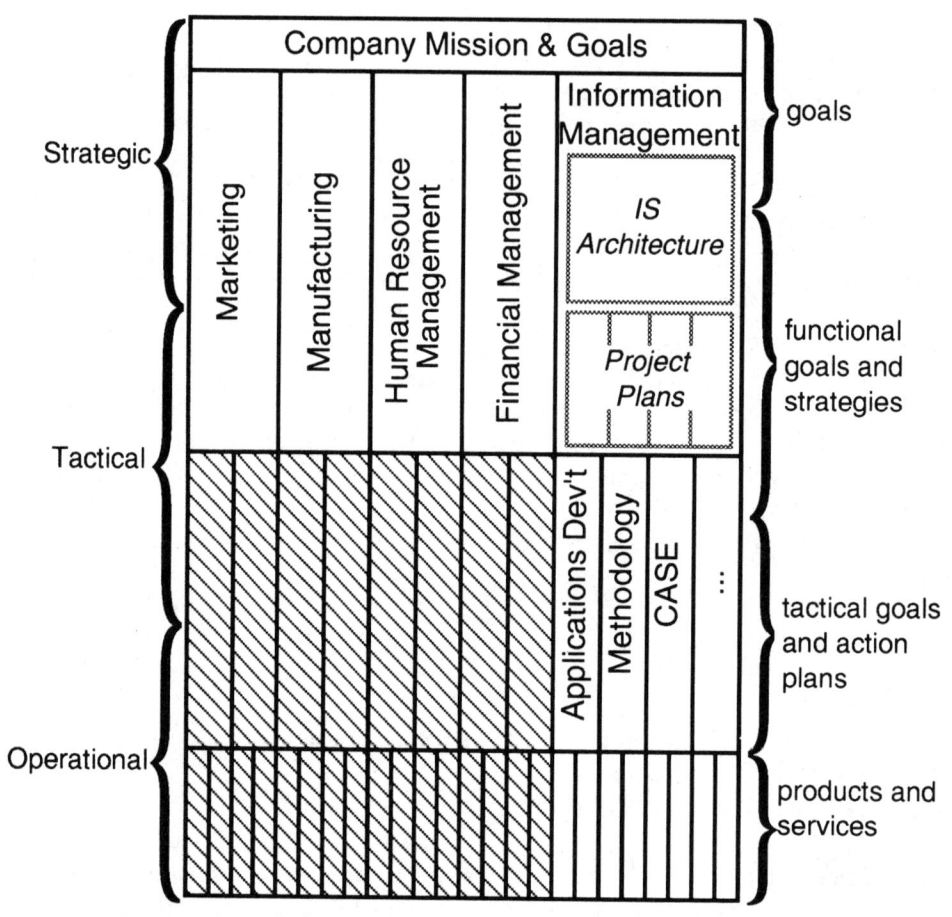

Fig. 7-3. *IS planning within the company planning structure*

At the operational level, these projects create products and services, integrated applications for managing data about software development.

The IS architecture can be split into three main areas:

1. The Information Architecture, translating business strategies into a planned configuration of integrated business data and applications. This architecture will have two main subsets: the applications and data needed to support traditional business functions, and those needed to support the function of information management.
2. The Technology Architecture, describing desired hardware, software, and communications configurations to support the information architecture.
3. The Information Resource Infrastructure, addressing the organization of human resources needed to design and implement the other two architectures.

A generalized framework for IS planning is shown in TABLE 7-4. The different areas that must be planned correspond to the three architectures listed above: business strat-

Table 7-4. Strategic IS Planning Framework

Planning Area	Strategic	Tactical	Operational
Business	• Principles • Goals • Strategic opportunities	• Policies • Project definition	• Communication of principles, goals and opportunities • Definition of policies and standards • Periodic reevaluation
Applications	• Functions • Applications architecture • New software development paradigms	• Project plans and schedules • Migration plans • New development methods • Desired process measurements	• Application development and maintenance • Reusable module management • Release management • Methodology development • Metrics management
Data	• Conceptual data model	• Project plans and schedules • Conversion plans	• Database development • Data integration • Data storage management
Organization	• Optimal organizational structure	• Reorganization plans	• Reorganization
Human resources	• Desired skills inventories • New jobs and roles • Career paths • Allocation policies	• Training plans • Recruiting plans • Personal career planning • Allocation to projects	• Course development • Training • Recruiting
Technology	• Technology architecture • Technology forecasts	• Purchase plans • Upgrade plans • Installation plans	• Purchase • Installation • Maintenance

egies, applications, and data make up the information architecture, and human resources and organization structure comprise the resource infrastructure. The technology architecture stands alone addressing equipment, systems software, and communications requirements. Each area must be planned at three levels: strategic, tactical, and operational.

How much planning do you need?

Accepted methods for planning some of these resource areas already exist. Business strategies are often articulated on an annual basis for each functional area of the company, including IS. Staffing plans address the human resources aspect.

Building an IS architecture doesn't mean reworking all of the company's strategy and staffing plans. It means taking existing plans and tying them into a coherent framework based on business goals. Ideally high-level corporate goals and strategies will be set by top management in conjunction with the chief IS manager, ensuring a common vision for IS and the rest of the company.

Planning for the entire IS organization can be a daunting prospect for a project manager who simply wants to use a new CASE tool. While planning is necessary for widespread success of CASE, there are cases where small purchases can achieve narrow, targeted benefits. In crisis situations, managers often must trust a "gut feel" and decide to bring in CASE tools for immediate productivity or quality gain. Others might find it impossible to gain approval for an IS planning effort, and be forced to plan for CASE tools alone, out of context of the needs of the entire IS organization. In general, though, the random approach brings only short-term benefits to single departments or project teams.

A debate constantly rages about whether software planning is best done "top-down" or "bottom-up." Top-down proponents say it's the only way to tie software to strategic goals, and to ensure you get the consistency promised by a solid architecture. Bottom-up advocates say that top-down projects become too large, get stalled, and rarely provide solutions. They say the only way to get things done is to do them, then roll it all up to a higher level as you need to.

When discussing CASE, this debate has already been closed. Many companies have proven that bottom-up approaches to CASE don't work. Faced with truly chaotic new environments, some of these firms are trying to retrofit the tools they have into top-down IS architectures. Firms that start with top-down plans, spending a few months to map things out before starting their journey, will have a much smoother trip.

Continued company-wide success with CASE does require a certain level of IS planning. However, the planning process need not be exhaustive. William R. King and T. S. Raghunathan found after surveying 280 IS managers that above a certain level of resource commitment, further planning efforts bring no additional returns. "That a little IS planning is good," they say, "does not imply that even more is better."[7]

Effective planning for the software development environment can be done without addressing every detail of the IS architecture. But the more you can plan for up front, the better. Many questions must be answered before making the CASE decision, including:

- What level of data and applications integration is desired?
- Can CASE contribute to the achievement of strategic business goals?
- Are enough available to manage the transition to CASE, and the added support roles required?
- Will developers be able to learn the new tools?
- How much of the IS budget can be channeled for new development tools and associated costs?
- What are the plans for future hardware and software purchases?
- Should applications be developed for mainframe platforms, or for PCs and LANs, or for all of these in combination?

Few managers can answer these questions off the tops of their heads. The best way to respond to these questions is with a comprehensive architectural plan. Otherwise, managers planning CASE tool purchases are forced to make assumptions that lead to restrictive solutions. The chosen development tool might not help achieve the true goals of the IS organization.

Goals of strategic planning

In order to answer the questions listed above, you need a planning process that lets you:

- formulate common principles to guide IS activities
- tie IS plans to business strategies
- reengineer IS processes for quantum improvements
- involve the people most affected by the plans
- enable the prioritization of internal IS development projects
- outline development project costs, benefits, and feasibility
- effectively allocate resources
- plan transitions from the current environment to the desired one
- address the plan's context

These objectives hold true for any type of planning, and they are especially relevant when drafting an internal IS architecture.

Many consultants present the concept of architecture as something radical and new. In fact, IS organizations have built architectures for years. Architectures exist today at every IS site. Each functional IS department normally has a picture showing the interfaces between main departmental applications systems. Sometimes the pictures are annotated to show hardware or communications concerns.

Though useful, these architectures reflect the artistic expressions of a few enthusiastic developers rather than a coordinated plan for integrated systems. They are limited in scope and reflect past constraints rather than future directions. Usually these architectures reflect systems exclusively. They don't connect business strategies with the IS infrastructure needed to support them. Created ad hoc, these disparate operational blueprints confuse rather than clarify.

Tie to strategic business plans

To bring unity to these architectures, gather them together under the banner of common company goals. As TABLE 7-1 showed, IS managers generally recognize the need to align IS and corporate goals. Unfortunately, many managers find the two sets of goals hard to synchronize. A 1986 study by professors Albert L. Lederer and Aubrey L. Mendelow showed that the most common problem facing IS planners was a lack of information about top management's objectives.[8]

The nature of the IS planning process often stands in the way of corporate goal alignment. TABLE 7-5 shows a useful spectrum of planning integration created by William Synnott.[9] Synnott presents five levels of integration of business and IS plans. Most IS planning is currently done via reactive or linked modes. Both of these modes imply a

Table 7-5. Degrees of Planning Integration

Type of Planning	Description	Degree of Integration
1. No planning	No formal planning takes place, either business or information systems.	(No plan)
2. Stand-alone planning	The company may have a business plan or an information systems plan, but not both.	Business and systems plan
3. Reactive planning	A business plan is prepared and the IS function reacts to it—a traditional, passive systems role.	Business plan → Systems plan
4. Linked planning	Business planning is "interfaced" with information systems planning. Systems resources are matched against business needs.	Business plan ∩ Systems plan
5. Integrated planning	Both business and information systems planning occur simultaneously, interactively. They are indistinguishable.	Business or systems plan

Source: From *The Information Weapon* by William R. Synnott, Copyright © 1987 by John Wiley & Sons, Inc. Reprinted by permission of John Wiley & Sons, Inc.

one-way transfer of information. Goals are set first at the corporate level, and then accommodated by IS managers. Integrated planning, on the other hand, involves cooperative goal setting at the corporate level.

The easiest way to tie business and IS plans together at this level is by letting the IS manager actively participate in the setting of business strategies. In another study by Lederer and Mendelow, sixteen out of twenty IS managers cited the difficulty of finding out corporate goals as a barrier to effective IS planning.[10] The four executives who did not mention this problem were the only four in the group who actively participated in the setting of their companies' business strategies.

The goal model consists of both guiding principles and more directed strategic tactical goals. Principles define the organization's approach to information management by stating beliefs and behavioral constraints. Goals identify specific objectives that the business must achieve. Principles help set a common vision of the way IS should operate; goals indicate what must be accomplished for this vision to come about.

The toughest time will be had by IS managers in firms where no formal planning is undertaken. In these cases, the IS manager can sometimes step in to fill the gap. The manager can:

- Suggest that top management prepare a strategy plan. This may sometimes be seen as threatening by top management.
- Convince top management to participate in strategic information planning sessions. Business goals and strategies will be elicited at the start of these sessions.
- Request IS personnel to extract business goals from various printed sources (annual reports, financial plans, mission statements) or through serial interviews with functional managers.

In the absence of clearly articulated business goals, many IS managers are tempted by these latter two options. They can be executed by resources under IS control, often faster than a full-scale corporate planning project. However, goal models built by IS people lack two important qualities: appropriate vision and corporate credibility.

First, IS personnel can't possibly know the strategic directions and long-term ideas that functional managers haven't yet committed to paper. When IS people try to predict the goals of other functional areas, they usually go too far. Used to quantum technological leaps, IS professionals tend to think everything is achievable, and impose upon manufacturing, for instance, an instant desire to be fully computer-integrated. The plans of most functional managers are tempered by the many constraints which govern their functions.

Second, a goal model built by IS will rarely be taken to heart by the rest of the company. The IS organization has been distant for too long, and it is rarely perceived as having a solid handle on strategic issues. Few functional managers believe that the "techies" know as much about their business as they do. A goal model is only useful when shared, so a model built solely by IS can never be of lasting value.

When the IS planning scope is limited by time or resource constraints, or for political reasons, it might make sense to throw together a straw model of corporate goals. The adoption of an IS-created goal model as the official one for a firm is extremely rare, but not unheard of. These goals should be presented as assumptions and reviewed with those who will eventually approve the plan, long before the plan nears completion. Keep in mind that the goal model is a chief determinant of the shape of the architecture. If the goals are meaningless to those who will use the plan, the plan itself will carry little weight.

The best option is always to keep IS involved in the setting of company-wide principles, goals, and directions. When this is impossible, IS plans should always be based on commonly understood formal business plans. An IS manager forced to instigate the business planning process must ensure that top managers are invested in the plan. This paves the way for their later approval of the IS architecture, which grows from the seeds of the business plan.

Recognize opportunities to reengineer IS functions

Automating existing development methods increases productivity, but only incrementally. Incremental improvements can't produce quantum productivity gains. And most companies clearly need gains of five or ten times normal productivity to meet the demands on IS over the next decade.

Many IS groups now involve themselves in business reengineering, helping business managers radically restructure operations for major cost and customer service benefits. This same reengineering philosophy should be applied to IS. It's the only way to break through the software development logjam.

No strategic plan for the 1990s and beyond is complete without a discussion of strategic information systems opportunities. Competitive advantage rarely comes from speeding up existing practices. It derives from applying new practices or technologies in ways that competitors can't quickly imitate.

CASE tools are strategic information systems for software development organizations. Effective CASE relies on reeingineered development processes, as formalized by a methodology, and also improves the productivity of traditional development methods. IS planning should include a look at new ways of operating, and new processes that might better meet the organization's goals.

Reengineering efforts are often slowed by disbelief of the power of recent technologies. Strategic planning should include a look at new technological developments, leading to a visionary design for the technology architecture. It is always more comfortable to restrict discussions of technology to what's available now. But strategic systems arise from new technology, not old.

Forecasting the next generation of usable technologies sounds impossible, but it's not. Nearly all of the technologies that will hit the mainstream in the 1990s have already been developed and publicized. Many have already been used successfully by other companies. Object-oriented programming has been possible for over twenty years, yet it's only now gaining widespread acceptance.

The technological horizon for technology forecasting should extend at least five years. Simple scans of the industry press will tell you what some of the next big things will be. Specialized consulting firms will happily offer you their own predictions, complete with the odds of their occurrence. Occasionally, you'll find the perfect fit between an elusive corporate goal and a promising new technology. Thus are strategic systems conceived.

The technology architecture lays a generalized blueprint for the configuration of hardware, software, and communications equipment, now and into the future. You must be careful to keep this architecture visionary—an enlightening guide, not a dogmatic edict.

Don't introduce resource constraints prematurely. Doing so will limit the benefits you can achieve from planning, as well as the flexibility of the plan in the face of future changes. Plan conceptually, with an eye toward the future. Constraints like the types of hardware or development tools currently available shouldn't be considered during strategic planning; these constraints will be applied in detail during the later tactical planning stages. By the time you start implementing new systems to support IS, many of the technologies that don't seem "industrial strength" will be ready.

New technological capabilities will generate ideas for fundamentally transforming some IS functions, and creating new ones. For example, new rapid application-generator programs totally alter the development process for some small, self-contained programs. The old design-code-compile-test sequence gives way to a much swifter design-test loop. This is reengineering at its best, accomplishing the same or better results while eliminating a number of costly process steps.

New technology can catalyze the reengineering process, but it's not a prerequisite. Reengineering might entail a rethinking of current processes. Eliminate time-consuming "sign-off" procedures for voluminous systems specifications and you become a reengineer. With new tools or not, every IS group can benefit from reassessing its development process, based on new needs for productivity and customer service.

Involve the people most affected

Planning for the IS organization is normally done by the senior IS manager in conjunction with immediate subordinates. No one denies that these managers know the most about overseeing information resources. Yet isolated planning furthers the data processing "priesthood" and distances IS from the rest of the company. If information will be managed as a corporate resource, groups outside of IS must have a say in how it will be done.

Specifically, two additional groups should help IS managers build the IS architecture: other functional managers, (the audience for the applications architecture) and developers, (the targets of development environment changes). Involving senior functional managers helps bridge a sometimes vast communications gap. These managers are IS's ultimate customers; their needs should become some of IS's main goals. Get them to develop wish lists and then discuss which ones are most important to grant. Remember that this level of planning doesn't consider business applications. You want to gather the functional managers' views about IS services, the level of IS support they desire, and their preferences for centralized or decentralized software development. As a result of the IS planning process, a consensus should develop among functional managers about the IS organization's role in the company.

Non-IS managers don't need to be computer literate. In structured meetings, good facilitators can concentrate on the business aspects of information resource management. The managers should be briefed about strategic benefits of structured IS planning, CASE, and other new techniques and technologies that IS might potentially adopt. Part of the reason that non-IS managers find it hard to fathom what IS can do for them is their unfamiliarity with the capabilities of information systems. Once non-IS managers are included in the IS planning process, their appreciation of IS grows.

There is little need to talk in detail about hardware and software with functional managers, though some enjoy it. The best information from functional managers relates to goals, strategies, and requirements. Planning sessions should concentrate on these aspects, not technical details.

During strategic planning sessions, other managers can:

- provide information about business strategies that might not have surfaced otherwise
- gain a better understanding of the factors facing the IS organization
- relate strategic IS plans to those of other functional groups, leading to integrated planning
- feel some ownership of the ideas shown in the resulting IS architecture, and therefore be more likely to support it in the future
- break down barriers to communication between IS and other organizations

Some IS managers feel they lose autonomy by letting other managers put their fingers into IS plans. Though input from other managers is necessary, final decisions still rest with IS.

Programs to improve software development through CASE and other technologies can often be very costly, resulting in increased IS budgets and by extension, relative reductions in the budgets of other functional areas. By allowing other managers to participate in the decision-making process that leads to CASE, you smooth the way for their later approval of needed funds.

Gaining participation of other managers can be problematic. In most companies, the head of IS is rarely asked to sit with the planners of other functional areas. Cross-functional planning is an exception rather than the rule. Does marketing invite the CIO to participate in sessions to determine next year's campaigns? Not usually. Yet IS, by virtue of managing a corporate resource, is organizationally more similar to personnel or finance than to marketing. Personnel planners usually poll functional managers to determine staffing and skill needs. Finance planners work from business requirements set down by managers across the company. So must IS planners reach out to other departments, gauging the needs of each, before drafting strategic and tactical plans.

The first time cross-functional IS planning is attempted, it might be difficult to round up participants. A savvy CIO can usually persuade management peers to join in; without a CIO, such participation requires extensive lobbying. If the results are impressive the first time, next year's IS planning sessions should be well attended. It only takes one publicized strategic system to sell functional managers on the potential for strategic information planning.

Systems developers, on the other hand, radiate enthusiasm when asked to help plan for the IS organization. When developers know their management is discussing major changes to the organization, they get curious, and sometimes paranoid.

Admittedly, some decisions may be too highly charged for developers to participate. A discussion about whether to outsource all development and fire half of the IS staff might cause trouble even if no changes are made. Yet most discussions could benefit from input by the development staff. Even if the results of planning might be unpopular, developers will accept them better if they have at least been consulted during the planning process.

It's like a child who overhears his parents discussing whether to send him to boarding school. He wants to be consulted about it. If he's not, he'll rebel no matter which decision is made.

There's no point getting tools that developers feel incapable of using. How do the developers feel about changing their tools? Do they like the way projects are handled today? Do they think an integrated corporate database will be feasible? Do they fear losing their current level of expertise, or are they excited at the prospect of learning new technologies?

Even if the developers' opinions differ from management's, the planners will gain valuable insights into the developers' position. This helps dramatically during the migration from current to future environments. The developers are thankful for having been consulted, and more likely to support the resulting architecture.

Enable project prioritization

The scope of your planning effort depends upon your position in the firm. The CIO can commission broad IS planning efforts; the CEO or a corporate planning manager can sponsor suites of strategic plans for the entire company. IS department or project managers have narrower domains. They must either lobby higher-level managers to support architectural planning, or carry out more limited planning within their area of jurisdiction.

As with any strategic planning effort, the wider the organizational scope, the better. Broad scope makes it easier to find commonalities, to make changes at a macro level for greatest effect. It allows you to prioritize resulting projects across a wider range, enabling optimal resource distribution. As the planning scope narrows, planning directions become more tactical in nature, constrained to work within sometimes incompatible strategic frameworks.

To optimize resource allocation, the pool of resources should be viewed from the highest possible level. Organizational levels inhibit the performance of an information-based organization. Management hierarchies exist for control purposes, but they only build barriers to free information flow. In some companies, installation of an effective decision support system has led to attrition of middle management. It became apparent that some middle managerial levels existed only to control information collection, and summarize information for presentation to higher management.

Ideally, IS planning should be done from a company-wide perspective. Currently, most IS organizations are structured as a sort of mirror image of the overall corporate structure. If the company contains marketing, finance, and product development organizations, chances are it also contains marketing systems, finance systems, and product development systems departments. Each department normally gets personnel and computing resources contingent upon their functional counterpart's importance in the company. In other words, the business units making the most money also tend to get the most IS support.

Logical though this sounds, it can lead to misallocation of IS resources. The most profitable groups rarely have the greatest need for new information systems. In the age of strategic systems and process reengineering, the least stellar business units often need the most IS resources.

When choosing among possible business applications, this means identifying the areas where an application can have the biggest incremental impact. Within the IS organization, it means looking beyond automating software development with CASE tools. Perhaps your group suffers most from poor project management support, or disorganized training programs. The plan must identify which areas need the most immediate attention.

The information architecture presents a blueprint for future development projects. A planning horizon of five years guarantees a large set of potential projects from which to choose. No company has the resources to tackle all of the projects its managers envision. The IS planning process should enable managers to rationally choose which projects should be sponsored, staffed, and launched.

Understand project costs, benefits, feasibility

Linking each project to the business strategies it supports allows you to rank them in terms of overall value to the company. Yet to fully assess the projects' relative priorities, other factors should be considered as well:

- current systems support
- costs and benefits
- resource constraints
- feasibility
- sequential dependencies

Current systems support Some of the functions and data you describe will already be well-supported by existing systems. One could be a software system that streamlines the system testing function, for example, another an efficient manual system for tracking applications training courses. Functions and data that aren't managed well or automated today often deserve immediate attention.

Costs and benefits The financial benefits of application systems—especially strategic systems based on forging new links with customers and suppliers—can be nearly impossible to quantify. Costs are more tangible; values are easily attached to the resources needed to develop systems. Consequently, managers can't normally demonstrate convincing economic benefits of a new system. Quantifiable costs must be balanced against strategic and intangible benefits.

Resource constraints Some projects will require specialized resources. You may have a hundred developers available, but if only one can create expert systems applications, you're limited to developing one or two of these at a time. Aggregate resource usage can be quantified economically, but special resource conflicts should be examined as they arise. CASE implementation projects often require specialized knowledge about a company's development process, technological advances, corporate culture, and business goals. Methodology development projects require similar skills. If you're limited to a few people with this range of knowledge, you might need to stagger these two projects rather than run them in parallel.

Feasibility Many factors affect project feasibility. Feasibility combines two major categories of concern: risk and magnitude. The classic model lists the TELOS risk factors: technical, economic, legal, organizational, and schedule.[11] For projects internal to IS, the organizational and schedule factors carry the most weight.

Gigantic, complex projects stand less chance of success than do small, simple ones. For this reason, development projects should be made as manageable as possible. For instance, a CASE implementation project can be scoped either large or small. Some CASE implementation projects fail precisely because they are scoped too big. Projects that begin with software evaluation end up managing methodology development, metrics, organizational change, training, and hardware upgrades. Projects that explicitly include all of these aspects up front are too large and complex to ever gain approval. Spin off some of these efforts into separate, targeted projects, and you have far less risky project portfolios.

Sequential dependencies A final common sense determinant of project priority receives little attention in the planning literature. Some projects can't start until others have shown results. For example, you can't develop a system to manage customer orders before the project to define customer information requirements has done so. When every project interacts with others, such sequential dependencies are unavoidable. When business goals steer you toward integrated applications and development environments, dependencies sprout like stalks of grass.

Resource allocation

Project prioritization gives the IS manager guidelines for allocating information resources. At this point, aggregate resources can be allocated from the highest priority projects on down, until the resource pool is exhausted. Subsequent tactical planning will then ground these estimates in reality, assigning specific resources to specific projects.

Resources must first be allocated to maintaining existing systems, at an appropriate service level. The resources that remain are discretionary, available for use on projects defined by the architecture. Some of these projects fulfill mandatory legal or governmental requirements. Others that have little value by themselves will be required for the success of future projects. After allocating resources to these, you are left with a pool to use for strategic development.

First measure the factors to:

- determine the strategic goals supported
- identify other intangible benefits
- quantify economic benefits and costs
- assess project feasibility
- work out sequential project dependencies

Now select the feasible projects with the highest strategic and economic benefits. Sequence them according to the dependencies you've uncovered. Now you can allocate resources starting with the highest priority projects, and work your way down.

Plan transitions from current environment

When John Kennedy promised to put men on the moon by 1970, he didn't just set the goal and then ask NASA to find a way to do it. He had already seen plans describing how the goal could be accomplished in that time frame. A strategy was already thought out, and JFK provided the money and commitment to make it happen.

Likewise, the goals described in an IS plan aren't realistic until strategies for achieving them are defined. The simplest planning model of all lists three steps:

1. Set goals.
2. Assess current situation.
3. Figure out how to get there from here.

Most of the IS plan describes goals: blueprints for model software factories. To plan the migration from today's environment to the one sketched out in the planning architectures, the plan should also describe the current situation, and ideas about how to get there from here.

A detailed migration plan will be done at the tactical planning level. At the strategic level, you need to recognize the gaps between what you have and what you want, and suggest some overall strategies for achieving them.

TABLE 7-6 takes the strategic planning information from TABLE 7-4 and lists the current inventories that should be taken for each area, as well as some migration strategy options. These options aren't meant to be fully inclusive, merely illustrative.

Address context of plan

In addition to the content of the plan, you must also consider its context. Context is often more important than the contents. Context includes:

Table 7-6. Current Inventories and Migration Options

Planning Area	Strategic Plan	Current Situation	Migration Strategy Options
Business	• Goals • Functions • Strategic systems opportunities	• Current functions	• Centralize • Decentralize • Reengineer • Acquire capability • Outsource • Divest
Applications	• Applications architecture • New software development paradigms	• Current applications • Current development methods and tools • Existing measurements	• Continue to enhance • Continue to maintain • Reengineer • Rewrite • Retire • Continue to measure
Data	• Conceptual data model	• Existing databases and files	• Keep structure and data • Convert data to new structure • Throw it all away
Organization	• Optimal organizational structure	• Current organizational structure	• No change • Reorganize
Human resources	• Desired skills inventories • New jobs and roles • Career paths • Allocation policies	• Current skills inventories • Job descriptions • Career paths • Allocation policies	• No change • Retain • Shift to new job • Shift to new project
Technology	• Technology architecture • Technology forecasts	• Current hardware, software, and communications configurations	• Purchase new • Upgrade • Relocate • Sell or scrap

- corporate culture and its ability to assimilate the changes implied by new technologies and procedures
- role the IS organization serves within the company
- characteristics of the various divisions and departments that will draw on IS products and services
- accepted methods for allocating IS resources (including personnel, hardware,

communications capabilities, applications, data storage, and consulting support) to other parts of the organization
- level of risk that the firm's management finds appropriate

These contextual factors affect the contents of the plan, and influence the way you present it. For example, assume the IS organization established its role as a centralized provider of services to other functional areas. IS personnel are temporarily assigned to systems projects within functional areas, yet they report to IS managers, not functional managers. If the IS planning team doesn't have the power to alter the traditional role of the IS organization, then the plan must conform to it. Unless the planning team relishes a protracted battle to reorganize IS, the plan they create must be executable by a centralized IS group; it shouldn't place all its bets on a distributed end-user computing strategy.

Contextual factors should also influence how the planning results are presented. When IS is centralized, as in the example above, managers must make a stronger effort to make sure the functional organizations understand and buy into the IS plan. When software development is decentralized, functional managers will pay more attention to the IS plan; after all, you're messing with "their" developers now. Functional managers lose interest more easily when plans affect other groups' people and finances, but not their own.

Some of these contextual factors can be categorized and documented. Methods exist for characterizing and formally describing the external business environment. Yet most are intangible factors, obvious only to company veterans. Failure to address the context often leads to failure of the resulting plan, as many outside consulting firms have discovered. By including as participants some of those whom the plan will affect—software developers and functional managers—you've got most of the context covered. Though top managers understand the corporate culture, the developers and functional managers better understand the idiosyncrasies of their groups. They will usually demonstrate these same idiosyncrasies during planning sessions, subtly tailoring the results to better fit the groups they're meant for.

The next chapter walks through a structured planning effort for a hypothetical IS organization.

8

Designing an IS architecture

For all their knowledge of technology, IS organizations are often the least automated groups around. CASE automates the software development function, but this is only one of many IS activities. There are numerous opportunities to apply information technology within the IS group. The trick is knowing where to start.

For years, software development gurus have advocated structured techniques for strategically planning business applications. Many firms currently use these techniques to prioritize software development projects according to business goals. Yet almost none of them have planned at the same level for IS's own information systems. Information management activities can be planned and analyzed using these same structured techniques. The results then serve to support decisions to use CASE tools and other information systems. Before software developers subject their clients to intense analyses of goals and information needs, they should figure out their own strategic direction.

Information management should be defined and analyzed as a business function on a par with others like marketing or financial management. The importance of information management applications should be weighed against that of other business applications, as part of a company-wide information architecture. Such analysis helps decide whether you should abandon an accounting system rewrite in order to implement CASE tools, or if it's sensible to develop a new strategic marketing system using current IS development technology.

Because of the way most IS budgets are determined, planning for IS applications as part of a company "applications pool" leads to reduced emphasis on information management applications. Other functional applications directly address corporate goals, while information management applications affect them more indirectly, so the functional applications usually get higher billing. For instance, a goal of streamlining shop floor operations is met directly by an application that lets you simulate equipment and worker configurations. Yet applications for the IS group seldom address corporate goals so clearly. A methodology development project, for instance, will partially satisfy a goal to improve information systems reliability. This goal is likely less important to top managers than the one to streamline the shop floor, especially if production costs are rising.

IS goals have been hidden for so long that they aren't high priorities for many top managers, even when a CIO lobbies strongly for them. Management wants a responsive IS group which delivers timely solutions to business problems, on time, within budget, and matching quality standards. They feel this is their due (as it is), and that failure to achieve this is caused by basic incompetence on the part of IS, not a shortfall of technology.

By lumping information management applications into the selection pool with other business applications, funding for their development hinges on the importance of IS goals to top managers. This usually means information management applications get tabled until after many business applications are built. The business applications then suffer from the unstructured, inefficient development methods of the past.

I suggest that strategic IS planning occur prior to company-wide strategic information planning. If a company-wide effort has already happened, the chances are that the resulting applications portfolio did not include information management applications, so a subsequent strategic IS planning project can build on what was done already.

By separating strategic IS planning from corporate strategic information planning, the IS manager can draw a line between funding for business applications and funding for information management applications. IS planning usually results in very strong cases for the highest-rated information management applications. This gives the IS manager the support she needs to justify additional expenditure—often separate from the standard IS budget—to higher management.

Choosing a planning method

Theorists and consultants offer dozens of strategic planing methods. Many are outgrowths of traditional strategic-tactical-operational planning ideas taught in most business schools. Others are directed toward IS planning, whether from a high-level business perspective, or from a mid-level project planning view.

Every company plans uniquely. There are as many different approaches to planning as there are corporate cultures. For IS planning, any approach that fulfills all of the goals outlined in chapter 4 will be adequate. In most cases, pieces of many different planning methodologies must be combined to achieve all of these goals.

Figure 8-1 lists a selected set of formal and semiformal planning methodologies and shows how well each fulfills the planning goals mentioned in chapter 7. Of the methods listed, Information Strategy Planning (ISP) does the best job of business strategy alignment and uncovering strategic systems opportunities. IBM's Business Strategy Planning (BSP) methodology covers many of the same bases as ISP, but tends to ignore changes affecting the business environment.[1] Portfolio analysis concentrates on external market opportunities to the exclusion of internally driven strategies.[2]

The SISP and Booz-Allen Hamilton methodologies focus on cost/benefit analysis, feasibility studies, and allocation of information resources, and the Booz-Allen approach includes a sketchy migration plan from existing and in-process systems to the new architecture.[3]

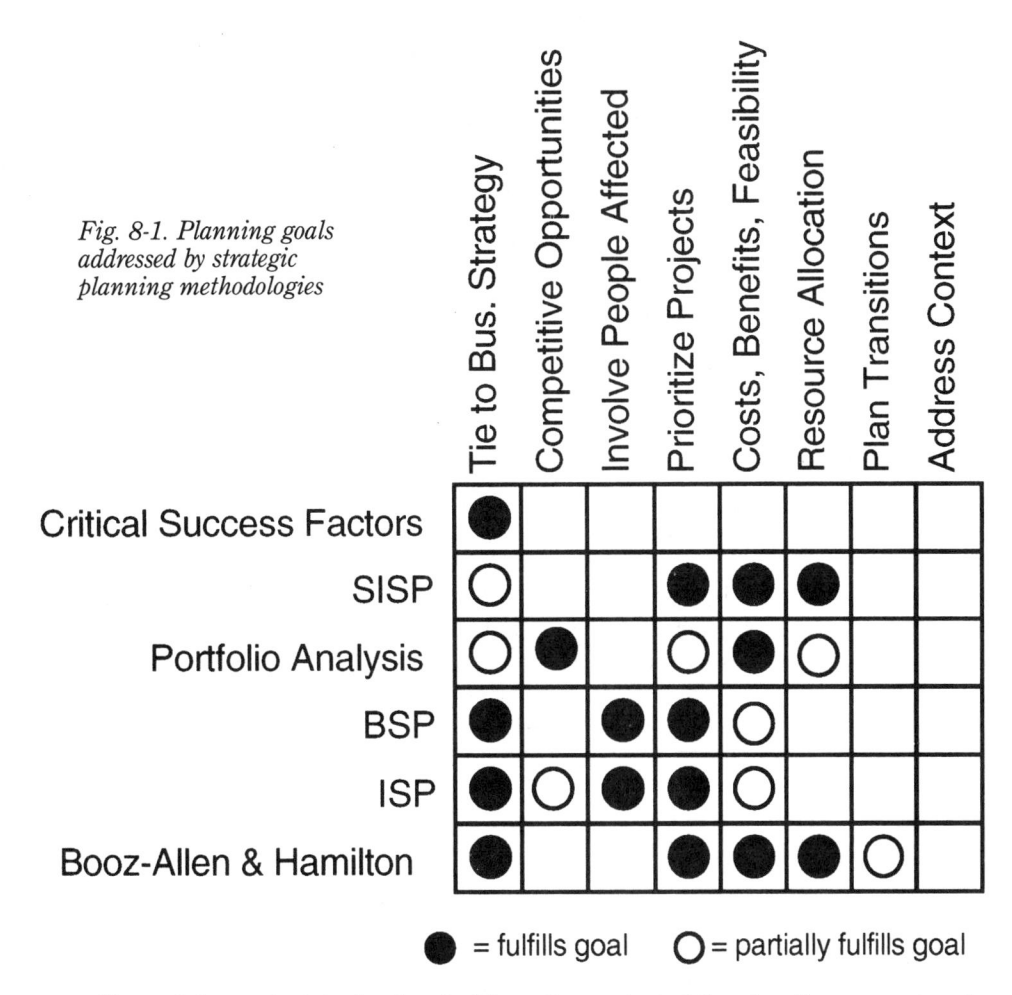

Fig. 8-1. Planning goals addressed by strategic planning methodologies

	Tie to Bus. Strategy	Competitive Opportunities	Involve People Affected	Prioritize Projects	Costs, Benefits, Feasibility	Resource Allocation	Plan Transitions	Address Context
Critical Success Factors	●							
SISP	○			●	●	●		
Portfolio Analysis	○	●		○	●	○		
BSP	●			●	●	○		
ISP	●	○	●	●	○			
Booz-Allen & Hamilton	●			●	●	●	○	

● = fulfills goal   ○ = partially fulfills goal

None of the methodologies listed address the context of the plan: the corporate culture, the role of the IS organization, its relationship with other divisions and departments, accepted methods for allocating IS resources, or level of risk preferred by top management. Many authors in the field of strategic planning discuss these factors, but none have described formal steps for doing so.[4]

The approach I suggest for strategic information resource planning borrows the best parts from many of these methodologies. The main steps of this approach are:

1. Describe the context of the strategic IS plan.
2. Draft a project plan for the strategic IS planning effort.
3. Recruit planning participants.
4. Determine guiding principles for the IS organization.
5. Define goals for the information management function.
6. Identify the major subfunctions of information management.
7. Brainstorm ways to reengineer IS processes.
8. Identify types of data needed for information management.

9. Analyze how well current development systems meet stated goals.
10. Form in-depth analysis projects.
11. Set general guidelines for analysis projects.
12. Assess project feasibility, costs, and benefits.
13. Prioritize projects according to goals supported, feasibility, and sequential dependencies.
14. Allocate aggregate resources to the projects listed.

The first three steps are common sense. Step 4 derives from principles-based techniques favored by Index Corporation, a management consulting firm with expertise in IS architecture. Steps 5, 6, 8, 9 and 10 are drawn from the ISP methodology. Step 7 is a synthesis of various strategic systems brainstorming methods. Steps 11 through 13 are modifications of SISP tasks. Figure 8-2 shows the flow of these steps.

Many of the steps outlined above—especially the ISP steps that are part of the information engineering methodology—are well supported by available CASE tools. This presents a paradox: How can you use a CASE tool to plan for implementing CASE tools? Most companies have some kind of CASE tool already; over 80% have experimented with the technology according to some surveys. What these companies lack is the architecture for making CASE tools productive.

If you don't own a CASE tool that supports strategic planning methods, you can either buy a single trial copy of one that does (some vendors will let you use one for months without paying), hire consultants who have their own CASE capability, or track the planning information manually. This last option isn't that enjoyable but it's definitely feasible.

An IS planning case study

This section presents a lengthy example that applies the above methodology to a hypothetical IS organization. The example concentrates on the information architecture component of the IS strategic plan. Most companies have established methods to identify and plan for new technologies (the technology architecture), and design organizational structures, and plan staffing requirements (the information resources infrastructure).

The techniques illustrated are often used to perform strategic planning for information systems across a company. This case study applies them to strategic planning for applications to automate the IS organization.

I won't describe every step of the approach in great detail. My main purpose is to illustrate the kind of information that makes up a strategic IS architecture, enough for a project manager to customize the approach for her own situation.

Describe the context of the strategic IS plan

The IS organization in question is a department within a mid-sized industrial manufacturing firm with gross sales of around $50 million a year for the past three years. At its headquarters in Seattle, Washington, the IS department manages an installed technology base of one large mainframe with more than 100 dumb terminals, and 30 personal

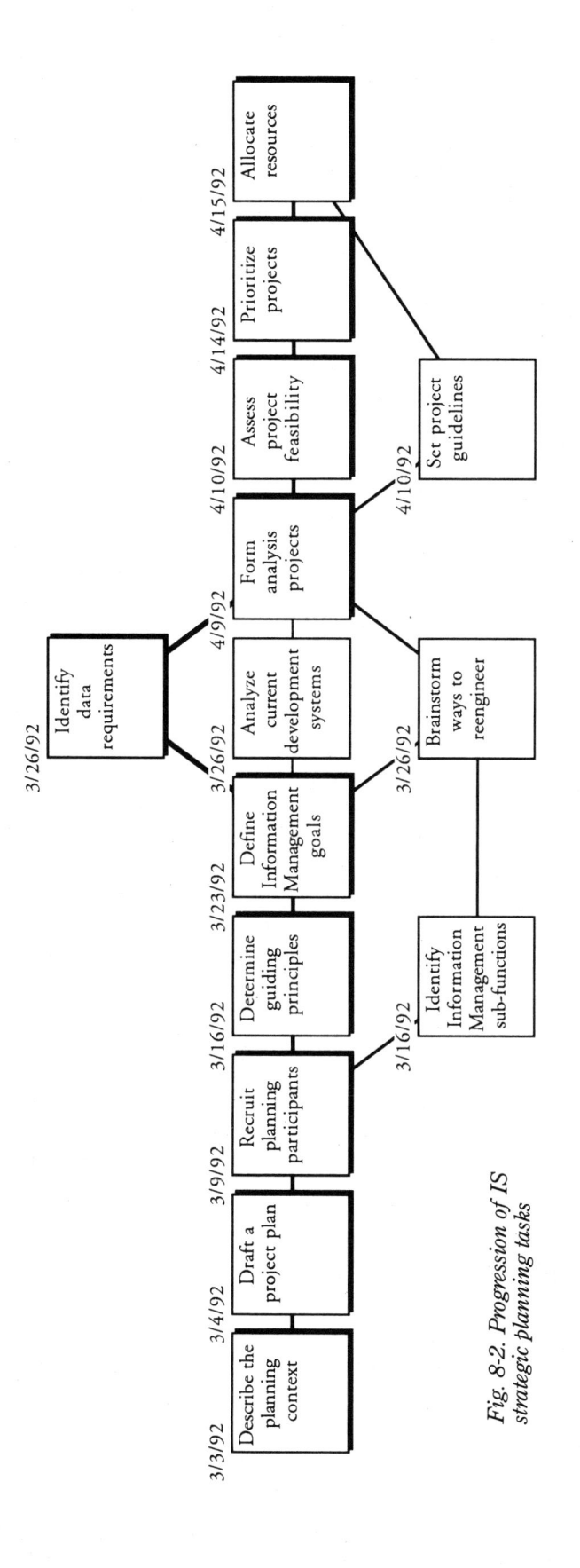

Fig. 8-2. Progression of IS strategic planning tasks

Date	Task
3/3/92	Describe the planning context
3/4/92	Draft a project plan
3/9/92	Recruit planning participants
3/16/92	Determine guiding principles
3/16/92	Identify Information Management sub-functions
3/23/92	Define Information Management goals
3/26/92	Brainstorm ways to reengineer
3/26/92	Analyze current development systems
3/26/92	Identify data requirements
4/9/92	Form analysis projects
4/10/92	Set project guidelines
4/10/92	Assess project feasibility
4/14/92	Prioritize projects
4/15/92	Allocate resources

computers, most of which are linked to the mainframe in some manner. The company owns three manufacturing plants and one distribution center, each of which own and operate their own minicomputer systems.

The IS staff numbers 50 developers and 15 technicians at the Seattle headquarters. In the field, each local IS group contains from 10 to 12 developers, and 5 or 6 technicians.

Figures 8-3 and 8-4 show the organizational structure of Normalco. The IS organization is divided into systems operations, systems development, end-user computing, systems standards, and information technology R&D. The latter three groups were created less than a year ago to address new trends in information technology. Each manufacturing and distribution facility has its own IS department, whose manager reports directly to the company IS manager.

The distributed data centers' main mission is to support systems created by the headquarters manufacturing and distribution systems group. They also create local systems for facilities operations and management.

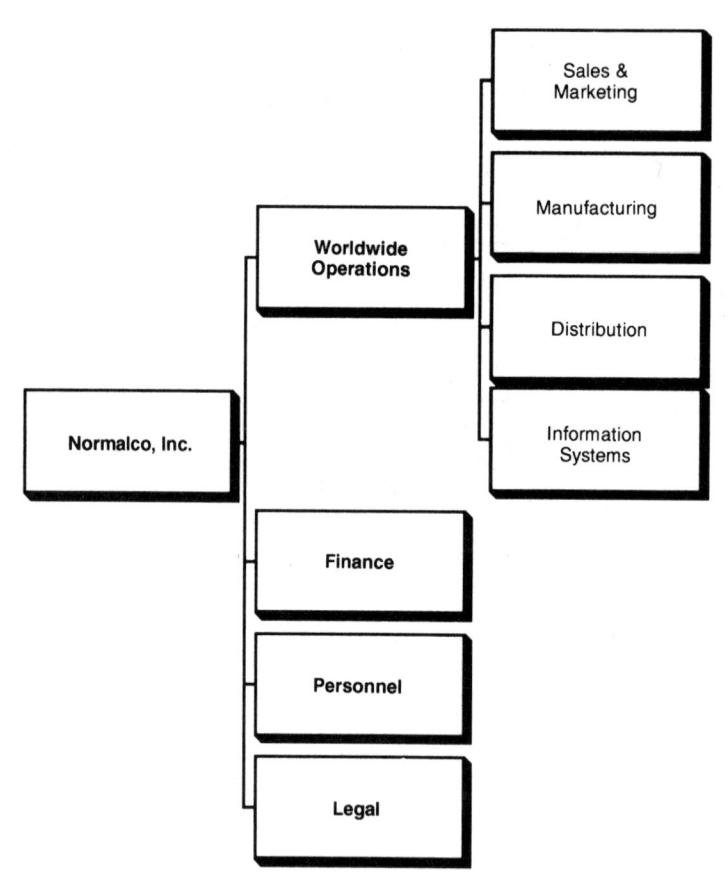

Fig. 8-3. Top-level Normalco organizational structure

An IS planning case study   **183**

Fig. 8-4. Structure of Normalco's IS organization

- **Information Systems**
  - **Systems Development**
    - Database Administration
    - Financial Systems
    - Marketing Systems
    - Manufacturing and Distribution Systems
    - Administrative Systems
  - **Systems Operations**
    - Seattle Data Center
    - Seattle Manufacturing Data Center
    - Omaha Distribution Data Center
    - Dallas Manufacturing Data Center
    - Calgary Manufacturing Data Center
  - **End User Computing**
  - **Systems Standards**
  - **Information Technology R&D**

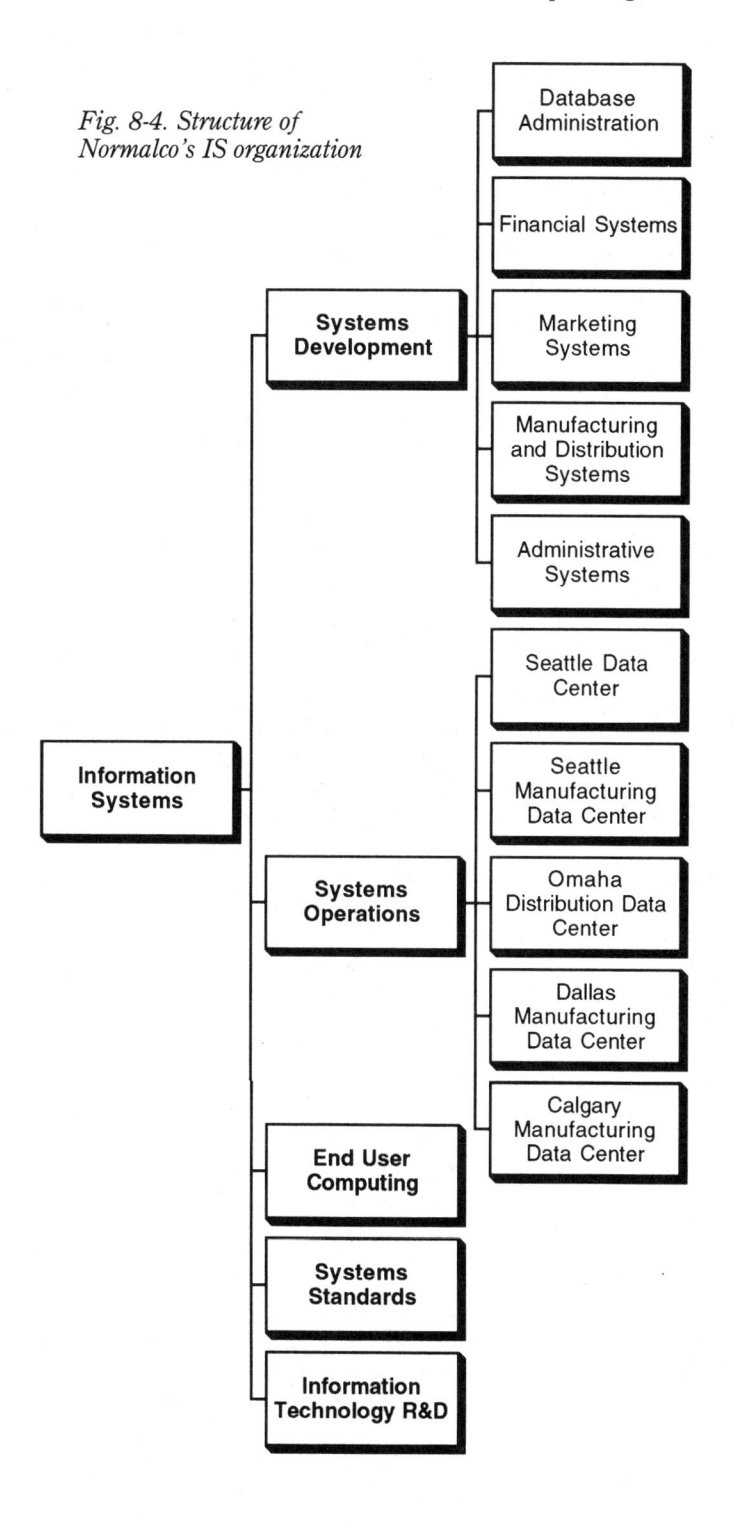

After a discussion the manager of systems development was chartered to develop a proposal for a strategic planning project for the IS organization. He began with a statement of the project's context, including:

- description of the IS organizational structure
- description of the geographic distribution of IS resources
- analysis of the role of IS within the company
- assessment of the organization's ability to accept and learn new technologies

Many planning methodologies include the description of the organization and its geographic locations during steps to define formal business strategy. This information is more useful before planning begins in earnest. It can be used to identify who must be involved in strategic planning. This information is easily gathered from official documents about the organizational structure or the company telephone directory.

A description of the role of IS within the company should give insight into dynamics of intra-organizational relationships, identifying every point where IS interacts with other organizations. This description can form a basis for later discussions about organizational changes.

Normalco's systems development manager drafted the following statement:

> The organization provides information products and services to all functional areas of Normalco. Products are software applications and paper reports produced by centralized applications that run on the Seattle headquarters mainframe. Services include applications maintenance, hardware and software installation, report distribution, applications training, and end-user computing consulting and support. For the most part, products and services are requested by the functional organizations, and these requests are prioritized and either granted or tabled by the systems development group. Each functional organization appoints user support liaison who puts developers in contact with appropriate systems users, and helps them define documentation and training requirements.
>
> The Seattle systems operations group forecasts computer and communications hardware needs for the entire company. It coordinates purchases of mainframes and minicomputers company-wide. Systems operations also maintains mainframe and communications hardware for the Seattle headquarters.
>
> Each distributed data center (in the manufacturing and distribution facilities) has a small operations team which maintains minicomputer and PC hardware and communications equipment for the facility. In some cases, they work closely with the facility industrial engineering group to set up and service computer-integrated equipment. The distributed IS groups develop localized information systems at the request of facility managers. They also provide end-user computing support within the facilities.
>
> Applications training courses are developed with the help of liaisons from personnel training. Systems developers provide information about the applications to personnel training course developers, and are responsible for validating the resulting course materials. Courses are given by trainers from the personnel training organization.
>
> Members of the end-user computing group act as internal consultants to the functional areas. They advise functional managers about purchases of personal

computer hardware and software. They also provide training for supported software packages, including packages, such as spreadsheets and PC database managers, that can be used to develop self-contained PC applications. All end-user computing purchases are made by the functional organizations, though training is provided free of charge.

The systems standards group (currently a single person) defines coding, documentation, testing, and installations standards for all systems developed at Seattle headquarters.

The information technology R&D group (also a one-person group) investigates new developments that can be applied to improving Normalco's information systems capabilities.

Much of this description will seem obvious to IS management, but it provides valuable information for IS planners, all of whom may not be familiar with every facet of the IS organization. This information is essential if an external consultant will be called in to help with the planning effort. In addition, it provides insight into IS's relationship to the rest of the organization, allowing planners to tailor the plan to its environment.

The description of organizational dynamics can be expanded to include:

- inventory of human resources and their skills
- description of the organization's ability to assimilate new technologies
- analysis of top management's feelings toward risk-taking
- ideas for marketing IS services to various functional organizations

These are useful additions to the environmental assessment. However, this first step toward IS planning should be a quick one. It is only a preliminary to the true planning effort, and shouldn't be overdone.

Draft a project plan

The proposal for the IS planning effort should include a first-cut project plan. The project leader should take the following steps to develop this:

- describe project goals and expected benefits
- delineate the planning approach and deliverables
- identify the planning team
- identify a management sponsor
- identify desired planning participants
- collect and assess existing strategic plans
- estimate a project schedule

The project plan can take any format acceptable to IS management.

Depending on level of participation from functional managers and level of detail desired, the planning effort can take anywhere from two to six months. It should not extend beyond six months in any case, since that will cause a loss of momentum and support for the resulting plan.

Recruit planning participants

The set of people needed for IS planning can be divided into four groups: planning team, reference team, executive sponsor, and steering committee.

The planning team, drawn from IS ranks, should include an experienced development project manager. Team members must understand the planning methodology being used, and be conversant with information technology in general. Someone should understand the CASE tool used to support the planning effort, if indeed one is available. An experienced planning facilitator from outside the organization can be called in to help run planning sessions. This option looks better when staffing is short, or when group dynamics make it undesirable for the project leader to facilitate meetings (for instance, when the leader feels uncomfortable about directing superiors).

Normalco's planning team was headed by a software project leader whose project was recently tabled due to user uncertainty about system requirements. It also included the systems standards person, who was a trained JAD facilitator, and a software developer familiar with the current development environment.

The reference team is a group of managers and technical specialists who are on call to the planning team. They will contribute specialized knowledge during specific planning steps. For instance, the manager of the information technology R&D group will help the steering committee brainstorm new strategic systems ideas, but won't attend the rest of the planning sessions. The reference team never meets as a group. However, their managers must allow them time to participate when called upon.

The executive sponsor can determine the fate of the planning project. Normally, the top IS manager or CIO sponsors this effort. He should begin the planning sessions by stating a vision for the IS organization, providing focus for the participants. They must see that the sponsor understands the project goals, and is committed to executing the resulting plan. He must empower participants to set ambitious goals and directions for achieving them. He can sometimes act as a participant, though he must take care not to stifle comments from his subordinates.

When the planning scope is limited to a single IS subunit, the CIO is still the best choice as a sponsor. His participation ensures that even localized results will influence cross-company IS plans.

The steering committee commission, contributes to, questions, and endorses the work of the planning team. While the planning team might disband at the end of the planning process, the steering committee can continue to oversee all follow-on projects. It should include people from both inside and outside the IS organization, specifically IS managers, functional managers, functional systems users, developers, and technicians. The group of IS managers should include the head of each main IS organizational subunit, and some representative managers from remote sites. Even if one subunit is driving the effort (for instance, if marketing systems conducts the effort alone because of an inability to marshal support on a broader scale), representative managers from other groups should be invited. Otherwise, the eventual push for common development environments might scuttle even the best architecture.

Participants should know that they represent their peers, and are entrusted to eventually present the plan's results to their respective constituents.

Participant selection is the trickiest of all tasks. Where possible, select visionaries who can extrapolate future goals from today's environment. Keep the group at most one or two levels apart in the organizational hierarchy. Lower-level employees tend to talk in details, frustrating higher-level managers. Some might feel unqualified to speak face-to-face with managers about management issues, and end up tuning out completely.

Define guiding principles for the IS organization

As hierarchical management practices become less effective in rapidly changing business environments, management by principles gains popularity. Principles don't define policies or strategies; they state overriding values of importance to the company. They also provide direction without enforcing structure, allowing individuals the discretion to form ad hoc structures best suited to the tasks at hand.

Few firms have explicitly stated the principles under which they operate. Levi Strauss and General Electric are notable exceptions, both companies publish statements of principles and encourage worker empowerment within these guidelines. As Levi Strauss' CEO Bob Haas relates, "In a more volatile and dynamic business environment, the controls have to be conceptual. . . . It's the ideas of a business that are controlling, not some manager with authority. Values provide a common language for aligning a company's leadership and its people."[5]

Values can be the cornerstone of an effective IS architecture. If corporate principles are published, IS principles should add to them. Otherwise the IS organization should define a full set of principles from scratch.

Statements about principles can't be trite catch-phrases or meaningless platitudes. They should give guidance about the trade-offs IS personnel face on a daily basis. A sample set of principles is shown in TABLE 8-1.

Define the goals of information management

Goals follow directly from principles. They identify specific objectives that the business must achieve, within the bounds of the stated principles. They sum up a company's mission and purpose, its *raison d'etre*.

Building an information architecture for IS before one is built for the company poses a problem: how can you align IS's goals with the company's if the company's aren't yet known? If top management has already created a structured strategic business plan for a different purpose, your project can draw corporate goals from it. If not, you will be forced to gather these goals yourself.

Some managers resist new planning projects, saying, "We already do strategic planning." Most firms do strategize on a periodic basis. However, the goals that arise from most periodic business plans fall short in three ways:

1. They understate the obvious. Many business plans assume a certain level of knowledge by the reader. Though the company's mission may seem obvious to top managers, it is rarely so to lower-level employees, including IS developers.
2. They state solutions rather than objectives. A durable goal model survives changing times with minor alterations. Many strategic plans present solutions ("Implement automated conveyor system in all plants") rather than goals

Table 8-1. Sample IS Principles Statements

Area	Statement of Principle
Process	• All new applications development projects should follow accepted development methods, and record results of these methods upon completion. • Every development project should attempt to reengineer business processes, not just automate current steps. • Information systems will be used to encourage a common face to customer, suppliers, and other external agents from every unit within the company. • Systems support and maintenance tasks are no less important than new development tasks, and will receive no less recognition.
Data	• Information belongs to the company, not to any specific employee or organizational unit. • Integrated information is more valuable than isolated islands of data. • Shared data must be stored in common data structures and formats. • Each authorized employee must be able to access all of the information he or she needs to do their job effectively and completely. • Information users must have access to development tools to let them add value to the data they receive. • We seek visibility about how each employee contributes to the improvement of customer service, and the profitability of the firm.
Organization	• Business users and systems developers alike are accountable for the quality of information systems. • The IS organization will lead the corporation in applying technology to improve its internal processes. • IS personnel must be business-literate. • IS personnel will be assigned to development projects on an as-needed. basis; they shall not be limited to a specific organization or business focus.
Technology	• We will manage a multi-vendor technical environment, with an emphasis on information connectivity. • We will keep the number of different technologies we use limited, to allow effective technical support. • Business effectiveness is more important than cost-cutting or technical efficiency.

("Reduce transfer times between plant stations by 30% by 1994"). True goals allow for alternative solutions.

3. They ignore the power of information technology to create and transform business processes.

If you have the wherewithal to convince top management to attend a strategic planning session, your first step should be to do so. During this session, brainstorm a list of corporate goals and then refine and structure them, creating a hierarchy of permanent, strategic, and tactical goals for the entire company.

If you are forced to pull corporate goals from published strategy documents, try to distill from them the most essential ones. Buttress these with the mundane day-to-day goals that were originally missed, and add to them new goals to improve competitive advantage by exploiting information technology.

Once you have a corporate goal framework, define subgoals for the information management function and relate them to the corporate ones. Strategic goals might already exist for IS, but they're susceptible to the same criticism: they are often incomplete, and predisposed to offering solutions rather than objectives.

The IS goal model must spring directly from the participants. Lederer and Mendelow rightly criticize both BSP and ISP, saying they "merely attempt to incorporate top management's objectives into the IS plan once the objectives are established for the organization as a whole."[6] To circumvent this criticism, first create the goal model from scratch with the participants, using only corporate business goals and visionary statements of the chief IS manager as your guides. Afterwards, compare this model to past strategic IS plans. Reconcile differences in favor of the new model, and bring forward valid goals from past plans that were omitted during recent planning sessions. The resulting goals will bear the stamp of the planning group, and be taken to heart by them.

Goal format Some advice for defining information management goals:

- Think ahead. The more visionary your goals are, the more value they bring. Encourage the participants to base goals on future desires rather than past struggles. Competitive advantage derives from creativity, not xerography (except for Xerox, that is). For strategic goals, employ a five-year window; for tactical goals, a two to three year window will suffice. Remember these are goals, not action plans. They don't need to be completely practical, just barely attainable.
- Transcend the organization. Functional goals remain long after companies reorganize. Goals should be stated for the information management function rather than the IS organization or its subunits. If a future decision leads to IS decentralization, information management goals will carry on while the organization expires.
- Don't prematurely limit your options. Try to remain neutral about potential technology platforms. "Purchase CASE tool" is not a good goal. It is an implied solution. After going through this process, you might find that a CASE tool is not what you need. These goals act like blinders, limiting the group's vision. Ask the question, "Where do we want to be?" before you ask, "How do we get there?"
- Be realistic. Don't let revolutionary zeal trigger far-fetched goals. There must be a real chance to achieve these objectives within the specific time frame.
- Be specific. The goals you create should be measurable, so you can track future progress. This implies a level of specificity, and a time element to each goal. Progress toward a goal to "improve the software development process" can't easily be measured. However, a goal to "reduce defects in installed systems by 50% each year until 1993" lends itself to easier assessment.

Normalco Goals Figure 8-5 lists goals defined during Normalco planning sessions. The planning team used a CASE tool that models goals as a hierarchy. At the top is the permanent mission for the organization; the next level contains strategic goals, and below these fall tactical ones. Each goal supports only one parent, and each parent goal is fully described by its kids.

IS Mission. Plan, develop, and manage information resources to support business strategies, meet the needs of customers of IS products and services, minimize impacts of rapid changes in the business environment, and enable open exchange of information throughout the company.

1. **Systems support business strategy.** Ensure that information resources are directed toward supporting business goals and improving the company's competitive market advantage.

    1.1 **Align systems with business goals.** Prioritize and develop new systems according to their potential satisfaction of key business goals.

    1.2 **Seek out strategic systems.** Proactively research and identify areas where information technology can enable new business processes, providing competitive market advantages. Develop and implement at least one system that enhances company competitiveness by 1994.

    1.3 **Reengineer business processes.** Critically evaluate existing business processes and redesign them to capitalize on advances in information technology.

2. **Improved IS customer satisfaction.** Increase the satisfaction of information system users by delivering products and services that meet their requirements for cost, timeliness, and quality.

    2.1 **Meet customer system requirements.** Proactively gather, structure, and analyze customer business processes and information needs, and ensure that delivered applications fulfil these requirements. Improve the appropriateness rating in postmortem reviews by 200% by June 1994.

    2.2 **Minimize system defects.** Strive for zero-defect applications, reducing the measure of defects-per-function-point by 300% by June 1994.

    2.3 **Minimize system downtime.** Fix all critical application failures (causing work stoppages) within 24 hours maximum, and 3 hours on average, by June 1994. Limit hardware or communications equipment downtime to less than one hour for 95% of all incidents.

    2.4 **Ensure data integrity.** Protect business data from corruption by unauthorized users, or technical glitches.

    2.5 **Consistent user interface.** Present business data using stable, recognizable, intuitive user interface elements that are similar across all delivery platforms.

    2.6 **Enable distributed data access.** Allow all authorized company employees, no matter how remote from the physical data storage location, to access and analyze integrated business data.

    2.7 **Support management decision making.** Store essential business information in ways that allow flexible access and analysis by company managers.

    2.8 **Provide applications training.** Accelerate customers' learning curves for new applications and information sources through concentrated education programs.

    2.9 **Respond quickly to customer feedback.** Maintain timely communications by responding to customer inquiries within 24 hours.

3. **Streamlined development process.** Optimize the software development process, improving the ratio of quality products created per man-hour and dollar expended.

Fig. 8-5. Normalco information management goal model

Fig. 8-5. Continued.

    3.1 Increase developer productivity. Reduce the time needed to produce high-quality software applications by 300% (compared to 1990 baseline metrics) by June 1994.

    3.2 Follow common methodologies. Establish, maintain, and use repeatable and effective development methods.

    3.3 Simplify project scope. Reduce business system complexity by encapsulating smaller projects and limiting the number of bridges and interfaces they require.

    3.4 Responsive application maintenance. Provide rapid answers to customers who request changes to installed applications. Prioritize change requests according to impacts upon business goals.

    3.5 Coordinate system installations. Package and install applications as integrated system release, minimizing customer's installation costs.

    3.6 Provide tool & technique training. Accelerate developer's learning curves for new techniques and tools through concentrated education programs.

4. Minimize impact of business change. Develop an infrastructure that allows us to respond quickly to changes in the business environment and advances in technology.

    4.1 Integrated data and applications. Minimize information and process redundancy to gain significant quality and productivity benefits. Encourage process reusability and data normalization to achieve this.

    4.2 Continuous process improvement. Strive for annual improvements of 10% or more in developer productivity and accuracy of project time estimates by measuring, reviewing, and enhancing development methods.

    4.3 Forecast resource requirements. Anticipate future needs for personnel and technological information resources, based on strategic alignment of resource plans and business goals.

    4.4 Discover useful new technologies. Seek out, test, and evaluate new products and methods that promise to improve software development processes, or delivery of information and software products to the customer.

Inspiration for these goals came from the personal experiences of steering committee members, and also from information drawn from:

- books and articles about ideal information management practices
- experiences of other successful IS organizations
- information about competitors' information management functions

The goal-brainstorming sessions also generated ideas for other areas of the company: goals about recruiting personnel and improving the manufacturing process. However, these goals pertain to other functions outside the scope of information management. They were recorded, but not included in the resulting goal model.

Often participants have a hard time thinking about goals. They relate better in some cases to the problems they experience day to day. By brainstorming problems first (call them "issues" if you want to keep the session a little more upbeat), you can then generate goals to address them. These goals will only address today's problems, though, so be sure to supplement them with some visionary brainstorming.

Once the goal model is complete, ask steering committee members to evaluate each goal's relative importance. Rank strategic goals by how critical they are to the information management function; rank tactical goals by how critical they are to fulfillment of their parent strategic goal. James Martin proposes a ranking scale similar to the one shown in TABLE 8-2,[7] though other schemes can also be used.

Normalco employed forced ranking techniques to rate their goals, as shown in TABLE 8-3. They gave a unique value to each strategic goal, and then to each set of tactical goals. They obtained the overall result by multiplying the strategic and tactical factors.

Table 8-2. Criticality Ranking Scale

Rank	Criticality
5	The function cannot continue if the goal is not met.
4	Failure to meet the goal will cause operational disruptions.
3	The goal supports but does not drive day-to-day operations.
2	The goal will only indirectly support day-to-day operations.
1	The goal is desirable, but not required to support the function.

Identify major subfunctions and data groupings

The IS plan's information architecture contains models of the subfunctions under "information management," and of the data needed to effectively manage business information. Be visionary about functions and data just as you were when defining IS goals. Include in the functional model activities that you haven't initiated, but think you should. Include in the data model information you might not need today, but probably will tomorrow.

Figure 8-6 shows a decomposition diagram for Normalco's information management function. Notice that this hierarchy is very different from the company's organizational structure. It describes what activities are done, not who does them. It's important to keep the functions rather abstract, not too detailed. For instance, the system construction function could be split into detailed code, compile, and link processes, but this detail adds little to the strategic planning process. To keep the planning effort manageable, keep your functions high-level. This helps you avoid another pitfall: the tendency to tie functions to a specific technology or implementation. For instance, in a CASE environment, the systems construction function might divide into "generate code" and "bind to database schema." If you go to this level now, you put limits on later solutions.

You might find it useful to supplement the functional model with a view of how the functions relate to organizational structure. A matrix can be used to show which subunits set policy, perform, or indirectly support which functions. This matrix helps identify the stakeholders in each function. It also provides a checklist for each subunit, identifying every function that they perform.

Table 8-3. Goal Ranking Worksheet

Parent Goal	Rank	# of Kids	Child Goal	Rank	Weighted Rank*
Improved customer satisfaction	3	9	Meet customer system requirements	1	47
Systems support business strategies	1	3	Align systems with business goals	1	47
Minimized impact of business change	2	4	Integrated data and applications	1	45
Improved customer satisfaction	3	9	Minimize system defects	2	43
Streamline development process	4	6	Increase developer productivity	1	43
Systems support business strategies	1	3	Reengineer business processes	2	43
Improved customer satisfaction	3	9	Ensure data integrity	3	40
Minimized impact of business change	2	4	Continuous process improvement	2	40
Systems support business strategies	1	3	Seek out strategic systems	3	40
Improved customer satisfaction	3	9	Minimize system downtime	4	37
Streamline development process	4	6	Follow common methodologies	2	37
Minimized impact of business change	2	4	Forecast resource requirements	3	35
Improved customer satisfaction	3	9	Support management decision-making	5	33
Improved customer satisfaction	3	9	Respond quickly to customer feedback	6	30
Minimized impact of business change	2	4	Discover useful new technologies	4	30
Streamline development process	4	6	Simplify project scope	3	30
Improved customer satisfaction	3	9	Provide applications training	7	27
Improved customer satisfaction	3	9	Enable distributed data access	8	23
Streamline development process	4	6	Responsive application maintenance	4	23
Improve customer satisfaction	3	9	Consistent user interface	9	20
Streamline development process	4	6	Provide tool and technique training	5	17
Streamline development process	4	6	Coordinate system installations	6	10

*Weighted rank = 50 − (Parent rank × Child rank × (10 / # of kids))

194 Designing an IS architecture

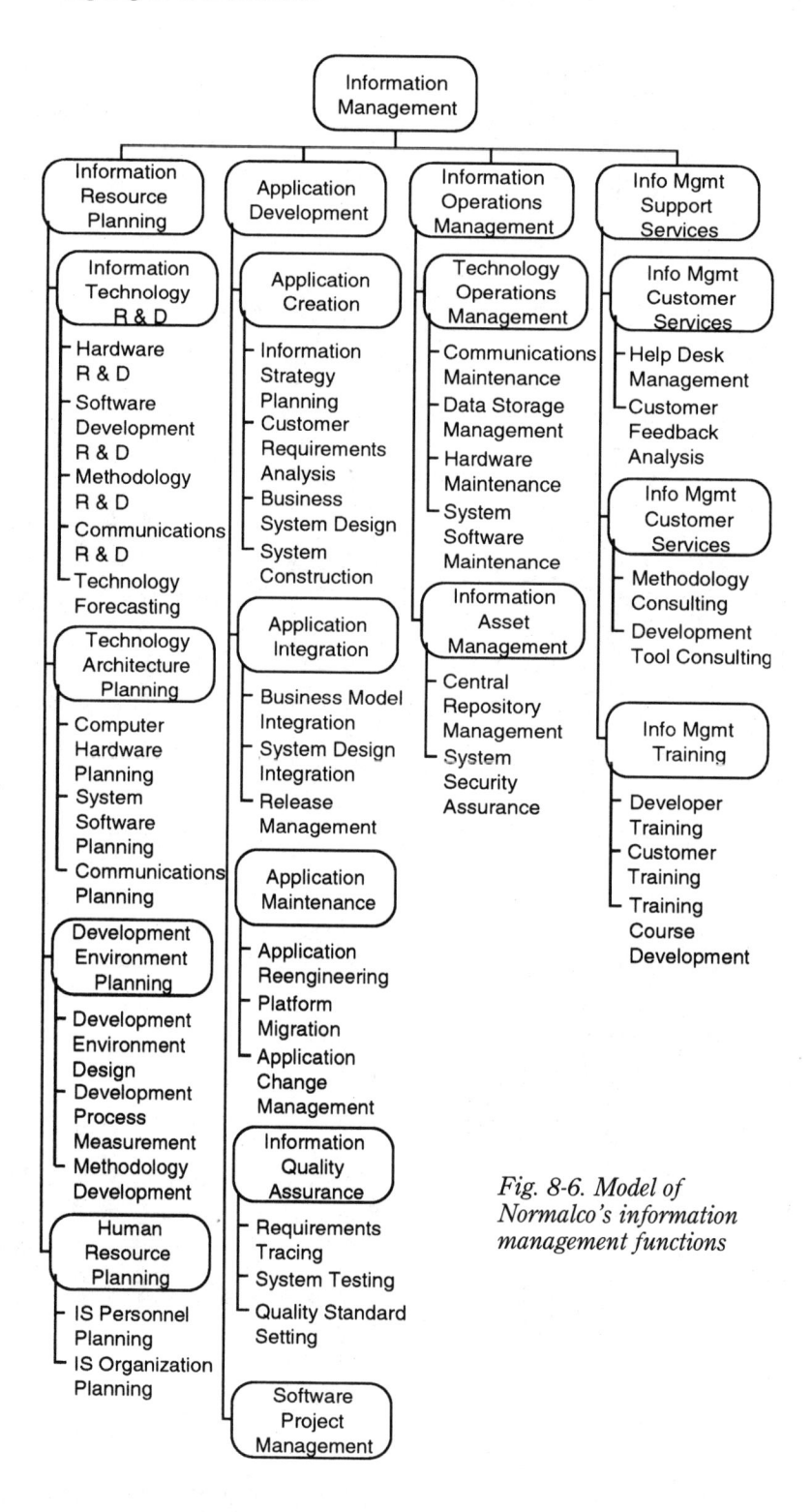

- **Information Management**
  - **Information Resource Planning**
    - **Information Technology R & D**
      - Hardware R & D
      - Software Development R & D
      - Methodology R & D
      - Communications R & D
      - Technology Forecasting
    - **Technology Architecture Planning**
      - Computer Hardware Planning
      - System Software Planning
      - Communications Planning
    - **Development Environment Planning**
      - Development Environment Design
      - Development Process Measurement
      - Methodology Development
    - **Human Resource Planning**
      - IS Personnel Planning
      - IS Organization Planning
  - **Application Development**
    - **Application Creation**
      - Information Strategy Planning
      - Customer Requirements Analysis
      - Business System Design
      - System Construction
    - **Application Integration**
      - Business Model Integration
      - System Design Integration
      - Release Management
    - **Application Maintenance**
      - Application Reengineering
      - Platform Migration
      - Application Change Management
    - **Information Quality Assurance**
      - Requirements Tracing
      - System Testing
      - Quality Standard Setting
    - **Software Project Management**
  - **Information Operations Management**
    - **Technology Operations Management**
      - Communications Maintenance
      - Data Storage Management
      - Hardware Maintenance
      - System Software Maintenance
    - **Information Asset Management**
      - Central Repository Management
      - System Security Assurance
  - **Info Mgmt Support Services**
    - **Info Mgmt Customer Services**
      - Help Desk Management
      - Customer Feedback Analysis
    - **Info Mgmt Customer Services**
      - Methodology Consulting
      - Development Tool Consulting
    - **Info Mgmt Training**
      - Developer Training
      - Customer Training
      - Training Course Development

Fig. 8-6. Model of Normalco's information management functions

The function-to-organization matrix also pinpoints inefficiences in organizational design. Ideally, policy for each centralized function should be set by only one group. For instance, every systems development group sets their own policy for development process measurement today, yet common policy would enable comparison of process effectiveness across subunits, not just within them.

Normalco's matrix, shown in FIG. 8-7, is limited to the IS organization. However, if significant end-user development occurs outside the IS group, you should include other organizational units.

Another matrix can help identify missing functions or neglected goals. By relating each function to the goal it supports, you can rationalize both. Once you've completed the matrix, cursory analysis points out gaps in both models. If a function doesn't support any of the goals listed, you have either omitted a goal, or discovered a function that's outlives its usefulness. On the other hand, if a goal has no functional support, you should figure out what you must do to achieve the goal, and add it to your functional model. Figure 8-8 shows Normalco's function-to-goal matrix.

Brainstorm ways to reengineer IS processes

The steering committee suggested visionary goals, functions, and data requirements, but the chances are they all represent incremental changes from current practices. Usually you must make an extra effort to break old paradigms and generate truly innovative ideas. Use some of the techniques below to drive brainstorming sessions about new and redesigned IS functions:

- Build upon information from advanced technology groups within the company. Invite research and development engineers to present a list of soon-to-be-available technologies. Brainstorm ways the IS organization might exploit each one.
- Find out what other firms are doing. The airline industry came up with the concept or rewarding frequent fliers with discounts and prizes. Since then companies in other industries—from hotels to video rental stores—have adopted the concept, using it to strategic advantage. Investigate the software development environments of other firms, and see how they've reengineered the process.
- Think of the most perfect way to handle each function. What if the end-users could record the system specification themselves? What if systems could anticipate the information a manager wants to see, and notify her when it's available? Though far-fetched, these ideas can be scaled back to realizable goals and functions.
- List the general ways information technology can be used to improve processes. A list compiled by Thomas H. Davenport and James E. Short is shown in TABLE 8-4. Ask how each capability might impact the Information Management function. TABLE 8-5 shows the ideas this exercise generated for Normalco's IS steering committee.

Update the goals, function, and data models to reflect results of these brainstorming processes, as appropriate.

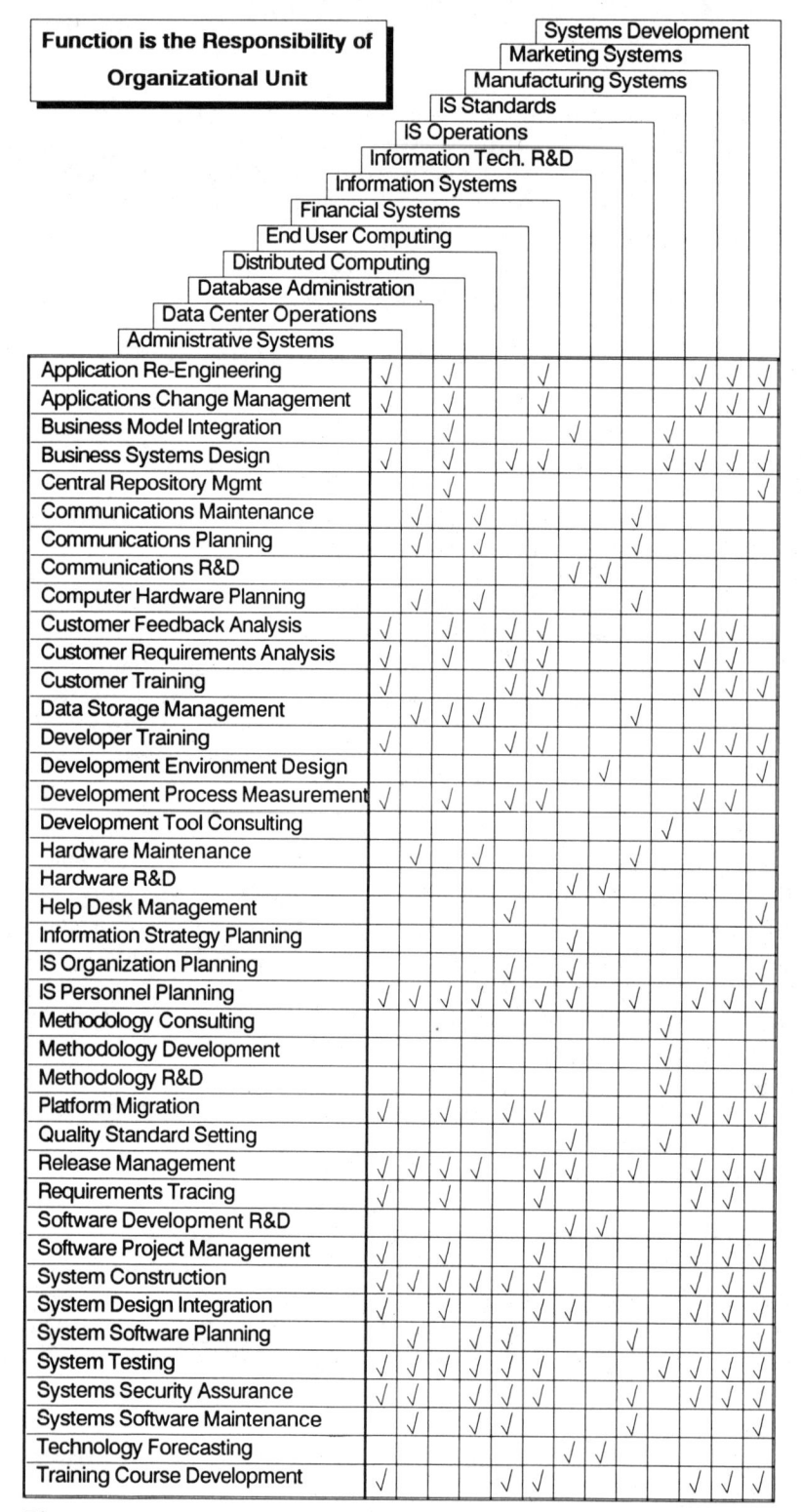

Function	Administrative Systems	Data Center Operations	Database Administration	Distributed Computing	End User Computing	Financial Systems	Information Systems	Information Tech. R&D	IS Operations	IS Standards	Manufacturing Systems	Marketing Systems	Systems Development
Application Re-Engineering	√		√			√					√	√	√
Applications Change Management	√		√			√					√	√	√
Business Model Integration			√				√			√			
Business Systems Design	√		√		√	√					√	√	√
Central Repository Mgmt			√										√
Communications Maintenance		√		√				√					
Communications Planning		√		√				√					
Communications R&D								√	√				
Computer Hardware Planning		√		√				√					
Customer Feedback Analysis	√		√		√	√					√	√	
Customer Requirements Analysis	√		√		√	√					√	√	
Customer Training	√				√	√					√	√	√
Data Storage Management		√	√	√				√					
Developer Training	√				√	√					√	√	√
Development Environment Design								√					√
Development Process Measurement	√		√		√	√					√	√	
Development Tool Consulting										√			
Hardware Maintenance		√		√				√					
Hardware R&D							√	√					
Help Desk Management				√									√
Information Strategy Planning							√						
IS Organization Planning				√			√						√
IS Personnel Planning	√	√	√	√	√	√	√		√		√	√	√
Methodology Consulting		√								√			
Methodology Development										√			
Methodology R&D										√			√
Platform Migration	√		√		√	√					√	√	√
Quality Standard Setting						√				√			
Release Management	√	√	√	√		√	√		√		√	√	√
Requirements Tracing	√		√			√					√	√	
Software Development R&D							√	√					
Software Project Management	√		√			√					√	√	√
System Construction	√	√	√	√	√	√					√	√	√
System Design Integration	√		√			√	√				√	√	√
System Software Planning		√		√	√			√					√
System Testing	√	√	√	√	√	√			√		√	√	√
Systems Security Assurance	√	√		√	√				√		√	√	√
Systems Software Maintenance		√		√	√			√					√
Technology Forecasting							√	√					
Training Course Development	√				√	√					√	√	√

Fig. 8-7. Matrix of organizational units responsible for information management functions

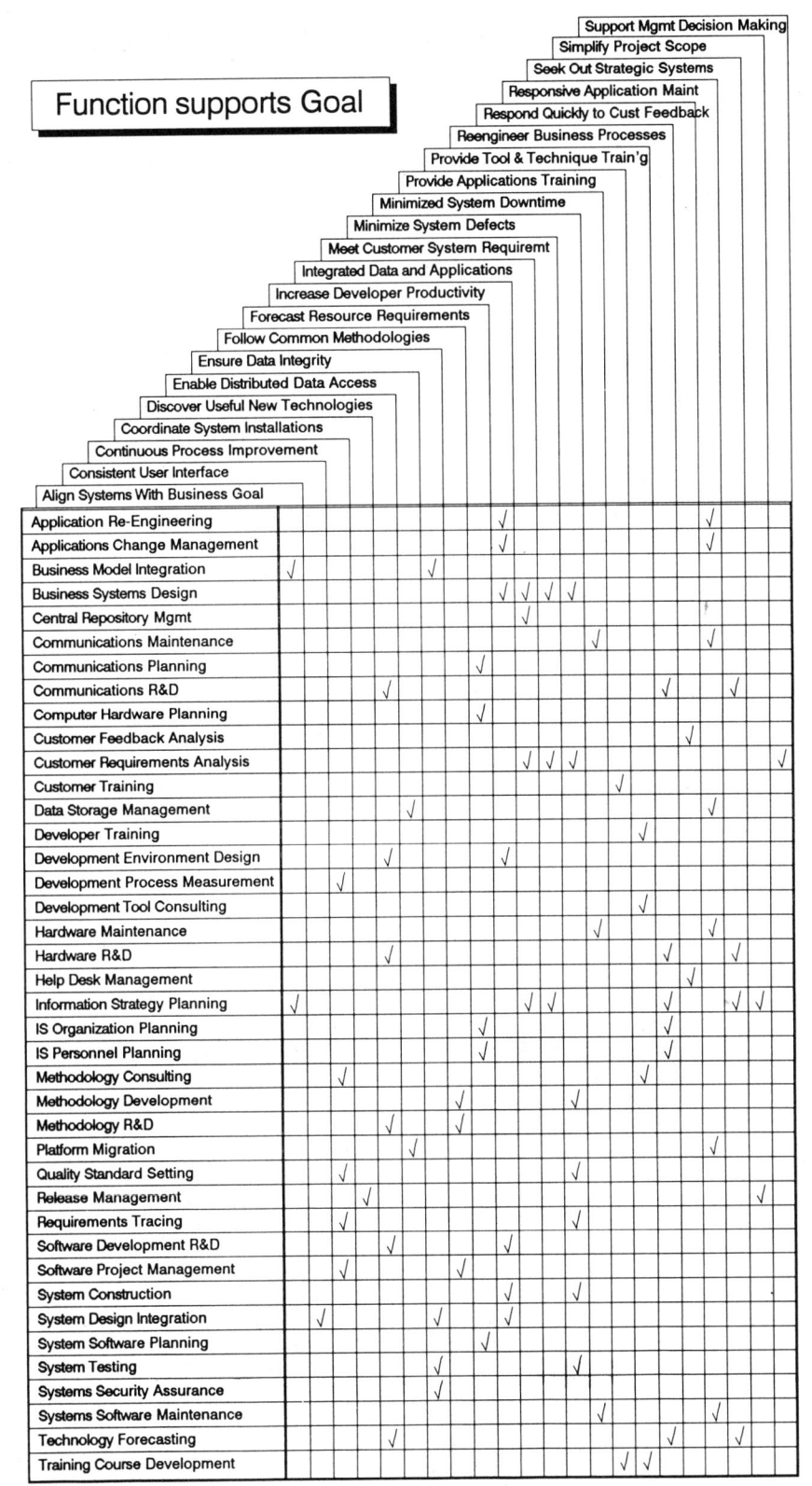

Fig. 8-8. Matrix of goals supported by functions

Goals (columns):
1. Align Systems With Business Goal
2. Consistent User Interface
3. Continuous Process Improvement
4. Coordinate System Installations
5. Discover Useful New Technologies
6. Enable Distributed Data Access
7. Ensure Data Integrity
8. Follow Common Methodologies
9. Forecast Resource Requirements
10. Increase Developer Productivity
11. Integrated Data and Applications
12. Meet Customer System Requiremt
13. Minimize System Defects
14. Minimized System Downtime
15. Provide Applications Training
16. Provide Tool & Technique Train'g
17. Reengineer Business Processes
18. Respond Quickly to Cust Feedback
19. Responsive Application Maint
20. Seek Out Strategic Systems
21. Simplify Project Scope
22. Support Mgmt Decision Making

Function	1	2	3	4	5	6	7	8	9	10	11	12	13	14	15	16	17	18	19	20	21	22
Application Re-Engineering											√							√				
Applications Change Management											√							√				
Business Model Integration	√						√															
Business Systems Design										√	√	√	√									
Central Repository Mgmt											√											
Communications Maintenance														√				√				
Communications Planning									√													
Communications R&D					√													√		√		
Computer Hardware Planning									√													
Customer Feedback Analysis																		√				
Customer Requirements Analysis										√	√	√										√
Customer Training															√							
Data Storage Management				√														√				
Developer Training																√						
Development Environment Design					√					√												
Development Process Measurement			√																			
Development Tool Consulting																√						
Hardware Maintenance														√				√				
Hardware R&D					√													√		√		
Help Desk Management															√							
Information Strategy Planning	√									√	√							√		√	√	√
IS Organization Planning									√									√				
IS Personnel Planning									√									√				
Methodology Consulting			√													√						
Methodology Development								√					√									
Methodology R&D					√			√														
Platform Migration				√														√				
Quality Standard Setting			√										√									
Release Management				√																		√
Requirements Tracing			√										√									
Software Development R&D					√						√											
Software Project Management			√					√														
System Construction										√			√									
System Design Integration	√						√				√											
System Software Planning									√													
System Testing							√						√									
Systems Security Assurance							√															
Systems Software Maintenance														√				√				
Technology Forecasting					√												√			√		
Training Course Development															√	√						

Table 8-4. Capabilities of Information Technology to Transform Business Processes

Information Technology Capability	Possible Process Impact
Transactional	• Transform unstructured processes into routinized transactions.
Geographical	• Transfer information with rapidity and ease across large distances, making processes independent of geography.
Automational	• Replace or reduce human labor in a process.
Analytical	• Bring complex analytical methods to bear on a process.
Informational	• Bring vast amounts of detailed information into a process.
Sequential	• Enable changes in the sequence of tasks in a process, often allowing multiple tasks to be worked on simultaneously.
Knowledge management	• Allow capture and dissemination of knowledge and expertise to improve the process.
Tracking	• Allow detailed tracking of task status, inputs, and outputs.
Disintermediation	• Connect two parties within a process that would otherwise communicate through an intermediary (internal or external).

Reprinted from "The New Industrial Technology and Business Process Redesign" by Thomas H. Davenport and James Short, *Sloan Management Review*, Summer 1990, p. 17 by permission of publisher. Copyright 1990 by the Sloan Management Review Association. All rights reserved.

Table 8-5. Application of Information Technology to Information Management Functions

Information Technology Capability	Impact on Information Management Functions
Transactional	• Formalize analysis and design processes.
Geographical	• Enable cooperative systems development across geographic distances (e.g., allow Calgary Data Center and Seattle Systems Development to work together on a software project). • Quickly share R & D findings among data centers.
Automational	• Automate the regression testing function. • Automate document creation.
Analytical	• Verify correctness and completeness of analysis and design models.
Informational	• Centrally manage large quantities of software engineering data.
Sequential	• Move away from a sequential, waterfall methodology towards a rapid, iterative one.
Knowledge management	• Distribute methodology information, and provide expert tutorial services for developers.
Tracking	• Streamline software project management functions. • Automatically compile software failure statistics and track production fixes.
Disintermediation	• Allow system users direct access to prototype software products. • Allow system users to create and manage their own information management issues, and system enhancement requests.

Identify types of data

The data portion of the information architecture can take two forms: a list of generalized subject areas, or a conceptual entity-relationship model. In many cases, a list of subject areas is enough. A subject area is a category of information centered on a resource, product, or activity that interests the IS group. For instance, "software applications," "development tools," and "computer hardware" described subject areas or interest to IS professionals.

A conceptual data model arranges these subject areas—or more detailed data classifications, called entities—graphically, identifying how they relate to each other. If you anticipate eventually developing your own information systems to support information management functions, then you will want to model your data this way. Such systems might help manage the development methodology, or track development progress, or streamline hardware installations. Normalco's planners intend to purchase and adapt their IS support systems, so they declined to model their data requirements in this format.

Once you've identified the subject areas of entity types, relate them to the subfunctions you created above. An association matrix serves this purpose well. Mark how each function will interact with the subject area or entity type: will it create, read, update, or delete the information? Most CASE tools that use matrices allow you to use a C, R, U, or D value to describe this relationship. Figures 8-9 and 8-10 show Normalco's CRUD matrix, as it's known in the vernacular.

Analyze how well current development systems meet goals

Having defined where you want to be, now take a look at where you are. Take stock of the systems you currently use to support the functions you've modeled. List development language and packages used to create software applications, productivity tools used by developers, and associated applications like project or issue management systems.

Identify the functions that each system performs, and rate how well it performs them. This can be done in matrix form, as illustrated for Normalco in FIG. 8-11. This example matrix is noticeably sparse; most IS organizations are very lightly automated. The systems IS uses concentrate heavily in the area of system construction.

Form projects from function and data groupings

Now that you've decided your high-level functional and data requirements, it's time to make something concrete out of them. Up to this point, you've defined the building blocks of your information architecture. The next step is to build project areas from these blocks.

A project area is a combination of closely related functions and subject areas. Information engineering methodologists know these as business or analysis areas. The shape of each area defines the scope for a further development project. Scope these project areas broad enough so that further analysis can uncover and exploit commonalities. Scope them small enough so that a project group can investigate them thoroughly within four to twelve months.

Function involves Subject Area

C=Create
R=Read
U=Update
D=Delete

Function	Applications	Business Goals	Customer Req'ts Issues	Databases	Development Tools	Hardware	IS Customers
Application Re-Engineering	U			U	R	R	
Applications Change Management	U			U			
Business Model Integration		R	U				
Business Systems Design	C			C	C		
Central Repository Mgmt	R				R		
Communications Maintenance	R					U	
Communications Planning		R				C	
Communications R&D		R				C	
Computer Hardware Planning		R				C	
Customer Feedback Analysis	R		C				R
Customer Requirements Analysis		R	C				R
Customer Training	R			R		R	U
Data Storage Management				U	R		
Developer Training				R	R	R	
Development Environment Design		R			C	R	
Development Process Measurem't	R				R		
Development Tool Consulting			C		R		
Hardware Maintenance	R					U	
Hardware R&D		R				C	
Help Desk Management	R		C		R		R
Information Strategy Planning	C	C					
IS Organization Planning		R			R		U
IS Personnel Planning		R			R	R	U
Methodology Consulting			C		R		
Methodology Development		R			R		
Methodology R&D		R			R		
Platform Migration	C			C	R	R	
Quality Standard Setting		R					
Release Management	U	R	R				
Requirements Tracing		R					
Software Development R&D		R			C		
Software Project Management	U	R		R	R	R	R
System Construction	U			U	R	R	
System Design Integration	R			R			
System Software Planning	U	R		U		U	
System Testing	U						
Systems Security Assurance	R			R			U
Systems Software Maintenance	R					U	
Technology Forecasting		R					
Training Course Development	R			R	R	R	R

Fig. 8-9. First part of matrix of subject areas referenced by functions

Function involves Subject Area	IS Developers	Methodologies	Software Dev't Projects	Software Engineering Objects	Software Quality Statistics	Technological Changes	Training Courses
Application Re-Engineering				C			
Applications Change Management			R	C	C		
Business Model Integration				D			
Business Systems Design				C			
Central Repository Mgmt			R	U	C		
Communications Maintenance							
Communications Planning						R	
Communications R&D						U	
Computer Hardware Planning						R	
Customer Feedback Analysis			R		C		
Customer Requirements Analysis				C			
Customer Training							U
Data Storage Management						R	
Developer Training	U	R					U
Development Environment Design	R	R	R			R	
Development Process Measurem't	R	U	R	R	C		
Development Tool Consulting	R	R	U				
Hardware Maintenance							
Hardware R&D						U	
Help Desk Management							
Information Strategy Planning			C			R	
IS Organization Planning	U	R					
IS Personnel Planning	U	R	R				R
Methodology Consulting	R	R	R				
Methodology Development	R	C	R			R	
Methodology R&D		C				U	
Platform Migration				C			
Quality Standard Setting					C		
Release Management			C	R			
Requirements Tracing			R	R	R	C	
Software Development R&D		R				U	
Software Project Management	R	R	U	R	C		
System Construction				C			
System Design Integration			R	C			
System Software Planning						R	
System Testing				R	C		
Systems Security Assurance	U						
Systems Software Maintenance							
Technology Forecasting						C	
Training Course Development	R	R					C

Fig. 8-10. Second part of matrix of subject areas referenced by functions

Function is implemented by Existing System

Function	Automated Batch Test Executor	Change Control Manager	COBOL Code Restructurer	COBOL Compiler	COBOL Subroutine Library	Database Optimizer	Flow Chart Tool	Mainframe 4GL	PC Database Manager	Service Request Tracking	Software Project Scheduler	Software Project Time Tracker	Spreadsheet	Test Data Management System	User Security System
Application Re-Engineering			√												
Applications Change Management		√						√							
Business Model Integration															
Business Systems Design							√								
Central Repository Mgmt															
Communications Maintenance															
Communications Planning															
Communications R&D															
Computer Hardware Planning															
Customer Feedback Analysis															
Customer Requirements Analysis										√					
Customer Training															
Data Storage Management						√									
Developer Training															
Development Environment Design															
Development Process Measurement															
Development Tool Consulting															
Hardware Maintenance															
Hardware R&D															
Help Desk Management															
Information Strategy Planning															
IS Organization Planning															
IS Personnel Planning															
Methodology Consulting															
Methodology Development															
Methodology R&D															
Platform Migration															
Quality Standard Setting															
Release Management															
Requirements Tracing													√		
Software Development R&D															
Software Project Management											√	√			
System Construction					√			√	√		√				
System Design Integration						√									
System Software Planning															
System Testing	√														
Systems Security Assurance															√
Systems Software Maintenance															
Technology Forecasting															
Training Course Development															

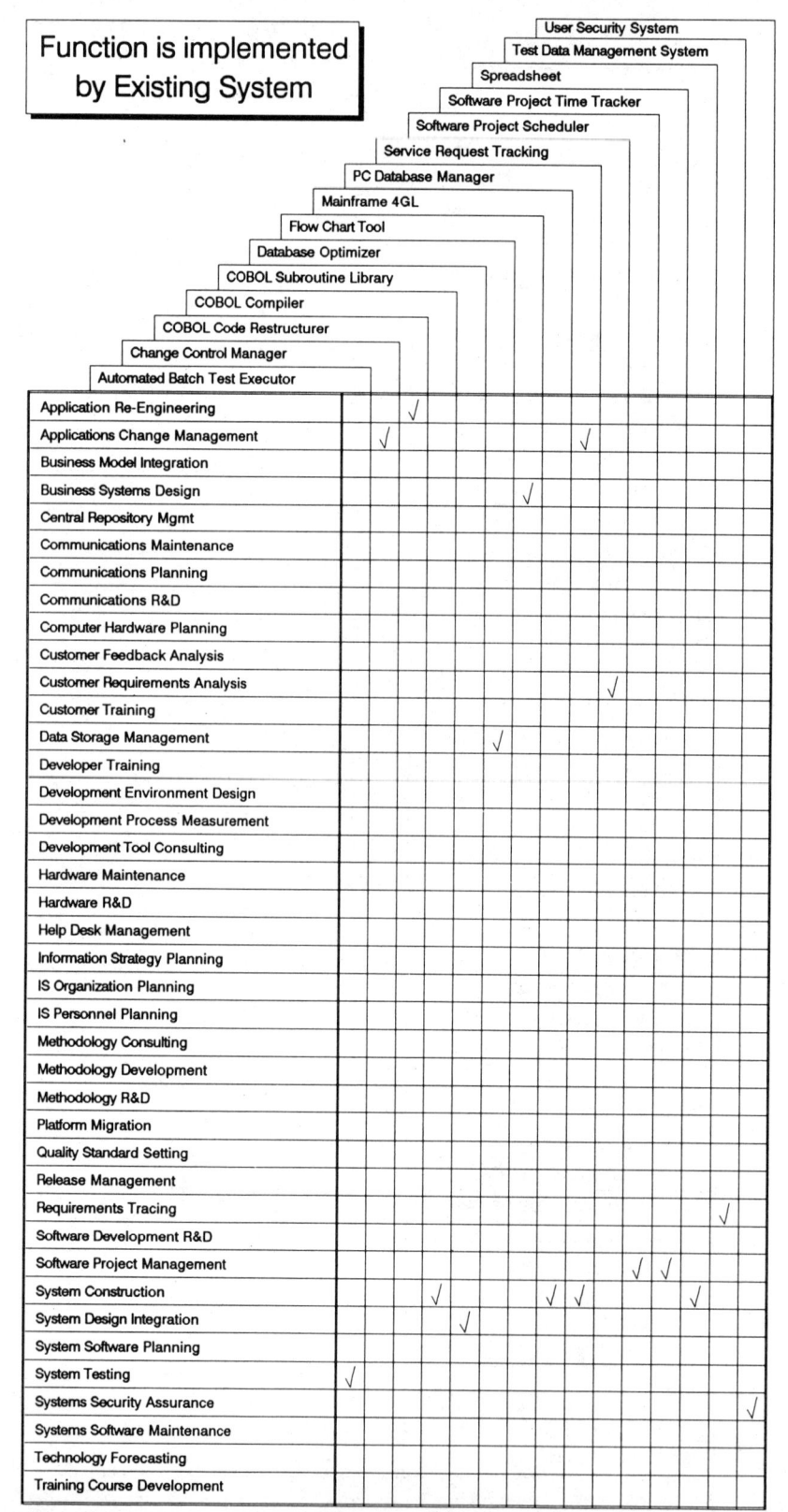

Fig. 8-11. Matrix of current systems that support functions

A technique called clustering can simplify the job of defining project areas. Clustering operates on relationships between functions and subject areas, grouping together functions that involve similar subject areas. Many CASE tools will automatically cluster these functions and subject areas for you, though the final groupings must usually be manually tweaked to make them more sensible. However, complex clustering algorithms overwhelm the pencil-and-paper planner. Without a CASE tool, it's best to group functions and data into projects "by eye."

The number of projects you form should vary according to the IS organization's size. The smaller the organization, the fewer the projects, and consequently, the broader the scope of each project. Information gathering is simpler in smaller companies. Broad survey projects can be done in the same time it takes a narrowly scoped project to finish in a large organization.

Keep in mind that not all of the follow-on projects will result in automated systems. It's safe to assume that investigation into the software development process will lead to some sort of automated tool creation or purchase. However, a project like methodology development might just lead to creation of methodology documents and guidelines on how to use them. When forming these projects, try not to presuppose the form of the final results. Pass these projects to competent analysts who can thoroughly investigate and recommend alternate solutions.

TABLE 8-6 shows the projects that Normalco formed. One very broad project addresses the entire software development life cycle, from requirements-gathering through application maintenance reengineering. Another broad project covers the entire planning sequence, from strategic planning down to planning for all sorts of information resources. The planners felt the wide scope of these projects would allow analysts the most freedom to streamline functions involved. Note how the projects fall into two distinct categories: software development (the first four in the list), and management thereof (the remainder).

Despite its name, Normalco has its idiosyncrasies. Their project list might differ wildly from something your company would create. Still, many analysis areas on this list should be at least considered by your company. Many industry analysts agree that the following areas should be investigated when planning for integrated CASE:[8]

- strategic information systems planning
- requirements analysis and systems design
- applications maintenance and reengineering
- information quality assurance
- methodology development
- project management and process measurement
- consulting training

When preparing IS plans, make sure you've considered all of the above. Throw them out if they seem like overkill, but think about them first.

Set guidelines for analysis projects

Before estimating costs and benefits for each project, it's best to set some ground rules. Are you considering developing your own CASE tools, or do you only want to think

Table 8-6. Normalco Analysis Areas within Information Management

Analysis Area	Functions Included
Information resource planning	• Information strategy planning • Hardware planning • Communications planning • System software planning • IS personnel planning • IS organization planning
Software development process	• Customer requirements analysis • Business model integration • Business system design • System design integration • System construction • Application reengineering • Platform migration • Application change movement
Information quality assurance	• Quality standard setting • Requirements tracing • System testing • System security assurance
Software project management	• Software project management • Release management • Development process measurement
Development environment design	• Methodology development • Development environment design • Central repository management
Consulting and training	• Development tool consulting • Methodology consulting • Customer training • Developer training • Training course development
Technology R&D	• Technology forecasting • Communications R&D • Hardware R&D • Methodology R&D • Development environment R&D
Technology maintenance	• Hardware maintenance • Communications maintenance • System software maintenance • Data storage management

about purchased solutions? Which hardware, software, and communications platforms should the projects consider, and which should they rule out? Do you only want preliminary investigations into each area, rather than full-fledged projects bent on producing automated solutions?

These concerns can be summarized as technology platform policies, make or buy guidelines, and suggested depth for analysis projects. It's best to record these policies now before eager analysts drive projects to unacceptable conclusions. Keep in mind that these policies are really more like constraints. They will limit the scope of projects that follow. Take care not to narrow things too much at this stage. Though a certain PC operating system is the accepted company standard, the software development process project might discover that the perfect software development tool runs on a different one. Had you narrowed their scope too much at the start, they would never have discovered the best solution.

Assess project feasibility, costs, and benefits

Having identified areas for further study, now estimate what the impact of each study might be. Assess the impact in three areas: expected benefits, estimated costs in terms of money, personnel, and technological resources; and the likelihood of success.

Expected benefits The subsequent projects will define the requirements for each analysis area, and recommend solutions for meeting these requirements.

Since you earlier related each function to the goals it supports, estimating benefits is less complicated than it could be. The set of goals supported by all functions within a project are the raw benefits. In some cases, the effect of achieving these goals will be quantifiable; in others, benefits will be qualitative and harder to put numbers to.

TABLE 8-7 shows the goals supported by each Normalco project. As an example, the information quality assurance area supports these goals: continuous process improvement; ensure data integrity; and minimize system defects. The effect of minimizing system defects can be quantified fairly easily. The monetary benefit will be:

(current defects per system − targeted defects per system)
× cost of fixing a defect

If your firm doesn't have standard measurements for defects per system and the costs of fixing them, industry standard numbers can provide a ballpark estimate.

Other goals aren't so easily judged in monetary terms. Continuous process improvement, for example, will be hard to pin down. Often such qualitative benefits must be presented as intangibles. Unfortunately, many managers won't take intangible benefits seriously, yet techniques exist for putting numbers to even the most intangible factors. Rather than simply listing qualitative benefits, you can attempt to estimate monetary benefits from them using expected value, incremental analysis, or excess tangible cost techniques.[9]

By ranking the goals as they did earlier (TABLE 8-3), Normalco planners can assess the qualitative gains promised by each project. To measure this they summed the scores of the goals each project supports. They felt this was a sufficient indicator of strategic benefits, and elected not to perform economic cost/benefit analyses. However, if your management favors quantitative analyses, you won't have this option.

This benefit rating doesn't yet consider how well the project's functions are currently supported. The figure you really want is an assessment of the incremental benefit the project will bring. Down-adjust the ratings of functions that have good systems support today. For example, if you already have project management software in place, the software project management function has some support today. The ratings of goals it supports should be correspondingly reduced.

Estimated costs Costs are much easier to quantify than benefits. Production facilities use Materials Requirements Planning (MRP) to extrapolate personnel and

Table 8-7. Goals Supported by Normalco Analysis Areas

Analysis Area	Goals Supported
Information resource planning	• Align systems with business goals • Forecast resource requirements • Integrated data and applications • Meet customer system requirements • Reengineer business processes • Seek out strategic systems • Simplify project scope
Software development	• Align systems with business goals • Consistent user interface • Enable distributed data access • Ensure data integrity • Increase developer productivity • Integrated data and applications • Meet customer system requirements • Minimize system defects • Responsive application maintenance • Support management decision-making
Information quality assurance	• Continuous process improvement • Ensure data integrity • Minimize system defects
Project management	• Continuous process improvement • Coordinate system installations • Follow common methodologies • Simplify project scope
Development environment design	• Discover useful new technologies • Follow common methodologies • Increase developer productivity • Integrated data and applications
Consulting and training	• Continuous process improvement • Provide applications training • Provide tool and technique training • Respond quickly to customer feedback
Technology research and development	• Align systems with business goals • Discover useful new technologies • Follow common methodologies • Increase developer productivity • Reengineer business processes • Seek out strategic systems
Technology maintenance	• Enable distributed data access • Ensure data integrity • Minimize systems downtime • Responsive applications maintenance

equipment costs. You can go through an MRP step for each analysis project, identifying the quantities of each type of resource you need.

Analysis projects involve two main types of resource costs: human resources, both direct and supporting; and technology resources, including hardware, software, and system timer. Estimate salary costs of managers and developers involved in the project.

Add to this partial salary costs for supporting people: specialists that will help out part-time, executive project sponsors, attendees of facilitated information gathering sessions.

For projects that are international in scope, travel and meeting costs should also be estimated. Gathering requirements from geographically distant stakeholders is never cheap.

Technology resource costs will only be significant if the project requires technological support that's out of the ordinary. Only add technological costs if the team will need special dedicated workstations or software, or inordinate amounts of system time to conduct their investigations.

Remember that the costs you're estimating at this point are those for running the analysis project, not for constructing or purchasing the project's recommended solutions. The project will evaluate the costs of alternative solutions during its course. As a result, you can't directly match up the costs and benefits of the project at this point. The benefits you've estimated are those of the eventual solution; the costs are those of deciding which solution to implement—they don't include the cost of building or buying the solution itself. These costs and benefit factors can only be used to prioritize among projects, not determine actual net present value or return on investment (ROI) for each project.

It is possible to come up with complete ROI figures for each project, but you must make some wild assumptions to do so. For instance, you can presuppose that a CASE tool will be purchased to improve the software development process, and factor a likely cost for the CASE tool into the expected project costs; but since the project hasn't yet defined your shop's development requirements, your estimate might vary widely from the eventual sum. True economic analysis is best done after the requirements are set, when it can be used as a tool for evaluating alternative solutions. I'll discuss economic analysis of CASE tool alternatives in depth in chapter 10.

As with benefits, not all costs are quantifiable. For instance, CASE implementation carries with it the costs of organizational change, much of which is unquantifiable. These intangible costs are often treated as risks rather than estimated monetary costs.

Realizing that these cost figures were most valuable in relative terms, and in order to compare them later against goal ranking scores, Normalco reduced its cost figures to a simple relative measure. They used a one to ten scale, with one being the cheapest, and ten the most expensive.

Project feasibility Many of the standard risk categories for assessing the feasibility of systems development projects won't apply here. Technical and legal risks, for instance, will be minimal. These projects are basically gathering and analyzing information about software development practices, data management, project management, and other IS concerns. They are not (yet) developing systems to address these.

The feasibility categories that do apply are:

- Cultural. Some project areas may contradict the prevailing corporate culture. For example, a group of assembly-language programmers who enjoy their work might resist discussions about new development methods no matter how much pressure management applies. Without prior awareness or education programs, the subject matter of some projects puts them at risk right from the start.

- **Organizational.** Most projects defined during the planning process will cover the entire IS organization. Very complex organizations impose barriers to information-gathering that can seriously hamper some projects. Similarly, it might be hard to staff certain projects in decentralized organizations. These centralized IS projects are new to most IS groups. They are structured along functional lines, and have few people available for centralized projects.
- **Resource availability.** When available resources haven't yet mastered skills required for the project, the project is at risk. For example, most analysis projects require some facilitated information-gathering sessions. If no experienced facilitator is available, there is no guarantee that the person assigned to "wing it" will do a good job.
- **Magnitude.** The larger the project's scope, the greater the likelihood of schedule delays.

Assess these feasibilities for each project. Normalco's feasibility estimates are shown in TABLE 8-8. To measure a project's magnitude, they counted the subject areas it would have to examine, based on the function-to-subject-area matrix created earlier. Organizational feasibility was rated according to the number of organizational stakeholders in the project's functions.

Normalco rated the other factors on a one to ten scale, with ten being the most risky, and one the most feasible. The final feasibility score is a summation of these factors, subtracted from 50 to give the most feasible projects the highest numerical scores.

Table 8-8. Feasibility Rating Worksheet

Analysis Area	Subjects	Organizations	Cultural Factor	Resource Availability Factor	Feasibility Score*
Software development	9	11	6	7	17
Information resource planning	11	11	9	7	12
Technology R&D	5	4	6	9	26
Development environment design	10	5	9	9	17
Information quality assurance	12	8	5	6	19
Technology maintenance	4	6	1	2	37
Project management	12	11	6	7	14
Consulting and training	12	8	5	7	18

*Feasibility = 50 − (Subjects + Organizations + Cultural factor + Resource availability factor)

Prioritize projects

By now, most planners feel like a child at Christmas time: surrounded by new toys, not knowing what to play with first. Prioritization becomes a matter of balancing how much fun a toy seems to offer (the benefits) against how much effort it takes to play with it (the costs) and how likely you'll be able to master it (the risks).

For a first-cut analysis of relative project priorities, simply match the benefits against feasibility factors. John G. Burch presents a proven technique for comparing project benefits and risks that can be easily adapted to this situation.[10] For each project, plot the benefits score, on one axis, against the feasibility score, on the other. Normalco's projects are compared this way in FIG. 8-12.

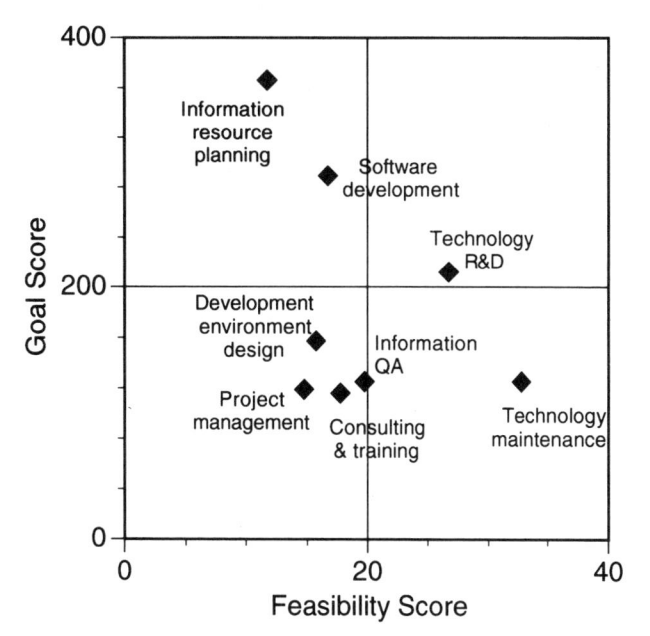

Fig. 8-12. Comparison of analysis area benefits and feasibility

The highest priority projects fall into the upper right quadrant on the graph. These projects support the strongest IS goals and are the most likely to succeed. For Normalco, only the technology R&D project area fell into this quadrant, though software development came close. Either of these is a good candidate for the first internal IS project. The bottom left quadrant contains undesirable projects, expensive and with few returns. At Normalco, the project management area fit here.

The information resource planning area had the highest strategic score, and also the lowest chance for success. Normalco might do best to put this project on hold until more appropriate resources are available, or until an educational process reduces cultural resistance to this area. Either development would increase the project's feasibility.

A final factor now comes into play: sequential dependencies. Some of the projects on the list depend on results of previous projects. Leave the dependent projects out of the running for the first-cut project sequence. Once the prerequisite project nears completion, the dependent project becomes available for sequencing against the rest.

Allocate aggregate resources to the projects

Now that you've identified which projects to pursue first, you need to see how many you handle. Strangely enough, most internal IS projects will be labor intensive. Human resource constraints will be the biggest obstacle to their completion. To allocate them, you must know:

- the number of each type of resource available (including the resources you'll depend on for providing information to the project teams)
- strengths and weaknesses of these resources
- other restraints upon fulfillment of the plan, such as budgetary limits, or potential delays caused by needs for personnel training or recruiting

Identify the discretionary pool of IS personnel by looking at applications development plans. Often you can draw personnel from applications projects that are stalled or floundering. If the problems faced by these projects can be traced to current development practices or poor organizational relationship between IS and its customers, you can often justify shifting resources to solve the real problems.

At this point, you just need to balance the internal IS projects against resource demands of current and planned applications development efforts. If benefits of IS automation are communicated effectively, pulling resources from other projects will be less difficult. But if the IS organization's "time crunch" mentality cannot be altered, even slightly, you'll have a tough time getting personnel to handle internal projects.

Working the plan

As a result of the IS planning process, most firms find that projects to streamline software development are extremely important to the IS organization. They also discover other internal IS projects that can greatly improve their working environment. The rationale for each of these projects is plainly justified by strategic goals and thorough analysis of costs and risks.

9

Reengineering the development process

After strategic planning for IS, the next project analyzes the software development process (SDP). The SDP is the backbone of the IS organization, the main assembly line of the software factory. The strategic IS plan defines multiple areas for further analysis, but almost all of them hinge upon a definition of the SDP. The manner in which you measure performance, manage projects, test software quality, or train developers depends completely upon the way you develop and maintain software.

You can approach this project many different ways, but results should be similar: a description of what the development process should be. This information will be the basis for subsequent efforts to develop standard methodologies, launch measurement programs, investigate project management needs, and of course to select and acquire CASE tools.

Why analyze?

Conceptual definition of SDP requirements is an important link between goals defined in the IS strategic plan and realities of CASE methods and tools. Many managers, eager for quick productivity windfalls, rush directly to CASE tool acquisition once they realize that CASE makes sense strategically. But as Peter Freeman relates, "If the process is not understood, then a tool will very likely not help the process and may impose quite a different process on the user."[1] A little patience in this area will pay off well down the line.

Development of an integrated software development environment should be managed like a software development project. It's not enough to adopt nuggets of knowledge from CASE consultants or advisors. You might know already that you need management commitment, lots of training, and a strong methodology for CASE to succeed. But the only way to ensure that these tactics pay off is to plan them carefully. We need to combine them all into a coherent, structured strategy.

Treating CASE acquisition as an internal software development project, it makes sense to follow a proven development life cycle to define CASE requirements. First identify your SDP requirements without prejudice toward specific methodologies or tools. People experienced with structured analysis are familiar with this concept: define the "logical" requirements before you design physical implementation. Analysis of the SDP area as a whole provides significant paybacks:

- So many factors surround the SDP that a single team might take years to address them all in detail. It's far better to take a high-level look at the development environment as a whole, and then tactically address the areas that will benefit most from CASE.
- A common, high-level definition of the SDP enables subsequent projects to spin off independently. Large firms benefit from splitting analysis of the development environment into small, manageable projects. Define the SDP first and other projects can proceed from a common base. Project management, software testing, and information resource planning will align to a well-understood development process.
- You want the methods and tools you decide upon to provide the best returns for the least cost. The total cost of CASE is far more than just the tool's purchase price. Analyzing your requirements will pinpoint related costs of CASE.
- You want a rational set of criteria for deciding among tools and methods. CASE vendors make most of their sales to companies that have never used CASE tools before. Frankly, they get away with a lot of claims that experienced CASE users easily repudiate. The more you know about your own environment before you negotiate with vendors, the more likely you are to weed out truth from hype.

The SDP analysis project will be followed by detailed projects to develop and document an in-house methodology (chapter 11) and to evaluate and select CASE tools that fit your environment (chapter 10).

It's important to note that the development process is not necessarily a methodology. It describes the essences of software development activities, including objectives, contributors, and data requirements. It takes the functions described in the IS strategic plan to a deeper level of detail, and sets the stage for future efforts to document methods, select tools, and alter the IS organization (FIG. 9-1).

CASE for process reengineering

Process reengineering is founded on a simple maxim: you can't get guantum gains in productivity by making incremental changes in the way you work. Spectacular gains require drastic measures.

The push for CASE gives you an opportunity to reengineer the software development process. As many firms have shown, the introduction of new tools doesn't always speed up SDP. New tools don't eliminate the need for information-gathering sessions, formal reviews, test plan creation, or any other tasks that keep developers from producing software nonstop. SDP analysis involves documenting these many activities. Reengineering involves obliterating some of them, and streamlining the process.

Fig. 9-1. Centrality of the software development process

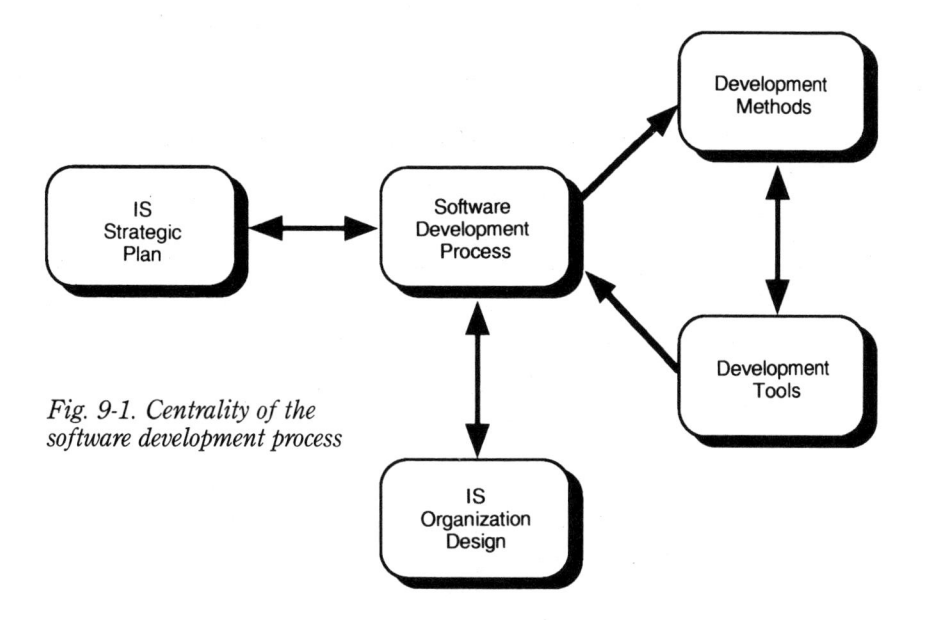

Though change is never easy, don't make "minimizing changes to the current environment" your highest priority, as some observers suggest. This approach will never grant you ambitious vision. A reengineering approach encourages you to set ambitious goals and take forceful steps to meet them. You don't need to meet every goal in the first year; look forward many generations to where you want to be, then plan an evolutionary transition from your current environment.

Unless you must, don't start the SDP analysis project with a preconceived life cycle or waterfall framework. It might soon be imposed, since most people feel comfortable with the framework already. But it stops you from seeing new development models, such as evolutionary development or rapid prototyping.

To reengineer, you should try to uncover assumptions that underlie your current methodology. Ask yourself how current methods came to be, and whether these causes are still valid in the current environment. Some of these assumptions include:

- Methodology exists to control developers. This leads to form-based methodologies, where every step requires a review, checkpoint, proposal, justification, or sign-off. When methods are seen as tools for developers, instead of shackles, they will use them to great advantage.
- Development technology doesn't support better methods. For example, previous tools could not document user requirements as part of a system, thereby guaranteeing requirements traceability. This led to a need for voluminous specification documents. Today, CASE tools can capture these requirements in simpler form.
- Change is dangerous, especially in user requirements. Specification freezes and contracts with users are ways of saying "we defy change." As project sizes shrink, and generating systems from specs becomes easier, the costs of change are lessened.

- A developer's job is defined by his tools. Most programmers identify most with tool-based tasks, such as code editing, compilation, and debugging. Other tasks, like gathering user requirements or discussing system interface issues, are treated as distractions, or unproductive tasks. When high-level development goals are agreed upon, though, specific tools become less important. A developer is no longer a FORTRAN hacker; she's someone who uses the best tool for each particular job.
- The last thing you do is test the software. This sentence can be read two ways, both of them pertinent. By saving testing for the end, you catch errors when they are the most expensive to fix. When quality assurance is part of each development task, the final testing steps won't be nearly as intense.
- Methodologies must be split into phases. Phases exist to simplify management control. They are arbitrary divisions of the development cycle, set up for managers' convenience. They complicate the development process by erecting barriers to task iteration. Phase divisions are the reason prototyping and object-oriented development cause such havoc. Goal-driven methodologies can remove much of this phase dependency.
- Isolated projects deliver systems faster than integrated projects. This is only true when the systems don't need to interact with anything once they're installed. Retroactive integration is far more difficult than proactive integration, and will take much longer. By applying the concepts of evolutionary delivery and coordinated application releases, integrated systems can get out the door quickly.

You can also consider redefining the boundaries of the software development process. Should it start as a reaction to a user-written request for a system, like today? Or should it start earlier, in conjunction with strategic business planning? Should users be able to design and implement their own systems? Might business customers be included in the list of IS's software development customers?

Reengineering must start with goals, and then lead to the best ways to achieve them. Ronald Henkoff, writing about ways to improve office productivity, describes a similar approach:

> Corporations are changing the way they motivate, measure, and reward white-collar workers. They are stressing a pair of concepts relatively new to the world of desks and chairs: quality and customer service. In practice this means minimizing errors and rework, eliminating excessive inspections and approvals, and delegating authority. It means focusing on only those activities that . . . add value for the customer—even when the 'customer' is a person in the department down the hall.[2]

IS faces identical challenges. By analyzing the development process, with an eye toward major improvements, these challenges can be conquered.

An analysis methodology

Your shop might already have an accepted methodology for analyzing business requirements for potential software systems. If so, you should apply that methodology to analysis of SDP. You have people skilled in those methods already, and the project's audience will be comfortable with the deliverables produced.

However, the SDP project is unique in some ways: it involves process redesign on an unprecedented scale, and it will probably lead to a CASE system purchase rather than a software design project. The general steps you should follow for the SDP analysis project are:

1. Sketch the overall project strategy.
2. Define the analysis methodology.
3. Identify the analysis team.
4. Refine the goals of software development.
5. Analyze functional and data requirements for software development.
6. Identify design or acquisition projects.

Starting from the strategic IS plan, first map out the SDP project and its relationship to other internal IS projects. Then take a look at your current analysis methodology, and decide how to apply it to SDP analysis. After identifying the project team and participants, gather the requirements for software development in your company, and then define subsequent projects to design or acquire specific solutions to these requirements.

Depending on the project's scope, SDP analysis can take weeks or months. In large organizations, gathering participants together for facilitated sessions will cause the greatest delays. The amount of strict analysis work will be determined by the number of different development methods in use today. Firms with one or two standard methodologies, strictly followed by all developers, will find the analysis project very simple. Those with many autonomous development groups, each creating different types of systems in different ways, should plan on a fairly lengthy analysis project.

You can use a chart like the one shown in FIG. 9-2 to get a rough estimate of the number of development methods in use in your organization. Fill out one of these tables for each autonomous development group that falls under the analysis project's scope. An autonomous group is not subject to (or simply doesn't follow) the same development standards as other groups. For instance, many U.S. companies split IS into two major departments: domestic and international. The international group is rarely subject to the same development standards as the domestic developers. Other firms have completely separate divisional IS groups: one for marketing, one for finance, one for manufacturing, for example.

The left side of the chart lists the physical platforms the group builds applications for. If the division is a single vendor hardware shop, the three categories shown should suffice. Otherwise, you might want to customize the list to include different brand names and operating systems. For instance, the left side might list IBM Mainframe, Hewlett-Packard minicomputer, and Prime Minicomputer if those are the three primary platforms for the group. It could even say IBM Mainframe/MVS and IBM Mainframe/TSO, for example, if significantly different methods were used to develop applications for both platforms.

The types of applications the group creates are listed across the top. Each type of application listed requires significantly different development techniques. The "Other"

Development Path Worksheet

Group or Division: _____   Date: _____

Delivery platform	Types of Applications Developed			
	Transaction-based (online or batch)	Real-time, embedded	Knowledge-based, expert systems	Other
Mainframe or Mini, with dumb terminal				
Self-contained PC or Intelligent Workstation				
Distributed system (LAN or client/server)				
Other				
Total Paths				

Fig. 9-2. Development path worksheet

category is a catch-all and can include neural networks, fuzzy logic systems, or any other type of system you create on a regular basis.

For each division, simply check off each type of development that applies. Each check mark implies a different development path. By summing the totals for each division, you have the number of development paths in use in your organization. As a very rough estimate of how long an SDP analysis project might take, you can use the formula:

$$1.5 + (\text{the number of development paths} \div 2)$$

The result gives you the estimated number of months an SDP analysis project will take using an appropriately-sized project team (as described in the next section).

This is an extremely rough estimation, but it illustrates a simple point: the more autonomy given to different groups of developers, the harder it is to distill the basic requirements for software development. If the total number of development paths is 10 or more, consider narrowing the analysis project's scope to make it more manageable. You might limit the project to a certain type of applications development, or to a specific IS department or division. Ideally, an SDP analysis project should run between two and six months. If it goes much longer, you stand to lose both momentum and management support.

Some reengineering efforts can be kicked off with concentrated sessions geared to breaking people out of their current paradigms. In another example from Motorola, Henkoff writes, "The company sequestered four auditors and two managers in a room for two weeks. Their charge: to identify and eliminate those tasks that were not essential to producing quality products for the 'customers' . . ."[3] The results of this effort were improved quality and timeliness, one third less staff, and a savings of $1.8 million per year in external audit fees. Those aren't bad returns from a two-week project.

In discussing some detailed project steps, I'll point out other shortcuts for keeping the project short and manageable.

Sketch the project strategy

If you recently completed a strategic IS plan, this step involves little more than review of the plan's published project strategy. As part of the IS plan, the planning team set out some general guidelines for analysis projects, including:

- technology platform policies
- make or buy guidelines
- suggested depth for analysis projects

They also scoped the SDP project in terms of functions, subject areas, and goals supported. Sufficiently detailed scope and guidelines might provide you with enough direction to start staffing the analysis team right away.

You should still take time to plan the analysis project itself, to:

- refine the scope of the SDP analysis project
- decide whether it will trigger subsequent projects to select or design technical solutions, or whether it will include these tasks in its scope
- define deliverables of the project

If no IS plan exists, you will need to articulate this information from scratch during this step.

The planners defined the SDP area's scope in terms of information management goals, functions, and data. Ideally this scope should be inherited by the analysis team, a signpost for their first foray. But first those plans should be evaluated pragmatically, in view of other demands upon the project.

In the case study in chapter 5, the company defined a fairly narrow view of the SDP, excluding quality assurance and project management functions. Medium to large size companies must restrict the project's scope this way to increase its chance of success within a reasonable time frame. Smaller firms can combine these three project areas—SDP, information quality assurance, and project management—and minimize coordination costs of running separate projects.

In some cases, there might be a real sense of urgency to bring in CASE tools or provide fast, small solutions. You can trim a little piece of the larger SDP project and analyze it first. This isn't the best long-term move—it can limit your options in other areas later; but it can help keep the dogs of criticism from snapping at your heels.

Small projects often pop up in the software maintenance area. You can gather requirements for source code documentors, analyzers, and restructurers fairly easily. Implementing these changes won't radically alter the way most developers work. If you extend this mini-analysis to areas of software testing, change control, or reverse engineering, tread more lightly. These weave through the entire development process, and should be analyzed as part of the whole.

In any case, don't let political pressure force you into premature technology decisions. Even if you carve a small bit to analyze, examine it thoroughly before you commit to tools or methods. Many CASE failures start with impetuous purchases. Always understand your requirements fully before you buy, even if your manager already has her heart set on a certain product.

Once you've provided one quick, effective solution, you should be granted the time to take a thorough look at the rest of the SDP. The size of your shop will determine whether you let the same team analyze SDP requirements, and research or develop technical solutions for these requirements. Large organizations need more time to gather requirements from their many managers and developers; they usually develop many different types of systems, and can benefit from multiple solutions targeted toward specific requirements. These organizations should tackle SDP analysis as a separate project. Once they've captured a full set of requirements, subsequent specialist projects can pursue various solutions as needed. For example, one subsequent project could investigate CASE tools that support real-time, embedded systems design. Another might be commissioned to formalize a standard development methodology, and another to discover how best to automate the testing process for each type of system.

Decentralized IS organization can use the analysis project to set company-wide requirements for centralized development support. For instance, it might specify types of information that should be captured about software development, and types of repositories that should be used to store this information. Then each division can start its own project to select and implement methods and tools, within these boundaries.

Smaller firms can often roll everything into one project. The same team can analyze development requirements, and also evaluate tool and method solutions. A team of 2 or 3 people in a shop with 30 or fewer developers can usually do this in a few months. If they decide to develop custom CASE tools, it will take much longer.

Define the analysis methodology

Once you have an idea of the analysis project's scope, you can define the analysis approach and expected deliverables. The approach you choose depends on:

- which techniques are best suited to the subject matter
- whether an IS strategic plan was done
- how much detail you desire
- skills of potential project team members
- accepted means for presenting system requirements to management

Treating the SDP project as an application development project, it makes sense to apply the techniques you normally use to model business requirements. You can assign developers already skilled in these techniques to the project.

Structured analysis techniques lend themselves well to defining the development process and the structure of software engineering data. Structured deliverables might include:

- goal decomposition models
- process models (decomposition diagrams, data flow diagrams (DFD), process dependency diagrams, structured pseudocode)
- data models (entity-relationship diagrams)
- current systems assessment

If your company is not familiar with structured techniques, you can gravitate toward textual documents such as:

- goal descriptions
- process narratives
- data dictionary descriptions

The main advantage of the structured approach also carries its greatest cost. The detailed models you'll create will take a lot of time, especially without a CASE tool to manage them. The details they'll describe might be excessive. Like any software development project, CASE entails the inevitable "make or buy" decision. Though some people advocate full structured requirements analysis before purchasing software, the SDP analysis project rarely warrants such an intense effort. Don't create fully normalized data models or perfectly balanced DFDs unless you plan to develop your own CASE tools. Just gather enough information to decide which approaches will fit best your environment.

This fit goes beyond the mechanical input-process-output picture you get from diagrams. Many of your development requirements won't surface during an objective look at the software assembly line. They will come from the likes and dislikes of developers and managers, or business and economic imperatives. For these reasons you should take a critical look at your software development goals before describing the ideal SDP.

The strategic IS plan will provide the starting point for many of these deliverables. Your approach will differ if no plan was done previously: you will need to identify goals, processes, and data from scratch rather than building upon previous information.

The initial statement of approach should also suggest how deliverables should be formatted and presented. The project's deliverables should be packaged in familiar requirements document formats, if accepted ones exist. IS managers and developers will be more likely to read and understand projects findings if they follow familiar presentation guidelines. If current formats don't support everything the project produces (for instance, many "external specification" documents today don't include statements of goals), then amend them, but keep the overall format as familiar as possible.

The following requirements document outline covers most of the deliverables mentioned above (listed in brackets):

1.0 Project scope and charter
2.0 Goals of software development [goal model]
3.0 Current software development processes
   3.1 Description [process models, data model, current systems assessment]
   3.2 Assessment of goal coverage
      3.2.2 Acknowledged problems and bottlenecks
      3.2.1 Areas of strength
4.0 Future software development requirements
   4.1 Statement of detailed software development requirements [data model]
   4.2 Comparison of proven methodologies to requirements
   4.3 Recommended future process flow [process models]
5.0 Subsequent project strategy
   5.1 Prioritized project list
   5.2 Project descriptions and estimates

Section 4.2 in the outline illustrates a difference between this project and most applications development projects. Usually business processes are well entrenched, and applications are developed to improve their execution. Current development processes, however, are sometimes wholly deficient and must be redesigned. This section will present an analysis of other methods that could be applied by the firm.

The outline's final section presents a list of subsequent projects that will take the requirements and determine specific solutions for them.

No matter which approach you decide on, make sure that it covers three major steps:

1. States the software development goals.
2. Defines essential software development requirements.
3. Identifies and prioritizes projects to provide specific solutions.

The main objective remains: define the essential requirements for software development, independent of technical concerns, in a way understandable to developers and managers alike.

Identify the team

Armed with a project definition and suggested approach, your next step is to choose the best team for the job. Typical roles and responsibilities for an SDP analysis team are listed in TABLE 9-1.

The SDP analysis project leader must fully understand current development methods, support directions set by the IS planning team, and communicate well with IS

Table 9-1. SDP Analysis Project Roles and Responsibilities

Role	Duties
Management sponsor	• Recruit team members and participants • Communicate project's importance to other managers • Buffer project team from unrelated distractions • Set high-level directions during project sessions
Team leader	• Recruit team members and participants • Define project method path • Create and manage project schedule • Buffer project team from unrelated distractions • Set up facilitated project sessions
Project team member	• Records information gathered during facilitated sessions • Performs structured interviews with participants • Documents requirements using structured analysis techniques
Evaluation committee member	• State essential software development requirements • Convey project information to respective groups • Review eventual project publications

managers, functional managers, and developers. The higher this person sits in the chain of command, the better, as long as they have some fairly recent experience managing or contributing to software development projects. This person should have a senior management sponsor who acts as a liaison to other top managers, and who communicates the need for this project to those who will participate in it. If this same team will be chartered to select and purchase CASE tools once the requirements are defined, the project leader should also be able to evaluate specific tool features and negotiate with vendors.

Some of the team members, and many of those tapped for information about the SDP, should be developers themselves. Developer participation up front will minimize developer resistance to new solutions. The SDP analysis project examines the main assembly line for the IS factory. While manufacturing managers usually include those most knowledgeable about operational tasks in the decision to acquire new production technology, top managers in service organizations rarely do so.[4] When deciding how to automate the SDP, IS managers must admit they lack detailed knowledge of current processes, and encourage developers to state their requirements and concerns.

Remember that you want to identify the best future environment, not just whitewash today's. Unfortunately, most developers have a hard time thinking in futures. They are often so busy with their day-to-day work that they don't have time to research or test out new techniques. Yet there are always some developers who revel in new technologies and methods. You want some of these on the analysis team, to keep the group thinking ahead, especially if you want them to investigate new development methods including prototyping, iterative development cycles, object-oriented development, and expert systems creation. A mix of crusaders and pragmatists is best.

Business experts or user liaisons should participate when requirements are being defined. A business expert familiar with software development methods also makes a good project team member. Their jobs will be affected by changes to the SDP. They might be asked to review new types of documents in the future—perhaps diagrams and pseudocode instead of lengthy narratives about system requirements. Switching to an iterative prototyping methodology radically alters the business expert's job, since he must work closely with the developer while screen layouts and behaviors are designed. You will also want to consult business experts for requirements about system delivery, interface characteristics, documentation, and training.

IS managers should also help define requirements. Management methods should change along with development methods. CASE tool productivity gains are often nullified when developers find themselves handcuffed by inappropriate and inflexible management practices. The developers struggle to produce new types of deliverables, but managers still want to see the old stuff, too, because that's what they understand best. The projects sink under the weight of two sets of deliverables, one developed using CASE, one created the old way to make managers happy. Get the managers involved up front, so they'll be more satisfied when things change later on.

Other project participants can be drawn from groups closely attached to the IS organization. A shop developing embedded systems will want to tap the brains of an equipment expert or two. Specialized IS groups, such as standards or software testing should also be represented.

Refine the goals

You have already identified objectives and requirements of the software development organization during IS planning. At the start of the SDP analysis project, you will want to elaborate on the goals, bringing them to a more relevant level of detail. As Peter Freeman says, "Clear objectives for [a software development process] can energize it more than any one thing."[5]

As an example, take the set of goals defined for Normalco's SDP project during the planning case study in chapter 5:

- align systems with business goals
- develop consistent user interfaces
- enable distributed data access
- ensure data integrity
- increase developer productivity
- integrate data and applications
- meet customer system requirements
- minimize system defects
- provide responsive application maintenance
- support management decision-making

This is a robust set of goals, but not detailed enough to thoroughly justify any methodology or CASE system selection. These goals should be broken down one or two levels further, providing operational objectives that can be later matched to tool and methodology features. To do this, evaluate strategic goals in the context of your environment. Gather information about developer likes and dislikes, productivity bottlenecks, quality problems, and successes of other groups and companies, and use these to tailor your goals.

The productivity goal could be detailed as follows:

3.5 Increase developer productivity
    3.5.1 Promote and manage reusable software components
    3.5.2 Automate tedious processes
    3.5.3 Support rapid application development methods
    3.5.4 Specify systems at high levels of abstraction

These operational goals can be prioritized just like the strategic IS goals they are descended from, to indicate those with highest relative importance.

Analyze the requirements

Once your goals are defined, you can describe what you must do to achieve them. Unless your goals are conservative, your current methods probably won't fulfill them all. When gathering requirements, you don't just want to capture today's environment; if it was working excellently, you wouldn't be doing this project. You want to identify the ideal future development environment. Later, you'll use this as a yardstick by which to measure CASE tools and other solutions.

The way you execute these steps can differ according to your penchant for reengineering the process. If you already have a good, repeatable methodology that just needs some automation, and you want incremental productivity and quality gains, you can analyze your current process using basic structured analysis techniques. Then pinpoint areas that can benefit most from incremental changes.

You can use any number of structured diagrams or narratives to describe the current development process. However, if you believe the process must change significantly in the future, this effort might be misplaced. Do a good job detailing future requirements, and you'll have little need for diagrams of today's process. Most teams will be better off just recording the basics of the current process, and spending more time describing future needs.

If you don't have common methods in place, or you want quantum productivity gains, take a reengineering approach. This approach consists of three tasks:

1. Identify essential processes.
2. Research and model the best methods for achieving objectives.
3. Assess how well current processes meet stated goals.

Identify essential processes Analysis works best when done broadly. Despite guidelines handed down from strategic planners, most teams are tempted to narrow analysis scope and churn out quick deliverables. Some political situations make this prudent, but normally you should keep your scope as wide as possible. Address everything you think you can handle within the suggested six-month project window.

Requirements should cover all types of development performed within the organization, not just the most popular. Some companies discover internal pockets of efficient development that can be exploited to everyone's advantage. Currently marginal methods, such as object-oriented analysis or rule-based knowledge acquisition, might gain importance in the future.

Before you can model the SDP requirements, you must understand the critical processes involved. Try to identify the value added of each process, not necessarily the mechanism used to implement it. For instance, the screen prototyping process enables early user verification of systems design. It doesn't matter whether a sophisticated tool is used, or whether the "prototypes" are done on paper. An essential process will live on even if its current mechanism becomes irrelevant.

You can use the functions handed down from the strategic IS plan as starting points for this step. Brainstorm the processes that make up these functions. Weigh each one against the goals you've listed. Processes that support none of your goals are clearly not essential.

You might want to solicit information from those who perform many of the processes. You can hold structured interviews to discover the steps developers take to create new software. Do this even if you have an official development methodology in place. Pay particular attention to the shortcuts or unofficial steps they take—these are the areas where the current process falls short. Interview at least three separate developers. Each one will follow different paths toward working applications.

Ask the developers open-ended questions, designed to elicit free-form responses:

- What do they like and dislike about the current development systems?
- If money were no object, how would they improve the development environment?
- Given perfect development technology, what functions would they still perform? What information would they still need?

Once you've identified the main processes, try to put together a picture of how they fit together. Use a format that shows some of the process dynamics, such as a data flow diagram. You can also illustrate the various actors in the process, such as systems users, developers, and IS managers, and show how they interact with the processes. By helping the participants visualize the process, you encourage new analogies and ways of thinking about software development.

Research new methods Even if you're happy with the current SDP, take some time to investigate new methods. Read up on development techniques that have worked elsewhere. Don't rule out methods that sound too avant-garde or risky. A few firms got into object-oriented programming years ago, when most IS organizations scorned the idea. Many of these firms now have powerful libraries of reusable software that let them cut development times in half. Start upon a learning curve early, and you'll be an expert when everyone else is still debating.

Don't limit your research to just one or two popular methodologies. What fits the majority might pucker or sag when you wear it. You're looking for advantages, not conformity.

On the other hand, you might not have a standard methodology, or the one you have might need improvement. Many CASE consultants, having read books on managing organizational change, will advise not changing your methods when you move to CASE tools. One of the most common tenets is "CASE should be evolutionary, not revolutionary." Minimizing the changes you force upon the developers, they say, makes it easier to impose those changes. This is true if you already have successful methods in place. For example, a shop that uses structured analysis and design techniques with little automated support is well poised to trade up to an integrated, repository-based CASE tool. But a tool that automates object-oriented methods will appear far more threatening to developers. It will make many of their current skills seem obsolete, and definitely spur resistance.

When you don't have common methods in place, CASE forces you to change the way some people work. The alternatives are to maintain the status quo or allow each developer to get special tools to support the way he works, which leads to CASE tool anarchy. Given the inevitability of such change, you might as well switch to new methods with the most promise for quantum leaps in productivity and software quality.

This doesn't mean you should throw new methods and new tools at the developers in one overwhelming bundle. It means you should set your sights high, not try for everything at once. Some of the biggest CASE failures were with firms that changed all the methods and tools at once, without adequate planning or preparation. Instead, you want to set out toward revolutionary goals at an evolutionary pace. Zoologist Richard Dawkins makes a case for gradual evolutionary steps that sounds almost word for word like the advice of many CASE gurus: "Because of the astronomical odds against success, a series of small steps, each one building on the accumulated success of previous steps, is the only feasible way."[6]

Unfortunately, most CASE implementors take this to mean: "Don't try to change things too much because it will never work." This leads many IS managers to settle for timid, low-cost CASE tools that automate one or two developer tasks. Yet Dawkins also points out that evolutionary steps would be more effective if they were directed toward fixed goals. For instance, there might be thirty genetic differences between an insect and a scorpion. If the genes knew they wanted to be a scorpion, they could get there in thirty generations. Since they don't have this goal in mind, it can take thousands of generations, and might never occur.

So rather than simply automating a few development methods in random evolutionary fashion, you should practice directed evolution. Plan the mutations ahead of time; make the revolution seem evolutionary. For example, the systems you build might be well tailored for object-oriented development techniques. Yet your developers don't know the first thing about object-orientation. Proceed toward the vision in small evolutionary steps: early education in concepts, articulation of management's vision, a few development tools to play with on a trial basis, one or two pilot projects. Handled well, this progression lets you realize your vision while minimizing stress and turmoil.

Revolutions only scare those who are satisfied with the status quo. If you are wholly dissatisfied with the software development process, minor improvements won't bring much. Even small changes to the ways developers work require large doses of management support, educational programs, and cash. Why go through these efforts for small paybacks?

This analysis project gives you unprecedented power to improve the development process. It would be a shame to waste this chance by defining requirements that involve miniscule improvements. Keep the best of your current methods if they meet the goals you've set up; obliterate the rest, and design something great.

Assess current methods   How well you describe and document your current methods depends upon how many development paths fall within the scope of the project, and how these methods work today. When the scope includes many different kinds of software development, you can waste a lot of time documenting each in detail. It's better to concentrate on critical assessment of the methods, highlighting what works and what doesn't, and using this information to drive your future requirements.

Useful in this regard is the Software Engineering Institute's Process Maturity Framework, presented in chapter 5. Through an in-depth survey process, you can discover how advanced your software engineering practices are, and which improvements you should concentrate on first. Roger S. Pressman presents a similar survey in his book, *Making Software Engineering Happen*.

Self-assessment surveys can be valuable if you're not already sure what you do well and what you don't. However, they don't help you describe the dynamics of your software process. If you plan to reengineer the SDP, you will need to understand the development forces at work today.

If you have just one or a few development paths currently being used, documenting them can be useful. If these methods are entrenched and reasonably effective, chances are you'll simply want to amend them to describe an incrementally better future environment.

If you feel the current environment should be completely overhauled, though, documenting current processes won't buy you much. You won't be able to carry any of this documentation forward to help define a better future environment, so don't waste your time.

Still, few environments are so poor. Usually you can pinpoint some strengths of your current situation. Perhaps your developers provide high-quality systems today (though they overrun project schedules to do so). Or the software testing process has become highly efficient (to cover for quick-and-dirty development techniques). You want to capitalize upon the things developers do well today.

Be sure to tap the knowledge of managers and developers during the current process assessment step. Gather as many facts and opinions about current methods as you can. Discover what they like most, and what they abhor.

Start by looking at the ways you perform the essential processes and seeing how well they support your goals. The strategic IS plan contained a list of current software development systems and how well they met strategic IS goals. This list can be used as input to this step.

High priority goals that have little or no current support are the ones you should concentrate on. Well-supported goals need not be addressed immediately by new tools or techniques. Once you've identified the gaps between today's environment and your picture of the future, you can muster projects to fill them.

Identify the projects

You now have a picture of your target development environment: the processes that developers go through and the information they manage. This picture serves as a guidepost for subsequent projects to find concrete solutions that fit your requirements.

You should find that the number of development paths you've just documented is less than the number you started with. You should have identified commonalities in the ways that different IS groups work that allow you to generalize certain practices. This will make the subsequent tasks of developing common methodologies and selecting CASE tools that much easier.

Were this a standard software development project, the next phase would involve designing an application that fulfills the business requirements identified during analysis. Those planning to build their own CASE tools should do exactly that: use structured design techniques to automate the requirements you've just described.

However, most firms prefer to buy CASE tools. They can use the SDP requirements to drive the evaluation and selection of development tools, becoming the most sophisticated customers most vendors have ever seen.

Depending on the scope of your analysis project, you can initiate a number of design or acquisition projects at this point. You can follow a process similar to that at the end of strategic planning: group the subfunctions and processes you've described into manageable project areas.

Two main projects all firms can pursue are: methodology design and CASE tool acquisition. The methodology design project formalizes the SDP for your organization. It creates a common source of information about your development process, available to all developers.

The CASE tool acquisition project uses the requirements you've specified to evaluate and select the CASE tools you really need.

If the analysis project was broad in scope, you might spin off some additional design projects:

- process measurement design
- automated testing tool acquisition
- software project management support

In larger firms these three projects might be tackled first as separate analysis projects, as mentioned in chapter 8.

Firms in search of highly integrated solutions should actually analyze all of these areas before starting up a methodology design or CASE goal acquisition project. Process measurement, quality assurance, and project management are all tightly related to the SDP. Some CASE tools automate these functions in addition to the basic design and creation of software. Whether created together or separate, the requirements for all of these areas should be compared and reconciled. The SDP can act as a common thread, weaving all of these aspects into a coherent, textured whole.

10

Retooling the software factory

CASE tools are capital equipment for the IS organization's software factory. They should be selected and purchased with the same care given to purchases of manufacturing machines.

The CASE purchase for most firms is a question of asset replacement. The IS group already owns compilers, linkers, database managers, and other tools. They seek more efficient tools based on new technologies, to increase product quality and productivity. Despite the great gains many CASE users have experienced, most firms investigate CASE tools reluctantly. As management professor W.J. Fabrycky relates, "A decision to replace is much more binding than a decision to continue with the present asset. Continuation . . . is a course of action that can be reviewed at any time, whereas a decision to replace is a commitment for a longer period into the future."[1]

Developers are often happy with the tools they use. Faced with technical shortfalls, clever developers create work-around solutions, and enjoy the tinkering that these entail. Management complaints about missed deadlines, unresolved business issues, or poor quality software can usually be traced to organizational or communications problems, not code compilers or testing tools. As a result, managers often delay tool replacement decisions.

Yet there comes a time when development tools become scapegoats for software problems. Not because the tools don't work, but because their throughput is low or their outputs are lacking. As Fabrycky puts it, "A machine or other asset may be incapable of meeting the changing demand required of it . . . The usable piece of equipment may be in excellent condition, with consideration of its replacement being forced by the need for greater capacity."[2]

Much of this book discusses handling the organizational issues that surround development tools before you worry about the tools themselves. Before deciding which CASE tools to use, it's advisable to:

- set strategic business directions
- set strategic direction for the IS organization that support the business goals

- develop an IS architecture, identifying needs for automated software development, information quality assurance, project management systems, and support for other aspects of software development
- document and assess your firm's basic software development requirements
- define the software development process as a standard methodology or method pool

Now it's time to make the asset replacement decision for your development tools.

Cooperative CASE tool selection

The decision to investigate CASE was made at a strategic level during IS planning. Your functional requirements for development tools were developed during an SDP analysis project. The findings of this analysis project will be inputs to the project to evaluate and select CASE tools.

Other related factors will influence the CASE evaluation project as well, specifically:

- organizational change impacts
- cost and resource constraints
- findings of other analysis efforts regarding information quality assurance or project management
- results of the ongoing methodology or method pool development group

CASE evaluation involves more than simple feature-matching and cost calculation. It also means evaluating impacts upon the IS organization and the development methodology, and finding workable combinations of CASE tools when one tool isn't enough.

The methods can't be defined, in fact, until specific CASE tools are chosen. Many specific steps depend upon CASE tool idiosyncrasies. Similarly, the impact of CASE upon the organization can't be fully evaluated until the tool itself is known.

Why should you treat CASE evaluation as a project instead of a few days in the life of an IS manager or a newly-appointed specialist? First, one person alone might take forever to complete a systematic CASE tool evaluation. Tools number in the hundreds, and you might need to gather requirements from just as many people. A project tends to get more concentrated support than does a single specialist engaged in his day-to-day duties. The specialist doesn't have the same weight behind him when he calls asking for interviews or for help testing a new CASE tool. He doesn't have the committed support of other developers that a project leader receives automatically.

Second, you want to spread the responsibility for the final selection decision. By letting other managers and developers participate in the selection process, you increase their stake in the tool. They will work harder to make its application successful. Group decision-making also prevents a single person from "taking the fall" if the tool doesn't work as well as expected.

A final reason for running an evaluation project: projects get results, while part-time duties don't often produce. Projects require management support and commitment from team members and participants. The supporters will require results; the contributors will be motivated to produce them. Project planning requires up-front effort, but it also increases the chance you'll soon get a solid report on the CASE tools best suited for you.

Run as a project, CASE evaluation should happen more quickly than it might otherwise. Gathering tool and vendor information and scheduling vendor demonstrations will be the lengthiest tasks. Scheduling and preparing for group sessions also takes time. Estimates for the length of the evaluation project will depend upon how broad your requirements are, and how wide a field of CASE tool candidates you'll consider. Once again, you can use a very inexact formula to get a primitive estimate. Based upon the number of development paths your analysis project settled upon (as discussed in chapter 6), the following formula provides a rough guess about how many months the evaluation project should take (excluding pilot development project using the new tools):

$$2 + (\text{the number of development paths} \div 2)$$

If you have only one well-documented methodology, a good evaluation process should last about ten weeks. A project to define comprehensive CASE solutions for many different types of development can run to six months and beyond.

The six-month "ceiling" isn't as important for this project as it was for the strategic planning and analysis projects, though—as long as you provide some interim results during the course of the project. Once you've defined the requirements of your total development environment, you can start targeting specific solutions to high priority requirements, and bring these in as you find them. As long as you show progress, the project can continue unabated.

A CASE evaluation methodology

The CASE evaluation project starts with a clear charter: investigate and recommend the most cost-effective tools for improving the software development process.

One sequence of steps for a simple CASE tool evaluation project is:

1. Define evaluation scope.
2. Identify evaluation team.
3. Identify cost and resource constraints.
4. Define qualification criteria.
5. Gather product information.
6. Identify candidate CASE tools.
7. Define evaluation criteria.
8. Analyze remaining tools in depth.
9. Issue requests for proposal.
10. Analyze CASE economics.
11. Select and purchase CASE tools.
12. Review evaluation process.

Start by making the project's charter more specific, refining the SDP requirements, identifying monetary and technical constraints, and prioritizing the tool features you desire. Then evaluate CASE tools in light of these requirements. Narrow the field of candidates according to how well they cover the most important features you need. Ask for proposals or quotations from vendors, and evaluate tangible and intangible costs of each option. Convince CASE vendors to provide demonstrations or trial copies of their products. If you have the time and staff, run pilot projects to compare detailed capabilities of each tool. Dependencies between these tasks are shown in FIG. 10-1.

Once you've completed the project, you'll know which of the available CASE tools can do the most for you. How far you take this methodology depends on the type of commitment you'll be making to CASE. If you're planning to invest millions to build an integrated development environment, each of the following steps will apply. If you're a smaller shop or independent developer after more limited tools, the most relevant steps will be defining requirements, prioritizing them, and seeking out CASE information. I'll discuss these steps in more depth.

Define evaluation scope

Once again, start by determining the techniques you'll use to gather information, compare tool features against your requirements, and assess costs and benefits of each package. The tasks you decide upon will determine skills needed by the project team. I've provided one possible set of tasks; you should review these steps, see what makes sense in your environment, and add or subtract tasks as necessary.

The main questions to answer are:

- Are you after full development environment solutions, or isolated benefits?
- Will you consider developing CASE tools or additional utilities?
- Must you follow formal procedures for evaluating and purchasing hardware and software?
- Will you rely upon vendor-supplied information, or seek out independent sources?
- Will pilot projects be part of the evaluation process?

Development scope Up to this point, I've discussed the need to document and understand the entire development cycle. But that doesn't mean you need to automate the whole environment. For some firms, a comprehensive, integrated CASE environment will be the answer; for others, a few well placed single phase tools will be more cost-effective.

At this point, the project sponsor should decide whether the evaluation project will consider full-scale solutions, or just look at isolated development areas. There are three general strategies you can follow:

- Targeted strategy. You want to improve specific development tasks or phases, without worrying about comprehensive, integrated solutions.
- Component strategy. You want full development cycle CASE coverage, but don't want to pay high-ticket prices for integrated CASE tool suites.

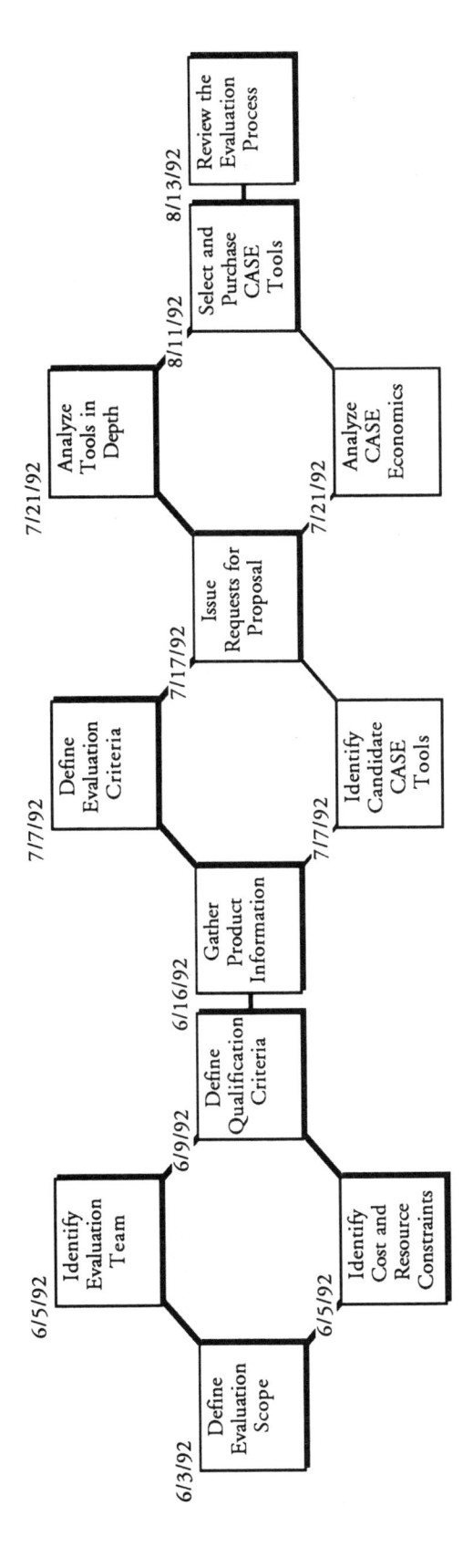

Fig. 10-1. PERT chart of CASE evaluation tasks

- Integrated strategy. You want full-cycle CASE coverage, but don't want to hassle with interfaces between different vendors' tools. You prefer a single integrated CASE tool from a reputable vendor, and will wait for that vendor to supply full-cycle solutions.

The targeted strategy is usually quick and cheap, bringing narrow benefits. Even if you're only planning to bring in a self-contained tool or two, it pays to do some broader analysis up front. You don't want the engineers getting used to a tool that doesn't fit in with future plans. If you follow a targeted strategy, acknowledge its limitations. Don't let the success or failure of a single tool invalidate the entire CASE concept.

If you seek integrated tools, you must decide whether to introduce an entire suite of tools at once, or ease into a full environment a step at a time. The latter approach is less risky, but has a smaller chance of drastically improving the situation. Some vendors sell their tools as separate components (though they normally give a significant price break for the entire suite). Regardless of how you purchase a tool, you can implement it a step at a time. You're not forced to use every facet of a new tool.

The component CASE strategy assumes that no single vendor will provide the total CASE solution for your firm. It is a mix-and-match strategy to link various "best of breed" tools together into a streamlined development environment. Gaps in some tools will be plugged by other tools or homegrown utilities. You can deliver new tools incrementally, adding new capabilities as people become ready for them.

Don't attempt a component strategy unless you have a solid, central tool you can use to anchor the other components. Most vendors tell you their tool interfaces with other CASE products, but usually these interfaces are clumsy, one-way feeds that transfer partial information. Try to build an integrated environment on these interfaces, and you'll end up with a web of leaky interfaces that might actually hamper productivity.

The best anchor is an open repository tool. Those with extensible metamodels and interfaces that can be customized let you plug various tools into a truly integrated CASE database. They support an integrated, rather than interfaced, component CASE strategy.

Of course the price of most repository tools makes them unattractive for smaller shops. Newer LAN-based repository tools have lower price tags, but none of the products currently offered have open architectures. Smaller shops that hope one day to have integrated CASE tools can start with a few targeted tools interfaced together. If these component tools are part of a larger set offered by a single vendor, so much the better. This means you can add new functionality from the same set in the future, guaranteeing a modicum of integration.

Many vendors offer integrated full-cycle CASE tools today. The main advantage of these tools is the automatic integration they provide: you don't need to customize metamodels or interfaces. Beware of vendors who promise more integration than they deliver; there are quite a few of them.

The integrated strategy ties your fate tightly to that of the CASE vendor. Unfortunately, vendors' agendas rarely match your own. Some vendors feel driven by market pressures to add new bells and whistles to their tools before they firm up the basic functionality. Some of IBM's business partners in the drive toward AD/Cycle have been paralyzed by the new demands. In their zeal to help IBM define its repository and AD/Cycle strategy, they have delayed much-needed enhancements to their own tools.

Buying an integrated CASE toolset is the fastest way to get an effective, full-cycle development environment. It's not the cheapest, nor the safest, but it promises the greatest immediate returns.

If you're following an integrated CASE strategy, the evaluation team should specify requirements for automating the full SDP. If you're after targeted tools, you can limit the set of requirements to specific parts of the development cycle.

Those following a component CASE strategy are advised to write requirements for the full environment, not just one piece of it. These broader requirements can act as guidelines for future evaluation efforts, ensuring consistency between various components.

Homegrown tools Some companies, especially computer manufacturers, prefer to create their own integrated tools from scratch. While this assures you of a snug-fitting solution, the size of such a project makes it untenable for most firms.

Large companies can analyze whether to create their own CASE tools or buy them from outside vendors. Many commercial tools started as in-house development projects, TI's IEF and McDonnell Douglas's Pro*Kit among them. It's tempting to run a standard "make versus buy" analysis for CASE just like you would for a business software package. But many of the advantages of homegrown business applications don't really apply for CASE.

Custom CASE tools will conform to unique development requirements. Though many firms follow special development methods, most of their idiosyncrasies represent procedural hold-overs, not essential development steps. Homegrown CASE tools can entrench inefficient processes, while outside tools can provide impetus for a change.

Custom CASE tools can be easier to maintain, since company employees know the internals in depth. However, CASE systems are notoriously complex and difficult to maintain. Costs of maintenance will skyrocket, no matter how well each developer knows a piece of the system.

Add to these factors the high cost and risk of in-house development projects, and the "make" option doesn't look good. However, many companies still choose this option for one compelling reason: most commercial CASE tools have severe limitations.

Though most firms don't want to develop their own tools from scratch, many are prepared to extend or customize the tools they buy. To appeal to this market, some CASE vendors tout the pliability of their tools. They publish data structures, export data in popular text and graphics file formats, or create "public interfaces" to allow customers to add features or utilities to the CASE environment.

The most popular homegrown utilities improve upon the CASE tools' often disappointing reporting capabilities. Other utilities create standard documents directly from CASE information (often to conform to DoD document standards), automatically gather and report metrics, or interface to popular project management tools or spreadsheets. Firms that want the "perfect" environment must usually customize or add value in this way. Even the best integrated CASE tools don't include every feature you'll need.

Add-on utilities carry a significant maintenance burden. Unless the vendor commits to support your additions—an unlikely event—you will need to upgrade your custom utilities whenever the vendor changes the CASE tool's data structures. Some vendors insulate you from such changes by providing a "public interface" or by following industry standard data structures. But even these must change eventually, so be prepared.

Be sure to carefully evaluate customization requests before someone starts hacking out utilities. Many of the requests will come from easy developers who want to replicate everything they had before CASE. Will the addition add value within the future framework? How will it fit with the method paths you'll use with CASE? Ideally, you should treat the creation of add-on CASE utilities as true systems projects.

If you plan to customize the CASE product, or to develop specific add-on utilities, your evaluation method path should include tasks to identify which utilities to build, and to estimate costs and development times for them. You will want to include the people that might develop these utilities to the project team or participant group.

Scope of information search How much will you rely upon vendor-supplied information? Some managers are naturally more skeptical than others; they will want to rely upon independent information sources, and will therefore incur some additional research costs. Others prefer to deal directly with vendor representatives, questioning and cross-questioning them until they've got the answers they need. Each preference implies slightly different approaches to gathering product information.

You might also be forced to limit the number or types of vendors you can select from. Many governments force their agencies to choose preapproved vendors, for example. Other firms have preferred vendor relationships that might restrict whether, or in what sequence, you can contact other suppliers.

Be careful not to prematurely limit the range of candidate tools you'll evaluate. I've known IS managers who constrained the evaluation process by telling people up front to "decide between tool X and tool Y." These recommendations are normally based on little more than hearsay, or impressive advertising campaigns. Try to go into the evaluation project with an open mind.

Formal selection procedures Some companies have formal policies governing software and hardware evaluation and selection. You might normally send a request for proposal (RFP) or request for quotation (RFQ) to each vendor whose product you are considering. Any steps that these transactions require should be built into the project's approach from the beginning.

CASE tool dogfights How much effort are you willing to spend to find the right CASE tools? The true test of any CASE tool is a pilot project: a small self-contained development effort that will put the tool, and the methodology you follow, through their paces. Only by using the tool to develop a real-life, working application can you really gauge how well it will work. Up until this point, you must rely upon vendor information, independent advice from people who may or may not have developed systems with the tool, and sales demonstrations. None of these will point out what a pain it is to debug the code generated by the CASE tool, or how long you have to wait for a workstation-to-mainframe-repository file transfer.

The best evaluation process pits CASE tools against each other in a pilot project battle. Use each tool to develop a similar application, from start to finish, and compare notes. One or a group of tools will certainly emerge a winner. However, few firms have the time or human resources to run such a test.

The most prudent approach (described below) starts with a comprehensive "paper evaluation" of the products. Then the preferred set of tool candidates are brought in-house for demonstrations. Finally, you select a tool and purchase it—on a trial basis. Then use the tool for an intensive pilot project. Take any criticisms of the tool to the vendor and see how they respond. If you're not satisfied, send it back, and bring in the next tool on your list.

Identify the evaluation team

At the end of the SDP analysis project, you sketched out a strategy for subsequent projects: one to create a development methodology, another to evaluate and select CASE tools. Smaller organizations probably combined these two projects into one, obviating the need to select a new evaluation team at this point.

In any case, the structure of the evaluation team can be similar to the structure of the analysis team, including a management sponsor, project leader, project team, and evaluation committee.

If you run separate projects, you'll want some of the same people who worked on SDP analysis and methodology projects to participate in the CASE tool evaluation. CASE tool evaluation should follow directly from SDP analysis. Those who define requirements are more inclined to see them met. The evaluation committee might be the same group that helped define the SDP. It consists of high-level IS managers, software project managers, software developers, and technology experts.

The committee solidifies a set of CASE tool requirements. The project team surveys available tools, seeking single tools or combinations that match the evaluation criteria. They narrow the field to a few candidates, and define costs, benefits, and potential impacts of each. The committee debates the merits of each scenario, and recommends one for implementation.

TABLE 10-1 shows typical responsibilities for each project role. In addition to skills needed for earlier projects, the evaluation project team must be able to: expertly assess technical tool features, perform financial cost/benefit analyses, and negotiate with vendors.

The CASE evaluation project team can evolve into an official software development support organization. This group becomes the caretaker of the strategic IS plan, the SDP analysis results, and the method pool. They are familiar with tools and methods in use, and their communication skills enable them to be effective internal consultants. This option will be discussed in more detail in chapter 9.

Once again I'll stress that some of the people who will use the tools should help decide which tools to acquire. IS shops already know the value of letting users help design application systems. In this case, the users are software engineers, and the application is CASE.

Identify cost and resource constraints

The evaluation team should start with an idea of how much money can be spent, and which types of changes can be made to the IS organization to support CASE. Cost limi-

Table 10-1. CASE Evaluation Project Roles and Responsibilities

Role	Duties
Management sponsor	• Recruit team members and participants • Communicate project's importance to other managers • Buffer project team from unrelated distractions • Set high-level directions during project sessions
Team leader	• Recruit team members and participants • Define project method path • Create and manage project schedule • Buffer project team from unrelated distractions • Set up facilitated project sessions • Negotiate terms with CASE tool vendors
Project team	• Record information gathered during facilitated sessions • Perform structured interviews with participants • Gather product information • Fill out feature checklists • Run cost/benefit analyses • Obtain, set up, and test CASE tools
Project participants	• State physical tool requirements • Help prioritize tool requirements • Help review and test CASE tools • Convey project information to respective groups • Review eventual project publications

tations can severely limit the range of tools to choose from. Integrated tools in particular carry fairly high price tags. Mainframe repository tools typically range from $150,000 to $500,000. Repository tools that run on minicomputers or LANs might be a half to a fourth of this cost.

Self-contained workstation-based tools might cost as little as $300 each. However, their functionality is normally very limited. Some tools are sold in modular form. You can purchase the modules one by one, or all at once. Without a central repository, though, the integration of these modular tools is limited.

Two of the biggest cost factors are computer hardware and CASE tool training. To limit these costs, take advantage of what's already available.

Available hardware The computer and communications hardware you own or plan to buy will greatly influence the CASE tools you consider. Operating systems and other supporting software also restrict your possibilities. You need to consider these physical system requirements from two perspectives: the physical platform you'll use for development, and the target environment for developed applications.

In both cases, you want to leverage off of the hardware and software you already own. New workstations generally cost more than CASE software to run on them. Minimizing hardware expenses will keep total CASE expenditures reasonable.

Current skills Now is the time to run a reality check against the current skills of software engineers. The greater the gap between your current methods and the ones espoused by the new CASE tool, the greater your education and training costs.

This doesn't mean you should rule out new tools that require additional developer training. Factor this in as an additional cost. Tools that significantly increase productivity will always require retraining. From a cost/benefit point of view, such tools might come out ahead of those that parallel current techniques more closely but only bring slight productivity increases.

For example, training COBOL programmers to use object-oriented languages like Smalltalk can be very costly. Switching to an object-oriented paradigm is difficult for many programmers, and the learning curve can be steep. Yet once the programmers master the new techniques, productivity gains can be dramatic. Four months of lower productivity, as they track up the learning curve, will be more than offset by the next year of more efficient development.

Define qualification criteria

No single tool will handle all of your software development needs. Many companies get paralyzed once they realize that there is no single "silver bullet." Frederick Brooks used this metaphor in a supernatural context: the silver bullet that slays a werewolf. Another context is just as appropriate: the silver bullet of the Lone Ranger. There is no one weapon that helps the Lone Programmer always win. But a team can put together an arsenal of weapons, each one targeted at the problem it can attack best.

Finding tools to automate all aspects of development is like building a jigsaw puzzle. You know how it should look when put together, but you need to find the right pieces.

The SDP analysis effort determined the essential needs of developers in your environment. These needs prescribe a fundamental set of CASE tool features. Basically, the tool must support essential development processes.

Yet the SDP analysis is still somewhat abstract, a broad-brush sketch. It defines basic process steps such as data modeling or screen design, but none of the specifics about how you want the processes done.

If this were a project to design and construct your own CASE tool, this step would make the general features concrete. It would document which data fields needed to be on which screens, or whether you'd tell the system to quit by clicking somewhere with a mouse, or by typing "Q" in a command field.

Since you'll be purchasing tools, though, it makes no sense to go to this level of detail. You need enough information to make an informed decision about available CASE tools. This means embellishing and refining the broad-brush SDP requirements, to create a concrete set of prioritized CASE tool capabilities.

The requirements you identify will fall into two categories: qualification criteria and evaluation criteria. Qualification criteria describe features that a tool must have in order for it to be considered. Evaluation criteria represent detailed requirements that let you select one qualified tool over another.

Before you start gathering information about CASE tools on the market, list the basic features a tool must have for it to qualify as a candidate for further evaluation. Qualification criteria normally fall into seven categories:

1. development task coverage
2. development platform

3. target system characteristics
4. delivery platform
5. development paradigms and methodologies
6. tool integration
7. flexibility and extendability

Development task coverage Development task coverage refers to the basic CASE functionality you seek. Do you want to automate structured analysis or design methods? Do you want code generation capability? Do you want to improve code testing capabilities? Start by listing the basic functions you'll require, such as data modeling or interface design. This gives you enough information to weed out many CASE tools from the evaluation field.

If you've analyzed the essential SDP requirements, you already understand your basic process in depth. Use this as a guide to the basic functions a tool must support to qualify for further evaluation.

Development platform If your budget won't allow for new hardware purchases, you should only consider tools that run on development platforms you already own. This platform includes programming languages as well.

Make sure that the tools you evaluate created source code that your platform can handle. For example, the best CASE tool you evaluate might generate Ada code. But a new Ada compiler could cost you an extra $50,000.

Another platform consideration is the need for distributed access or storage of software engineering data. If you're looking for ways to promote cooperative software development, you might restrict the candidates to LAN-based tools.

Firms looking for additional tools to augment ones they already have will list tool compatibility as a qualification criterion. Today AD/Cycle compatibility is a popular CASE vendor claim. Actually all that vendors can claim today is that they will follow AD/Cycle developments, and hope IBM and its partners won't pull the rug out from under them.

Until 1993 or 1994, AD/Cycle won't involve great customer gains. IBM and its business partners are struggling to define a common metamodel for the repository. The biggest challenge will be using this model as a standard exchange format while still allowing vendor product differentiation. Depending upon the model, AD/Cycle might end up hindering further progress toward software productivity, rather than facilitating it.

While AD/Cycle compatibility is an admirable goal for the future, don't base your CASE tool decisions upon it. If AD/Cycle becomes an industry standard, all vendors will be forced to conform to it. If it doesn't, it will simply become another proprietary repository specification, and compatibility won't be an important issue.

Target system characteristics The types of systems to be created will also determine a tool's suitability. Some tools can help you develop both online and batch transaction systems. Others specialize in real-time, embedded applications.

Application content—the business data and processes being automated—can also influence CASE tool considerations.

As code generation from structured design becomes a reality, some CASE users are offering to sell application models. A company buying a design model can customize it for its own environment fairly easily. Then they can generate it to run within their own hardware and software configurations. I worked with one client, a large airline company, that purchased a template for a frequent-flier management system. With a small team, they developed a complex, strategic application from this model in just under eight months, using Texas Instruments' IEF product.

If you are planning to develop specific applications with your new CASE tools, ask whether any design templates are currently available. A strong template could influence which tool you buy.

Some CASE vendors provide vertical market niche products. For instance, products are available that only generate CIM applications. Unless these types of applications are all you do, these products aren't usually a good idea. They foster departmental separation—the CASE tool anarchy I discussed earlier. Since the marketing group can't make use of manufacturing-only CASE tools, they'll buy different tools for themselves.

Delivery platform The most restrictive criteria of all might involve the targeted delivery platform for your business applications. It's unlikely you'll want to buy new computers just because a CASE tool generates applications that run on them.

The delivery platform's hardware components include computers, display terminals or workstations, communications lines and networks, and other hardware or instruments. Software components include operating systems and database management systems.

Development paradigms and methodologies A development paradigm is a fundamental view of software structure. Most programming languages represent a procedural paradigm: software is a set of sequential instructions. Other object-oriented or rule-based paradigms have proven more effective for certain types of applications. Unless you're planning a major retraining effort, you probably want to stick with the paradigm your engineers are already familiar with. However, good CASE tool support can simplify a jump to object-orientation or rule-based development methods. It is much easier, for example, to build good expert systems using a sophisticated expert systems shell than it is to write them in C++.

The methodology supported by the tool should only be a qualification factor if most developers already use standard, structured methods. Methodology authors normally tout their techniques as the best and only ways to develop systems. Yet when choosing an effective CASE tool, theory doesn't carry too far. To deliver applications, you sometimes need to compromise the theories. I recommend waiting until you're evaluating candidate tools before imposing methodology restrictions.

Tool integration Many people still consider CASE tool integration to be a luxury. As long as it generates code, who cares what happens to information lost along the way? I've already touted the benefits of integrated development environments. Without some measure of integration, productivity, quality, and management support benefits will be limited. Any company pursuing a component or integrated CASE strategy should put tool integration high on its list of qualification criteria.

Most vendors now providing fully integrated development environments are those who have taken a single view of systems development and extended it vertically to cover the total life cycle. Texas Instruments calls this a "narrow path" implementation.

By limiting the range of development methods, it becomes much easier to generate working systems from analysis or design specifications. This breeds an important trade-off: as the need to generate systems increases, tool flexibility decreases.

Flexibility and extendability Many prospective CASE customers demand flexible software that will bend to their every whim. They want extendable metamodels and the ability to patch each tool into every other. Vendors respond gladly with claims of methodology independence and flexible software development.

Yet flexibility can be as much a cost as it is a benefit. As professors Stephen R. Rosenthal and Harold Salzman of Boston University observe, "To the extent that interactive, mission-critical software is flexible, the burden of software design is passed from the software developer to the customer."[3] Tools that are methodology independent, in other words, force their users to have more self-discipline.

Flexibility per se should not be a qualification criterion for CASE tools unless the things you plan to do with the tool are truly unique. CASE tool flexibility takes a few basic forms:

- Interface flexibility. Screen and report formats can be altered, or "hot key" shortcuts added, but basic processes don't change.
- Parameter-driven processing. Users can choose from lists of options that alter software processes along predetermined lines. These often let you set up diagramming standards, or select methodology rules for consistency-checking.
- Feature extendability. Given source code or data structure information, users can create their own add-on software, effectively extending the system's set of features.
- Customization capability. The vendor provides full source code or CASE models, allowing the user to alter and maintain any portion of the software.

These capabilities can give advanced users some development leeway. But to the extent that they lessen the rigor of the tool, they can be costly as well.

Gather product information

Armed with a list of qualifying features, you can now gather information about CASE tools. Most CASE products aren't on display at the local computer software store, so you must actively seek information about them.

As the CASE industry has grown, so have information sources, including:

- advertising, and direct vendor information
- magazine reviews
- books
- CASE tool directories
- conferences
- consultants
- other CASE users
- vendors of software you currently own
- electronic research services

Advertising and direct vendor information Most computer or software magazines carry CASE tool advertisements. Some advertisements carry more information than others, though nearly all suffer from buzzword overload. Terms like integration or flexibility are cited regularly, but rarely in the same context. Be wary of similarly pliable buzzwords in ad copy: they may not mean what you think they do. See TABLE 10-2 for some buzzwords that are often taken in vain.

Table 10-2. Misguided Meanings of Common CASE Buzzwords

Buzzword	Should Mean	Often Means
Integrated	All data managed by one tool can be used by others without file transfers or reformatting	• One-way file transfers or data translations • Common user interface
Methodology support	Allows creation of a set of diagrams or documents in accordance with a proven set of techniques, and prohibits actions that subvert the intended purpose of the techniques	• Allows creation of specific diagrams or documents that follow the visual conventions of a specific technique
Methodology independent	Allows customization of the tool's methodology standards, while still prohibiting subversive actions	• No restrictions on modeling style or process specification syntax • Conglomeration of tools loosely tied together, with no overriding vision behind them
Central repository/ encyclopedia	Single, active source of software engineering information, simultaneously accessible by all developers with an approved interest in the information	• Passive data dictionary • Workstation data file that different developers can access one at a time
Code generation	Produces a complete software application, in the form of full source or object code, with associated interface objects	• Creates skeletal source code shells • Creates a hollow interface: screens without underlying processing capability

The best part of most CASE tool advertisements is the vendor's address or telephone number. Every vendor will send product descriptions and brochures if you request them. Some of these information packages simply rearrange the magazine ads on heavier paper. Others are extremely valuable, including position papers written by the product's developers and copies of independent product reviews. Many vendors will also include demonstration disks upon request.

The direct contact method of information-gathering has one serious drawback: your name gets forwarded to vendor sales representatives who will thereafter bother you periodically.

Magazine reviews Most magazine reviews concentrate on personal computer software. They are often written from the viewpoint of independent programmers, who rarely have the time to go through a full life cycle. None of the reviews discuss large-scale corporate rollouts of CASE tools before they write their reviews. Reviews discuss user interface issues and basic analysis and design features, but little else. Still, they can provide valuable first impressions of tools, and point you toward tools for further investigation.

Books The number of CASE books on the market has blossomed along with the industry. Most books with the CASE acronym in the title contain lists of tools and vendors. Due to publishing lead times, though, these lists are always somewhat out-of-date.

CASE tool directories Some consulting and publishing firms compile CASE tool information in directories for sale to the public. Most directories list basic tool features and vendor information. A few include reviews of each tool, or surveys of people who have used it. A list of CASE directories is provided in appendix C.

Conferences CASE tools are on display in the exhibition halls of most software development or computer conferences. Some CASE-only conferences have also sprung up in recent years. You can learn about more tools in a half-day at one of these exhibitions than after weeks of calling vendor sales representatives for information.

Often CASE implementation concerns are topics of lectures or seminars at these conferences. Such sessions can provide excellent insights into the realities of CASE, especially when given by software engineering veterans. Beware of consultants who treat lectures as extended advertisements for their services.

Consultants Many consultants now specialize in CASE tool evaluation and implementation for client companies. They make it their business to stay on top of industry developments, and often have contacts in vendor organizations. They can be valuable sources for CASE information, and their experience can help speed your evaluation process.

However, some consultants might try to limit the range of tools you evaluate. They might be familiar with one or two tools and steer you toward them, hoping for follow-on development work. Others have partnerships with specific CASE vendors, and might act more like sales representatives than objective advisors.

Other CASE users Vendors of the most popular tools often support users' group organizations. If you're thinking seriously about buying a specific tool, ask to attend a users' group meeting. Other customers will talk frankly about the tool's pluses and minuses provided no vendor sales representatives are around.

CASE Research Corporation sponsors an International CASE User Group (ICUG) dedicated to all varieties of large-scale automated development tools. ICUG has branches in many U.S. cities. A listing of national user groups involved with CASE is given in appendix C.

Vendors of currently owned software Some vendors of programming languages and database management systems broaden their product line by introducing CASE tools or development aids. Companies following a targeted CASE strategy can get quick returns from such tools, while expending a portion of the normal cost. Assume you own a fourth-generation programming language. The 4GL vendor might offer a structured diagramming tool or screen designer that creates 4GL code as an end product. Your developers are already familiar with the 4GL, so you only need to train them in the new tools and methods. Plus the CASE tools should fit your current development environment.

The CASE products offered by some 4GL or DBMS vendors aren't very robust however. Analyze these products as thoroughly as you do any others. But when searching for candidate tools, make sure you inquire about tools from vendors you already deal with.

Electronic research services Another option for information-gathering is an electronic research service. These often provide CASE tool feature information, and capsule product reviews.

Connect time for these services can run from $30 to $250 an hour or more, with additional charges each time you call up specific reports or articles. TABLE 10-3 lists some of the electronic options available.

Table 10-3. Electronic Sources of Information about CASE Tools

Database	Service	Type of Information	Charges ($)
Business Software	• Bibliographic retrieval service • Dialog	• Selected product listings	• $6 – $30 per hour connect charges (depends on subscription options)
Computer Database Plus	• Compuserve (COMPDB) • Dialog	• Articles from computer periodicals	• $24 per hour connect surcharge • $1 per article abstract • $1.50 per full-text article
Computer Directory	• Compuserve (COMPDIR)	• Specific product information, including hardware requirements and list prices • Vendor names, addresses, phone numbers, product lines	• $24 per hour connect surcharge • $1 per menu of matching products or vendors • $0.25 per product or vendor listing displayed
INSPEC	• Bibliographic retrieval service • Dialog	• Abstracts from journals, books, and conference proceedings	• $6 – $30 per hour connect charges (depends on subscription options)

As you wade through this sea of information, keep your qualification criteria close at hand. Avoid compiling lists of every imaginable type of tool. Trace through the sources with an eye toward your requirements, and you'll end up with a list of viable candidates.

Identify candidate CASE tools

Your list of qualification criteria should let you sift through piles of CASE tool literature with relative ease. The depth and breadth of your information search will determine how long this process will take. One company found a thorough process of narrowing prospective vendors took them four weeks.[4] I've known IS managers who spent six months gathering information about tools before bringing in vendors for demonstrations—though this was done independently, and not as part of an evaluation project.

If your requirements are wide in scope, you might find that no single tool fulfills them all. Don't give up; you'll need to consider multiple tools in combination. One way to do this is with a matrix of tools to qualification requirements. Match each requirement with the tools that support it. An example matrix for development cycle coverage requirements is shown in FIG. 10-2. You can produce other matrices showing hardware or software support requirements too.

Referring to these matrices, combine the tools into sets that together support all the requirements. As you proceed to evaluate tools in more depth, treat each set as a separate option.

You can at this point rule out some sets as being too costly or complex. You might also need to adjust the qualification requirements. If you can't find any tools that qualify, you've probably set your sights too high.

	Product A	Product B	Product C	Product D	Product E	Product F
Information Strategy Planning	●	●	○	●		○
Business Area Analysis	●	●	●	●	●	●
Business System Design	●	●	●	●	○	●
Database Generation	●	●	○		●	
Application Generation	●	●	○		○	
Automated Testing Support	○					
Reverse Engineering: Databases			●			
Reverse Engineering: Applications			○			
Central Repository	●	○	●	●	●	○
Coordinated Release Support						
Software Change Control	●		●	●	●	
Project Management Support	○			●	○	●
Methodology Support				○	○	○

● = supports feature   ○ = partially supports feature

Fig. 10-2. Simple CASE tool feature matrix

So far you've only evaluated surface capabilities of the tools. If you end up with a large number of candidates, you'll need to look at some of the features in more depth. You don't want to continue past this point with more than eight or ten options. Each option will be the subject of in-depth study. If you can limit the field to three or four candidates, you can devote lots of time to each one.

Define evaluation criteria

To choose from among the tools that fit your environment, you'll need to define your requirements in more detail. This involves elaborating upon your rough qualification criteria, and then prioritizing the requirements.

Expand requirements As you evaluate the remaining tools in more depth, each of your qualification criteria can be given more detail. To this information, you can add less crucial technical, user interface, or vendor factors. You should fully define all your demands before approaching CASE vendors.

For data modeling, for example, you might prefer a tool that helps draw entity-relationship models, using the Bachman diagramming conventions, with support for subtyping and automatic data normalization. For code generation, the list of specific questions to ask is much longer:

- How complete is the transformation? What, if anything, must you manually add to the generated code to create a working system? Productivity is much less when the generator doesn't produce 100% of the code.
- How detailed must pre-generation specs be? Does it work from high-level analysis or design specs, or low-level source code? From graphical diagrams? Look for the highest level of abstraction without performance penalties.
- Must the CASE tool be present for the generated system to run? This forces you to install copies of the tool everywhere you install production systems.
- Is the code compiled automatically, or not at all (interpreted)? How long does it take to generate, compile, and test an application?
- What are the performance statistics for generated systems? How do they compare to hand-coded systems?

It's not enough for a tool to have a feature in name; it must support that feature to the degree you require. The more specific you are in your requirements, the less able vendors are to appease you with buzzwords.

Appendix B presents a comprehensive list of CASE tool evaluation criteria. This list is divided into three major categories:

1. CASE tool features, including development cycle coverage, other development and technical services, and physical characteristics of the CASE software
2. development path criteria, which describe development paradigms and platforms, and the types of systems you plan to build
3. vendor criteria, including product costs, training, and technical support

Don't try grading each CASE tool against the entire list of criteria in appendix B. It's a comprehensive list, designed to describe most possible tool features. If you attempt to fill out a checklist of this size for every candidate tool, you'll be a year older before you finish. A list of evaluation criteria is most valuable when it's short and well prioritized.

Prioritize requirements Some industry analysts suggest standard approaches for evaluating and selecting CASE tools.[5] Most of these mention that you should first define your CASE tool requirements, then run through lengthy feature checklists to find the tools with the longest lists of capabilities.

This approach involves detailed classification of CASE tool features, but little description of what your own needs are. CASE tools with the longest feature lists aren't necessarily the best. Rosenthal and Salzman discovered from interviews with software vendors that "the features and functions considered advantageous are often the seductive bells and whistles attractive to managers."[6] Since most managers make simple comparisons of product features before they articulate their true operational goals, Rosenthal and Salzman find that "the software supplier with the longest list of features often wins the sale."[7]

Before you start counting features, decide which ones matter the most to your company. Why determine how twenty tools fare in each of one hundred categories when you can rate a few of them by fifteen or twenty criteria that you truly care about? If you've taken time to plan IS goals and analyze development requirements, you have a basis for effectively selecting the most appropriate features.

You can use some of the following tactics for prioritizing requirements:

- Focus on weirdness.
- Refer back to IS planning goals.
- Understand IS management's motivation.
- Perpetuate what you do well today.

Focus on weirdness Concentrate on the things your shop wants to do differently from the norm. Do you have special documentation requirements? Development or delivery platforms from niche computer vendors? Extreme requirements for application reliability or data integrity? A staff well trained in specialized development techniques? Focus on the oddest aspects of software development in your shop, and you can quickly narrow the field of available tools.

Explicitly state why unique features are unique. Vendors will need to know some background. Question whether these idiosyncrasies represent true requirements, or convenient habits. If the latter, you might give some thought to reengineering your development process.

Refer back to IS planning goals During the IS planning effort, you developed a comprehensive list of IS goals. These goals are prioritized, and can tie directly to certain CASE tool features. TABLE 10-4 shows some of the features that support the goals developed in the planning case study in chapter eight.

Of course this tactic isn't available to those without time to plan for the future of the IS environment. TABLE 10-5 shows some of the CASE tool functions with the greatest effects upon the basic benefits discussed in chapter three.

Table 10-4. CASE Tool Features Implied by Strategic IS Goals

Normalco Goals, in Order of Priority	CASE Tool Features
Meet customer system requirements	• Strategic planning capability • Support for structured analysis and/or design methods • Interface prototyping • Simulation of real-time systems
Align systems with business goals	• Strategic planning capability • Seamless tool integration • Applications generated from business analysis and design specs
Integrated data and applications	• Central repository, with extensive services and reporting capabilities • Model sharing facilities (check-in/check-out and object-level locking) • Change impact analysis • Seamless tool integration
Minimize system defects	• Model consistency-checking • Automated testing support • Seamless tool integration
Increase developer productivity	• Seamless tool integration • Code generation • Database generation • Automatic transformation or creation of other software engineering objects
Reengineer business processes	• Strategic planning capability
Ensure data integrity	• User security features • Referential integrity enforcement for databases
Continuous process improvement	• Metrics calculation and recording • Methodology customization, or method pool management
Seek out strategic systems	• Strategic planning capability
Minimize system downtime	• System diagnostic tools • Automated testing support
Follow common methodologies	• Tightly coupled methodology support • Methodology customization, or method pool management
Forecast resource requirements	• Project management support
Support management decision-making	• End-user development capability
Respond quickly to customer feedback	• Software change control
Discover useful new technologies	• (No support available)
Simplify project scope	• Affinity analysis or clustering features • Function point analysis, or other calculations of software size and complexity

———Continued———

Table 10-4. Continued

Normalco Goals, in Order of Priority	CASE Tool Features
Provide applications training	• Automated document creation
Enable distributed data access	• Ability to create distributed applications • Ability to share software engineering information

Table 10-5. Best CASE Tool Types for Desired Benefits

Main Benefits	Type of Tool
Productivity	• Automated testing tools • Code generator • Reuse library • Reverse engineering • Screen prototyper
Quality	• Automated testing tools • Code generator • Methodology support • Screen prototyper • Simulator • Structured analysis and design
Management support	• Central CASE repository • Metamodel access • Methodology support • Project management
Strategic alignment	• Strategic planning

Understand management's motivation Is there a crisis underlying the push toward CASE? Was an application rejected by users for poor quality? Perhaps CASE quality assurance functions are most important. Are there constant complaints about late projects? Project management support might be a high priority. If the tools you bring in don't address the problems that spurred the CASE evaluation, the tool might not succeed.

Perpetuate what you do well today If you're jumping straight into CASE tool evaluation without redesigning the software development process, you should decide how important maintaining current procedures are in relation to productivity and quality goals. Let's take the creation of software documentation as an example.

As Barry Boehm points out, more than 60% of development effort in large firms goes to create, review, and maintain product documentation.[8] Obviously cutting down documentation requirements could vastly shrink project time. Are your shop's documentation standards, as written today, extremely important to uphold? They certainly are for military contractors. But might there be other ways to achieve the same goals? Perhaps you can distribute online, electronic documentation, drawn straight from the CASE repository, instead of compiling, formatting, and printing voluminous paper documents. Perhaps most people really don't care about the detailed design documents you send out today; they'd be happy with a five page system overview.

Suppose, however, that everyone is currently very happy with the documents your group produces. You have a system of template files and word processor macros that generate well designed documents, and you don't want to lose this capability. Make the ability to export to this word processing software an important requirement for new CASE tools. Leverage off what you do well today, and no one will see the new tools as a setback.

How to record priorities The simplest way to prioritize requirements is a two-tiered approach. Separate them into "hard," or "must have," requirements, and "soft," or "nice to have," ones. Most of the hard requirements will correspond to the qualification criteria, involving hardware platforms, methodologies, and levels of integration.

Technical features aren't as crucial as basic development functions, and often fall into the category of "nice to have." Some analysts suggest you only consider tools that support mousing and multiple windows, for example, because they can make it easier to manipulate complex information. But I believe the type of interface makes very little difference, as long as the man-machine interaction is well designed.

Some people shy away from mouse and window environments because their developers aren't used to them. True, the first time you use a mouse you can feel lost. But it only takes a day or two to adapt to such interface changes. Poor functionality stays with you forever.

You shouldn't make a particular type of interface a "hard" requirement. Sometimes a reliance upon a specific operating system forces a certain interface type—not many Macintosh applications, for instance, don't use a mouse. Otherwise let the interface be a "soft" requirement. It will force you to pay more attention to the tools' functions, and leave you less apt to be bowled over by a seductive interface.

Remember that the shorter your list of requirements, the faster the evaluation process will be. Don't list requirements that you don't care about. Give more weight to a critical feature than to a pile of trivial ones. Don't be swayed by a product's bells and whistles. These are less like church bells than they are like a bell on a cat, warning that the marketers are ready to pounce.

If this evaluation marks your first foray into the world of CASE, don't go overboard defining requirements. Just getting started with structured methods and tools is a big accomplishment. As you gather more information and test out more tools, you'll learn which features are most valuable. Don't try for everything the first time you get a CASE tool. Start by matching basic requirements, then learn as you go.

Some evaluators find it useful to grade each requirement according to its importance. A simple one to ten scale is usually sufficient. Hard requirements rate a nine or a ten. Soft requirements play the rest of the scale. These scores can act as weighting factors when you evaluate how well each tool fulfills the requirements.

Analyze tools in depth

So far you've selected candidate CASE tools, and compiled a list of the criteria by which to judge them. Next you need to evaluate each tool against this criteria, to form a basis for choosing one winner from the pack.

This means seeking out new information about the tools, and getting as close to hands-on as you can without spending any money. To help grade the suitability of each tool, you can use any of the following techniques:

- Scan product information.
- Obtain demonstration software copies.
- Send out vendor questionnaires.
- Schedule vendor demonstrations.
- Check customer references.

Scan product information You've amassed a wealth of CASE tool knowledge during your product information search. So far you've used it to identify candidate tools. Now you can cull details from it, about each criterion you value. Closely read the product literature to see which diagramming standards are used for data models, or how DFDs get transformed into program structure charts.

Some vendor literature doesn't carry this kind of information. If not, call your vendor sales representative. She will find the answers for you, or refer you to technical people directly.

Obtain demonstration software copies Many vendors will send demonstration copies of the software to you for free, or for a nominal charge. Demo disks can give you a sense of the look and feel of a product. Some demos are simple slide shows of CASE tool screen displays. Others give you most of the functionality of the actual software, with the exception of "print" or "save" commands.

Because of these limitations, you can't pretend that demonstration software is close to the real thing. There's no way to test them under real-world conditions. Demo disks can help rule out some tools, though. One look at an archaic user interface or unreadable diagram graphics can put a tool right out of the running.

Send out vendor questionnaires Once you've articulated your requirements, you can easily format them as questionnaires for CASE tool vendors. The main advantage of this approach is that it puts a lot of the burden of the CASE tool analysis onto the CASE tool vendors themselves. There are some disadvantages too.

First, there is a lot of room for misunderstanding when dealing with the written word. Make sure you've expressed your criteria well. Second, you limit what you learn about the tool. A tool might have a marvelous feature—say automatic generation of processes from a data model—that you didn't think to ask about. Shrewd CASE vendors will sneak all of their selling points, regardless of relevance, into their responses. But you can't count on this.

Finally, some vendors, especially smaller ones, or those selling single-task CASE tools, are put off by lengthy questionnaires. Vendors of full-cycle integrated tools are accustomed to lengthy dialogues with prospective customers. Companies selling $295 diagramming tools have fewer sales resources, and less time to spend filling out twenty page documents. Take a little time to tailor questionnaires to the intended vendors and you'll get a much better response.

Questionnaires are best used as preliminaries to more in-depth contact with vendors. Use them as a springboard to talk with vendor representatives about the strengths and weaknesses of the product.

Remember to highlight your strangest requirements. Most vendors have pat answers to the standard questions. It's the odd questions that test the limits of their products.

State why you're asking each question. A question like "Can you customize the diagramming icons?" doesn't mean much from a vendor's point of view. Perhaps you really need rectangular process icons on certain diagrams because your users are currently used to them. A vendor might have exactly what you're looking for, but be forced to answer "no" because of the way you framed the question.

As part of the questionnaire, ask them how their vision of future development environments matches up to yours. You'll want to make sure they're pulling in the same direction you are.

Often these questionnaires can be combined with formal requests for vendor bids or proposals.

Check customer references Reputable vendors will refer you to their existing CASE tool customers. If no references are available, the vendor might be hiding something.

Existing customers can often give you a very balanced view of the tools, both advantages and disadvantages. Naturally the vendor will only direct you to satisfied users. Yet most satisfied CASE customers traveled a jagged path to get where they are now. Every tool has its drawbacks, and make sure you find out a few of them.

Also quiz the customers about their IS and user organizations, their developer skills, and their technical environment. How closely does their environment match yours? Some CASE tools that work well in small- to mid-sized shops buckle under the weight of heavier demands. Tools favored by a scientific research organization might meet a cooler reception from developers at a consumer goods company.

Schedule vendor demonstrations When you start getting serious about a product, it's time to call the vendors in. If you represent a large company, convincing representatives to visit you is no problem. Smaller firms might be forced to attend demonstration sessions at conferences, or special seminars that some vendors set up in larger cities. Conference or seminar demonstrations don't provide as much information as on-site ones. You're competing with a dozen other people to get your questions answered, and learn about your high priority features.

An on-site demonstration can last from an hour to half a day. Most vendors will send you a sales representative and a technical support person. They usually want someone there who can talk "techie" with the best of them.

Vendor demonstrations are often slick and scripted. Sometimes the caliber of the presenter indicates the vendor's level of interest in you as a customer. Top priority prospects aren't sent rookie representatives who can't deviate from the script; they get veteran salespeople who have answers for everything. If the demonstration team seems inexperienced, it can mean the vendor company can't get enough people to support rapid growth.

You'll hear a lot about the vendor's future plans during the demonstration, especially in response to your toughest questions. CASE tools are more complex than most software packages, and are constantly being added to and improved. The vendor company's strategic direction matters a lot if you plan to commit to their tools for the next few years. Is it their goal to provide integrated full-cycle software development environments? Do they plan to provide the ultimate programmer's workbench, or tools that any fool can use to build business systems? Or do they position the tool as a small, targeted product—a component in someone else's grander scheme?

The vendor's vision will guide development efforts for the next few years. Don't base your CASE decision on promised features that can't be demonstrated. Especially beware of the claim that "if enough customers ask for it, we'll make it a high priority." But learn what you can about their plans. With luck, you'll find a vendor whose direction paces yours. As you need more functionality, they'll have grown to provide it.

To learn more about the vendor's commitment to CASE, ask how they developed their CASE tool. Did they use their own methodology and tools to develop their products? I have asked this question many times, and never heard an unqualified "yes." A few vendors use some structured techniques to help develop tools; others use early modules to help analyze requirements for later ones. But for the most part, CASE vendors developed their software using the same seat-of-the pants methods they tell you not to use any more. I don't know a vendor who can generate a CASE tool using a CASE tool, though the most visionary CASE companies state this as a strategic goal.

The most frustrating part of vendor demonstrations is when the reps say, "Well, we can't show you that feature right now. But trust us, it works." Try to prepare the representatives before the demonstration. Tell them specifically which features you want to see demonstrated. From your research you already know more about their product than most prospective customers do. You don't want to hear an hour-long talk on every small feature of the tool. Tell them you want to see how to transfer data between the analysis and design toolsets, or how to create a process action diagram, or how many steps go into generating COBOL code. You're not trying to make life hard for the vendor. You're simply trying to make the demonstration more valuable for both parties. They get insight into your concerns, and you learn about your highest priority features.

Even the best demonstrations show a small fraction of CASE tool features. They will familiarize you with the product, but they can't recreate real-world situations. The only way to learn all about an integrated CASE tool is to take it through a full-cycle development project.

Finding the best fit As you scan vendor literature and watch product demonstrations, you'll be flooded with CASE product details. Most tools are so different, and so wide ranging in their capabilities that comparing them seems impossible. The two tactics you can take to manage this are to focus on only the few most important aspects of the tools and capture the information in a standard, structured format.

You've already narrowed your criteria according to importance. To capture the information, I suggest a spreadsheet approach. List each criterion, and rate how well each candidate tool fulfills it. Weigh the scores according to the importance of the criterion, and the degree of support provided by the tool. The resulting weighted score provides a good indication of the value of the tool.

Spreadsheet analysis A simple spreadsheet analysis of CASE tool features is shown in TABLE 10-6. Each feature is weighted from one to ten, with ten being most important. Each tool is scored according to how well it supports each feature. The scores range from zero, meaning no support, to five, meaning the best possible support. The people evaluating the features must assess different aspects of the feature to come up with this score. The total score for each tool is an approximate measure of how well it fits the requirements.

A more complex rating mechanism, illustrated in TABLE 10-7, lets evaluators select various degrees of feature support, and then extrapolates these into ratings of productivity, quality, management support, and strategic benefit. This lets you choose tools that maximize certain benefits. The excerpt shown in TABLE 10-7 concentrates on the code generation aspect of the tools. Each degree of feature support implies different levels of various benefits. The evaluator checks off each tool's support level, and the spreadsheet calculates aggregate scores for each type of benefit. By applying a weight to each type of benefit, you can select the tool that maximizes what you most want to achieve.

This is a complex approach that takes time to set up. However, it makes the evaluators' jobs easier: they check off features instead of applying subjective values. It ensures that different people rate tools the same way.

TABLE 10-8 shows how four tools fared in each feature category. The evaluators chose to limit their evaluation to what they considered the most critical functions: strategic planning, structured analysis, prototyping, code generation, and repository integration. Products C and D both fared well in this comparison. Because their scores

Table 10-6. Simple CASE Tool Rating Worksheet

Crucial Tool Features	Weight	Product A Score	Product B Score	Product C Score	Product D Score
Strategic planning	10	3	5	5	4
Analysis					
Entity-relationship modeling	9	3	4	5	5
State-transition diagrams	7	4	0	0	0
Process modeling (DFDs or PDDs)	8	4	4	4	4
Business process specification	6	1	2	5	5
Prototyping					
Screen prototyping	7	4	1	3	3
Simulation (finite state machine)	5	0	0	0	0
Application generation					
Code generation	8	3	2	5	5
Database generation (DB2)	5	3	3	4	4
Integration					
Level of integration	9	4	3	5	5
Central repository features	7	3	3	5	5
Total score (= weight × score for row)		**247**	**216**	**318**	**308**
Weighted average rating		3.0	2.7	3.9	3.8

Table 10-7. Detailed Feature Rating Matrix

Rating for: Product D	√	Prod	Benefit Value Qual	Mgmt	Stra
1.1.7. Code generation					
1.1.7.1. Completeness of code generation					
• Full code, including data access		5	2	2	0
• Full code, except for data access	√	4	2	1	0
• Skeletal code		2	1	1	0
• Able to link in external object code	√	1	0	1	0
1.1.7.2. JCL generation					
• Complete JCL generation for batch programs		4	2	2	0
• Skeletal JCL generation	√	2	1	1	0
1.1.7.3. Detail of pre-generation components					
• From graphic models		5	3	1	2
• From high-level pseudocode (4GL-level)		4	2	1	2
• From detailed pseudocode or source code macro lang	√	3	2	1	1
• From actual source code stored with CASE objects		1	1	1	0
1.1.7.4. Completeness of pre-generation components					
• Everything for generation is stored in repository		3	1	3	0
• From repository objects and additional code specs	√	1	0	0	0
1.1.7.5. Number platforms the tool generates for					
• Single hardware/OS platform	√	3	0	1	0
• Multiple hardware/OS platforms		5	0	3	0
1.1.7.6. Number of generated programming languages					
• Single language	√	1	0	0	0
• Multiple languages		2	0	0	0
1.1.7.7. Runtime environment					
• Fully independent programs	√	0	0	3	0
• Requires CASE tool to run		0	0	0	0
1.1.7.8. Runtime performance					
• Worse than most hand-coded programs	√	0	0	0	0
• Equivalent to most hand-coded programs		0	2	0	0
• Better than most hand-coded programs		0	4	0	0
1.1.7.9. Development performance					
• Executable specifications; no generation necessary		5	2	0	0
• Local workstation code generation		4	1	0	0
• Seamless host code generation from workstation		3	1	0	0
• Code generation requires simple file transfer	√	2	0	0	0
• Code generation requires multiple file transfers		1	0	0	0
Code generation scores:		**17**	**5**	**8**	**1**

Table 10-8. Detailed Feature Rating Comparison

	Prod	Qual	Mgmt	Stra	Weighted Score
WEIGHT	10	8	1	5	
Product A					
Strategic planning	5	9	21	14	
Structured analysis	10	13	11	9	
Prototyping	7	6	3	1	
Code generation	15	6	7	1	
Integration and repository	17	19	22	1	
Total:	**54**	**53**	**64**	**26**	**1158**
Product B					
Strategic planning	9	18	33	26	
Structured analysis	6	12	11	14	
Prototyping	3	5	2	2	
Code generation	12	5	7	0	
Integration and repository	12	9	14	0	
Total:	**42**	**49**	**67**	**42**	**1089**
Product C:					
Strategic planning	11	21	42	31	
Structured analysis	9	12	19	14	
Prototyping	5	5	2	1	
Code generation	25	9	13	2	
Integration and repository	17	18	18	1	
Total:	**67**	**65**	**94**	**49**	**1529**
Product D:					
Strategic planning	8	18	38	26	
Structured analysis	10	13	17	11	
Prototyping	16	17	5	1	
Code generation	17	5	8	1	
Integration and repository	15	16	15	1	
Total:	**66**	**69**	**83**	**40**	**1495**

were so close, they rate further investigation. Rating schemes can give a good indication of a tool's potential, but they can't make your decisions for you. In this case, the company might consider running parallel pilot projects with each tool to learn more about them.

Issue requests for proposal

Many companies issue requests for proposal (RFPs) or requests for quotation (RFQs) to vendors when preparing for large-scale software purchases. Sometimes RFPs only request economic information from the vendor. Others are packaged with informational questionnaires, as described above. Most vendors of integrated CASE tools will respond to even the most lengthy requests, provided you tempt them with hints of volume purchases.

To get good information from the vendor, you'll need to estimate how many tools you'll need, how many people will be trained, and other factors. You can ask for information about other customers' implementation plans. How fast was their CASE tool rollout? How many developers were trained in the first year? Did they need one central repository for each one hundred workstations, or for each ten?

Once the vendor responds, you'll have enough data to do some financial cost/benefit analyses of the CASE tool options. If you don't send out RFPs, you'll want to contact vendors directly for cost information.

Analyze CASE economics

Having gauged the benefits of the tools, it's time to analyze the costs. Financial analysis of the CASE tool purchase serves two purposes: to compare costs and benefits of various tool options, and to justify CASE tool purchases to senior IS managers.

Financial analyses can be simple, or horribly complex. Because of the complex nature of CASE tools, simple financial analyses don't tell the whole story. For example, the spreadsheet in FIG. 10-3 calculates initial investment amounts for four different products. It illustrates an important point: CASE tool costs go way beyond the purchase price. When extrapolating costs, include the price of:

- hardware, including new machines, upgrades to old machines, and communications equipment
- supporting software, such as operating systems or DBMS's
- training and consulting

However, FIG. 10-3 misses two important points: CASE costs don't stop after the first year, and CASE benefits can more than offset these costs over time.

The first problem is easily reconciled: add ongoing costs to the calculation. These costs include:

- hardware maintenance
- software upgrades and maintenance
- new staff required (if any)
- ongoing training costs

The next problem, quantifying CASE benefits, is more difficult. In the first year, high start-up costs make most CASE implementations seem like bad investments. But the beneficial effects of CASE increase over time. It usually takes more than a year for a CASE investment to break-even.

Figure 10-3 provides a useful comparison of tool costs, but it won't help you cost-justify the CASE investment. To do this, you need to assume some financial gains due to CASE. Your spreadsheet model can show these sums a number of ways:

- staff reduction while maintaining existing service level
- more software produced by constant number of developers

Simple analysis: Integrated CASE tool cost

	Product A	Product B	Product C	Product D	
Staff Costs					
CASE Development staff	3	3	3	3	
CASE Support Staff	2	2	2	2	
Total CASE Development Staff	5	5	5	5	
Loaded Cost/CASE Developer	$90,000	$90,000	$90,000	$90,000	
Loaded Cost/Traditional Developer	$85,000	$85,000	$85,000	$85,000	
Total Salary & Benefits Differential	$10,000	$10,000	$10,000	$10,000	for CASE support staff
Training Cost per CASE Developer	$3,500	$8,500	$10,000	$10,000	
Total Training Costs	$17,500	$42,500	$50,000	$50,000	for all CASE staff
Total Staff Cost	**$27,500**	**$52,500**	**$60,000**	**$60,000**	
Development Tool Costs					
Hardware					
Number of New CASE Workstations	5	5	5	5	
Workstation unit cost	$9,500	$9,500	$13,000	$13,000	
Total hardware cost	**$47,500**	**$47,500**	**$65,000**	**$65,000**	
Software					
Central Repository Cost	$95,000	$180,000	$225,000	$250,000	
Repository Upgrades and Maintenance	$10,000	$18,000	$20,000	$25,000	
New central supporting software	$25,000	$0	$0	$0	
Total Central Software Cost	$130,000	$198,000	$245,000	$275,000	
CASE tool cost per workstation	$4,500	$2,995	$8,500	$8,000	
Supporting software per workstation	$0	$400	$0	$0	
Total Workstation Software Cost	$22,500	$16,975	$42,500	$40,000	
Total Software Cost	**$152,500**	**$214,975**	**$287,500**	**$315,000**	
Total Hardware and Software Cost	**$200,000**	**$262,475**	**$352,500**	**$380,000**	
Total Development Env't Cost	**$227,500**	**$314,975**	**$412,500**	**$440,000**	

Fig. 10-3. Simple CASE tool cost spreadsheet

- less time spent on maintenance, and more on new development, as better quality software gets rolled out
- financial impact of better systems support for strategic goals

Figures 10-4 and 10-5 illustrate more advanced financial models for gauging CASE impact. Figure 10-4 shows a baseline scenario, extrapolating development environment costs over the next five years, assuming no CASE tools are employed. This model is based on assumptions that:

- Application demands and complexity will increase at a rate of 10% per year.
- Developer salaries keep pace with inflation.
- Every new developer hired requires training and a new workstation outfitted with development software.

Figure 10-5 shows a scenario involving the purchase and deployment of integrated CASE (ICASE) tools. This model uses the same assumptions as the baseline model, plus:

- A goal for penetration of CASE tools into the IS organization has been set. This represents the percentage of developers actively using the tools.
- Estimates of productivity gain are conservative, given the ICASE tool's potential for three to five times normal productivity. Productivity starts slowly, in deference to learning curves and implementation snags, and plateaus at twice current levels.
- The IS organization will not try to increase the level of service it provides. Productivity gains will be offset by staff reductions.
- A small group of developers will form a central support group.
- CASE developers demand slightly higher salaries than traditional developers.
- CASE workstations cost more than non-CASE workstations because of the tools' demands on memory and the central processing unit (CPU).

The productivity assumption has the biggest effect upon the model.

To compare different CASE tools, you need to create separate spreadsheets for each. Substitute different cost figures and productivity estimates for each. Tools that scored higher on productivity benefits in the spreadsheet feature analysis can be assumed to provide greater financial gains from productivity.

Since CASE should be treated as a capital investment, rather than a one-time expense, you can state the benefits of CASE in terms of net present value over time. Figure 10-6 compares the baseline and integrated CASE scenarios. During the first year, the CASE scenario is more expensive. Over time, however, savings increase dramatically. In six years, the net present value of the money saved by ICASE amounts to over five million dollars at a discount rate of fifteen percent.

Projected Development Environment Costs
All amounts in thousands; some amounts are rounded

Baseline: No CASE tools

Year	1992	1993	1994	1995	1996	1997	Notes
System Complexity	1.00	1.10	1.21	1.33	1.46	1.61	10% annual increase
Inflation Rate		5%	5%	5%	5%	5%	
Staff Costs							
Development Staff	50	55	60	66	73	80	increases according to complexity
Loaded Cost/Person	$85	$89	$94	$98	$103	$108	inflation
Total Salary & Benefits Cost	$4,250	$4,909	$5,623	$6,494	$7,542	$8,679	
Training Cost per New Developer	$3	$3	$3	$3	$4	$4	inflation
Total Training Costs	$0	$16	$17	$21	$26	$27	
Total Staff Cost	**$4,250**	**$4,925**	**$5,639**	**$6,515**	**$7,568**	**$8,706**	
Development Tool Costs							
Hardware							
Number of Workstations Installed	45	50	55	60	66	73	
New Workstations Needed	5	5	5	6	7	7	per new developer
Workstation unit cost	$8	$8	$8	$8	$8	$8	price cuts counter inflation
Total workstation cost	$40	$40	$40	$48	$56	$56	
Software							
Mainframe Compiler Upgrade Cost	$15	$16	$17	$17	$18	$19	inflation
Development Software Unit Cost	$3	$3	$3	$3	$3	$3	price cuts counter inflation
Development Software/New Developer	$15	$16	$15	$18	$21	$21	
Total Tool Costs	$33	$35	$35	$38	$42	$43	
Total Hardware and Software Cost	**$73**	**$75**	**$75**	**$86**	**$98**	**$99**	
Cost of Baseline Scenario	**$4,323**	**$4,999**	**$5,714**	**$6,601**	**$7,666**	**$8,805**	

Fig. 10-4. Projected development environment costs without CASE tools

Projected Development Environment Costs
All amounts in thousands; some amounts are rounded

Integrated CASE (ICASE) Scenario
Assumes staff reduction with constant service level

Year	1992	1993	1994	1995	1996	1997	Notes
Parameters							
Application Complexity	1.00	1.10	1.21	1.33	1.46	1.61	10% annual increase
Inflation Rate	5%	5%	5%	5%	5%	5%	
CASE penetration goal	10%	20%	40%	60%	80%	80%	% of developers using CASE
Productivity Improvement	20%	40%	70%	100%	100%	100%	compared to current productivity
Staff Costs							
CASE Development staff	5	9	18	23	25	22	
"Traditional" Development Staff	41	39	28	15	6	6	10% annual increase
Total Development Staff	48	49	46	38	31	28	see formula below*
CASE Support Staff	2	2	4	5	6	4	1+20% of CASE developers
Total Development and Support Staff	50	51	50	43	37	32	
Loaded Cost/CASE Developer	$90	$95	$99	$104	$109	$115	inflation
Loaded Cost/Traditional Developer	$85	$89	$94	$98	$103	$108	inflation
Total Salary & Benefits Cost	$4,115	$4,530	$4,782	$4,430	$4,037	$3,594	
Training Cost per CASE Developer	$10	$11	$11	$12	$12	$13	inflation
Total Training Costs	$50	$42	$99	$58	$24	$0	training for new CASE developers
Total Staff Cost	**$4,165**	**$4,572**	**$4,881**	**$4,488**	**$4,062**	**$3,594**	
Development Tool Costs							
Hardware							
Installed Base CASE Workstations	0	5	9	18	23	25	
Number of New CASE Workstations	5	4	9	5	2	0	
Workstation unit cost	$13	$13	$13	$13	$13	$13	
Total workstation cost	$65	$52	$117	$65	$26	$0	
Software							
Central Repository Cost	$250	$0	$0	$0	$0	$0	
Repository Upgrades & Maintenance	$25	$50	$50	$50	$50	$50	
CASE Tool Cost per Workstation	$8	$8	$9	$9	$10	$10	inflation
CASE Tool Upgrades per Workstation	$1	$1	$1	$1	$1	$1	inflation
Total Workstation Software Cost	$40	$39	$89	$67	$47	$32	
Total CASE Software Cost	$315	$89	$139	$117	$97	$82	
Total Hardware and Software Cost	**$380**	**$141**	**$256**	**$182**	**$123**	**$82**	
Total Development Env't Cost	**$4,545**	**$4,713**	**$5,137**	**$4,670**	**$4,185**	**$3,675**	

*New staff total = previous total * (application complexity / ((CASE penetration * productivity improvement) + % traditional developers))

Fig. 10-5. Projected development environment costs with integrated CASE tools

Net Present Value Analysis of CASE Scenarios

Year	1992	1993	1994	1995	1996	1997	Notes
Cost of Baseline Scenario	$4,323	$4,999	$5,714	$6,601	$7,666	$8,805	
Cost of ICASE Scanario	$4,545	$4,713	$5,137	$4,670	$4,185	$3,675	
Savings (Loss)	($222)	$286	$577	$1,931	$3,481	$5,129	yearly
Net Present Value @ 15%	($193)	$23	$403	$1,507	$3,237	$5,455	cumul.

Fig. 10-6. Net present-value analysis of development cost scenarios

TABLE 10-9 compares the net present value figures for the four CASE tools. Product C, which was the second most expensive option in the simple cost analysis, now proves to be the biggest cost saver.

Table 10-9. Comparison of NPV Results

	NPV of Six-year Costs	NPV of Savings vs Baseline
Product A	$18,340	$4,348
Product B	$20,723	$1,965
Product C	$17,035	$5,653
Product D	$17,154	$5,455

This kind of financial analysis can go a long way toward convincing senior managers of CASE benefits. Yet results are never unequivocal. Pure financial analysis also understates many of CASE's biggest advantages.

Sculpting the intangibles By the time software decisions reach a certain management threshold, say Rosenthal and Salzman, "assessments are usually reduced to some type of financial payback calculation, while substantive issues associated with the proposed technology are submerged."[9]

The many financially intangible benefits of CASE, mentioned in chapter 3, are rarely discussed with senior managers. Edward Rivard and Kate Kaiser note that "typically, project proposals simply include checklists of intangible benefits, such as higher accuracy of data and improved customer service, with minimal description."[10] They add that "qualitative benefits also may sell systems that do not have early paybacks and that management probably would have rejected otherwise."

To get people to pay attention to intangible benefits, you often need to quantify them. Brief descriptions of intangibles are easy to ignore. Solid, numeric estimates tend to make a greater impact. Two techniques used with other qualitative business decisions are the expected value method, and sensitivity analysis.

Expected value method You determine the expected value of an option by estimating a set of possible outcomes, and assigning each one a probability. For example, CASE tools purport to lessen the number of software defects, thereby reducing maintenance costs. TABLE 10-10 shows how to calculate the expected value of maintenance savings given a range of estimates about software defect rates with CASE.

Sensitivity analysis Set up a model based upon assumptions about productivity and quality gains (this can be similar to the spreadsheet models shown earlier, or

Table 10-10. Expected Value of CASE Quality Benefits

Total function points to be developed this year			12,000
Average number of defects per function point			2
Average cost per defect (7 hours × $25/hour salary)			$175
Estimated cost of fixing defects			$3,780,000

Possible Reduction in Defects per Function Point	Probability of Occurrence	Cost Reduction	Probable Savings
0%	10%	$0	$0
5%	20%	$189,000	$37,800
10%	30%	$378,000	$113,400
30%	25%	$1,134,000	$283,500
50%	10%	$1,890,000	$189,000
80%	5%	$3,024,000	$151,200

Expected savings from CASE	$774,900
Expected reduction in defects	20.50%

altered to return a different target measure than NPV (net present value) of costs saved). Do "what if?" analyses using the model, finding the thresholds where CASE implementation changes from a good idea to a bad one. Now estimate the probability that these assumptions will come true.

For example, if the productivity gains from the ICASE tool in FIG. 10-5 never reach 45% or more, the ICASE scenario becomes just as costly as the baseline scenario. How likely is this outcome? Since other customers of this tool reported gains ranging from 40 to 200%, chances seem slim. The ICASE scenario still seems good. You can use this approach to test assumptions about less quantifiable benefits as well.

Estimates are never right You can spend weeks or months building the best models, counting each imaginary penny. But such detail is rarely warranted. Financial estimates will never come true, they'll just be varying degrees off the mark. The main purpose of financial analysis for CASE is to choose among competing tools. There is a large margin for error here. You just need enough information to rank the alternatives, not to figure costs exactly.

Top managers will be more enthusiastic about tools with a financial edge. But if you present intangible benefits well, even expensive tools will seem like bargains.

Select and purchase CASE tools

Armed with estimates of costs and benefits, you can make a well informed choice. If you have set up an evaluation steering committee, it's time to present the analyses to them, and help them reach a decision.

Once the best tool or set of tools is selected, you'll need to start vendor negotiations. The contracts you'll need to deal with might extend to:

- license agreements for software purchase
- volume purchase agreements
- lease options for high-priced tools
- service agreements for training and consulting

Most vendors will negotiate substantially lower prices for volume purchases, and for packages that include future training or consulting services. Lease options often attract smaller customers who want a high-priced tool.

Be sure to specify that the tool purchase is contingent upon successful completion of a pilot project. Despite your best research, you can't really know a tool until you use it. Though pilot project training and consulting costs won't be refundable, reserve the right to get the rest of your money back if the tool doesn't perform as advertised.

This step will end most evaluation projects. In most companies, the next step—running a pilot project with the new tool—should be handled independently, as an actual software development project.

Review the evaluation process

This won't be the last time you select new development tools. If you buy into an open repository, à la AD/Cycle, you'll frequently evaluate new CASE components in the future. Even the best integrated tools will one day bow to new technologies, which you'll need to evaluate in similar ways.

Record the best ideas arising from this evaluation project so you can apply them to future efforts. Did the evaluation steering committee work well? Were people happy to be included in this momentous decision? Once the tool has been used for a while, revisit the feature analyses and financial estimates. Where were they wrong? How could you do better in the future? Like any other process, technology evaluation benefits from continuous improvement.

11

Shaping the method pool

Software developers seem doomed to repeat the mistakes of history. Without project histories, they can never exactly duplicate essential processes, or gauge their effectiveness. Today very few IS organizations keep project histories, run postmortem project evaluations, or even document the steps followed during the development process.

Never is such introspection as important as when you first introduce CASE. It involves significant cost, a measure of anguish for all people involved, and, depending on who you listen to, mixed benefits. The potential benefits are extraordinary, but the actual ones haven't been obvious. IS managers proclaim major productivity gains in the press, but few can really back up their numbers. Others brand CASE a failure without looking at the full range of its effects.

By the end of a CASE-driven software project, most participants realize a need for formal methodologies and process measurements. Developers struggle with new techniques and discover that there's no "autopilot" setting on the CASE tools. Managers try to justify massive outlays with rough feelings that things are going better now than they were before. They pray for the one criterion that will supposedly prove everything: shorter project duration.

Two simple provisions can greatly reduce this mid-project angst: a well documented methodology and a program for measuring the development process. This chapter discusses each subject in turn, in context of the overall 12-step CASE implementation process presented in chapter 7.

Up to this point you have:

- Decided that automated software development makes strategic sense for your organization.
- Reengineered the software development process for maximum speed, quality, and management support.
- Analyzed basic software development requirements.
- Evaluated and selected CASE tools.

Now you need to document ways to meet the development requirements using the chosen CASE tools.

Building the method pool

In chapter 5, I described the need for more flexible methodologies, able to change with the technological times. With the variety of new development options available today, traditional single-path methodologies simply cast old practices in stone. They can retard the adoption of new techniques and tools.

A sturdier model that supports rapid change is the modular method pool. This collection of standard development methods lets project managers derive unique methodologies for each new type of development. Yet it encourages standardization of each technique, and common practices for building quality into every product. It also provides a framework for measuring and improving software development processes.

NASA's Michael Evans describes a possible scenario in his book *The Software Factory:*

> As methods are applied, and as tools are developed and acquired to support them, they are made available for use by other projects. Through the software environment, rules for using methods are developed, tools are shared, and the experience of one project team becomes available to others.[1]

I hope to show that such a scenario can be easily constructed and used to support software creation.

Like many other aspects of CASE implementation, method pool development should be handled as a full-fledged development project, with dedicated resources. If it's handed to someone as a part-time, unofficial duty, chances are it will never be completed.

As mentioned in chapter 5, buying a packaged methodology doesn't absolve you from documenting your own development process. No packaged methodology will fit your environment exactly. You should still pursue a project to adapt purchased methodologies to your situation.

The project can follow a sequence of steps like the one below:

1. Plan the method pool project.
2. Design the method pool.
3. Document the software development objectives.
4. Identify a baseline method path.
5. Select alternative methods.
6. Document method pool components.
7. Review the methods with stakeholders.

The numbering implies these steps are sequential, but in fact many of them can occur simultaneously. Figure 11-1 shows the dependencies between these tasks.

Building the method pool **269**

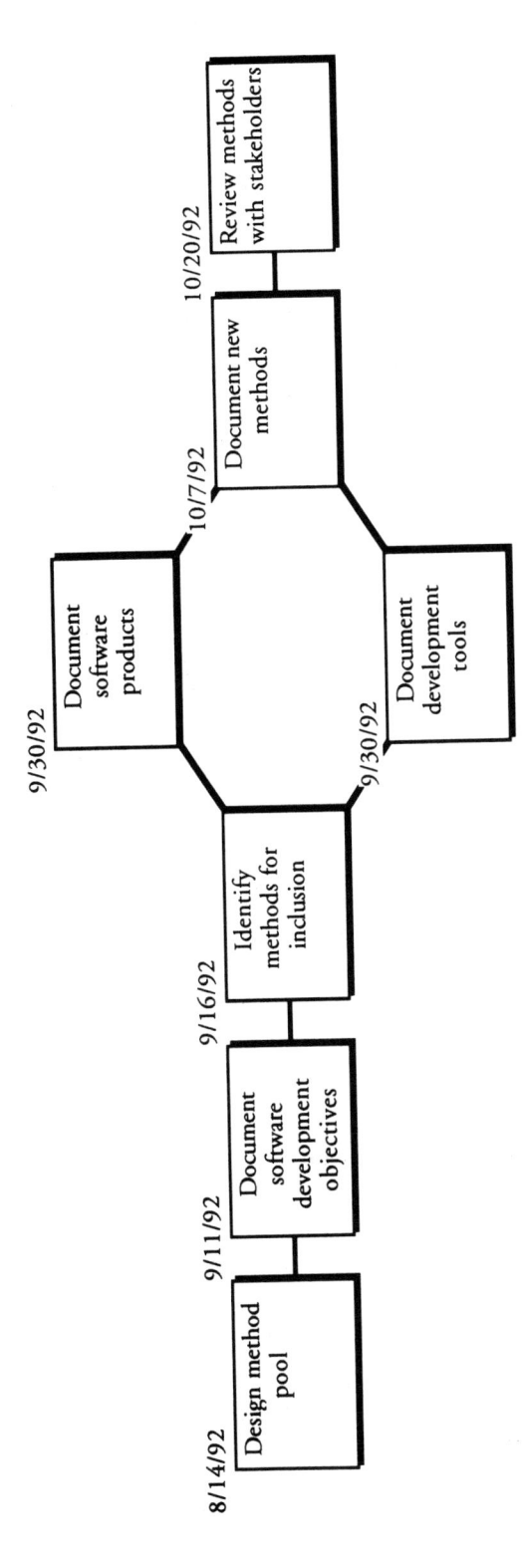

Fig. 11-1. Dependencies among method pool development tasks

Plan the method pool project

This project, like most, should start with a planning step. During this step you should set the project scope, select an approach, determine contributors, and estimate a schedule.

Set the project scope The scope of the method pool project can be defined in four parts: goals, development paths, organizations, and deliverables.

TABLE 11-1 lists some of the more far-reaching objectives of a methodology. At this point you should decide how many of these (and others) you can achieve right away. These should be clearly stated as part of the project's charter.

Table 11-1. Objectives of a Method Pool Development Project

Category	Objective
Quality	• Ability to select highest quality development alternatives • Build quality assurance into the development cycle
Productivity	• Ability to select most productive development alternatives • Repeatable methods, to build expertise and reduce learning curves
Management support	• Aids for better project estimation
Strategic benefit	• A framework for continuous process improvement

One indicator of how much to strive for is how mature your development process is today. For example, if your company hasn't set up guidelines for project management and quality assurance, it might not be ready for continuous process improvement practices. This doesn't mean you shouldn't strive for as much as you can. You can design a method pool that allows for advanced functions, but only delivers basic capabilities right away. The evolution of the method pool can pace the maturity of the organization.

You should also determine whether the method pool will start out as a vehicle for all development paths, or merely for one specific approach. The broader the scope, of course, the more robust the eventual process architecture will be. Cost constraints and approval processes often hinder such ambition.

Often a single project triggers method pool development. For many, the introduction of CASE points out a need for formal methodologies. As long as flexibility is a goal, the method pool can start off supporting a single project. Later projects can then modify the pool, drawing from the first team's experiences and adding new ideas of their own.

The development scope chosen will determine the range of participants, as well. People familiar with each development path must be interviewed or brought together. The participants should also represent a wide range of development skills, including project management, quality assurance, training, and technical services.

The final scope parameter involves the project's deliverables. Will the project team develop an automated method pool system, or a bound volume of process documentation? This decision will determine the overall project approach, as discussed in the next section.

Select an approach   The steps I've outlined so far are broad, with lots of room for tailoring. Your own software development requirements will shape the method pool, and no generic approach to building it will handle every case.

The biggest up-front decision is how to design the overall structure of the method pool. In chapter 9, I postponed discussion of how the pool will be implemented. Now is the time to consider whether you will document things on paper or online.

Most firms publish methodologies on paper and distribute copies to every developer. Yet methodologies can be easily managed as database or hypertext software systems. Either medium can convey the information, but an online solution encourages interactivity. If your developers all have access to PCs or terminals, they might find online documentation more interesting. This can put documented methods just a few key clicks away from the CASE tool itself, and in some configurations on the very same screen.

You can pick a solution that combines the best features of both mediums. The main drawback of paper-based method manuals is their necessarily serial nature. Organizing them with separate sections describing products, methods, and goals forces people to madly flip pages to follow interconnections. You can also create separate manuals for separate method paths, but this is more difficult to maintain and removes most of the method pool's flexibility.

One solution is to publish in a combination of formats. You can print comprehensive paper manuals to describe methods, products, and goals. Then supplement this with a relatively simple computer-based tool that lets people explore the information at a high level. This tool need not include all of the details behind the methods. It can help them view, organize, and build method paths from high-level descriptions, referring them to printed manuals for further details.

At this point, you should specify whether or not there will be a computerized component. This decision will affect both the project's scope and people assigned to it. Software development might require a structured design approach, perhaps using available CASE tools. It definitely requires active involvement by software developers.

Define contributors   Method pool development is not a one-person job, for many reasons:

- One person can't know the details of every technique and tool.
- Everyone will be using it, and they'll be predisposed to do so if they helped build it.
- Each technique will improve as more people contribute new ideas about it.

Though one person alone can be responsible for managing the method pool, the entire IS organization must be involved to make it a success. Larger firms with many development styles might need a team of four or five developers and technical writers to build a solid method system.

Don't overlook the need for writing skills on this project. Concise, expressive text will interest people more than bland passages that sound like instructions for building a furnace.

Someone involved in the project, normally the project leader, should be pegged to manage the method pool, on a full-time basis, once the project itself is complete. If it's going to evolve, it needs constant support.

Estimate the schedule It's a good idea to start developing the method pool before you run CASE pilot projects. You can set up the method pool structures and support before you define the actual contents. Then during the pilot project you'll know exactly what information to capture.

How far you take it before running the pilot depends upon your level of commitment to the tools and techniques. If there's a chance you might junk everything if the pilot doesn't go well, you shouldn't try to document everything up front. Capture information along the way, but don't solidify anything until the project pans out.

The method pool project can take weeks or months depending upon your organization's complexity. The duration will vary according to the number of development paths and size of the IS organization. In a small group with only one basic way of building systems, one person could document a methodology in six to eight weeks. Large companies could require years to document all the ways they write software. If you approach method pool as an evolving system, though, you should be able to deliver an initial structure within four to six months from the time the SDP analysis is completed.

Lynn Brooks of the Library of Congress reports that their methodology development project took four full-time people roughly 14 months.[2] This included the time needed to gather general development requirements, create documentation and online systems, and review the results. A similar effort at Levi Strauss & Co. is nearing completion, having taken one full-time person nearly 18 months.

Design the method pool

Few examples of good method pool exist today. Some vendors sell tools that provide some of the functions you need. But fully functional pools must evolve in-house. Method pool design involves two main steps. First, decide whether or not to build the pool yourself. Then design the method pool system, be it manual or automated.

Like any development project, this one should start with a look at general requirements before launching into detailed design. During the SDP analysis you identified the software development requirements. Now you must look at requirements for a flexible method pool to support these.

A good method pool has four main characteristics: it is simple to use, flexible, goal-driven, and comprehensive.

Simple to use Despite many IS managers' best efforts, most existing methodology documents sit in dusty binders atop office shelves. I remember pulling one of these binders onto my desks many years ago. Upon joining the company as an entry level programmer, my new boss had suggested I become familiar with the official methodology. A month later, after already hacking out an emergency program or two, I browsed the binder, perplexed. According to it, I should have filled out a form for every program and subroutine I wrote. But I had never seen anyone else do this. I asked a colleague and he laughed, saying if we followed those procedures we'd never get anything done. The presence of a methodology made managers feel secure, but it had little effect on programmers. Their case against it was too strong: something so difficult to follow certainly won't improve the process.

Switching to standardized methods is difficult enough when the methods are clear and concise. One place I worked purchased a methodology that filled 14 very large volumes (it must have been voluminous to justify the price—who would pay $50,000 for a single 500-page book?). People were too impressed by the magnitude to even browse the information. However, a quick-thinking manager extracted a 70-page abbreviation of the methods (excluding many of the bureaucratic forms and approvals). This document soon became the de facto methodology for the entire organization.

The main advantage of the second version was its simplicity. People could browse through it in under an hour. It gave people ideas about what to do next without trudging them through minute process steps that smacked of Taylorism.

Though the structure and content of a method pool can be complex, there's no reason for you to present it this way. High-level overview documents can convey general concepts and direct the reader to other documents for further details. Information can be structured so that database administrators, for example, see only the details of those tasks they're immediately involved with.

Everyone who might use the method pool should be able to access it at a moment's notice. Because of cultural difficulties, you should remove every barrier between people and the process information.

If your CASE workstation supports windowing or multi-tasking, you might devise an online system that lets developers call up method information as they work. Ideally, they could open a window into the methodology right next to the window for the CASE tool.

The easier the method pool is to use, the more value it will bring.

Flexible Building a single method path to handle all software development is like defining a dessert-making methodology in order to bake a pie. You create an analysis phase for analyzing the type of pie desired, and how its flavor will interact with other dishes. You design the pie: its dimensions, deep dish or shallow, and whether to bake it in a conventional or a microwave oven. You might break the design phase into three sections, for separate crust, filling, and topping subsystems. Finally, you define a construction phase for assembling and cooking it, and an implementation phase for serving it.

You could create dozens of pies following this methodology, but what happens when you want to bake a cake? The crust subsystem doesn't exist. So you mark the crust steps optional. But next time you want to make custard, so you make the topping steps optional, too. And when you want a spread of fresh fruits and cheeses, you have to redesign the entire methodology.

This frivolous example has parallels in the IS world. Most methodologies describe a process for building a narrow subset of systems. The methods you use to build batch file processing programs simply won't work for designing an expert system or a hypertext application. Michael A. Jackson and Daniel D. McCracken put it well when they held that "to contend that any life cycle scheme, even with variations, can be applied to all system development is either to fly in the face of reality or to assume a life cycle so rudimentary as to be vacuous."[3]

New technologies are available, and system users know it. The emphasis on end-user computing raised their consciousness. Many use more sophisticated software on their personal computers at home than they use in the office.

The intransigence of current techniques can be faulted for some of the delay in adopting new techniques. It's hard to challenge the expensive, voluminous writ of wisdom that most groups call their official methodology. Yet if the IS's goal is to please systems customers, it must improve the range of its product offerings. It must open up its methods, and speed the way to future changes.

The manufacturing world responds to a similar need with modular product assembly. The systems world already accepts the concept of modular software as a way to promote component reuse and application flexibility. Modularity facilitates change. The concept applies as easily to methodologies themselves: modular processes used as ingredients for custom method paths.

Fabrycky describes modular manufacturing well:

> It is possible to achieve a broad product line and at the same time enjoy the fruits of standardization through utilization of modular design. Modularity involves the development of component "building blocks" that can be assembled in many different combinations and configurations in order to provide a variety of products ... [Modularity] is an effort to reconcile the need for product diversification with low processing cost.
>
> Each individual order can be translated into a unique assembly configuration. Although each assembly is unique, the final product is composed of standardized parts and components.[4]

Instead of adopting an entire methodology as standard, then, you should standardize at the modular method level.

A method in this context is a technique for creating a single product or set of products to fulfill a stated goal. Methods aren't a series of techniques for creating groups of intermediate and final products, but a single technique with one or a few major outputs. Defined this way they become process blocks for building customized methodologies. Each methodology is unique, but composed of standardized method components. When one method doesn't work well, or something better comes along, the new one can plug in to replace the old.

Goal-driven You don't want to make stuff just for the sake of making it. SDLC methodologies often fail for this reason: they list tasks whose only apparent purpose is bureaucratic, and unproductive. Followed to the letter, they add clerical tasks to the programmer's workload. The mountain of paper that results obscures the real goals of software development.

I've already talked about discerning the real goals of software development before choosing the tools and methods you'll use. By building these goals into the method pool you rationalize every part of the process. Goal visibility makes future improvement more likely. People can only suggest new and better methods once they understand the true objectives.

The Hartford Insurance Company pioneered a method pool approach in the 1980s. John Crawford, director of information management, described the underlying development goals as the "systems essence":

> The selectable life cycle says, "Whatever path is taken, there are certain minimum requirements for systems essence to complete the formal models that are required

in application generation. The techniques used to get there may be changed, but unless those objects are completed, the application cannot be generated.[5]

The method pool's essence derives from an ambitious and comprehensive model of software development goals.

Comprehensive Many current methodologies focus exclusively on transformation of business requirements into software programs. This ignores the vital link between these methods and the rest of the work that surrounds them. Other life cycle approaches arose solely for management convenience, listing control steps for pounding discipline into reckless programmers.

A method pool needs to balance all aspects of systems development. Few if any methodologies include steps for quality assurance, process and data integration, project management, and development process measurement. Yet all of these functions bear heavily on project success.

Methodologies that ignore most of the real world will never be seen as practical. They don't help you estimate new projects, because they leave out a number of crucial steps. They don't provide a reliable source for finding out what to do next. A method pool should include all tasks needed to meet software development goals.

Make or buy? Some vendors offer packages that support facets of a method pool, as shown in TABLE 11-2. These tools let you define one or more methodologies, with customization points. Generally these tools work well for setting up a single stan-

Table 11-2. Sampling of Methodology Management Tools

Methodology Tool —Vendor	Base Methodology	Features
Project Management Template —Texas Instruments	Information engineering	• Export data to project management tools • Requires IEF CASE tools • Customizable tasks within preset phases • Estimation support
IE Expert —James Martin Associates	Information engineering	• Export data to project management tools • Requires IEF CASE tools • Customizable tasks within preset phases
MethodManager —Manager Systems Products	Multiple	• Integrated interface with MSP's open repository and project manager tools • Automatically invoke CASE tools on developer workstation • Customize tasks and phase • Manage multiple methodologies • Estimation support
firstCASE —AGS, Inc.	Life cycle	• Integrated interface with MSP's open repository and project manager tools • Automatically invoke CASE tools on developer workstation • Customize tasks within preset phases • Manage multiple methodologies • Estimation support

dard methodology with approved variations. However, they don't support modular methods, nor are they goal-driven. They normally let you document a "purpose" for each technique as a text description. They are all phase-based as well, forcing tasks to fall within predetermined work categories. The benefits of modularity and continuous process improvement won't materialize soon with these tools.

Yet depending upon available resources, buying such a tool might be preferable to developing one of your own. If you've never had a methodology before, setting up one or two basic ones is a great step. In addition, some of these tools provide task estimation support, and direct links to CASE and project management tools. Such links are not easy to build or maintain.

Some more comprehensive tools might emerge over the next few years. In Europe, where every country that cares has chosen a different official methodology, efforts to develop a common process architecture have been underway for years. An early ESPRIT project called Hector created a basic methodology framework. A newer Euromethod project will try to build this into a common method architecture for the European Community. However, solid results aren't expected before 1994 or 1995. IBM's AD/Cycle efforts could also lead to tools to manage methods and process architectures, probably within the same time frame.

For now, if you only need to support one or two popular development paths, and your ready cash outweighs your development resources, you would do well to choose one of the available methodology management tools. But if you're looking for flexible ways to manage many types of development, and you're ready to devote some resources to doing it right, build your own method pool. You'll want in-house understanding of process architectures anyway, and purchased tools still need full-time, dedicated support.

Method pool structure Much of the method pool's value lies in the way its data is structured. It should be built with an "open architecture" to support future developments. As Ron Radice and his colleagues, developers of IBM's Programming Process Architecture note, "Without a clearly defined and accepted architecture for the process, the tools and methodologies can only come together in a loosely coupled manner, with reduced effectiveness."[6]

You can solicit ideas from managers and developers about what they'd like a methodology to do for them. Their expectations for a methodology will be low, and some of them might be hostile to the idea. Still, their requirements can form a baseline measure for initial functionality. Be wary of building past limitations into a system designed to support change.

The method pool should not lock in the arbitrary phase breakdowns of current life cycle methodologies. For example, some integrated CASE tools make the construction or coding phase of old life cycle models virtually obsolete. If the system is generated directly from high-level designs, why do you need a coding phase? Object-oriented development can also break down boundaries between traditional phases. Some people feel that object-oriented analysis and object-oriented design are indistinguishable—the latter is merely a second iteration of the former.

A phase-based approach forces sequential dependencies that might not exist in reality. It suggests that you can't start any tasks in the next phase before this one's phase review. It also implies that full system scope is known during planning, or that all requirements are complete after analysis. Sequential phases leave no room for iteration or rework.

If you categorize methods according to certain phases, you should allow those phases to change over time. In other words, don't "hard code" specific phases into the method pool up front. Let them arise as natural task groupings, based on types of goals supported.

This same principle applies to the ubiquitous work breakdown structure (WBS). A WBS can be a valuable project management aid, but it also parcels tasks into somewhat arbitrary categories. New techniques must be force-fit into WBS categories that were never meant to hold them. Let your system derive a WBS on demand from customized method paths (perhaps based on goals rather than tasks), instead of building method paths based on numbering schemes.

When gathering data requirements, keep in mind that the method pool can also provide decision support for IS managers. In particular, the entity types describing projects, method histories, and metrics will give IS managers unprecedented visibility into the development process.

Figure 11-2 presents a high-level data model for a method pool system. This can act as a starting template for your own efforts. The fundamental entity types describe goals, products, methods, method paths, contributors, and development tools.

Method pool functionality A breakdown of method pool functionality is shown in FIG. 11-3. The fundamental system must manage all basic method pool information. You can gather project experiences and measure effectiveness manually, incorporating these findings into future versions of the method pool as warranted.

The system must also provide guidelines for charting method paths for specific projects. Manual systems usually include predetermined method paths for each popular form of development. The project managers then must identify and document all exceptions to the official method path.

A more sophisticated system lets you capture metrics and project experiences as part of the method pool. A database system will let you update existing methods with this information.

Project managers will benefit from an additional feature: automated support for creating method paths. This lets them dynamically generate new method paths to fit specific projects. The manager specifies project goals and constraints. The system responds with a list of known methods that meet these requirements. The manager pulls methods from this list, pulling the ones that fit best with the team's skills into a project method path.

Additionally, the system can apply task iterations according to project estimates and export the data to project management tools. Figure 11-4 illustrates a method path drawn from the pool, and how various tasks multiply according to number of products required.

The advanced functionality is not trivial. The most successful systems I've seen use some form of rule-based logic.

Incremental delivery I don't suggest that everyone design and build a fully functional method pool right away. If you can document some standard methods on

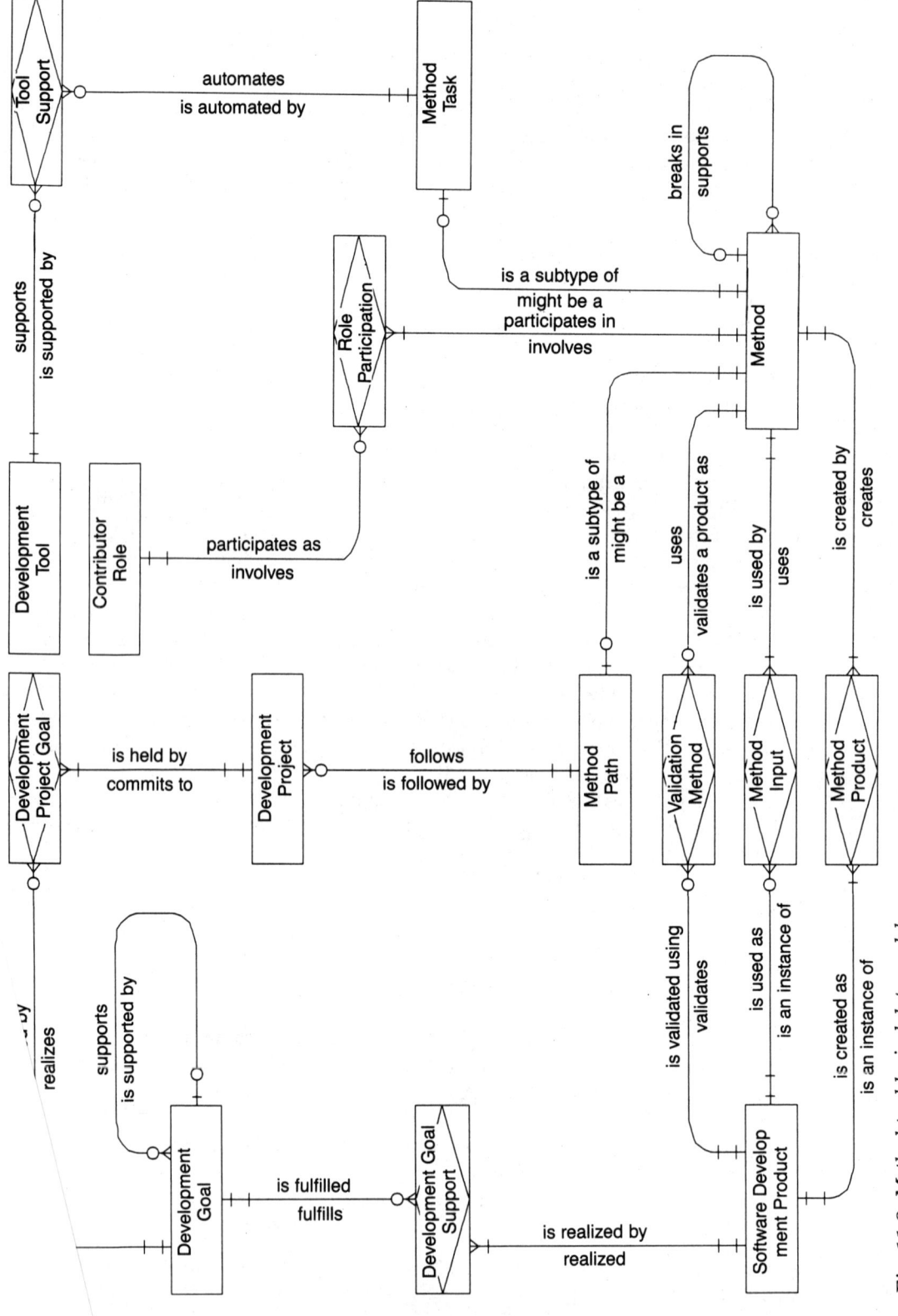

Fig. 11-2. Method pool logical data model

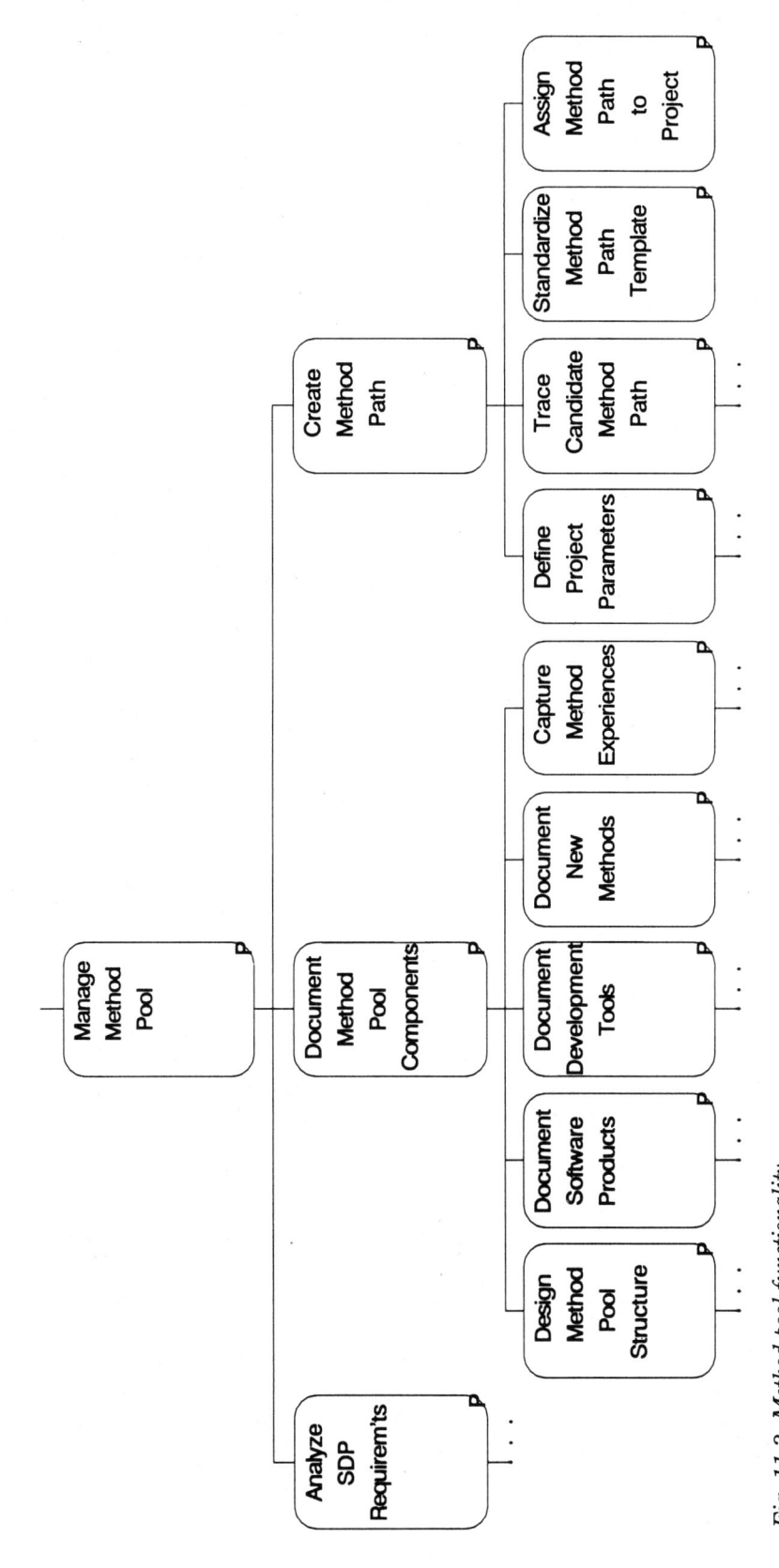

Fig. 11-3. Method pool functionality

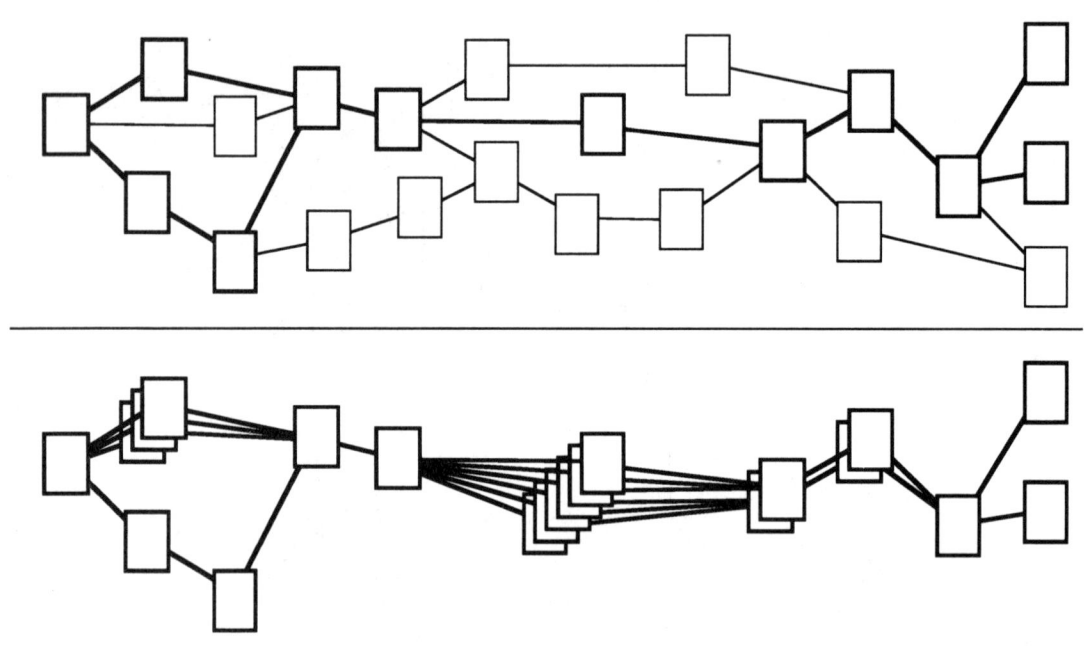

Fig. 11-4. A method path drawn from the pool, with repetitive tasks multiplied

paper, you've made a great start. From there you can jump to a simple, relational database or hypertext system that allows ad hoc inquiries. Build advanced functions onto these as you progress.

You don't even need to document all available methods up front. When the concept of methodology is new, sketchy methods can be better than fully detailed ones. This puts a burden on the early practitioners: they must figure out and write down the best ways to perform each technique. Yet it lets you start small, delivering a bounded method pool framework to build upon.

Starting small lets you practice evolutionary development of the method pool. Evolutionary development removes the temptation to make the method pool so complex and all-encompassing that it becomes unusable. You can develop a streamlined, high-level method pool framework very quickly. Then use early project experience to flesh out the best approaches to each method. Soon you'll have a practical, effective, and fully documented set of method paths.

TABLE 11-3 shows one progression for incrementally delivering method pool functions. Incremental delivery lets you deliver basic functions quickly, while designing systems with an open architecture to aid future enhancements. For further information about incremental delivery, refer to Tom Gilb's book, *Principles of Software Engineering Management*.

Only the first subset in TABLE 11-3 can be easily implemented on paper. Nonlinear information doesn't comport itself well in linear documents. If you will create a paper-based methodology, the main chore you'll face is making the information easily accessible. Usually this means organizing the information into separate volumes. One provides an overview of the method pool—development objectives, standard method paths, con-

*Table 11-3. Evolutionary
Delivery of Method Pool Functionality*

Subset	Functions	Data Structures
1	• Basic entry and update capability • Reporting for single, standard method path	Goal, product, method, method path, tool, and contributor
2	• Dynamic method path creation	Project
3	• Export data to project management tools	
4	• Ability to capture project method histories	Method history
5	• Process and product measurement	Process metric and product metric

tributor roles—with references to other documents that provide more details. Supporting volumes include reference documents for:

- deliverables, including evaluation criteria
- methods, including estimation criteria and detailed procedures
- development tools
- training courses, or self-paced tutorials

Figure 11-5 shows the relationships between these volumes.

Each set of method pool functionality forms the basis for small, directed software design projects. You can use whichever structured design techniques you favor to create each subset in turn.

Document the software development objectives

During the IS planning and SDP analysis efforts, you developed a structured set of software development goals. These goals should be the first information to populate the method pool. They provide the rationale for the products and methods that follow.

If you want some ties to previous development phases, you can derive some high-level goals from the objectives of each phase. For example, one goal implied by a requirements specification phase might be understand business area dynamics. You can then tie management checkpoint or review methods to the fulfillment of this goal. As a result, project management will depend upon the fulfillment of common objectives, not upon creation of convenient documents.

While you expect technologies and methods to change rapidly, your strategic goals should remain relatively stable. Process improvement becomes a search for methods that achieve the same goals more cheaply.

One approach is to reverse engineer your goals from the methods you use today. But you end up with shortsighted goals this way, defined by the nature of today's tasks.

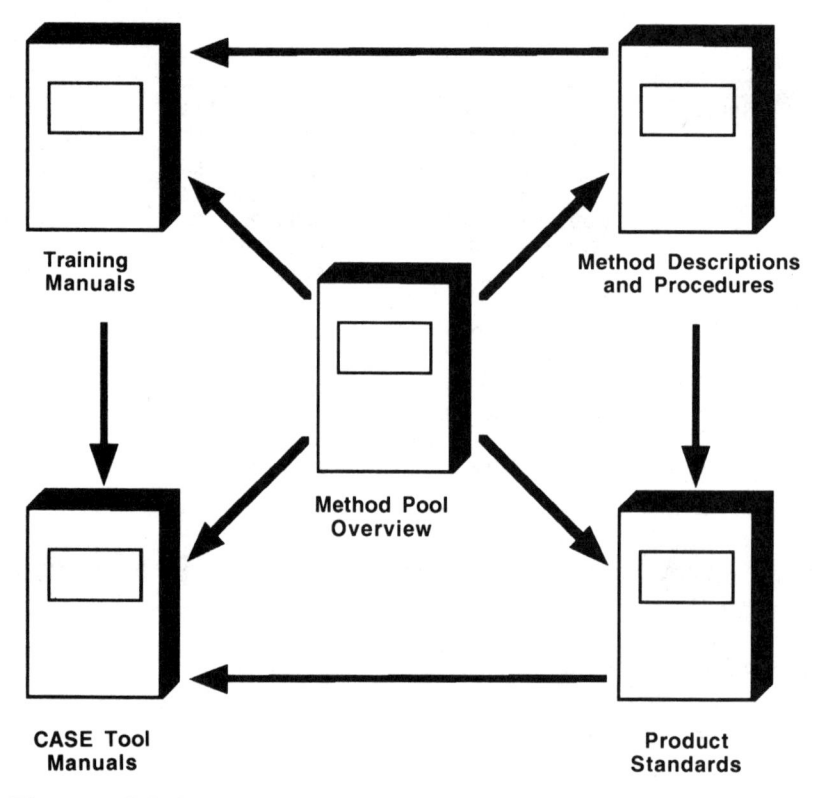

Fig. 11-5. Relationships between methodology documents

Since the goal model will drive future improvements, it must be visionary. If goals aren't ambitious, neither will future improvements be.

Identify a baseline method path

The next step involves seeking ways to reach your objectives. Most likely your current methods aren't meeting them all. Yet you can build upon the things the IS group does well today.

Your analysis of the SDP gives you a benchmark in the hunt for method paths. It indicates the conceptual data and processes your environment should contain. Now you must make the conceptual real, and look for the best implementations possible.

Method paths will vary according to many factors:

- Developer skills. In many cases, project managers will select techniques because they are already familiar to the project team. It pays to keep some traditional methods in the pool, especially ones you do well today, even if they're not as exciting as newer ones.
- Development paradigm. The object-oriented paradigm, for instance, entails a different set of paths and techniques than does the traditional process-centered perspective.

- Project schedule. There are cases where the schedule can drive the project. These situations call for rapid development method paths that incorporate prototyping, timebox, or evolutionary delivery techniques.
- Size and complexity. Small systems projects can skip many of the coordination and project management tasks that larger ones go through.
- Type of application. Screen-driven database applications, expert systems, and real-time embedded systems all require different tasks.
- Concurrent hardware development. The method pool concept will apply to other kinds of development, too. The paths for concurrent hardware and software development vary dramatically from software-only projects.
- Integration priorities. Creating suites of integrated applications requires many new coordination tasks.
- Entry point into the development process. Many teams switch to CASE or structured techniques midway through the life cycle. The disadvantages of this approach often outweigh the benefits. If you anticipate this situation, create special method paths for these teams The teams must know which of the earlier techniques to complete before they move to the next phase.

To satisfy all of these conditions, you'll need to pull methods from many different sources.

Finding method paths An incredible number of designer methodologies are out there, each touted as the solution to all your development problems. Most of them do solve some of the problems developers face. In addition, each IS organization has a repertoire of tested techniques and people to perform them.

If you're not attempting to reengineer the software development process, but merely documenting what you do today, you can start with a survey of current techniques. This can take the form of a search for best practices. Present a generic framework for your method pool—identify commonly recognized phases and some essential tasks—and then ask people to fill in the blanks. Who knows a clever way to generate test data? Who's got a good method for gathering business information from users? Have a jury review the methods, select some of the best, and reward the submitters. Then use these best practices as the start of the method pool.

The pool can then frame the evolution of your development process. Encourage new ideas, and institute a frequent review cycle and you can move toward the future a task at a time.

Other approaches to method gathering include:

- Purchase a packaged methodology. These are normally very expensive and thick with bureaucratic steps. However, some provide creditable technique descriptions, and many have automated support. Don't just bring in the books and put them on people's desks; recast them into your own format. Otherwise people will never attempt to improve the methods. Packaged methods often come in some biblical format, and one does not rewrite the Bible.
- Buy an integrated CASE tool and adopt the methodology that comes with it. Some vendors plug the methodology gap with their own offerings, tied directly to their CASE tools. This can be a fine way to jump-start a methodology project.

Remember, though, that you must still customize the methodology to match your environment. Plus, unless you plan to use this vendor's CASE tools for life, you'll need to expand it to manage multiple paths in the future.
- Adapt your current SDLC methodology for CASE and structured techniques. SDLC methodologies don't often adapt well to structured design techniques. Usually this just adds new deliverables on top of existing ones, increasing workloads. If you take this approach, be sure to radically redo the deliverables, replacing obsolete ones. Adapt the SDLC to new techniques, not the other way around.
- Survey the software engineering literature. Many of the best methods are published in books that cost a hundred times less than packaged methodologies. Few single books cover all aspects of software engineering, but with a small set of volumes about strategic planning, different styles of software development, project management, and process measurement, you can cover the full spectrum.
- Contact CASE vendors. The information you gathered while investigating CASE tools is invaluable. It shows you which methods already have automated support.

Select from these sources the methodology you feel will support the largest part of your software development efforts. Though the method pool is modular in design, while setting it up you need to see it from the full development cycle perspective. The pool must start off with at least one complete path to use as a basis for future improvements.

To set it up initially, you can take the following steps:

1. Start with a single method path. If you're planning incremental improvements within an existing methodology, use it as a basis. If you're starting from scratch, or you want to shift to a new development paradigm, pull a new path from one of the sources above. Pick a popular one, if possible, one well supported by advanced tools. To date, the information engineering methodology has the widest automated support base. If the method pool is a prelude to a CASE pilot project, make sure you choose a path that the pilot can use.
2. Match the products of this method path against the goals you've defined. A DFD, for example, will support a goal to define the interactions between business processes.
3. Discover which goals this method path doesn't support. An SDLC methodology normally fulfills most management goals, but fails miserably to support rapid development. Most CASE vendors' methods, on the other hand, address better quality and efficiency goals, but completely ignore management aspects.
4. Seek additional methods to fill the goal gaps. A book like Tom DeMarco's *Controlling Software Projects*, for example, can generate plenty of ideas for new management techniques. Other gaps can be filled by bringing in supplemental CASE tools. Be sure to include methods for validating products, such as reviews or structured walk-throughs. Also add methods for assessing process effectiveness, such as postmortem project reviews.

5. Once complete, you have a baseline method path. Consider adding alternative techniques for meeting some of the goals. Look for those that will meet the same goals at lower cost, or with higher quality. This way the method pool can start as a testing ground for new development ideas.
6. Document all the products, CASE tools, and methods in your method pool systems or documents.

These steps will help you establish the method pool's foundation. If you're rushed, you can limit the investigation of new methods and tools. The path you use to start doesn't need to be the ultimate development methodology. It can leave room for improvement; the pool's structure encourages it.

Select alternative methods

Most advantages of a method pool come from its ability to handle multiple, standard techniques. Competing ways of working should be encouraged. Still, there are limits to how frequently people can change things.

Be careful about adding every variation as a new method. As Roger Pressman cautions, "Because methods are closely aligned with the creative process, and everyone 'creates' differently, it is difficult to achieve consensus in this area."[7] Some people might feel that producing an entity-relationship diagram using one notation is totally different from drawing one using other conventions. In essence, these tasks both create the same product: a diagram of data relationships.

There is no point defining methods to use or create products that have only fleeting value. Each method and product provide avenues for managing the software development process, and evaluating substantial products. If a product need not meet any quality standards, and if it isn't required as input to another method, there is no need to document it. Similarly a method that creates nothing of value need not be defined. Most likely such a method is really a step within a larger method.

Say your data modelers normally interview business experts to gather business data requirements. If they follow a structured interview format, and wish to store interview notes for future reference, you might create a method to gather data requirements through structured interview. If these interviews are informal, though, creating a separate method isn't necessary. It would imply that you want to track and manage the data modeler's interview notes (which might be in illegible chicken-scratch on notepaper). Instead you would set this up as a step within a larger method:

- Gather initial business data requirements through structured serial interviews, or facilitated data discovery sessions.
- Synthesize data requirements into rough, high-level data model.
- Verify high-level model with select business users.
- Normalize data model to third normal form.

The follow-up task might then be a formal review of the data model with business experts and other members of the data modeling staff.

Generating alternatives Drumming up better techniques can be as simple as asking people, "How could we make this product better?" Perhaps screen interfaces would improve if they were created cooperatively during JAD sessions. Perhaps a screen prototyping tool could automate an even better process.

Other techniques arise from nonstandard development efforts. What about the team that needs to rewrite some old FORTRAN programs to transfer them to a new machine? With the addition of some reverse engineering tasks, they could follow a slightly different method path, but still perform most of the same techniques as their colleagues.

The method pool can also be used to combine the best parts of different packaged methods. I've worked with projects that used information engineering techniques for strategic information planning, and followed them with analysis and design tasks pulled from other methodologies.

The method pool intends to manage many different techniques, but you don't want to taint it by pouring in bad data. Evaluate techniques and paths for addition to the pool, and don't throw in every method that comes to mind.

As Michael Evans states, "The question to be asked when selecting or applying a method is: How does the method support the needs of the environment as a whole?"[8] Consider the factors that affect a technique's effectiveness:

- Integration with other methods. The first time someone tries object-oriented development, for example, many previous management methods become invalid. Make sure the methods you choose provide continuity from early planning through to software construction.
- Technical support. Are there good tools available to use this method? Are they integrated well with other tools you have?
- Developer skills. Can anyone do it well? If not, is training available? Your developers have lots of experience with certain techniques today. Sometimes keeping these techniques is a good solution.
- Imposed standards. For example, can the method produce documents that meet DoD-STD-2167A standards?
- Validation and verification. Is the method's output reviewable or testable? Do you need a separate technique for verifying the results of a previous one?
- Time constraints. Can the method be completed within allotted time limits? Does it contribute to a goal of rapid development?
- Reputation. Has anyone else used the method successfully, either in the company or in the industry?
- Cooperation with new groups. Forging new relationships with other subunits can be costly. Before involving these groups in your methods, prepare yourself for the coordination effort.

You want to encourage alternatives. But the effort involved in cataloging and measuring each method is not trivial. Make sure you pick the ones with the best potential for success.

Document method pool components

Once you've selected paths and methods for inclusion, it's time to fit them into the process architecture. You'll need to document the products, CASE tools, and detailed procedures for each method.

Document software products Products can be specifications, software objects, such as programs or database structures, or other deliverables like diagrams, documents, approval forms, or compiled survey results. Most products are created by one or more alternative techniques, and used as inputs by others.

You should work backwards from development goals to find supporting products. Sometimes you'll be forced to include products that don't support the objectives you've set. For example, your clients might request documents from you in an antiquated format, to conform to slow-changing corporate standards. I've seen cases where full internal specification documents were created for systems that were 100% code-generated. Hundreds of pages of machine-written code, virtually unintelligible to most humans, were distributed to dozens of business folk, simply because of corporate standards. If you find yourself in this position, fabricate a goal for conformance to client standards, and tie these products to it.

You should capture some basic information about each product:

- Description. Try to provide illustrations of sample diagrams or documents.
- Expected format. Must a diagram be printed, or can it reside in a CASE repository? This can also specify whether the product must be distributed to managers or project stakeholders.
- Evaluation criteria. What are the quality guidelines for this product? What kind of measurements can be taken to ensure product and process quality? This should describe criteria for product completeness (how to know when the task is done), and quality (the factors that make this a good product).

Some evaluation criteria can't be specified in detail until the project begins. Customer requirements might call for exceptional levels of reliability or usability that can't be anticipated ahead of time. You should allow for ways to describe these additional requirements for specific project paths.

Document CASE tools The methodology can't be complete without references to CASE tools. Tools, methods, products, and goals form a dynamic system: without one component, the others won't form a useful body of knowledge.

It would be nice to catalog every feature of every tool, so everyone can know what's available. Normally the effort involved is too great. You'll probably have your hands full just documenting the features you plan to use, without adding the ones you don't.

You can habitually document new tools when you launch pilot projects to test their feasibility. Later inject the results of the completed pilot project: whether the tool was effective, whether it outperformed alternative tools, and whether it will be available in the future.

The information to capture about tools is pretty basic. You need just enough to classify the tool's environment and availability:

- name and description
- hardware and software requirements, for both the development and target environments, which can be matched to the parameters of each project to help people select the right methods for their circumstances
- availability, noting whether the CASE tool is under limited distribution within the company

Details about how to use the tool will be captured as part of the procedures that describe each method.

Document detailed procedures The method information links the goals, products, and development tools. For each method, you should specify:

- Description. A high-level explanation of the technique and how it differs from alternative ones.
- Work breakdown structure. Classify methods by work type, using an accepted numbering scheme, if your management so requires.
- Estimation guidelines. How long should it take to conduct one iteration of this technique?
- Detailed procedures. Step-by-step instructions for preparing for and executing the method.
- Project experiences. Histories of actual applications of the technique, including hints and suggestions for better execution.

Beware of making your procedure descriptions too involved. The more detailed they are, the more often you'll need to change them. Avoid listing specific instructions about how to use the automated tools. Refer the reader to the tool's reference manuals instead.

Review methods with stakeholders

There is no point in capturing all of this information if you won't use it to improve the process over time. The first step, once the pool is built, is to present it for review. You'll need to review both the system itself and its content. Then you should set up a framework to review and improve the pool contents on an ongoing basis.

Testing the water Once you've filled the pool, test it out. By the time you've built the pool, you probably have a project or two poised to use it. Let a project manager try to build a path for an upcoming project. Test the dependencies between goals, products, methods, and tools. Are there any products that get created but never used? Are there any that don't support any goals?

If you've compiled paper documents, have people see how easy it is to find information. Are the descriptions readable, and the illustrations useful? If you've developed a computerized pool, you can apply standard testing techniques to determine acceptability.

Maintaining the method pool Before you start people running with the new methods, make sure they know their new responsibilities to the development process. From the very first project, people should start measuring how well each technique works. They must know that they can change the methods if they like. If they find the suggested methods inadequate, let them propose their own.

Some Japanese software firms promote continuous improvement in a similar fashion. Each project team must follow an approved method path, but is allowed to substitute one new technique. The only restriction: they must document the steps they followed, and measure their effectiveness.

The method pool won't evolve on its own. It needs constant support from dedicated employees. Some new roles include:

- Software development process steering committee. This group can convene periodically to evaluate method alternatives and suggest new entries into the method pool.
- Full-time method pool manager. This person will manage the information in the method pool, and help people become proficient at using it. This person can also perform analyses upon collected process measurements, and pass this information along to the steering committee and other interested parties.
- Software process architects. These people design modular methods and method paths. They capture method information and seek combinations of techniques that optimize the overall process. In smaller companies, the method pool manager can play this role as well.

Once the method pool falls into common use, it will affect the dynamics of the entire IS organization. Successful new methods will generate demand for new tools and new skill training. The method pool manager should be able to coordinate these effects with others who manage tool procurement and training programs.

The net result should be steady progress toward your ambitious software development goals. Of course, to be certain of this progress, you need to start measuring the value of the methods you use.

12

Measuring the splash

You can't know if new methods work better than old ones unless you measure the results. The only way to prove that CASE helps you is to quantify its effects. Most claims of greater CASE productivity are rough and unsubstantiated, and unmeasured advantages are difficult to sell.

Process improvement is the strongest reason for process measurement, but it's not the only one. Better measurement lets you capture actual development costs, to better determine profitability. It also enables better estimation of schedules and costs for future projects.

Despite these benefits, very few companies even try to measure IS performance. In a 1988 survey, less than 4% of IS managers could say how productive their department was, and less than 2% could assess the quality of their delivered systems.[1] But measurement is essential to CASE success, and should not be overlooked.

Most measurement approaches in the past concentrated on specific benchmarks for software defects and volume of software produced. These benchmarks are valuable, but they alone won't tell you how well you're doing. The true measure of IS success is positive business impact and customer satisfaction achieved with efficient use of resources.[2] As metrics guru Howard Rubin says, "The ideal measurement program design must be robust enough to satisfy both IS and business needs."[3]

I won't expound upon specific metrics in this section, since the subject is already covered well by other authors.[4] However, I will suggest some general principles for measuring CASE effectiveness and IS performance:

- Base measurements on IS goals and customer-defined criteria, not on software size.
- Focus on simple measurements, especially those that can be handled using CASE tools.
- Start measuring current projects so you have something to match new ones against.
- Devote full-time resources to the measurement program.
- Constantly review and improve the measurement process.

Good metrics don't fall on your lap. Because there are few common guidelines for measuring the software process, you'll need to develop most of your own. Once again, this takes a concentrated project effort.

Poolside metrics

As with method pool creation, process measurement can start as a project, and roll into an ongoing program. Because of the overlap between goals, methods, and metrics, this project can run in conjunction with the method pool project.

A rough set of steps for this project include:

1. Plan the metrics program.
2. Determine what to measure.
3. Measure current and past projects.
4. Measure effectiveness of methods.
5. Analyze and distribute metrics.
6. Review the metrics and measuring process.

As I describe these steps in more detail, I'll focus on the metrics you'll need to evaluate new tools and methods, and the ways in which CASE tools can help you measure.

Plan the metrics program

The planning step outlines the measurement scope, the approach for determining metrics, the people needed, and the metrics project schedule.

Set the measurement scope   The two predominant reasons for starting a measurement effort when you alter the development environment are to evaluate the performance of CASE technology and to gauge overall IS performance and enable continuous process improvement.

If all you're after is a quick assessment of a CASE pilot project's productivity, then you can narrow your immediate measurement scope. In this situation, you need to show that performance is better with CASE than without, based on current, well understood measures. You don't want to hold off a CASE pilot project while you congregate to decide which metrics to use. You can get a decent idea of the benefits of CASE without measuring all dimensions of the IS environment ahead of time.

A narrow measurement scope won't serve you well beyond the initial CASE pilot projects, though. If you've been keeping historical metrics, chances are that they measure software productivity, but ignore quality, business impact, and customer satisfaction. To improve the development process, you need to track progress against IS and business goals. This implies taking a very wide view of metrics, one that surveys the breadth of IS.

A poolside view   The scope for an ongoing measurement program should be identical to that of the method pool. Your goal model will drive the metrics just as it drives products and methods. The IS goal model follows directly from strategic business goals, so this will tie your measurements directly to the company's bottom line.

The stated purpose for the measurement program should be carefully prepared. You might say at the start that it's only to compare the new CASE techniques against previous development methods. Then you can grow the program into a more all-embracing effort to monitor essential IS activity.

Be careful to defuse rumors that these new measurements will be used as a form of control. Sandhiprakash Bhide, life cycle process manager at Mentor Graphics notes, "One of the main reasons for the resistance to . . . metrics by the engineering community has been the misuse of metrics as a ranking and rating tool."[5] If you plan to judge people with these metrics, you'll find that measurement itself will be much harder to accomplish. Convincing people that the measurements are a benign attempt to improve the process will be one of the most difficult tasks you'll face.

When to start? The metrics program should be started before you make major changes to the development environment. Ideally, you can gather some basic metrics before initial CASE pilot projects begin.

You don't have to wait until you select a CASE tool. Good metrics aren't gathered overnight. You'll need time to put them together. Even if you don't plan any CASE projects soon, you should start measuring your current environment today.

Once you begin measuring effects of new tools, allow sufficient time before judging their overall productivity or quality benefits. Initial pilot results indicate general acceptability, but they aren't an accurate assessment of what you can do once you know the tool well. CASE learning curves are long. It will take more than one project to demonstrate the lasting effects of CASE.

Who will measure? The effort involved in a comprehensive measurement program can keep people busy full-time. Many firms have set up separate metrics groups within the IS organization. Initial tasks involve deciding what to measure. These require participation from representatives throughout IS.

Like so many other efforts, metrics programs work best when participation is broad. Solicit input from those whose work will be measured. They are the ones who will be most affected by the program. In many cases, they will be the ones doing the measuring.

Because of the political sensitivity of measurement programs, make every effort to let developers drive the process. A measurement decision made without developer involvement is akin to taxation without representation. Don't try to impose it, or you'll face a revolution.

The actual measurement tasks are often suited to a few diligent metrics specialists. Another approach hands all metrics responsibilities to a separate quality assurance group. This ensures some consistency across projects. However, as metrics gain popularity, this can cause a measurement bottleneck. It can also inject new politics and bureaucracy into the measurement process. Developers might feel the metrics group is dogging their heels, slowing them down, or even misinterpreting the data.

A good long-term approach is to transfer measurement responsibility to developers themselves. People who feel accountable for their performance want to know how they're doing. If they know that the measurements are done to improve the process, not to punish laggards, they'll be inclined to collect them. They will also push to keep the metrics simple, understandable, and easy to collect.

Determine what to measure

A dozen people in a room can brainstorm hundreds of ways to measure IS performance. But measuring for its own sake won't take you anywhere. You don't want metrics to be a resource and productivity drain.

Roger Pressman remarks that it is "essential to limit the measurements to those few items that will really be used. Measurements are both expensive and disruptive; over-zealous measuring can degrade the processes we are trying to improve."[6] It's more important to select a few meaningful metrics and start collecting them than it is to capture every measurement possibility.

So how do you judge which metrics are most appropriate? The best metrics are those that:

- enable comparisons across multiple projects
- represent true goals
- can be simply presented and understood
- can be easily collected

Comparisons to current environment   Initially, your choice of metrics can be limited to what you need to measure a CASE pilot project. If your shop currently keeps standard metrics, measure early CASE projects against the same scale. For example, many shops gather information about effort expended per line of code (LOC).

If you're out to sell people on CASE, LOC measurements can be a great sales tool. CASE-generated LOC metrics almost always exceed those from hand-coded systems efforts. As an example, novice students using TI's IEF tool each routinely generate over 100,000 lines of working COBOL code during a two-week class exercise. Even the best COBOL hackers have a hard time matching this pace by hand.

However, CASE-generated programs normally have inflated LOC counts. Since code generators must handle every eventuality, they often build in lots of overhead and idle code (stubs for unused functions). This makes direct comparison to pre-CASE LOC metrics less valuable.

Other metrics, like function points or DeMarco's Bang calculation, approximate software functionality without language bias. They can be more appropriate for comparing CASE results against previous projects, or projects from other companies. Function points are rapidly becoming the industry standard for evaluating software size and complexity, and data on industry averages is readily available.[7]

Unfortunately, none of these measures translate well across different development paradigms. Lines of code statistics vary widely according to the programming language used and many other factors. Function points and Bang metrics are only valid for certain types of software functions; they don't make much sense for expert systems, neural networks, or in many cases, object-oriented systems.

These metrics all weigh software quantity without regard to quality or customer satisfaction. Yet better productivity—creating more software in a shorter period of time—is only one potential CASE benefit, and often the last one to emerge. Without methodologies or quality assurance tasks, CASE lets you generate mountains of code, much of it trash. Yet mountains of trash look great viewed through function point or LOC metrics. Your initial set of metrics should also assess software quality.

Most IS shops can gather data about the number of bugs found in delivered software. However, most pilot projects don't attempt to build a polished final product, so this figure isn't directly comparable. In fact, a cursory pilot project can do little to demonstrate the quality of CASE-generated software. Some quality gains, such as elimination of typographic or code syntax errors, can be assumed with certain tools. To really gauge CASE's quality boost though, you need to run a full-scale development project, and take a much broader view of metrics.

Based on goals Every metric implies the maximization of certain development aspects. To succeed, you need to maximize the factors that let you meet your short- and long-term goals.

Make sure that the metrics you choose are truly important. Measurements are policies in action. In the absence of strong shared values, measuring can skew the process. For example, if you tie project productivity measures to the volume of software produced, using LOC or function points, you encourage people to build large, complex systems. If you tie it to some measure of customer satisfaction or business impact, on the other hand, you encourage small, relatively powerful systems.

If your highest measure is function points implemented per unit of time, you still maximize the wrong thing. A developer who works an extra hour to remove a redundant data access, for example, adds time while reducing function points. The metric's value will be lowered while producing a faster, higher quality product.

Unless you've defined a goal called "create humongous quantities of source programs," function points and lines of code shouldn't be your primary measures. Even more complete measurements of software content and complexity, like DeMarco's Bang metrics,[8] can't assess the business value of the system, or guess how much people enjoy using it.

If you start defining projects whose only outputs are strategic plans and diagrams, for example, lines of code isn't a useful measure. You need to capture metrics at meaningful points throughout the development cycle.

What you really want to know is:

- Do the delivered systems improve the customer's competitive or financial position?
- Do the systems meet customer standards for timeliness, usability, learnability, and reliability?
- Are the users happy with the way they are treated by IS (and vice versa)?
- Is the IS group responding fast enough to meet the users' needs?
- Does the development environment meet the needs of software developers?
- Are project managers close to the mark with their estimates of project cost, benefit, and duration?

In short, is the IS group making progress toward its strategic goals? And is CASE helping?

Unfortunately, there aren't many standard approaches to measuring these kinds of objectives. All the firms that have done so successfully have had to define their own metrics. With a clear idea of IS's strategic direction, this is not hard to do.

If the goal model was built with measurability in mind, deciding what to appraise won't be difficult. Each goal should have some sort of measurement attached to it. The metrics for higher level goals will summarize the value recorded for all subordinate goals. This produces a metrics hierarchy that parallels the goal model. It ensures that lower level measurements serve the desired purposes: to help accomplish the IS organization's strategic goals. After all, why measure lines of code if doing so won't help tell you whether you met the customer's business needs?

IS managers will be more interested in the summary level metrics, and developers and project managers will benefit from the specific, method-level measures. This structure also helps protect developers from abuse of metrics by management. Instead of only knowing how many lines of code they produce, engineers can start seeing what their impact is upon the company as a whole.

Quality goal example Suppose you define a high-level goal to double software quality within two years. This might break into three supporting goals:

1. Reduce errors in delivered software 100% by 1994.
2. Increase customer satisfaction by providing systems that meet or exceed negotiated customers' business requirements.
3. Improve the perceived ease of use of software systems 100% by 1994.

To decide what to measure, simply work backward from these goals. First clarify ambiguous parts of the goal statements. What does "errors" mean in the first goal? It could refer to defects caught during final system testing, or the number of software bugs reported after installation, or the number and frequency of work stoppages due to software failures. You might need more information from the IS planning group before you can answer this. Whichever measure is chosen becomes your benchmark for the first goal.

The next two goals aren't so easy to quantify. How can you measure adherence to requirements? Studies can be done to trace system components back to the original analysis model upon which they are based. But this can't account for user's requirements that never made it into the model because of communication problems, or a premature "freezing" of requirements gathering efforts.

To measure goals like these, you have to cross traditional barriers. It's a common assumption that things you can't gauge accurately aren't worth measuring. Hence the propensity toward lines of code and function points: these can be counted easily and accurately. Many burning goals can't be answered with ready numbers. To quantify them, you need to send out surveys, ask people questions, or gather information about business performance. This raw, subjective data can then be mapped to common, simple scales that let people publicize and compare results.

A good way to measure customer satisfaction, then, is with a survey. Does the system do everything the customers wanted it to? Do they find it easy to use and learn? A standard questionnaire with responses fit to a numeric scale will let you compare survey results historically and across projects.

With lower level goals set, the highest level goal—to double system quality within two years—can be measured a couple of ways. You can create an index that combines the value of the subordinate measures, or you can simply report each of the component metrics separately, and require each of them to double within that time frame.

The process of matching metrics to goals helps firm up the goal model too. You can put solid numbers to previously nebulous objectives. You might also discover some goals that were previously overlooked.

Depending upon your goal model, this approach could leave you with a few dozen types of metrics to collect. But you don't need to start measuring all of these at once. If you've prioritized your goals, you can stagger metrics implementation according to the same priorities.

Some obvious measurements might not be stated in the goal model. A basic goal of measuring is to provide project managers with a basis for estimating future endeavors. You should keep track of the effort it takes to complete each task, and make these numbers available to project managers throughout the firm.

Figure 12-1 lists measurement ideas for the Normalco goal model presented in chapter 8. Note how each high-level goal summarizes metrics from its children. At the level of the topmost goal, the IS Mission, the group's total performance can be summed up with a half-dozen measurements, easily analyzed and presented.

The ideas listed in FIG. 12-1 constitute more than 20 separate measurements, but these are too many to institute at once. Based on the goal rankings carried out during IS planning, the metrics group can select six to ten measurements with which to start. Over time, other metrics can be added as you fine-tune the development and measurement processes.

Simple to present and understand When many people think about metrics, they cast back to statistics courses they hated in school. But process measurement need not involve linear regressions, or even standard deviations. The best metrics are simple and visible.

Manufacturers have known for years the value of visible measurement.[9] They post simple graphs and charts that illustrate important performance measures: the number of product defects per month, or the time-to-market for an average product. Managers can gauge how the plant is doing at a glance, and workers have goals to strive for.

You can apply the same principle to software process measurement. Select metrics that people can relate to: average turnaround days for software bug fixes, for example, instead of a complex maintenance performance index. Publish overall statistics in news letters, or post them in central locations. Raise the visibility of benefits shown by CASE projects. Let teams that do high-quality jobs gain recognition for their efforts.

Simple to collect The most popular criticism of metrics is: "I don't have time to worry about them." People facing harsh deadlines don't enjoy stopping their real work to measure how they're doing. Does an ambulance driver stop to ask observers how well she's handling the turns?

If a project's in mortal jeopardy, there might be an excuse for not measuring. Yet most project crises are imaginary, brought on by underestimation of project size and effort. This starts a vicious circle, since by not measuring you ensure continued underestimation in the future.

IS Mission. Plan, develop, and manage information resources to support business strategies, meet the needs of the customers of IS products and services, minimize the impacts of rapid changes in the business environment, and enable the open exchange of information throughout the company.

1. **Systems support business strategy.** Sum lower level metrics in terms of quality improvements, cost savings, and new sales generated. Report other measures as appropriate.

    1.1 **Align systems with business goals.** Grade each delivered application according to the goals it meets. Compare against goals it was designed to support during the ISP.

    1.2 **Seek out strategic systems.** Grade each system on its contribution to competitive advantage: number of new customers generated, or increased barriers to entry for competitors.

    1.3 **Reengineer business processes.** Compare business process efficiency just before and six months after the new system is put in place. Report results in terms of time savings, quality improvements, or monetary gain.

2. **Improved IS customer satisfaction.** Overall customer satisfaction survey ratings for IS responsiveness, system quality, and system appropriateness. Summarize costs of fixing system errors and failures, and data integrity problems.

    2.1 **Meet customer system requirements.** Capture average appropriateness rating from post-project satisfaction surveys.

    2.2 **Minimize system defects.** Monitor errors detected during each validation step in the method path. Count defects per function point discovered during final system and integration tests. Do monthly counts of production errors, both fatal and nonfatal. Track time needed to fix errors.

    2.3 **Minimize system downtime.** Track the time it takes to fix all critical application failures (causing work stoppages). Track nonplanned hardware or communications equipment downtime per month.

    2.4 **Ensure data integrity.** Record the number of errors that arise due to data corruption.

    2.5 **Consistent user interface.** Survey users about the consistency of application interfaces.

    2.6 **Enable distributed data access.** Track the percentage of installed systems that manipulate data residing in geographically distant locations.

    2.7 **Support management decision-making.** Analyze the usage patterns of data warehouse information.

    2.8 **Provide applications training.** Course evaluation scores from student surveys. Follow-up survey three months after course to reevaluate student proficiency with new systems.

3. **Streamlined development process.**

    3.1 **Increase developer productivity.** Function points per installed application divided by the man-months of effort expended during development.

Fig. 12-1. Possible metrics for Normalco's goals

Fig. 12-1. Continued.

> **3.2 Follow common methodologies.** Percent of active projects following common documented methods, by month.
>
> **3.3 Simplify project scope.** Average complexity rating of new projects, per month, calculated using project risk analysis worksheet. Alternate measure: average function point count of applications at installation time.
>
> **3.4 Responsive application maintenance.** Average time taken to respond to customer change request inquiries. Average turnaround time to resolve change requests, either by negotiation or by software development.
>
> **3.5 Coordinate system installations.** Cost of release installation, per customer, summing personnel support costs and lost production time. Compare to current baseline of installation costs for each independent system.
>
> **3.6 Provide tool and technique training.** Course evaluation scores from student surveys. Follow-up survey three months after course to reevaluate student proficiency in techniques.
>
> **4. Minimize impact of business change.** Aggregate financial contribution of newly introduced technologies or tools, based on improvements in productivity, quality, and strategic systems alignment. Rates of change of these improvements. Estimated financial savings from software reuse.
>
> **4.1 Integrated data and applications.** Number of currently automated redundant processes eliminated during integration efforts. Percent of each installed application drawn from reusable design or code libraries (derived from CASE repository). Percent of production systems using standard enterprise data definitions.
>
> **4.2 Continuous process improvement.** Number of additions to the method pool per month. Also track the rate of change of measurements of productivity, quality, and project estimation accuracy.
>
> **4.3 Forecast resource requirements.** Anticipate future need for personnel and technological information resources, based on strategic alignment of resource plans and business goals.
>
> **4.4 Discover useful new technologies.** Number of new technologies or tools piloted per year. Effect of new technology implementation upon development quality and productivity.

Since schedule crises remain a fact of IS life, people will only measure if the process is simple and quick. Given equivalent metrics, select the ones that are easiest to gather. CASE tools can simplify the gathering process for some metrics.

For example, function point and Bang metrics require complicated formulas. Few engineers will want to take time to calculate these by hand. Some CASE tools help by automatically calculating function points of a software design model. If the CASE tool won't calculate them automatically, you can write a simple program of your own to do so (ironically, the same developers that complain about the time it takes to measure will spend hours hacking out a utility program to do it automatically).

Metrics you can draw from a CASE repository include:

- business area or application complexity, in terms of function points or volume of software engineering objects
- percent of objects shared with other applications (reusability)

- number of analysis or design flaws, according to methodology rules known by the CASE tool

Many of these measures can be used in the future to generate project estimates. Some CASE tools have project management components, tied to specific methodologies, that help you estimate future tasks. Some estimating techniques for CASE-based projects will be discussed in chapter 13.

Even with the help of CASE tools, you can only quantify a narrow range of information. For instance, it's relatively easy to see how much software you're creating, based on LOC or function point metrics. Errors aren't that hard to track, either. But how do you put a number to customer satisfaction, or the degree to which systems support business goals?

Most companies must develop their own ways to collect such information. Often you can distribute standardized surveys to system users to gauge satisfaction, or system usability. In other situations you can observe direct effects of a system upon company sales or expenses. You'll need to define creative ways to track unquantifiable costs and benefits.[10] As long as you keep your goals in sight, the measures you choose will be effective.

Measure current and past projects

Few companies have kept track of past IS development performance. Before observing new CASE-based projects, you should first take stock of past and current ones. The metrics you collect from these will be a benchmark for comparing the new CASE methods.

You should capture metrics for at least two past or current projects. If you have time, try to measure at least six different projects. Projects vary widely in size and complexity, and will show corresponding productivity variations. If you already know the scope of a proposed pilot project, try to measure some past projects that are about the same size.

If you don't have a standard development methodology in place, collecting current metrics will be difficult. The only figure most IS shops record is how long it takes to deliver a system. In addition, you can discover how big the installed system is by counting lines of code or function points. Function points are better than lines of code because they can be compared across projects that use different languages or construction steps. With a standard methodology, you can track time to specific phases and deliverables.

Try to capture some data about system quality, as well. If system test results are archived somewhere, dig them up. Gauge the quality of older systems by analyzing error reports and change requests submitted by users.

When measuring the efficiency of the development process, keep the new CASE methods in mind. The things you measure now should match up with the things you'll measure with CASE. For example, monitoring the time it takes to compile a program won't do much for you when future tasks involve code generation. You'll get more value by measuring how long the entire program construction and testing cycle takes. Then you can compare this directly to the equivalent CASE construction cycle. Figure 12-2 illustrates this point: Though generation time is longer than compile time (which

Poolside metrics 301

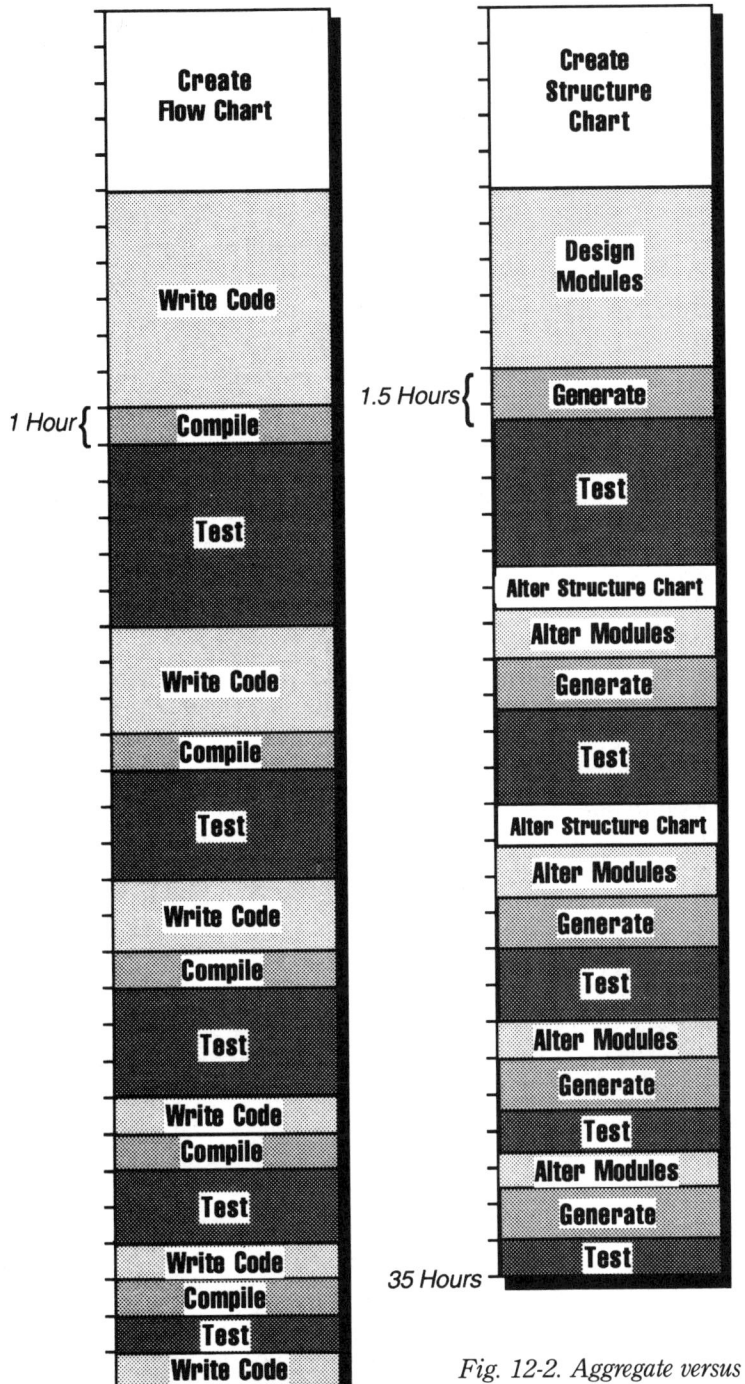

Fig. 12-2. Aggregate versus detailed measurements

includes removal of syntax errors in this implified model), it takes less total time to create and debug the program.

In summary, early benchmarks should concentrate on fundamental measures that can be gathered from existing systems, and that can be compared against future development methods. Some of these measures are:

- time to complete deliverables, or reach certain stages of development
- developer satisfaction with development tools and methods
- user satisfaction with systems and IS service
- quality of installed systems

To measure things like quality or satisfaction, you might distribute surveys to users and developers of installed base systems.

You might find it tough to convince people of the need to measure old systems. Pilot teams expect to be put in a fishbowl; developers of older systems probably hope never to think about them again. Yet most developers and users don't mind telling you what they think of the systems. You'll probably be the first person ever to ask about them.

Measure effectiveness of new methods

Measurement is an important aspect of every pilot project for new technology. Everyone involved should record how the new tools and methods affect their jobs, and the quality of the work they produce.

The toughest political challenge for the caretaker of a metrics program comes after the initial pilot projects finish. The pilot team takes measurement in stride, as part of the project's experimental nature. Engineers designing business systems might feel that measurement will hold the project back, and fight strongly against it. To sell them on the idea, share benchmark and pilot project metrics with them. These figures lend important decision-making power to IS managers and developers alike. They "proved" the worth (or worthlessness) of new tools in an experimental setting. Now you want their help gathering similar proof in a mainstream environment.

Start by helping developers and users record their own metrics. If you tell them to in a memo, they probably won't. If you work with them at first, though, and help them analyze and understand the results, they should fall into the habit themselves.

Don't limit yourself to metrics you were able to collect from existing systems. Take advantage of the added measures the CASE tools can give you. This will give you more analytical capability in the future. Use the CASE repository to the hilt: The more automatic measurements you take, the less work developers have to do.

Analyze and distribute metrics

Analysis makes metrics worthwhile. Many metrics programs fail because no one uses the resulting numbers. People begin to wonder why they're spending time measuring when the results aren't made public.

Use charts and graphs to breathe life into numbers. Visibility breeds improvement. Post them centrally, or in newsletters, so everyone knows how projects are progressing.

Publicize spectacular results, like systems that show almost no errors during testing, or notable jumps in overall development productivity.

As you compare metrics from various projects, try to discern why they differ. Did the project finish faster because of the CASE tools, or because most business issues were resolved during facilitated sessions with users? Did delays result from inefficient methods, or unanticipated personnel shortfalls?

Note extenuating circumstances as you collect the metrics. When you post aggregate results, display appropriate notes as well. Though you're not using the metrics for personnel reviews, project members will feel accountable for them. When projects lag for unanticipated reasons, qualify the numbers so people don't feel unfairly accused.

Metrics play an active role in method pool improvement. Each method can be measured, and the results used in two ways. First, fine-tune each method based on project results and experiences. Second, compare alternative methods using common measurements. For instance, is it faster to develop an entity-relationship diagram with tool X or tool Y? Are there fewer defects in the generated code, or in the code that was written by hand?

As the method pool system evolves, use it to capture metrics for specific goals and methods. If you don't use a method pool system, then PC spreadsheets or database packages make ideal vehicles for metrics analysis.

Metrics will also improve project managers' abilities to estimate future tasks and costs. This topic will be covered in depth in chapter 13.

Review the measurement process

The main purpose of metrics is to improve the development process. Following a similar philosophy, you should take steps to continuously improve the measurement process too. It's not enough to select a few measures and order people to record them. Those who will measure should help to decide what to measure. They should also suggest changes to the metrics and the measurement process as things progress.

Once the first sets of metrics get published, convene a forum to evaluate the measurement process. This can be the same bunch that planned the program in the first place, or a wider group of new stakeholders. Try to determine how useful the process has been so far, and what the prevailing attitude toward metrics has become. Ask questions that include:

- Did the metrics speak to people? Have any of the measurements become part of the developers' vocabulary? When asked how big a system is, do people respond in terms of function points (or other standard measures)?
- Are the metrics useful for improving the development process? What have people learned so far about various tools or techniques?
- Do people feel they measure the right things? Are there other things that should be recorded?
- Did the measurement tasks annoy people? Do they feel these tasks slow them down? Did anyone keep track of how long it took to measure things (a common oversight)?

As the metrics program grows, it will become impractical to hold town meetings. You can formalize the metrics evaluation with developer surveys, filled out at the end of each project. If you throw measurement tasks into the method pool, they can be evaluated simultaneously with other tasks.

Larger companies will want to assign a metrics program manager(s) to coordinate the ongoing effort. Many firms establish centralized groups to manage measurement data, and provide training and consulting to project teams.

If you set up a central group, make sure they are metrics lobbyists, not metrics police. Measurement can't easily shake the stigma that shadows it. Engineers, managers, and users alike will fear the misuse of the metrics, until their usefulness is proven.

Most measurement programs fail within a year or two. Still, those companies that persevere gain an invaluable body of information about their development process. Make sure you follow through with the program. Publicize the measurement and openly discuss their value and their implications. Give those affected by the metrics a voice in deciding what gets measured, and how.

Do it all well and you can have a brief career as a conference speaker, telling others what you've done. Better still, you'll be investing in productivity insurance. For the first time, you can make semi-objective decisions about the best ways to create software. Productivity drops won't survive long; you'll know the best ways to combat them. All it takes is a little investment up front.

13

Stacking the deck

Few things are more frustrating than getting a new toy that you can't play with. Once you've made a decision to use a CASE tool, and planned for its introduction, don't wait to put it to work. Acquire it (with no obligation), install it, and use it, soon. It could be the best thing you've ever used, meaning delay has an opportunity cost.

Of course, I don't advocate rushing in blindly. Design an architecture, build a personal support structure, and select your tools very carefully. But there's no reason to hold back once the elements are all in place. Have no fear that the new tool will fail—it might, but no matter. With a broad and flexible strategy, each tool becomes a single cog in a well balanced machine. Failure is never fun, but you'll have built enough fail-safe measures to insure continued progress. And you can always go back to doing what you do today.

Enthusiasm is no substitute for experience. The first team to use CASE will pioneer more than just technology. They will forge new management methods and communication patterns as well.

Watts Humphrey has remarked that three quarters of the organizations surveyed by the Software Engineering Institute "haven't instituted the kinds of rudimentary management practices they need before tooling up."[1] In other words, most groups try to use CASE without first learning good project management habits. CASE doesn't make project management passé; it increases the project manager's challenge.

CASE alone won't suddenly spark clear objectives or happy customers. These factors still need to be managed, along with the new factors CASE interjects. The challenge goes beyond the need to learn new tools and techniques. The first CASE project team also weathers realignment of personal values and political pressures, under the greater scrutiny of senior IS management. Add this to the normal problems of a moderately sized software development effort, and you create an uncontrollable project.

Most firms control their first CASE effort by making it a pilot: a small, self-contained project designed primarily to judge the worth of new development technology. By removing the pressure to create a production-quality application, the team can concentrate on making new tools and methods work.

There is no one accepted way to set up and run a pilot project. They can be simple, week-long tool tests, or substantial development projects a tiny step from the norm. Project goals vary widely from company to company, and project management needs differ accordingly.

Don't burn the house down

You detach a pilot from mainstream development for the same reason surgeons don't perform medical experiments on the President: the consequences of failure are too great. As Tom Gilb says, "If you don't know what you're doing, don't do it on a large scale."[2]

Depending on the tools you're testing and resources you can bring to bear, your pilot project can take one of many forms. They range from tiny projects to test tool feasibility to large-scale efforts to create installable systems.

Feasibility pilots

Sometimes you simply want assurance that a product will do what it's advertised to. You want to see a code generator spit out compilable programs, or a repository handle a half dozen simultaneous updates. You want your own people to test and observe, so you don't have to rely solely on the salesperson's word.

A feasibility pilot is a cross between a sales demonstration and a full-scale development project. From two to four developers simply road test the product, using some well bounded test cases. Perhaps they'll take two weeks to design and generate a few online programs, or reverse engineer some COBOL programs and see how they come out. You get enough hands-on experience to know that the tool works—or that it doesn't, as the case may be.

Feasibility pilots can sometimes replace proposals. The internal proposal process, in which a CASE champion must repeatedly justify the idea of endless levels of company management, stifles many ideas before they can be tested. Because of their low cost, simple feasibility pilots can often be done before running the proposal gauntlet. Successful results can then be used as solid justification for a subsequent proposal. And should the pilot fail, the champion can save his energy.

Most companies run simple feasibility pilots if they run a pilot at all. These involve the least outlay by the company, and results are usually good enough to silence skeptics. However, you won't learn enough in this short time to understand all of the tool's impacts. You won't discover if users like looking at the new diagrams, or if developers find it hard to meet documentation standards with the new tool. You won't know for sure if the tool produces higher quality software that requires less maintenance.

Full-cycle pilots

To test the tool in context, you need to run a pilot that covers the full development cycle. As Robert H. Wallace and his colleagues suggest, "The pilot project should be planned and executed as a miniature of a large project. The large project's documentation and timing constraints, appropriately scaled down, must be applied to the pilot project."[3]

Such projects carve out a self-contained piece of a real development effort. They plan to deliver a functional system—though not one intended for operational use—while testing out the new tools and methods. They follow a complete method path and cover many peripheral tasks like software documentation and quality assurance. As a result, they provide a thorough measure of most aspects of the tools and their impacts.

Usually the project team is given some special dispensations to smooth their progress. They might be absolved from certain documentation tasks, or allowed to assume solutions to difficult business issues, in the interests of speeding the project along.

The biggest barrier to running a full-cycle pilot is cost. Even if the vendor gives you the tools free for the evaluation period, the pilot expense is high. You'll be funding a full team of engineers for a few months, to develop a system that will never be used. Setting up tools like a central repository, especially on a mainframe computer, can draw technical support resources away from other important duties. Some vendors will let you use their facilities—mainframes and terminals—to reduce the cost of a pilot project. But this option is usually tendered to only the largest potential CASE buyers.

Live pilots

Most people are tempted to put the tools to work on a real project as soon as possible. Few have the resources to devote months of effort to a potentially throw-away project. This means, though, that you will buy the CASE product without fully understanding its workings. Tell the vendor this, and ask the vendor to give you the product on a trial basis for the duration of your first development project.

Sometimes it makes sense to apply the tools directly to an actual development project. Full-cycle pilot projects can be very costly. If you're going to invest a lot, shouldn't you get something in return?

Live pilot projects represent calculated risks. Before you try one, make sure the risks are manageable. These projects work best when:

- Failure is not deadly. If the project's about to derail, you should be able to quickly switch to another set of tracks. This project should be subject to the same go and no-go assessments as other projects.
- The tools and techniques have been proven elsewhere. If a similar company or another division has used the tool successfully, you might be better off just running a real project with it. Many projects are called "pilots" so managers can put off making a decision about new choices. If the tool has been proven many times over, and you know your situation favors its success, don't be timid. Bring it in and make it work.
- The new stuff isn't far removed from what you do today. A new compiler for a familiar programming language rarely warrants a full-cycle pilot project. If you're just inching forward, you don't need the weight of a pilot project to slow you down.

Though live pilots are risky, sometimes that risk can work in your favor. Canadian Airlines' first large CASE project was a crucial one for an airline: a frequent-flier system. Yet the system was successful, installed a year after development began, thanks in part to the purchase of an analysis-level CASE model from Trans World Airlines. IS managers at Canadian Airlines believe that the importance of the project generated intense commitment from everyone involved, thereby assuring the success of CASE.

Sehame Gouveia, director of data administration for the Home Office Reference Laboratory, led another successful mission-critical CASE project. "We believe strongly that a pilot project provides an out for the IS staff," says Gouveia, "and management loses interest. When people know the project is extremely important to the company, it's amazing the productivity you can get."[4]

If you plan to run a live pilot, select the project with care. A failure on its first attempt normally spells doom for CASE.

Match the pilot to the situation

TABLE 13-1 summarizes the major differences between the various types of pilot projects. To decide which type to run, ask yourself some questions:

- Will the CASE tool be allowed to fail? If the project must deliver an installable system, the answer is usually "no." Failure also isn't a popular option when the new tools are already bought and paid for.
- If the system must be installed, will the pilot team be subject to all of the same standards and restrictions? Sometimes current standards can detract from a pilot's results. For example, they might force the team to produce documents that the CASE environment doesn't require. This leads to duplicated effort and a loss of pilot productivity.
- Must the pilot team be fully trained? If you're running a feasibility pilot, you don't want to invest thousands of dollars in training courses. You might get money-back guarantees on tools, but rarely on training! But the larger the project's scale, the more important training becomes. How can you gauge a tool's eventual learning curve if you force developers to learn on the job?
- Is anyone's reputation riding on the pilot's success? Sometimes a manager or other CASE champion bets their reputation on the success of the new approach. In these cases, it's best to run a project with a small chance of failure, usually a simple feasibility test. Make sure the person at risk has a say in how the project is scoped.

Sometimes the best approach is to follow a graduated series of pilots. Start with a small feasibility test, and then run a reasonably sized, self-contained development project with the new tools. When you're ready to apply them to mainstream development, you'll have in-house experience and a documented set of best practices to draw upon.

A scientific approach involves running parallel projects. One project pilots the new technology, while the other produces similar products using traditional means. This approach reduces the effects of failing with the new stuff. You end up with a working product, no matter what. It also provides a "control" against which the new technology can be measured. Such results are irrefutable compared to those of a singular pilot project. No one can invalidate the results by claiming that a parallel pilot is unique.

Table 13-1. Characteristics of Pilot Project Types

Aspect	Feasibility Pilot	Full Cycle Pilot	Live Pilot
Training	Initial courses, or on the job	Initial courses, or on the job	Full training program
Team	1 or 2 developers	Full project team	Full project team
Deliverables	1 or 2 important outputs (e.g., generated programs, documents, diagrams	Full suite of deliverables, including user reviews, documentation, quality verification	Full suite of deliverables, including user reviews, documentation, quality verification
Deliverable standards	Not followed	Followed with some exceptions	Followed completely
Disposition of deliverables	Throwaway	Throwaway	Released into production
Process	Minimum to achieve final result	Full cycle method path	Full cycle method path
Potential benefit	Cursory evaluation	In-depth evaluation	Superior software application plus in-deth tool
Cost	Low	High	Very high
Consequences of failure	Don't purchase tools	Don't purchase tools	Lose face with customers

However, parallel pilots are doubly expensive. They are best used as a contingency plan for a live pilot. Say you're confident the technology can be used to create a superior application. Plan the effort as a parallel pilot, to be done sequentially by the same project team. Run the new technology project first. If it's an unqualified success, forget about the parallel project. If it fails, or doesn't provide spectacular results, proceed with the traditional effort. At the end, you'll have a working system and a wealth of directly comparable measurements.

Deciding where to fly

The project's subject matter greatly influences its chances of success. Some projects will never succeed, regardless of tools and methods used, because they are too large or ill-defined. Pilot projects should tackle safer subjects than most, especially when careers are at stake. The more your reputation depends upon the pilot's success, the smaller and tamer the subject area should be.

Pilot projects are like scientific experiments. You limit the number of variables in order to observe important causes and effects. You protect the pilot arena from outside disturbances that might corrupt the test. You must be able to measure the results.

However, you don't want to turn the pilot project into a quarantined, sterile effort. You don't want uncontrollable external forces to bias the pilot's results, but you do want enough realism for results to be relevant to your normal environment. Remember that you're not just piloting CASE or a set of methods. You want to understand the effects they will have on the people who will use them: how communications with users improve or deteriorate; whether strains are put on organizational roles or relationships; whether the tools or techniques cause developers undue stress or frustration.

To choose a good pilot subject area, consider this advice:

- Pick an application that's not crucial. A pilot project should be able to fail without dire consequences to the business itself.
- Pick a project that doesn't have a history of failures. Often people use CASE to try and revive doomed projects. There were probably good reasons why the project failed in the first place. As Alan Fisher relates, CASE "is not a technology that is easily retrofitted to a project failing due to poor requirements analysis, bad design, or bungled management."[5] Instead of breathing new life into a dying project, you might be sending CASE to an early grave.
- Pick a project that's reasonably sized. The intense resource coordination effort that gigantic efforts require can overshadow the effects of the new tools and techniques. Smaller projects are easier to learn from.
- Make sure underlying business issues can be resolved. New technology can't overcome problems of shifting scope or protracted issue resolution.
- Don't select reverse engineering or technical reimplementation projects as pilots, unless it's what you're piloting. You can't run a reverse engineering project and then say you've piloted CASE technology. You'll have only tested one aspect of it. From a business perspective, the systems you get from reverse engineering are no better than the ones you started with.
- Select a project that's similar to those you've done before. You want the results to be comparable with other development projects. For example, don't try to write a new electronic funds transfer application as a pilot if all you've done before are general ledger accounting systems. Problems learning the new type of application structure and the new communications technologies might totally invalidate the new CASE tools, even if these new tools perform admirably. Sometimes you must run a pilot for something completely new—a neural network development project, for example. In these cases, try not to compare results to previous methods. Neural network development fills a niche of its own, and won't be in competition with other method paths.
- Don't take a project that's half-done and retrofit it to use CASE. If the project has problems, you won't know if they sprung up before the CASE tool was brought in, or happened because of it.
- Keep the process scope familiar. Many CASE-supported techniques will be completely new to some shops. For example, if your company doesn't do strategic information planning today, then an ISP isn't the best thing to pilot. Though it's one of the most valuable projects of all, its value isn't immediately apparent to many software developers. You'll have a hard time saying a top-down methodology is superior to current methods unless you run a pilot that produces something familiar. Something like an ISP is a good candidate for a live trial by fire. If it works you have a major achievement. If it doesn't you can ignore the results.

Some people use pilot projects to try to impress naysayers. They go overboard to make the pilot project a success, even to the point of ignoring evidence to the contrary. Treating success as a *fait acompli* reduces the value of the pilot's results. In addition, it can lead to costly surprises.

As a pilot was being run by one group, a different project manager approached me to ask about training and preparing his team to use the new tool. I asked why he couldn't wait until the pilot project showed results. "Everyone knows the project will succeed," he responded, "whether the thing works or not. The CIO wants it to work, so it will." The pilot team finally gave the product a bad review, and the time the other project manager spent preparing his team was wasted.

You should go into a pilot project with an open mind, aware of the chance that the technology might fail. Still you want to give the pilot project team every opportunity to make a change for the better.

Pilot project success hinges less on the feasibility of the technology than it does on the project manager's skills. The best technology can fail when it's poorly managed. The key to a successful pilot is formal project management directed toward satisfying all stakeholders.

Making everyone a winner

Every project manager follows a different style. Some roll up their sleeves and hack out code with their subordinates; some give people basic goals and trust them to achieve them; others try to motivate through pressure and fear. All styles succeed in certain situations, but only when they follow certain essential practices. Style isn't the real issue: management practices are.

Common sense dictates that a project is successful when everyone involved in it is satisfied. Recently Barry Boehm and Rony Ross presented a theory of software project management that fits well with theories about managing change and transition:

> The primary job of the software project manager is to make winners of each of the parties involved in the software process: the project manager's subordinates and managers; the customers; the users and maintainers of the resulting product; and any other significantly affected people, such as the developers or users of interfacing products.[6]

The trick is to make sure that the definition of project success aligns with the self-interests of the people involved. CASE introduces new motivations for many of those it affects. It holds out the promise of attaining the previously infeasible, and gives rise to new hidden agendas. The tasks of identifying these agendas falls to the project manager, the one finally accountable for CASE success.

To keep everyone happy, the project manager must systematically negotiate with stakeholders and coordinate the fulfillment of their concerns. Even a feasibility pilot project commands a large audience. No matter how skilled a negotiator is, he will fail if he doesn't plan to negotiate with everyone involved.

Project planning is usually limited to defining a list of tasks, identifying a project team, and setting up a kick-off meeting. As projects grow in complexity, though, project management must grow accordingly.

Project management for everyone

The same forces pushing you toward CASE tools also call for formal project management:

- greater systems complexity
- rapid environmental change
- long learning curve for first-time project managers
- need to delegate tasks more effectively
- need for continuous process improvement

Project managers need to steer a straight course through a hurricane of changes. They will rarely face an identical project twice; each time, some major features will change. Still, there are some formal project management steps you can apply to any situation. The following list of general project management tasks is a good place to start:

1. Identify project goals and scope.
2. Select development methods and tools.
3. Identify the project team.
4. Draft a project schedule.
5. Monitor the project and communicate progress.
6. Publicize project success.

These steps apply to both pilot and mainstream development projects. Full-cycle pilots aren't that different from most projects, and need just as much project management support.

During this process, you need to constantly balance the need for management control against the need to achieve something worthwhile, and learn something new. Many feel that project management means riding herd on maverick programmers. In fact, it means figuring out how to give the mavericks free rein, while also appeasing top management's need for accurate estimates of project status.

Consultant and author P.J. Plauger makes an important point when he states: "Every software project must be just slightly out of control."[7] Projects that simply trample old ground bring few benefits. Every new CASE project, by definition, generates new knowledge. As a result, it will never be fully "in control." The project manager's job is keeping enough control to prevent any misstep from being fatal.

Identify project goals and scope

The time to start satisfying the stakeholders is before the project even begins. The first thing every project manager should do is clearly define the project's goals and scope. The next thing is to tie the goals back to the interests of the people involved.

Boehm and Ross provide a four-step process for achieving these win-win conditions:

1. Understand how people want to win.
2. Establish reasonable expectations.
3. Match people's tasks to their win conditions.
4. Provide a supportive environment.

People's win conditions for a CASE project differ in many ways from what they were previously. The managers that bring in CASE have a new stake in seeing the technology work. Developers have an interest in learning new and marketable skills. TABLE 13-2 summarizes some of the win conditions for various players.

Table 13-2. Winning Conditions for CASE Implementation Stakeholders

Group	Winning Conditions
IS Managers	• Better quality software • Projects completed on schedule; status known throughout • Prove CASE feasibility • Projects within budget
Developers	• Easier to build interesting, high-quality systems • Fast career path • Learn marketable skills • New tasks are fun; fewer tedious chores
Software maintainers	• No software failures • Good system documentation • Easy to find problems and solutions
Application users	• Help for doing job faster or better • No software failures • Easy-to-learn software
Customers	• Systems fulfill business goals • Responsive software delivery • Projects within budget

These conditions both affect and are affected by the stated goals and scope of the project. CASE and a switch toward applications integration can drastically change the way you scope projects. There are two main aspects of the project's domain: the business scope and the software engineering or process scope.

Process goals The type of pilot you decide to run presupposes certain goals: whether you plan to install the final application, or test more than just the tool. Process goals are the stated IS objectives for the project. They describe the baseline criteria for project success. For instance, if a project must be done by a specific date, for a solid business reason, this should be stated up front. If a pilot project must show 100% productivity improvement for the new tool to be successful, write this down at the start. If it becomes clear that critical objectives can't be met, you can take corrective action early in the project—even kill the project if need be. Why take six months to definitely prove a tool won't bring the returns you need when you could draw the same conclusion two months along?

You also need to balance process goals against the stated business goals. These often conflict when pilot projects also attempt to deliver business value. TABLE 13-3 shows how vastly these priorities can differ for various types of projects. For a feasibility pilot project, the primary goal is to improve the development process. Delivering business value is last on the list, since the resulting systems will never make it into production (and might, in fact, be a failure from the start).

Compare these to the ideal priorities for customer-driven software projects: deliver business value first, keep quality high, and provide prompt delivery. Proving new development technologies falls last on this list.

An extended pilot project that uses new technologies to deliver installable systems mixes these priorities up. Business value should still be paramount, and quality a close second. Without delivering these, no new technology can be called beneficial. Normally, the need to evaluate the pilot technology will supersede the need to deliver quickly.

Table 13-3. Goal Priorities for Various Projects

Feasibility Pilot	Ongoing Application Development
1. Improve the development process	1. Deliver business value
2. Meet software quality standards	2. Meet software quality standards
3. Keep the project on schedule	3. Keep the project on schedule
4. Deliver business value	4. Improve the development process

Extended CASE Pilot Project	Many Projects Today
1. Deliver business value	1. Keep the project on schedule
2. Meet software quality standards	2. Meet software quality standards
3. Improve the development process	3. Deliver business value
4. Keep the project on schedule	4. Improve the development process

Unfortunately, most CASE-based projects proceed without a clear idea of the trade-offs between business and process goals. Schedules often drive projects, leading managers to take shortcuts toward delivering something—no matter how trivial—on the promised date. These shortcuts tend to skip past business analysis and quality assurance tasks. Depending on directions handed down from IS managers, proving CASE viability becomes more important.

It can even be hard to rank a project's process goals. Wise IS managers will accept project delays if team members are gaining valuable experience as a result. Even if a CASE tool proves useless, the knowledge gained about the technology—and how not to use it—can make the project itself successful.

In fact, many CASE project managers can't tell you which project goals are most important. There is no way to maximize them all. Concentrate too much on one, and something else has to give. If it's important to make a new technology work, then schedules make good ballast. You can throw some of them out to keep the project afloat. But you can rarely justify throwing out business functions or skimping on quality.

This is why many CASE projects have a rough time. They attempt to do everything, and spread themselves too thin. It's crucial to state up front which goals take precedence for each project. This provides a set of guiding principles for the project team, and makes it easier to evaluate the sticky trade-offs that inevitably arise.

Most of these trade-offs balance potential achievements against resource constraints. Limitations on budget, time, and personnel should be plainly stated at the start of the project. Strict limitations can be a liability for a CASE pilot project; unforeseen expenses crop up because you weren't that familiar with the technology when you started. I've seen many an emergency memory upgrade bought when developers complained loudly about a CASE tool's slow performance.

In any case, the project manager shouldn't assume what the resource limits are. She should negotiate them up front, and prevent unpleasant surprises later on.

Process scope Software projects traditionally take a narrow business scope and follow it from requirements-gathering straight through system construction, as shown in FIG. 13-1. Yet projects also can be bounded by the type of information they produce. As FIG. 13-2 shows, strategic planning project P1 covers the entire business

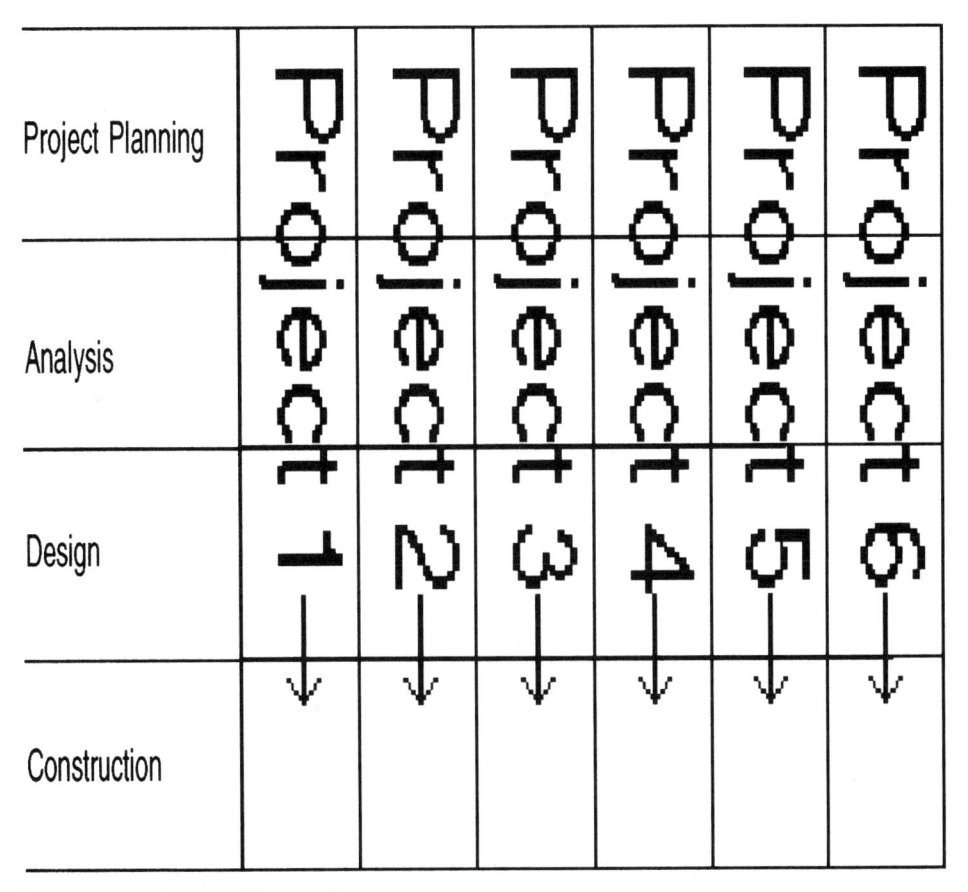

Project Planning	Project 1	Project 2	Project 3	Project 4	Project 5	Project 6
Analysis	↓	↓	↓	↓	↓	↓
Design						
Construction						

Fig. 13-1. Linear, ad hoc projects

scope, but only to a shallow depth. Analysis projects A1 to A4 then adopt narrower business scopes, expanding the planning information to a deeper level. Finally, design projects narrow the business scope even more, to produce useful, well bounded business systems.

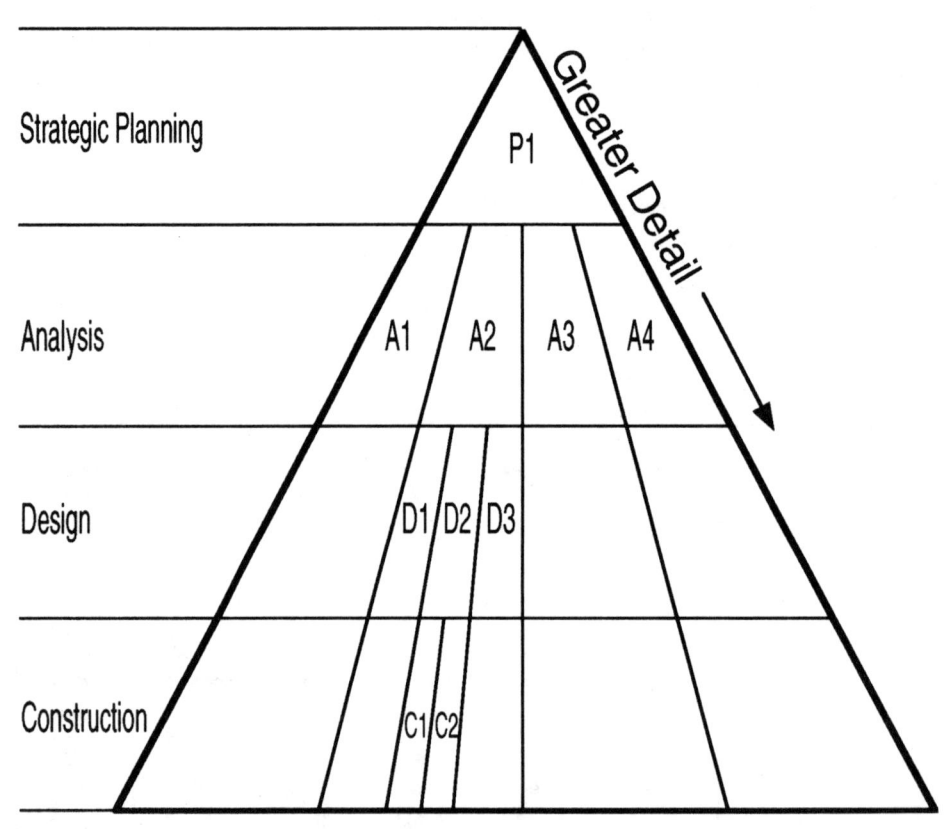

Fig. 13-2. Telescoping projects, differentiated by level of detail

Depending on your approach, a project's process scope differs radically. If you're running a pilot project to compare against traditional ones, you should probably take a similar straight-line approach. If you're using tools that concentrate on one phase of a top-down development path, you can limit deliverables to those products produced in this phase. In other words, to pilot strategic planning tools, you don't need to carry information into actual software applications. You can judge the deliverables on their own merits.

It's difficult to compare new top-down techniques to traditional straight-line approaches. To really test the value of the top-down approach, you need to start at the top with strategic information planning. This effort alone takes from three to nine months. It can take more than a year following top-down methods by the book before you produce even a small production application. The resulting application might be of high strategic value and impeccable quality, but it doesn't make for a swift pilot.

If you're planning a switch to top-down strategic methods, you might just want to pilot the tasks that cover the same ground your current methods do. For example, if your engineers use structured analysis methods today, pilot new tools that cover similar tasks. If they don't do analysis, but do use structured programming techniques, start with tools for structured design or flowcharting. The results from these pilots will be comparable to current experience. Favorable results will pave the way for additional tests of newer techniques. Once they're comfortable with one set of the top-down methods, you can more easily introduce the entire framework.

If you're running a pilot project, you should clarify which tasks your team is expected to perform. If the pilots are designed to test CASE in its true context, then peripheral tasks like document preparation or quality reviews should not be overlooked. There's a temptation when the word "pilot" is used to assume that these tasks can be skipped. But knowledge about the best techniques to use with CASE is one of the biggest benefits of early projects. If you're documenting a method pool, such knowledge is indispensable. It shouldn't be limited to purely technical tasks. You want to understand the best ways to manage, integrate, document, and ensure the quality of CASE projects as well.

The more things you change at once, the harder project success will be. You don't want to simultaneously foist full-cycle integrated CASE, JAD, rapid prototyping, and design inspections upon an unsuspecting project team. How will you know which of these contributed most to the project's success or failure? Part of the difficulty people have applying James Martin's concept of Rapid Application Development, for example, is the wide range of simultaneous changes it implies.

You can sometimes adopt a number of new techniques at once, but only with the help of experienced practitioners. Even then, you won't learn much from failure. It's like running an experiment while altering a dozen variables simultaneously. The chances of a significant result are slim.

Business goals Many projects fail because people chase after the wrong goals. Understand up front exactly what the business objectives of the project are, and how they differ from the process goals described above.

An ideal goal statement indicates some ambitious business goals but few solution constraints. Such constraints are often misconstrued as goals. For example, "write a C program to print payroll checks," includes one veiled business goal and two solution constraints. The business goal is "pay employees and contractors." The developers' power to solve this goal is hampered by the constraints that the system must be written in C, and that printed checks are the only way to pay people. Unchallenged, these requirements would prevent the team from designing a direct electronic deposit payment system using a highly productive CASE tool that doesn't generate C code.

Make every effort to weed out these solution constraints when embarking upon a CASE-based project. The people injecting these constraints probably don't understand the capabilities of CASE, and might force you to build archaic systems with brand new tools. It's like asking a modern urban architect to design an adobe hut.

Business goals identify the win conditions for the software customers. Meeting those goals makes the project successful. If process goals, such as a need to prove CASE technology, are very important, make sure that customers agree. Too often the process goals are an informal contract between IS managers and developers. The customers still think their goals are paramount, while in fact the project team spends more time working out kinks in the tool than analyzing customer requirements.

Business scope Business scope is inextricably linked with business goals. You can't achieve the goals without analyzing and automating a certain subset of the business.

Yet far too often simple business goals translate into elephantine software projects. Multiyear development projects are costly, and make scope-shifting a certainty. This can be remedied, for the most part, with up-front dialogue aimed at limiting project scope while delivering products of real value to the user. Usually this requires examining the users' goals in depth, and figuring out which subgoals would make the most immediate impact. You might still need to define a large system architecture, but then plan to deliver it bit by bit, in manageable chunks each with tangible business benefit.

Tom Gilb describes the main rationale for this approach, which he calls evolutionary development: "It is easier to see and deal with the effect of one small increment of the solution, than it is to understand the impact of the entire solution at once."[8]

As Gilb relates, most objections to this approach are of the "I can't possibly make it any smaller" variety. Yet most project managers, when pressed, really can split projects into manageable pieces. This task gets even easier when supported by CASE tools that matrix software objects against user goals, or allow you to run clustering processes to form logical, self-contained groups of data and processes.

The smaller the pieces, the easier things become to manage. You can better estimate the completion time for a system made of ten modules than for one containing two hundred.

Evolutionary development is also a good way to address many IS managers' "When will you start coding?" mentality. Try separating every project you're given into at least three subprojects. Work with the users to define the most important goal. Tell them if they can help you do so, you can deliver something to them in half the time. The entire project's business scope can remain unchanged; you'll simply create some smaller subscopes within it.

It still pays to do some up-front analysis on the original, wide business scope. But once you have an adequate big picture, it's time to cut and run. Take one subarea through to code generation as a pilot subproject within your project. As you do this, your team will learn about the full development path. This will let you improve the process before you even start on the other two subprojects. It also proves the feasibility of the process before you've invested years in the project.

This approach guarantees that CASE projects won't require two years to show results. Few IS groups can afford to wait this long for a payoff from new methods and tools. By the time these projects finish, the tools they use may well be outdated.

Keep project sizes small and you'll be able to improve the development process more rapidly. You'll also end up with happier customers. They'll receive something useful much sooner than they expect.

Select development methods and tools

The more tool and technique choices you have, the tougher it gets to decide which ones to use. For a pilot project, the biggest choice will be made for you. The new CASE tool will be poised for its test drive. Yet there will be other choices to make up front. How will you gather user information? Will you attempt to integrate the resulting system with others?

Other projects might be able to choose from among competing CASE options. As Michael Evans suggests, "A different CASE configuration may be required for each software project. Tailoring the CASE configuration must include the methods, tools, and libraries that are appropriate to the products to be developed."[9] With a method pool in place, divining a development path becomes much easier. Without one, you'll need to balance a few factors, among them developer skills, cost, and compatibility with current approaches.

Most vendors can suggest a methodology to follow when using their products. Some will insist that you hire their consultants to teach you the methods, or refer you to expensive third-party consulting groups. If you have the money to spend, external consultants can be initially helpful. As I said in chapter 6, though, don't let them force you into their way of doing things. Use consultants as a resource, but once you learn the techniques, adapt them to fit your specific circumstances.

Don't just read the CASE tool manual and then start developing things. Read up on the techniques that the tool automates. Some vendors can recommend texts that discuss the methods they support. Normally, the CASE vendor advertises the approach using the names of those who designed the methods in the first place. Look up these names—Yourdon, Martin, Jackson, Gane and Sarson, Warnier and Orr, McMenamin and Palmer, Hatley and Pirbhai, and so on—at a good library, and you'll find a wealth of information about the goals and principles that underlie these approaches. For information engineering methods, seek out texts by James Martin or Clive Finkelstein. Other methods identified by acronyms or obscure names are harder to learn about, but the information's out there somewhere.

It usually pays to document the tools and methods you plan to use. This can be part of the initial project statement or proposal. It gives people an idea of the planned project steps, and lets you start mobilizing resources to support tools and methods.

In some cases, you should avoid documenting tools up front. You can postpone some decisions until you learn more about the subject area. You don't want to limit the developers' choices too much up front. Let them select the best tools to fit the problems they uncover. If they find an expert system is the best solution, don't force them to write it in assembly language.

Occasionally, a project manager might be forced into surreptitious pilots. Strongly conservative managers often stifle the introduction of new tools into an organization. Sometimes the only way to convince people of a tool's worth is to sneak it in and prove its worth before anyone can object. The risks to this approach are apparent, and I don't recommend it except in extreme cases. It usually succeeds only with low-priced tools targeted to a specific task or two. For example, you might purchase a $195 screen mock-up tool in order to experiment with rapid prototyping techniques, or a $395 hypertext tool to create some self-paced training applications. If these go over well with users and developers, then you can make formal proposals with strong support.

When you have new tools for a pilot project, test fully. Many companies fill out lengthy feature checklists when surveying CASE tools. But when they pilot the tools, they exercise the minimum set of features needed to produce a specific outcome.

CASE tools are software, and should be subject to the same rigorous testing that you give to your other software applications. I suggest creating an actual pilot test plan for the CASE tool. You can base it upon the prioritized feature list you used to select the tool in the first place. It needn't be as detailed as a formal software test plan. But it should indicate the main benefits you are seeking. It will act as a guide for the project manager who sets up the project task plan, and for the developers who actually use the tool.

A pilot test plan encourages you to draw the most from the CASE tool. I saw one pilot project "fail" when the tool didn't provide expected productivity gains. Yet the developers never assessed the quality of the software they created, nor how well it could be documented, nor how well the customer liked the resulting online screens. All seemed to me far superior to the systems this firm currently used. But the damning evidence came from one small group of developers who looked only at development speed.

In the test plan, you can specify that the tool should be used during a JAD session to see if it can aid the information-gathering process. You can state that the generated software should be subject to standard testing procedures, and error rates compared to those of other systems. Tie the test plan to the IS group's strategic goals, and make sure you judge it in this context.

Identify the project team

The people on the project matter more than the tools. A good team can do wonders with a mediocre product, and a poor team can drive a great tool into the ground.

The roles to be filled for a CASE project are:

- project manager
- project team members
- CASE specialists
- project sponsor
- business experts

Project manager Many authors stress that you need a vocal champion to make CASE work. It's true that a persuasive advocate can speed CASE's acceptance. Yet no firm ever rides to success on one person's back. If you peg the technology to a single person, it lives or dies with that person. It's far better to build a body of grass-roots CASE supporters, so that others can carry the torch when one person fades.

Still, many a career has been made through successful CASE usage. Managers who rally developers to get the most from CASE get hailed as the first of a desirable new breed. Developers who impressively speed development while increasing system quality will also get well deserved recognition. Often these developers get more responsibility as they move to subsequent projects.

CASE needs a champion less than it needs a fair chance at proving its mettle. A skilled project manager can give it this opportunity.

Communication and negotiation skills rank high on the list of desirable project manager abilities. To discover the win conditions of each stakeholder, the project manager must be an astute observer; to satisfy them, he must be a master of coordination.

The pilot project manager should be pro-CASE, or at least neutral, not someone out to see the technology fail. Often this means assigning a less experienced project manager, someone whose reputation stands to gain from successful CASE use. Be wary of appointing someone who's heavily vested in the status quo development environment.

Finally, the IS manager or project sponsor should pay some attention to the win conditions of the project manager. If the chosen person feels they're being put in a no-win situation, the project is doomed to failure. The project manager achieves personal acclaim when they complete a "successful" project. In most firms, this simply means delivering systems on time and under budget. If standard definition of success doesn't change, the project manager will feel people have added to her burden. They are making it more difficult for her to meet schedules and budgets by adding the uncertainty of new tools.

The project manager should plan with her bosses to determine the true goals of the CASE project. Then she can concentrate on the most important aspects, and gain insight into her managers' win conditions.

Team members In general, the team you select for a CASE project shouldn't differ much from a standard project team. If any engineers have prior experience with the new tools or methods, they should rate a spot on the team. Since most folks won't have such experience, you can look for a few more general qualities:

- A willingness to learn. A team of pessimists makes for a short, depressing project.
- A healthy dose of skepticism. Some people choose team members according to their propensity to agree with the project manager. A team of yes-people won't provide the most balanced evaluation of the new tools.
- Familiarity with current methods and tools. You want some people who can compare the new tools to the old, and discuss the differences later with their peers. It helps if these folks are respected for their work with the old methods. You can also include a novice developer if you wish to test how easy the tools are to learn.
- Appropriate technical skills. New tools can cause unforeseen problems that non-technical people can't correct. Even if the vendor advertises that anyone can use their tools, make sure you have one or two people who can tweak an AUTOEXEC.BAT file, or hook up a new printer.
- Something to gain from the project. Don't pull reluctant people onto the project when you think it won't be in their best interests. Often a respected senior developer is thrown onto a case project to give it an air of credibility. But frequently the most senior people have the most to lose from the adoption of new technology (or they think they do, which amounts to the same thing).

The project team members are the ones who will get their hands dirty with the tools. They might well be the final arbiters of the CASE tool's value. People with the qualities outlined above can adapt quickly to the new tools, and make informed assessments of their worth.

CASE specialists On all but the smallest projects, the team will work better when backed up by competent supporters. For a CASE project, these support roles include:

- CASE consultant. Often external to the firm, consultants can bring a wealth of knowledge about methods and tools. Make sure they concentrate on transferring skills to project team members, and not on hacking out systems on their own.
- Methodologist or method pool manager. This person audits the process, documenting methods used. He also conducts process reviews, and suggests improvements for next time. This role often grows out of existing jobs that manage coding or development standards.
- Support technician. Someone must be able to support the installation of the tools, and provide technical support throughout the pilot. The CASE vendor will usually supply telephone support for free during this time, but check this out beforehand.

Depending on the project's scope, you might assign additional people to fill these roles. If you're running a feasibility pilot, these roles can be filled by actual project team members, instead of on-call specialists. If the new tools succeed, these roles could grow into full-time job positions.

Management sponsor A pilot project shakes things up in unanticipated ways. An active management sponsor can quell troubles that might otherwise shoot down a pilot.

For example, a client's pilot project team once fell afoul of their technical services group. It seemed that the team's frequent use of the mainframe CASE repository was slowing down other development teams' database response time. The technical services manager tried to force the CASE pilot team to access the mainframe only at non-peak hours. This would have wiped out the project's chances of showing any productivity gains, not to mention totally frustrating the team members. Luckily, the project had an active sponsor, a divisional IS manager, who reached an agreement with technical services (they moved the repository to another machine). Without such sponsorship, the project team would have had little recourse.

This sponsor can mobilize people who are beyond the project manager's influence. An active sponsor can also be a successful pilot project's greatest pubic relations resource.

Business experts Few people challenge the need to involve business experts throughout the development process. Early CASE projects are often insulated from such "distractions." Yet if you introduce CASE to ease the information gathering process, shouldn't users help test this?

IS groups often feel that the way they develop systems is their own business. As long as users get a system they like, they shouldn't care how it was created. But many new methods alter the relationship between users and developers, usually requiring greater user participation. Business experts should be involved in every new CASE project. They should review the created software and turn a critical eye upon the development process itself.

Handling transition At the start of the project, you should start preparing people for the personal transitions they are about to face. The importance of this varies according to the project's scope.

Transition pain won't have a heavy effect upon a feasibility pilot team. Since the new methods aren't seen as "permanent," the team won't be forced to reorient themselves. They'll have to adapt their habits, but not their value system.

For subsequent projects, though, transition begins the moment people are picked. Meet with them right away and discuss the differences between this project and others they've been involved with. Talk with them about the new opportunities this might bring, or the ways it might make their jobs easier. Find out what their win conditions are, and see how you can tailor the project to increase their odds of success.

Above all, don't underestimate the need for training. Everyone will need some kind of training or education, even management sponsors and business experts. Arrange for people to attend third-party courses or seminars if you haven't yet set up official training programs. Distribute books or videotapes that discuss the concepts you'll be piloting. Make sure everyone gets trained before the project progresses too far, and not as a reaction to problems along the way.

Draft a project schedule

I'm amazed when project managers blindly agree to develop a complex system in a few months time—before they even develop their own estimate of how long it should take. In *The Soul of a New Machine*, Tracy Kidder describes a perfect example of seat-of-the-pants project estimation:

> Ed Rasala asked Epstein, "How long will it take you?"
> Epstein replied, "About two months."
> "Two months?" Rasala said. "Oh, come on."
> So Epstein told him, "Okay, six weeks."
> Epstein felt as if he were writing his own death warrant. Six weeks didn't look like enough time, so he's been staying here half the night working on the thing, and it's gone faster than he thought it would. This has made him so happy that just a moment ago he went down the hall and told Rasala, "Hey, Ed, I think I'm gonna do it in four weeks."
> "Oh, good," Rasala said.
> Now, back in his cubicle, Epstein has just realized, "I just signed up to do it in four weeks."
> Better hurry, Dave.[10]

Using similar estimation techniques for some early projects I managed, I soon realized that hours of overtime were a high price to pay for hasty agreement to an unrealistic schedule.

Tom Peters lobbies for an appeals process that allows project managers to question deadlines or resource constraints handed down from above.[11] Few companies formalize such a process, but most IS managers will listen to a project manager's informed reassessment of a project schedule. Project managers shouldn't commit to delivery dates until they do a detailed schedule estimate, drawing on knowledgeable CASE sources.

Throw old schedules out the window Most people base estimates upon experiences with similar projects in the past.[12] CASE methods diverge greatly from previous ones, though, so this estimation technique will never be a good guide. Still, many project managers assume that their first CASE project will take at least as long as their previous endeavors.

Toward the end of a 6-month analysis project, a project manager asked me to review some schedules for the subsequent design and construction efforts. The team planned to use an integrated CASE tool to automatically generate all of the application code. Yet the manager estimated 9 months time to complete design, and then 12 months for construction. I reminded her that the firm's pilot CASE projects took less time to do design and construction than they spent in analysis. "Well," she replied, "those were pilot projects. This is a real one, and I know we'll hit obstacles no one has thought of yet. Besides, if it takes less time, then we'll look like gods."

Studies have shown that the most accurate estimates are made task by task, and then summed to achieve a project total.[13] This often tedious task can be automated using one of the project management packages on the market. There are two classes of automated project management tools:

- Project or phase estimators. These tools ask for project parameters and return project or phase time estimates. They are best for initial ballpark estimates, not official project schedules.
- Project schedulers. These organize tasks, relate them to resources and time estimates, and let you create Gantt or PERT charts. Some help you estimate low-level tasks. Total project estimates are arrived at bottom-up.

Few estimators have caught up with the CASE revolution. Most of these tools still base their estimates on assumptions about older development methods. Few consider newer approaches, such as information engineering or object-oriented development. Many tools base their results upon tens or thousands of project histories. However, few or none of these projects followed your new techniques, or used the same mix of CASE tools.

Nor are they designed for modular methods. Estimates are based upon assumptions about entire phases, regardless of specific steps performed within them. An estimation method that was proven on similar projects in the past can be projected forward. But when specific tools or techniques change, macro-metrics won't be very useful. They can tell you what you might expect were you not changing things, but they can't anticipate the changes. At best, you can build your own assumptions into the parameters you input to the estimation tool.

If you have a phase-based estimation tool with tailorable parameters, you can adapt it for use with new methods. Set up the parameters to reflect your early assumptions about the new development paths. Alter the parameters as you learn more from each project. Assuming you don't significantly change your development paths in the next few years, you'll eventually develop an accurate estimating tool.

Still, the most accurate estimates will always come from the bottom-up. You can closely guess how long it will take one person to perform one task. But guessing how long it will take a dozen people to do three hundred tasks is far more difficult. Project scheduling tools let you build schedules from the ground up, rolling detailed task estimates up to complete project schedules.

There are over 200 project scheduling tools available, able to run on any type of hardware you can imagine. Many CASE vendors now include task estimation support in their project management toolsets. These estimates are often based upon project experiences at other firms, and serve as an excellent guide for first-time CASE projects.

Shifting the workload In chapter 3, I discussed how most CASE approaches shift the workload forward to the planning and analysis parts of the development cycle. You'll spend more time gathering business goals and requirements, and less time designing and coding systems.

Some traditional software projects began with a set of programs already defined or presumed. The initial requirements specify solution constraints: the number of programs or screens to be defined. From there the project manager simply puts a number to each one—say three weeks per screen—and multiplies to arrive at an aggregate estimate.

However, nearly all structured analysis methodologies postpone the definition of these common system deliverables (programs and screens) until later in the development cycle. They aren't available up front to base estimates upon. As a result, managers facing their first CASE projects must come up with new estimation methods. Usually they revert to the most primitive method of all: the wild guess.

The first time I managed a CASE project, I assumed it would take about as long as the last project I worked on. (This was such an ingrained technique at the firm that project managers who derived more realistic estimates found themselves repeatedly justifying them.) Needless to say, this first estimate was way off the mark.

Yet with one project in hand, I now had a basis for estimating the next. Our team had been careful to measure progress at each step of the first project, and to couch these measures in terms of the CASE objects used as inputs to each phase. These measurements then provided the values needed to estimate the effort required for the next CASE project.

Assume, for example, you're running a project to analyze customer requirements in a certain business area. Your company has already built a strategic planning model, from which the analysis area was scoped. During analysis you will take a set of defined functions and information areas and transform them into more detailed processes and entity types. TABLE 13-4 shows a spreadsheet for estimating the effort involved in the analysis phase.

During previous analysis projects, each context process was broken down into an average of 22 elementary processes. Each subject area has been found to cover an average of 12 entity types. Since these are the fundamental objects for this kind of structured analysis, you can base the rest of your estimates upon them. The final estimate, of course, is in person-months of effort, not duration. The estimates you derive this way won't be exact, but they'll be far more accurate than guesswork. Plus, with each project you can adjust the multiplying factors, or even create new sets of them for different classes of projects. You can draw these factors directly from inquiries about actual CASE objects residing in the CASE repository.

Budgeting Some project managers are called upon to draft project budgets as well as schedules. This process changes little with CASE. It remains a function of resources assigned to a project, and how long they will be used.

Table 13-4. Estimation of Analysis Phase Effort

Historical Project Parameters:

Average elementary processes per context process	22
Average entity types per subject area	12
Average attributes per entity type	5
Average elementary processes per design area	15

Inputs:

Number of context-level processes	3
Number of subject areas	19

Estimates:

Number of elementary processes	66
Number of entity types	228
Number of attributes	1140
Number of resulting design areas (rounded)	4

Calculated Task Estimates (for object-based deliverables):

WBS Deliverable	Manhours / Per	Total
A100 Context diagram	15.0 / Context process	45.0
A200 Process decomposition diagram	20.0 / Context process	60.0
A220 Process dependency diagram	1.5 / Elementary process	67.5
A300 Process-to-entity matrix	1.0 / Elementary process	67.0
A400 Entity relationship diagram	16.0 / Subject area	304.0
A450 Entity attribute definitions	0.1 / Attribute	114.0
A500 Process action program	5.0 / Elementary process	330.0
A800 Design area risk analysis	2.0 / Design area	8.0

Total calculated estimate		995.5
Additional task effort estimate (non-CASE deliverables)		304.0

Total Manhours effort		1299.5
Total Man-days effort	8 / Day	162.4
Total Man-months effort	168 / Month	7.7

Depending on the scope of the CASE pilot project, though, it's sometimes wise to seek creative project funding. An IS department planning a CASE pilot might be able to defray some costs by soliciting participation of other departments. The pilot will benefit everyone if its results are publicized, so sharing its costs shouldn't be out of the question. It's better still if you can get developers from other departments to participate. This improves the odds of widespread acceptance of CASE.

Monitor the project and communicate progress

Once the project is underway, the project manager's workload doesn't slacken. Even if the project has been given every advantage—enlightened sponsors, meticulously selected tools, realistic project plans—surprises will crop up along the way.

No one can anticipate all the things that might befall a CASE project. Instead, I'll list a few principles for keeping the impacts of these surprises to a minimum:

- Manage risks and uncertainty.
- Measure as you go.
- Make every task a success.
- Have fun.

Manage risks Uncertainties aren't always damaging—only when they go unchecked. There are two basic techniques for managing risks: acknowledging them up front, and monitoring them along the way.

Risk acknowledgment can take the form of a risk management plan, as advocated by Barry Boehm. This plan, Boehm writes, "ensures that each project makes an early identification of its top risk items . . . develops a strategy for resolving the risk items, identifies and sets down an agenda to resolve new risk items as they surface, and highlights progress versus plans in monthly reviews."[14] Such plans are required for U.S. military contractors as part of DoD Standard 2167A. They are a good idea for every project manager, whether formally presented or informally drawn up for the manager's own benefit.

Some of the main risks facing CASE projects are listed in TABLE 13-5.

Measure as you go When your bosses ask you how the project's going, you want to say more than just "alright." Before, the answer was usually "the external specs are *almost done*"—a state they went into the day people started working on them!

CASE tools help you quantify progress in ways you couldn't before. Having estimated the number of entity types and elementary processes to emerge from the analysis effort, for example, you can track your progress against these numbers. If you estimated 80 entity types, and now have 50 fully defined and validated, tell your boss the data side is 63% complete. Though this figure can't convey the complexity of the data modeling effort, it certainly sounds more impressive than "alright."

Revise your estimates as you progress, so your numbers stay current. Many people feel that process measurement is something you do as a follow-on task once the project is done. In fact, you should record things as they happen.

Such measurements also let you know right away when you need to adjust earlier estimates. Avoid the temptation to try to make up for schedule slippage in later tasks. If you've estimated realistically all the way along, this probably won't happen. Confess the slippage now, while people aren't yet married to final delivery dates.

Quality assurance is another form of measurement. By measuring the quality of each product along the way, you can prevent small errors from triggering more, like a line of falling dominoes.

One project team I worked with was trained in how to write pseudocode, and then set out to describe some processes using it. At least 75 processes later, they came to me

Table 13-5. Major Risks of CASE Projects

Risk	Risk-limiting Techniques
Technical failure of CASE tool	• Contract for responsive technical support from the CASE vendor • Assign a full-time technical support person to the CASE project • Run feasibility pilot before larger project
Extended learning curves	• Provide extensive training before project begins • Encourage constant information-sharing among team members and with other projects
Resistant or cynical team members	• Identify members' win conditions up front, and attempt to satisfy them during the course of the project • Create transition plans and transition monitoring groups to help people raise and resolve problems caused by the new approaches
Unrealistic schedules and budgets	• Build both from the ground up, estimating time and costs for lower-level tasks and summing them to get total estimates • Limit project size
Vendor never delivers promised CASE tool enhancements	• Build a component CASE strategy around an open repository tool. Then buy another vendor's product to fill the void. • Ask another vendor to help you convert software engineering information from one repository format to another
Process goals overshadow business goals	• Explicitly state goal priorities at the start of the project • Create a pilot project "test plan" that indicates the features of the tool to be focused upon. This discourages developers from testing out every tool feature for just the fun of it.

for a review. For the most part, they had done a good job. But they forgot about the CASE tool's ability to reference actual data model objects, and ended up describing in painstaking text what could have been selected from a scrolling list in the tool. If they'd come back for review after one or two tries, they could have saved themselves a lot of rework.

Make every task a success Managers are always tempted to ask when you're going to start coding. If you're a project manager, don't let others get away with framing the question this way.

Code is only one of the deliverables of the new approach. Early diagrams capture and present business knowledge in valuable new ways. These deliverables are just as important as the final product. Your task as manager is to make every deliverable a small success. Format the diagrams nicely and present them to users and managers. Be ready to list other benefits of the new approach for your critics, including:

- better documentation
- closer adherence to business requirements
- knowledge about how the systems will affect business goals
- better software maintainability
- structured knowledge about the business

Admittedly, it will be difficult to sell people on CASE unless you one day deliver working systems. The first time through many developers will feel the philosophical angst of "What is all this buying us?" Once they see finished systems, though, it will all seem worthwhile.

Have fun   P.J. Plauger describes how fun, or the lack thereof, can actually affect the bottom line:

> Once upon a time, programmers worked for companies because computers were too expensive. Now, the average programmer can afford a comfy development environment at home. You will keep many programmers because they prefer a salary to the thrills of independence. You will keep a few more because they like to work on large projects as a part of a team. But it is harder than ever to keep programmers if the work isn't fun.[15]

The projects I remember most clearly are the ones that were the most fun to do. These were also, not surprisingly, the ones that were most successful.

CASE projects can be the most enjoyable ones your developers have participated in. They get to play with new tools, and they are empowered to discover the best tricks for making the new tools hum. Take advantage of these project characteristics, and build an atmosphere of adventure. With luck, the team members will carry the same atmosphere to future projects.

Publicize project success

Introducing CASE into a large IS organization is usually an uphill battle. You need to publicize every victory, no matter how small.

If a CASE pilot or mainstream CASE project succeeds, you should make sure everyone knows about it. An active management sponsor can usually handle a lot of this propagandizing; after all, the sponsor linked his reputation to the project from the start.

First, though, you need to determine whether or not the project succeeded. It isn't always as obvious as it sounds. In the absence of a final evaluation, some projects succeed simply by concluding. However, such victories are often Pyrrhic—win too many that way and you'll lose the war.

This time you have a list of project objectives determined at the start of the project. You can judge project success accordingly.

For example, if the CASE tool fails, a pilot project can still be successful. It has discovered useful information: tool X and technique Y don't work in this context. A pilot project only fails when no conclusions can be drawn, or when the conclusions are twisted to prove some political point. If objectives were to learn about the tools, rather than produce working systems, the pilot has prevailed. The lessons learned about CASE technology will balance the project's cost.

The goals stimulate questions to ask when you review the project.

- Did the project results support the business objectives?
- Did software quality perceptibly improve compared to prior projects?
- Was the project done faster than it might have been the old way (make sure you compare against actual historical metrics)?

- Will the resulting system be easy to maintain?
- How do the people involved feel about the new techniques and tools?

A good time to ask these questions is during a post-project evaluation. Research has shown that while 80% of IS organizations perform some kind of post-project evaluation, very few use this to improve development methods or management practices.[16] In most cases such evaluations seem like symbolic rituals for handing systems responsibility over to the users, and not a way to learn from the project's results.

Build the post-project evaluation step into each method path. Use it to evaluate the deliverables and the process used to create them. Roll the findings of the project team back into the method pool, by adding to the project experiences section of each technique. Also ask the pilot team to suggest alternative techniques that might improve upon their performance.

You can also revisit the personnel transition plan after the pilot project. Discuss how people feel about the new tools and techniques they just used. What were the major mental jumps each person made? What do they miss about the previous techniques? What do they prefer about the new ones? Were they given adequate training?

Take a look at how useful the metrics were. Were you able to say whether the pilot team was more productive than an average team? Were the deliverables better quality than most? When you can't answer one of these questions, think about how you might in the future.

You can base much of your evaluation on effective measurements. Results without metrics are easily washed away. If the project chalked up spectacular numbers, make sure they get publicized. You'll ensure a place for your project in the IS folklore, and set a new standard for the future.

14

Spreading the word

One successful pilot project doesn't end your CASE implementation. It catalyzes a host of further actions. Once you've settled on a set of tools and techniques, the rollout can begin.

The high-level change plan in chapter 7 lists these final rollout steps.

- Develop a training program.
- Organize for CASE and cooperative development.
- Roll out new tools and methods.
- Evaluate the IS architecture and transition plan.

Develop a training program

As Roger Pressman observes, "Education is often the stepchild of software engineering implementation. The need for it keeps surfacing, but no one pays much attention."[1]

Yet training is one of the most cost-effective ways for improving the development process. Not only do courses encourage common understanding of important development goals, they can also boost productivity. According to Curtis Plott, vice president of the American Society for Training and Development, investment in training has historically produced twice the productivity return of investment in new plant and equipment.[2]

When you install CASE tools, your need for training skyrockets. New tools bring an entourage of changes with them. Your training program should cover multiple aspects of software development, including fundamental skills and new areas of knowledge.

A list of the training program's offerings can include:

- Overview of the software development environment. This course presents all of the tools and methods currently in use. It discusses how to find and explore existing business models and reusable design libraries. It introduces people to

the method pool, and how to use it. This is the best jump-start course for new software engineers.
- Development methods and tools. If you have CASE tools, it's senseless to teach tools and methods separately. People must grasp the methods before they can make the tools sing. Depending on the methods you adopt, you might need one or a series of method courses.
- Method overviews. Geared toward managers and business experts, these short courses summarize the concepts behind development techniques and tools. They discuss the business rationale behind the methods. Participants will understand the major deliverables and milestones of software projects.
- Project management. This course can teach general skills, or it can be tailored to a specific development method path. Topics covered should include scheduling, task estimation, risk management, and budgeting.
- Facilitation skills. Everyone who will be asked to lead information gathering sessions with users, or integration meetings with developers should take this course. It covers effective presentation, and leadership skills.
- Repository management. This course discusses how to manage multiple CASE repositories and maintain a smooth flow of software engineering information throughout the firm.
- CASE technical support. Larger companies might want to provide internal technical support instead of relying upon the vendor. Large mainframe repositories will require on-site support. The course covers installation and maintenance of specific CASE tools.
- Sessions to present contents and meaning of integrated data and process models. Too often the business meaning of systems and models rests only in their creators' minds. Effective integration requires common understanding of these models. These sessions can present overviews of high-level goal, data, and process models, or they can concentrate on specific business areas.

These courses serve many different audiences. Figure 14-1 suggests which groups will benefit most from various offerings. You can compile a suggested training sequence for each group. For instance, developers might start with the overview of the development environment, followed by in-depth training in the methods and the tools, followed by education about the company's integrated business models.

Internal versus external

Education, like methodology, should be tailored to your environment. When courses say one thing, and reality another, reality wins.

The list of courses above is extensive. Unfortunately, only the largest IS groups have the time and resources to develop many of these themselves. Most firms must rely upon the CASE tool vendors or third-party training and consulting firms. But the more you can do internally, the better.

In-house courses Some IS groups get into the internal training business as a result of CASE. Informal meetings turn into seminars, and then into formal courses. Many IS managers resist this trend, saying, "We're in the software business, not the

Fig. 14-1. Suggested attendees for CASE course offerings

Courses	Software Engineer	Project Manager	IS Manager	CASE Consultant	CASE Tech Support	Active Business Expert	Business Manager
Development Env't Overview	●	●	●	●	●	○	
Methods & Tools	●	●		●	●	●	
Methods Overview (Users)			●			○	●
Project Management	○	●	○	○			
Facilitation Skills	○	●	○	●			
Repository Management	○			○	●		
CASE Technical Support	○				●		
Integrated Bus. Model Detail	●				○	●	
Integrated Bus. Model Overview			●				●

● = should attend training   ○ = on an as-needed basis only

training business." In today's environment, training is everybody's business. Continuous improvement requires continuous learning. If you rely solely upon third-party trainers, you can never advance beyond their capabilities—at least not on a large scale.

Courses aren't much easier to develop than software. Creating the materials requires good writing and layout skills. Getting the messages across requires presentation and teaching skills. You'll need to find people with these skills in your organization, or bring in contractors from the outside.

Some vendors will sell you their course materials for in-house use. By supplementing these with localized sections, you can build a customized course fairly quickly.

Hold off on customizing the methods and tools courses until you've stabilized the method paths you follow. The first few project teams can attend external, vendor-sponsored courses. Once a couple of projects have validated the CASE approach, you can develop your own in-house courses. If you do this too soon, you run the risk of frequent revisions to course materials.

External courses The number of consulting and training groups dealing with CASE seems to double every year. You'll have no trouble finding trainers, though it won't be easy to find ones who teach the same methods you've adopted. Look beyond the brochure blurbs about CASE methods or structured techniques to see which specific ones will be taught. Make sure that external trainers have experience teaching the specific techniques you plan to use, not just similar ones.

If you use outside trainers, ask them to tailor their presentations to your concerns. At least have one of your more knowledgeable people sit in as a training assistant. This person will answer questions like, "How do we apply this technique here?" or "What did project X find when they did this?" The assistant can also speak up when the trainer rolls past a point that's deemed important. For instance, a data modeling consultant course might use diagramming standards that differ from your company's standards. This assistant can briefly explain the company standards and compare them to the trainer's.

As an alternative, you can set up short debriefing sessions with people who return from external courses. Prepare some materials illustrating how in-house methods differ from those presented by the trainers. Present examples of how the methods have been applied by your organization. These few hours will make the training seem relevant, and are as valuable as the official course itself.

External courses can't address:

- in-house standards
- results from actual in-house projects
- hints about using the techniques in your environment
- how the techniques related to the company's CASE tools

Your challenge is finding ways to get this information across.

Informal training

When official courses aren't frequent enough, or don't carry enough information, informal training fills the gaps. You can provide for both ad hoc training, and informal knowledge-sharing forums.

Ad hoc training The various forms of ad hoc training include:

- Person-to-person instruction. Internal consultants can provide one-to-one instruction for project team members.
- Computer-based training programs. Self-paced training packages exist for many software engineering topics, methods, and some CASE tools.
- Instructional videotapes. These are available on a wide range of topics. They can be especially useful for introducing people to new concepts or advances in technology.
- Books. A well stocked software engineering library provides a wealth of information about CASE concepts, practices, and experiences of other developers.
- Study groups. Developers who want to accelerate the learning process can band together into study groups. They select topics, and meet periodically to discuss

them. Some groups walk through case studies; others do assignments and compare them. Study groups can also communicate electronically: Richard Cohen of StarSys, Inc. has run many successful software engineering study groups in the Computer Language Magazine Forum on CompuServe.

Knowledge sharing forums Formal training materials aren't easy to revise. Books and videos are static. Yet every day people pick up new knowledge about the techniques and tools they use. Unless there's a forum for easily sharing this knowledge, others will have to learn it themselves, the hard way.

In chapter 5, I discussed using the method pool to transfer knowledge about techniques. Provide incentives or recognition for people who contribute to the method pool, and you'll gather piles of valuable information. Chapter 6 suggested CASE user groups, user handbooks, newsletters, or electronic bulletin boards as vehicles for informal knowledge-sharing. All of these can help shorten learning curves and speed the acceptance of CASE.

Training sequence

Informal training forums are especially important in early stages of CASE implementation. Until you've stabilized your methods or developed internal courses, there will be no other way to spread new CASE knowledge.

Early CASE users will need to attend external courses. Try to train people right before they'll start using the methods and tools they learn about. Try to avoid what methodology expert Brian Dickinson calls the "sheep-dip" training strategy: "training every employee in all the techniques at once," whether they need it or not.[3] Months later, when people finally get around to using what they've learned, they'll be frustrated at their lack of recall and proficiency.

The biggest hurdle to CASE training is finding time for people to participate. Cougar and Zawacki found that data processing professionals have a "growth need"—for learning and extending themselves—that far exceeds that of other professions.[4] Software developers are motivated by learning new things. Every dollar or hour invested in effective CASE education will pay off manyfold in project results.

Organize for CASE and cooperative development

CASE can be a catalyst for reorganization. The demands of integrated, cooperative development usually require substantial changes to the reporting structure. Awareness of the need to manage the development environment also requires new groups and team structures.

But you should never reorganize at the same time you start using CASE. Take an ad hoc approach to CASE at the start: a team-based pilot project, drawing participants from various IS and functional groups. Don't formalize new techniques, communication channels, or work habits until you've worked the kinks out of them with small, informal groups. Once you've got a baseline of best practices, then take steps to change the organization for the better.

Reorganization rarely cures company ailments. Rather, it formalizes habits and lines of communications that are currently haphazard. But fundamental knowledge and skills must already be present. Reorganization simply cuts through old barriers, and lets the knowledge flow in more effective patterns.

Why reorganize?

Reorganizations often involve centralizing or decentralizing IS resources. CASE adds new fuel to the debate, but it contributes to both sides. Integrated CASE and the need to support new tools and techniques warrant new central support groups. On the other hand, some CASE tools simplify end-user development, contributing to decentralization.

This debate has no winner. All IS groups must balance centralized and distributed resources. Some functions, like consulting and training and architectural planning, must reside centrally. Others, like end-user computing support, must be distributed. Organizationally, the other functions—including analysis, design, and technical support—can fall anywhere. As long as task forces can be formed freely, it doesn't matter where developers and knowledge analysts reside in the organization. Every project will require cross-functional cooperation.

One imperative is clear, regardless of how you're organized: don't skimp on support resources. People churning out systems don't have a lot of time to investigate or apply new technologies. So dedicate some staff to doing just that. Peter Freeman, computer science professor and consultant, finds that "devoting ten percent of one's resources to a support activity is not uncommon today in sophisticated organizations that work on complex systems."[5]

The new generalists

When people talk of a software factory, they assume this means an assembly-line approach. For example, industry observer Alan S. Fisher suggests that:

> Software factories, like conventional factories, work in assembly line fashion with each group of workers specializing in one aspect of the manufacturing process. For software, this means specialized analysts, designers, implementors, and quality assurance professionals.[6]

However, the dehumanizing assembly-line approach is proving less productive in most conventional factories. The trend is toward cooperating teams, who follow the same set of products through the entire production cycle. Each team member must be skilled in many different operations.

Though specialists will always have a place, I believe the future will favor generalists. Managers of CASE consulting groups look constantly for people who can support the entire development cycle, people as comfortable talking business with top managers as they are designing online screens. General problem-solving, communications, and learning skills serve most CASE users better than specific technical talents. In addition, these skills let them jump smoothly from one technology to another, an important ability for the future.

New roles

CASE alters some current development roles, while creating a number of new ones. These roles fall into three categories: tool and technique support, integration, and software engineering. The software engineering roles already exist in most firms; CASE just changes their nature a bit. The other roles are, for the most part, specific to CASE and integrated system environments.

Tool and technique support roles include:

- Methodology trainer/consultant. An expert in new development methods and the tools used to support them. Needs good facilitation and consulting skills. Works closely with project teams to transfer needed skills.
- Methodology developer. Researches new development methods and tools. Manages the method pool and methodology documentation. Analyzes effectiveness of methods, and coordinates new additions and changes to the method pool.
- Repository manager. Monitors usage and performance of the central CASE repository. Coordinates integration of project-level repositories up to the highest-level repository. In larger organizations, this requires more than one full-time person.
- CASE support engineer. A specialized software engineer, entrusted with developing and maintaining the software development environment. Helps define development requirements. Evaluates and installs tools. Augment these by developing ad hoc utilities and "bridges" between development tools.
- Advanced technology researcher. Investigates new development technologies. Works with CASE support engineers to arrange demonstrations and pilot projects for new tools.
- Metrics analyst. Selects and establishes measurements of the software development process, and project management performance. Sets up measurement programs to capture baseline and ongoing metrics.

In the area of integration, the following roles develop:

- Information planner. This person helps facilitate and support strategic information planning sessions. Leads efforts to transform archaic business processes into streamlined ones.
- Integration specialist. Specializes in creation and upkeep of high-level business, data, and process architectures. Works to integrate various development efforts into common frameworks. Large groups might have separate release architects, software system architects, and data architects.
- Release manager. Coordinates multiple design projects to create an integrated release of multiple system segments. Might be a rotating position, falling to a competent project manager.

Finally, software engineering produces the need for:

- Knowledge analyst. This role represents the evolution of the programmer/analyst into a business and technology generalist. This person is a "knowledge engineer," able to extract information from business experts. Uses advanced development tools to capture and structure knowledge as business models, and to generate software systems from these models.
- Software designers. The closest role to the traditional programmer. Develops sophisticated, flexible module and system designs. Transforms requirements specifications into working systems.
- Technical specialist. Technical skills will be valuable for a long time to come. The technical specialist is an expert about specific target and development platforms. This is the person who can squeeze the last nanosecond of response time out of a system, or track down the most elusive bugs.

The names of these roles are not important. Many of them can be played by people who retain their old job titles. However, you should formally recognize the need for these new roles by altering job descriptions or employee performance objective. Most companies arrive at formal roles like these through trial and error. You can save some anguish by instituting some of these roles early on.

Roll out new tools and methods

You've planned and prepared as much as you can, following all or a few of the steps in this book. Now you need to get the tools into the hands of people who can use them. It's time to grab the elusive benefits of CASE.

I'll explore four aspects of the CASE rollout in more detail:

- drafting a CASE rollout plan
- installing CASE tools
- selecting and sequencing CASE-based projects
- integrating disparate projects

Drafting a CASE rollout plan

Because of the many people involved with the rollout, coordination requires a comprehensive schedule. The schedule should cover both hardware and software installations, and training for CASE users. These should show on the same schedule for two reasons.

First, you want people who attend training courses to have access to the tools. People retain knowledge better when they can apply what they've learned. Long lags between training and hands-on experience force people to have the tools without the training. This causes bad habits and frustration.

Second, you need to assign responsibilities for the installation, training, and central methodology support tasks. This implies changes to the organizational structure, or to specific job descriptions. These changes should be coordinated with the various rollout tasks.

Figure 14-2 shows an excerpt from a CASE rollout schedule. Before the first project team can start using CASE, their workstations and local software must be installed, the mainframe component must be set up, and all members must attend training courses.

This illustrates the incremental nature of CASE installations. You can stagger tool installations in order to reduce cost, resource demand, and risk at any one point. Some companies distribute CASE workstations on a project by project basis.

You can also stagger installations according to CASE tool components. For instance, to run a company-wide ISP, you only need one workstation copy of a strategic planning CASE tool. When the ISP generates new projects, though, you'll need analysis-level workstation tools and a central repository to enable information-sharing. Some CASE tools lend themselves to a modular installation approach, while others must be installed as a single package. In any case, staggering installations smooths the rollout process.

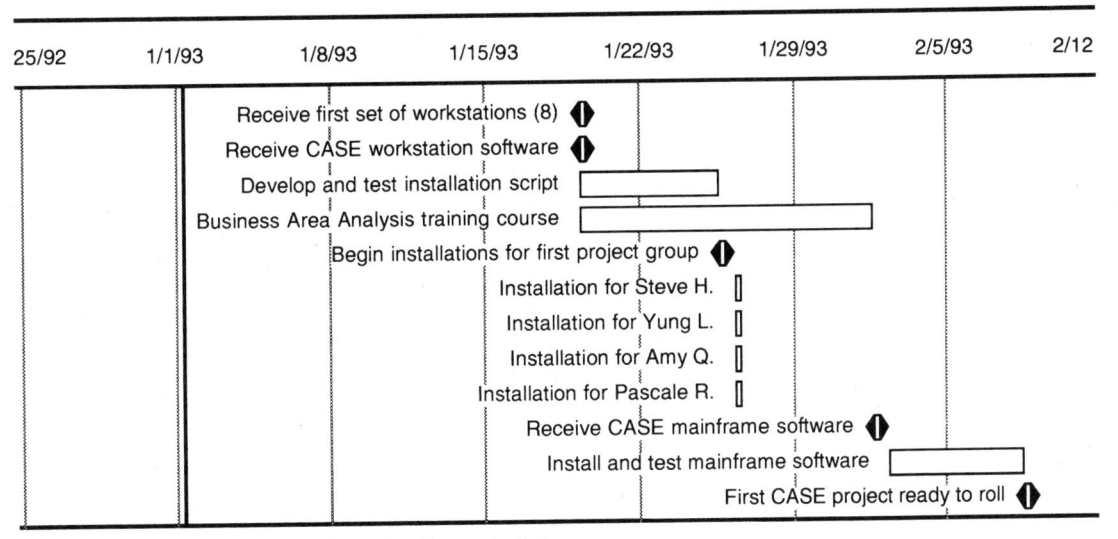

Fig. 14-2. Excerpt from CASE tool rollout schedule

Installing CASE tools

For the most part, CASE tool installations follow the pattern of other hardware and software installation jobs. The complexity and cost of most CASE tools makes the installation task challenging. The first thing to do is to decide where you want the tools; the next is to coordinate all the tasks for putting them there.

Physical layout The physical distribution of IS resources is an important factor that is often overlooked. Physical layout can affect attitudes toward CASE and cooperative development.

If possible, seat project team members near each other. Office seating is usually determined organizationally. Yet today's project teams have dedicated representatives from many different organizational units. For long-term projects, it makes sense to carve out an area where developers, business analysts, user representatives, and support personnel can work near each other. Sometimes this makes managers nervous— they can't look over their subordinates' shoulders as frequently when they're in a different building or on a different floor. Yet in the age of empowerment, shoulder-peering is an obsolete skill.

To promote team unity without rearranging everyone's desks, you can set up project rooms. A project room is a group workspace containing a CASE workstation, a white board or blackboard, and a meeting table. It provides a haven for a project team, where they can meet, compare notes, or even hold small information-gathering sessions with business experts. It also physically centers a team, and lets them develop a group identity.

Many project rooms become decorated in a prevailing style. One group I worked with created a Hawaiian project room. Each member brought in Hawaiian posters or knickknacks, and wore Hawaiian shirts to informal team meetings. Another team chose a "Star Wars" theme. In each case, the theme arose spontaneously from project members and gave them symbols upon which to base their group identity.

The project workstation shouldn't be the only one for the entire team, unless cost is critical. Usually the project workstation harbors the "project repository," from which each member carves subsets to work with on their own workstations. Ideally, a project has one project workstation plus another for each member.

Some firms try to limit their financial outlay by installing CASE tools on one or a few centrally located workstations. Since no one will use CASE for eight hours a day, they assume, people can share workstations. Yet this setup creates bottlenecks. As Pressman relates:

> If you decide to centralize CASE workstations for use by all interested parties, you are likely to encounter the same problems that occurred in the early days of centralized interactive computer terminals . . .: too many staff members waiting in line for too few workstations. This situation often results in lower productivity, staff frustration, and general dislike of CASE.[7]

The central workstation area only works well when CASE users are few. Once the technology spreads, centralized workstations can't keep up with demand.

Cooperative development puts a new premium on group meeting space. Many firms with overcrowded facilities make conference rooms into cubicles to pack more people in. When meeting rooms are hard to find, isolationist developers have an easy excuse.

Get equipment that supports group meetings. Cooperative development requires a common "group memory" of all facilitated sessions. One person taking notes on paper can't provide this. The information should be visible to all, so that people leave the session with a common view of topics covered. "Low-tech" recording equipment includes flip charts and white- or blackboards. Recent improvements on these include photoboards or new white board "cameras" that flash an image from a wall onto a piece of white paper. These save people from rewriting (and possibly reinterpreting) the group's information.

CASE tools augment to this information-recording arsenal. They are unparalleled for capturing and structuring information. A deft CASE tool "jockey" can record group information as it happens. With a workstation screen projector—a peripheral device that sits on an overhead projector—you can build CASE models with the entire group.

At the end, you can print the models and distribute them to participants. They leave with tangible proof that the meeting created substantial results.

Screen projection won't work for all groups. Some people get distracted by the technical wizardry in evidence, or end up nagging the tool jockey about where next to click the mouse, instead of discussing business requirements. In these situations, the CASE tool can still be used to capture the information, but it's not in full view of the group. You can print the models at the end for verification and refinement.

Coordinating installation tasks Once you decide upon the physical layout, you can plan for CASE tool installations. In most cases, installation involves more than loading CASE software onto a hard disk. Consider these additional items you might need to install:

- workstation hardware, or upgrades to existing hardware
- LAN hardware and software, including servers and communication lines
- supporting workstation software, such as new operating systems, or DBMS's
- hardware to support the central repository, or space allocations on existing host hardware for this purpose
- host repository and/or code generation software
- supporting host software

You should also check on availability of vendor technical support, delivery schedules of your hardware and software vendors, and training schedules of those who will use the new software.

Many rollouts stall at this point because technical support personnel get stretched too thin. Before you promise new tools to everyone, check with the people who will do the installations. Ask them to come up with a realistic rollout schedule.

Selecting and sequencing CASE-based projects

To select initial CASE projects, follow guidelines for determining pilot project candidates. Keep the first projects fairly small and self-contained, so you can take good measure of the value of the CASE approach. Make sure that any problems arising from the pilot project are solved before the first "real" projects get underway.

Once again, try not to impose CASE upon projects that are already underway. If a project team is already struggling, injecting new tools and methods can provoke toxic reactions. It will make their jobs harder before it makes them easier.

Try to distribute pilot team members across the first official projects, as direct contributors or internal consultants. Their hands-on experience will be invaluable to a new team.

The best way to select new projects, of course, is according to strategic business goals they support. With the right CASE tools, you can run a strategic information systems planning project to help decide systems priorities.

The need for strategic planning In one of my first jobs as a programmer for a major corporation, I experienced an important revelation: programmers can directly affect corporate policy.

Our programming team was rewriting a set of old information systems. We had to learn what the systems did by reading the old source code. We uncovered dozens of business issues, ranging from which codes were valid for certain offices, to how the entire pricing structures for certain services should be determined. We resolved about a third of these issues with system users, who made their decisions based on operational convenience, rather than strategic business knowledge. But issue management tasks took so long that our project fell behind schedule. In defense of our upcoming performance evaluations, based almost solely upon our ability to meet project schedules, we made a team decision to table the rest of the issues. We drafted solutions that seemed right based on our limited knowledge of the business, and tried to make the systems as flexible as possible, in case we guessed wrong. We finished the project just a few weeks late, and were commended for our performance.

I felt we'd overstepped our bounds by executing policy decisions, and casting them in source code concrete for years to come. But no one ever challenged us. In fact, many of the decisions we made were happily accepted by the user community, who for the first time had common rules for certain business situations.

Junior-level programmers, most of whom were new to the firm, ended up defining up important business policy. As I've learned since then, this scenario is common. Clive Finkelstein has called programmers and analysts "the final arbiters of corporate policy."[8] They fill a policy-making void that's better served by strategic information plans.

ISPs affect more than just system priorities. They crystallize the knowledge of key business personnel. They also trigger sweeping changes to the business.

Only through strategic planning will business processes get reengineered. Without strategic goals and principles, structured analysis methods work to automate current work procedures, not to rethink them. Competitive advantage is gained by transforming internal processes and forging new customer or supplier relationships in ways that competitors can't easily imitate. Leaps like these don't arise from fiddling with each little cog in the mechanism. They arise from fundamentally rethinking entire processes. When planners have set visionary goals, the question becomes "What can we do to achieve these goals?" rather than "What steps do we take in our work today?"

An ISP can be so useful that I recommend stalling all noncritical development projects until you've completed planning. An ISP project normally takes four to six months. If staff will sit idle in the interim, you can use the time to give them training in CASE methods and tools.

Ideally, you should run one company-wide ISP project. The breadth of vision this provides cuts through many of the organizational obstacles to competitive advantage. However, few companies can get senior managers to devote 10% of their time to this effort, over a six-month span. When you don't have the time or management commitment to run a company-wide ISP, you can try other options:

- Ask IS personnel to pore over strategic business plans and create an ISP from the information. This strategy has two major drawbacks. First, you must take the business plans at face value, with no chance to question or clarify the information. Business plans are often "trendy," listing numerous tactical goals, but few persistent strategic ones. Basic goals like "make and distribute products"— upon which most information systems are founded—are omitted in favor of goals

to increase sales in the Asia/Pacific region by 14%. In addition, ISPs done without business experts won't be accepted by them.
- Solicit strategic goals and principles from senior business managers. Build the remaining functional and data models with lower-level managers. This approach can limit time commitments of senior managers, but still provide high-level direction.
- Parcel the business into major functional areas, then run separate ISP projects for each one. This lets you dodge some of the organizational barriers to cross-functional decision-making. But it also creates a host of new issues to resolve. Each ISP will present different sets of goals and functions, and integrating them requires significant effort. In addition, multiple ISPs mean more work. Instead of one six-month project, you end up with eight four-month projects, plus integration time.
- Create one enterprise-level ISP, and them supplement it with functional area ISPs. In a few concentrated days with senior managers, you can model goals, principles, high-level functions, and information needs. This model will be necessarily shallow, but broad. It provides a framework for integrating subsequent ISPs, which will explore functional strategies in more depth. It still takes more time than a single company-wide ISP, but it avoids many of the integration problems of uncoordinated parallel ISPs.

The ISP will only be valuable if people champion its results. There's a temptation for IS managers to treat the ISP as a nice thing for users, but not a binding plan for IS. I've seen IS managers assert at the end of an ISP project that "it doesn't matter what the users say. We know which systems we'll develop first. We just want the users to buy off on them." This approach invalidates most of the findings of the ISP, and guarantees future credibility problems for IS.

The budgeting process can also undermine ISP directions. In some firms, development funds get distributed to those who clamor loudest, regardless of company strategies. To get the most of an ISP, you need to align funding practices with its results.

You should also make provisions for keeping the ISP alive. Once built, many companies pack the ISP away. They launch a few projects from it, but soon IS priorities shift and people fall back on old ad hoc project prioritization methods. Don't disband the management groups once the ISP is done. Get them back together periodically to discuss progress toward the plan, and manage aberrations. A living ISP provides a constant beacon for systems efforts, and a framework for systems integration. It also draws a map for CASE project rollout.

Integrating disparate projects

As part of the CASE project rollout, you might want to establish mechanisms for ensuring systems integration. A strategic systems plan is a prerequisite. Without up-front planning, the best you can hope for is widespread technical wizardry by technicians who must patch systems together.

You can also encourage integration through coordinated application releases, libraries of reusable software components, and common decision support databases—or data warehouses—as discussed in chapter 4.

Hopefully, you've already acquired the other prerequisite of systems integration: integrated CASE tools. Though they greatly simplify systems integration tasks, CASE tools can add new levels of complexity. With distributed CASE tools come distributed repositories, and new tasks for keeping all the information straight.

Managing multiple CASE repositories CASE models can reside in one or many separate repositories. Workstation CASE databases are repositories of sorts. Others reside on LAN servers, minicomputers, or mainframes. Large companies might store CASE information in any or all of these. As CASE projects proliferate, so will the models. The need to keep them all straight gives rise to the discipline of repository management.

Few companies set up a repository manager role when they start with CASE, but more should. Repository managers serve two basic functions. First, they help keep track of models and repositories. In large companies, the number of models will increase geometrically over time. One planning model begets six analysis models, which split into five design models each, and so on. Each model might be spread into a dozen different subsets, located on a half dozen machines. Without some idea of where these models lie, you run the risk of losing them.

A popular way to visualize CASE model distribution is with a tree structure. The shape of the tree depends upon the CASE tools' information-sharing capabilities. Central repositories with sophisticated object locking schemes allow many users to access CASE information simultaneously. Ideally, everyone could directly access a central company-wide model, creating a shallow subsetting tree (FIG. 14-3). Unfortunately, technological limitations of most tools prevent management of a single central model for the entire company. Some plan for splitting models up must be devised.

The simplest is to partition models by project (FIG. 14-4). A high-level enterprise model splits into a number of project models, all centrally located. Developers pull subsets of the project models for use on their local workstations. This scenario keeps the tree fairly shallow. Shallowness is good, for it means less time is spent transmitting data and reconciling discrepancies. The burden these tasks impose upon developers can be considerable, varying by CASE tool.

With tools that don't provide much repository management support, the subsetting trees can get very involved. I have seen shops with model hierarchies like that in FIG. 14-4. Because the tools provide few checks of model integrity, people must manage complex merging and subsetting paths. The effort involved in manually checking each upload or download can nullify most of the CASE tool's productivity benefits.

The second major duty of repository managers is to develop model merge and subsetting procedures. The biggest fear of a repository manager is lost information. Some CASE tools don't provide automatic check-in or check-out functions, which prevent people from overwriting others' work. These tasks then fall to manual procedures.

The procedures should address questions like:

- When should you upload your workstation model to the central repository?
- When should you back up workstation models?
- When should you back up or archive central repository models?

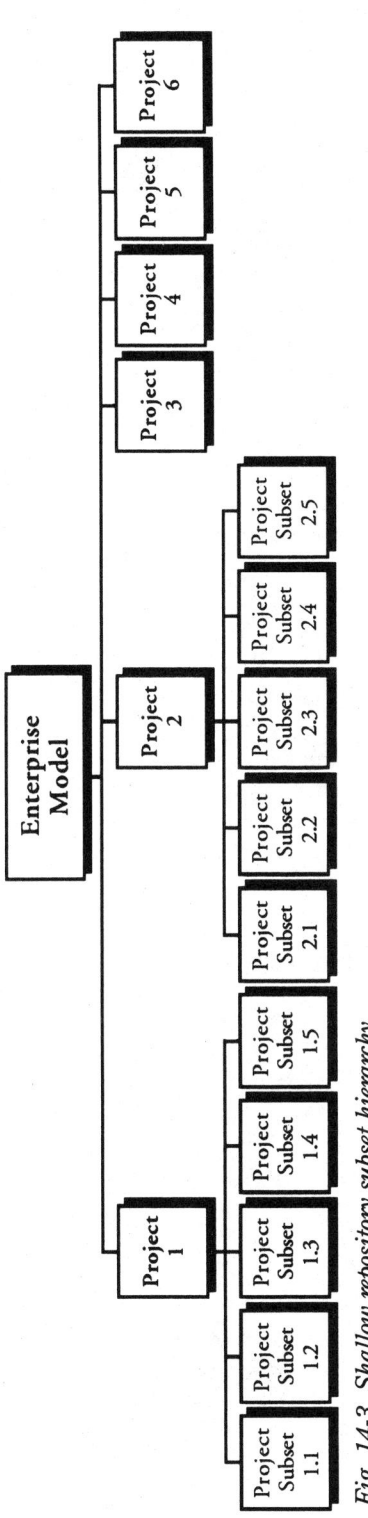

Fig. 14-3. Shallow repository subset hierarchy

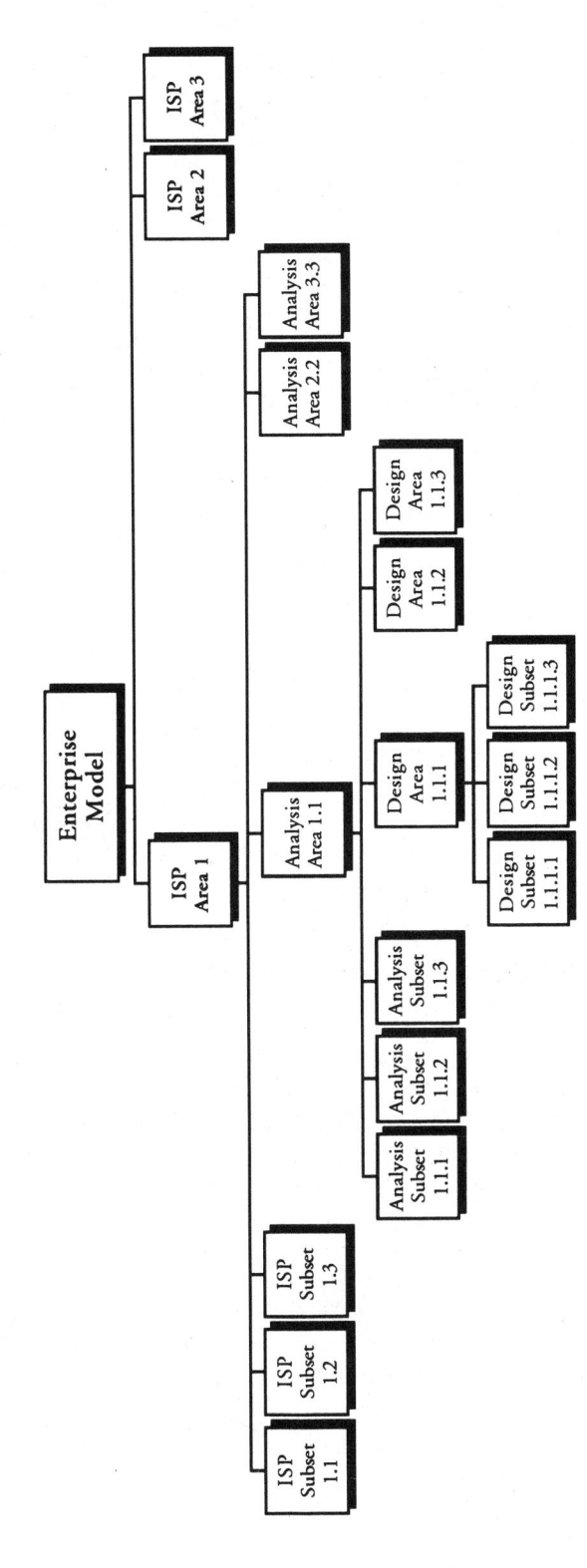

Fig. 14-4. Project-based repository subset hierarchy

- If you upload a model to the central repository, and it says other changes were recently made to the same objects, should you commit the upload or not? Who do you call to find out?
- What happens when you need access to a model or object, but you can't get it?

Internal CASE consultants can walk developers through the procedures, but the repository manager is the best person to write them.

Procedures, like development methods, will evolve over time. If you set them up initially, future effort will be incremental. If you wait too long, while the rollout speeds on, you'll end up scrambling to bring your repositories under control.

Coordinating application releases New integration tasks can complicate the model management picture. The "fan out" from strategic planning projects to analysis and design projects is countered by a progressive "fan in" to coordinated application releases. This implies a reshuffling of repository objects as old project lines blur. Usually a new release model is set up in the central repository, combining information from a number of projects. This model then moves as a unit through the design, construction, and implementation phases.

The introduction of reusable software engineering objects also affect model management tasks. Reusable objects can be held in a separate model—a reusable library—or they can be dispersed throughout models in the central repository. Their location is less important than their visibility. People must be able to quickly find and retrieve reusable objects, or they'll be tempted to rewrite them themselves.

Integration forces most developers out of old patterns of linear thinking. It adds new dimensions to the model management problem because it adds depth to the software engineering process. In some ways, integration tasks actually simplify repository management tasks. When you integrate disparate models, you end up with fewer to manage.

Evaluate the IS architecture and transition plan

The final step in the CASE implementation plan is an ongoing one. As CASE projects progress, as you learn more about the technology ways to manage its adoption, take time to reflect on how you've done. Roll lessons from CASE projects back into strategic IS plans. Adjust your picture of the software development environment when you stop using a tool, or introduce a new one.

A few months after you start rolling out CASE tools, review your progress in a number of areas:

- The IS strategic plan. Has the IS architecture proven valuable? Do people understand it? What is it lacking, and what parts of it were overkill?
- Budgets. Were rollout cost estimates accurate, or way off? How could this be improved next time? Have you been able to track implementation costs?
- Transition plans. Is the transition monitoring team working well? Which transition problems arose, and which could be avoided in the future?

- The method pool. Are people using standard methods or method paths? If you're now working with linear methodologies, will you want to build a method pool in the near future?
- The training program. Do people enjoy the courses? Have skills markedly improved? Do you see a need for any new course offering?
- The measurement program. Have you learned anything from the metrics you've gathered? Is the gathering process disruptive? What new things do people want to know now that measurement is possible?
- Organizational changes. Are people comfortable in their new roles? Should other roles be set up?

Reviews like these should become habit. Continuous improvement requires persistent scrutiny of your methods and performance. This applies to the introduction of new technologies as well as the creation of software.

CASE tool implementation isn't a one-shot project. By taking a holistic view of the CASE introduction, you'll have set up mechanisms to speed similar projects in the future. These include new functions to:

- Update the method pool frequently. Its structure lets you add and subtract methods as you please. You can incorporate new methodologies and tools as you need them.
- Evaluate new tools. A coherent IS tool architecture gives you a framework for plugging in new tools. By recording your experiences with CASE implementations, you can gradually improve the evaluation and selection processes.
- Monitor personal transitions. Once you've acknowledged the personal costs of change, you're poised for smoother changes in the future. By managing transitions, you reduce one of the greatest risks of new projects.
- Reorganize as necessary. Companies that reorganize frequently tend to be more responsive to environmental changes. Some of the shifts you make to support CASE can set precedents for future changes to the organizational structure.
- Keep an eye on new developments. Your CASE information-gathering skills will serve you well in the search for new and better tools.

CASE is the fastest growing segment of the software industry today. It's a rapidly changing technology that's synthesizing advanced artificial intelligence and object-oriented concepts. Today's CASE tools portend the integrated development environments of the future. They are a first and necessary step to that vision. By implementing CASE, and setting up the infrastructure to do it well, you're preparing your firm for future CASE technologies. You're building an environment that thrives on change. You will even get more software written in the interim.

Appendix A
Method pool management system

This appendix presents a small prototype method pool management system (MPMS). The system currently contains only a few of the features discussed in chapters 5 and 10, though it is rapidly evolving to handle most of the capabilities of a robust method pool. The system uses hypertext capabilities to travel along links between goals, products, methods, tools, and contributors. The hypertext features let users delve to any depth they wish in the method pool information.

Figures A-1, A-2, and A-3 show the initial screens a developer or project manager uses to select project goals, desired end products, and available input products. Once these are entered, the user then steps through the method pool to select or build paths that create all desired products, maximize support of the goals, and take advantage of the available inputs.

Figure A-4 shows a project summary screen after the user has worked backward from the structured analysis package deliverable to selected components of a tentative method path. From this summary screen the user can jump to details about methods, products, or goals. From the Product Description screen (FIG. A-5) the user can jump to an example of the product (FIG. A-6), or to a list of the methods that create, use, or validate the product (FIG. A-7). Through this last screen, the user can trace back from the product, through methods that create it, and to that method's inputs (FIG. A-8).

Methods also have description screens, as shown in FIG. A-9, which list supporting tools and contributors. Figure A-10 shows the method tool support screen, which describes specific steps within the method, and estimation guidelines.

As the user traces through the method pool, he or she can store a method path at any time for future reference. Figure A-11 shows a summary list of method paths created during the current session, and a rough idea of how well they cover desired products and goals. The details of each method path can be printed as a report. Future versions will allow export of information to project management tools.

This prototype system is still primitive, and functions best as a window into the pool of methods available to the firm. Even so, it is a powerful tool for raising visibility of development methods, and encouraging interactive learning and improvement.

Method Pool Management System

Select Project Goals:

- ☒ **1.1 Align systems with business goals**
- ☒   **1.1.1 Model business goals**
- ☒   **1.1.2 Relate goals to data and processes**
- ☐ 1.2 Seek out strategic systems
- ☐ 1.3 Reengineer business processes
- ☒ **2.1 Meet customer system requirements**
- ☒   **2.1.1 Model business data requirements**
- ☒   **2.1.2 Model business processes**
- ☒   **2.1.3 Model process and data interaction**
- ☒ **2.2 Minimize system defects**
- ☒   **2.2.1 Measure defects found in all products**
- ☒   **2.2.2 Early user validation of requirements**
- ☒   **2.2.3 Ensure requirements traceability**
- ☒   **2.2.4 Validate all interim and final products**
- ☐ 2.3 Minimize system downtime

Recommended goals indicated in bold.

Side buttons: Goal Hierarchy, Main Menu, Print List

Fig. A-1. Project goal selection screen

Method Pool Management System

Select Target Product(s):

- ☒ Integrated application package
- ☐ Stand-alone application package
- ☐ Single tested software program
- ☐ End-user decision support package
- ☐ Rule-based application package
- ☐ Neural network package
- ☐ User training course package
- ☐ User documentation package
- ☐ Business system design package
- ☐ Object-oriented design package
- ☐ Specification for purchased system package
- ☐ Structured analysis model package
- ☐ Object-oriented analysis package
- ☐ Information strategy plan
- ☐ Business strategy plan

Select final products only. Intermediate products will be determined later.

Side buttons: Product List, Main Menu, Print List

Fig. A-2. Project end product selection screen

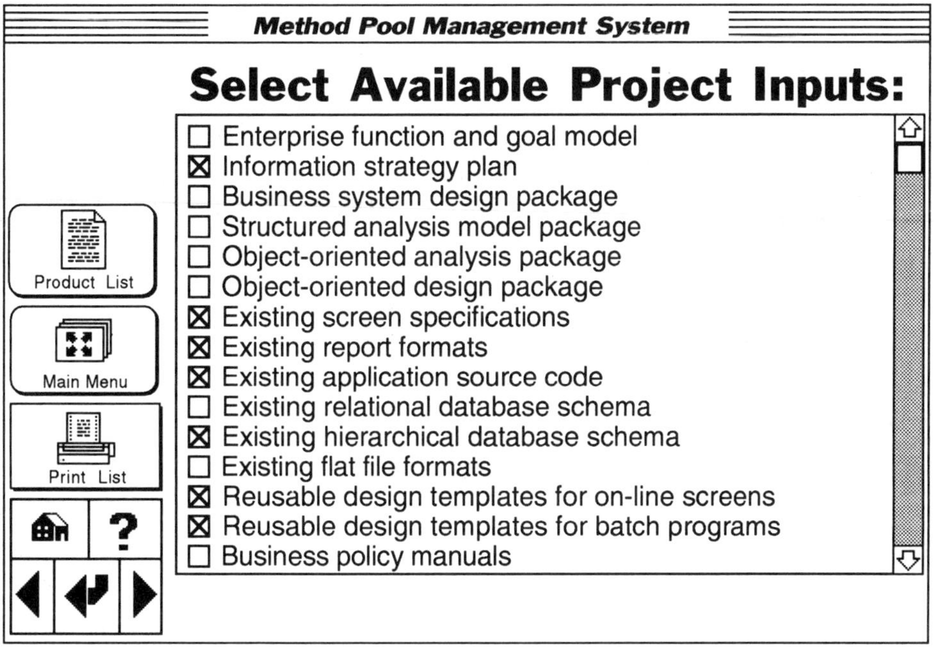

Method Pool Management System

Select Available Project Inputs:

- ☐ Enterprise function and goal model
- ☒ Information strategy plan
- ☐ Business system design package
- ☐ Structured analysis model package
- ☐ Object-oriented analysis package
- ☐ Object-oriented design package
- ☒ Existing screen specifications
- ☒ Existing report formats
- ☒ Existing application source code
- ☐ Existing relational database schema
- ☒ Existing hierarchical database schema
- ☐ Existing flat file formats
- ☒ Reusable design templates for on-line screens
- ☒ Reusable design templates for batch programs
- ☐ Business policy manuals

Fig. A-3. Project input product selection screen

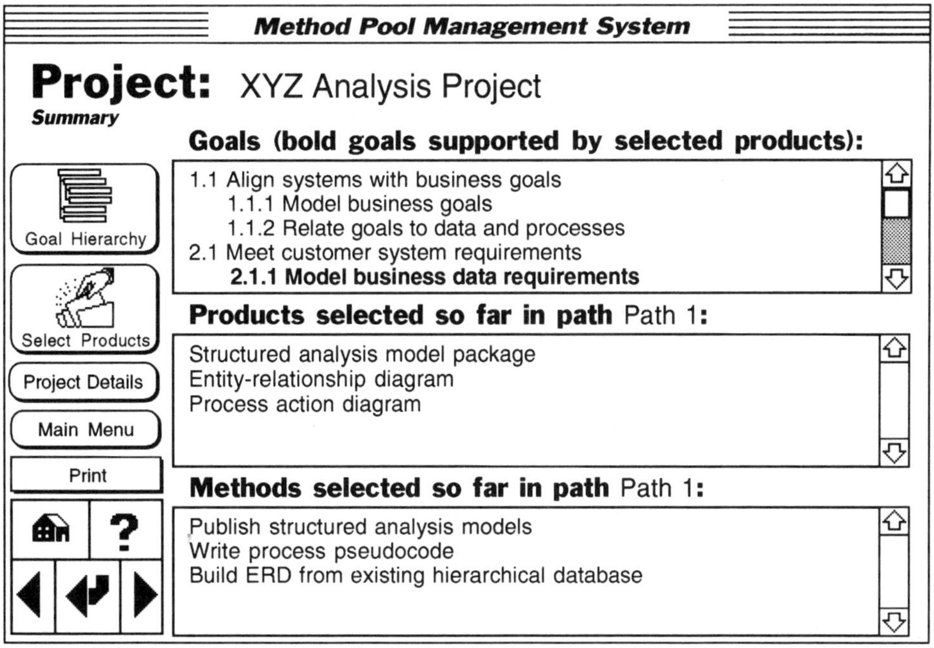

Method Pool Management System

Project: XYZ Analysis Project
Summary

Goals (bold goals supported by selected products):

1.1 Align systems with business goals
   1.1.1 Model business goals
   1.1.2 Relate goals to data and processes
2.1 Meet customer system requirements
   2.1.1 Model business data requirements

Products selected so far in path Path 1:

Structured analysis model package
Entity-relationship diagram
Process action diagram

Methods selected so far in path Path 1:

Publish structured analysis models
Write process pseudocode
Build ERD from existing hierarchical database

Fig. A-4. Project summary screen

352   Appendix A

Method Pool Management System

Product: Entity Relationship Diagram

Description

[Methods]

Description (click on bold words for more info):

The entity relationship diagram (ERD) is a graphical depiction of the business' information needs. It shows fundamental objects of importance to the firm (**entities**) and their status in regard to other objects (**relationships**).

[Examples]

Goals Supported (click for description):

2.1.1 Model business data requirements
2.2.2 Early user validation of requirements

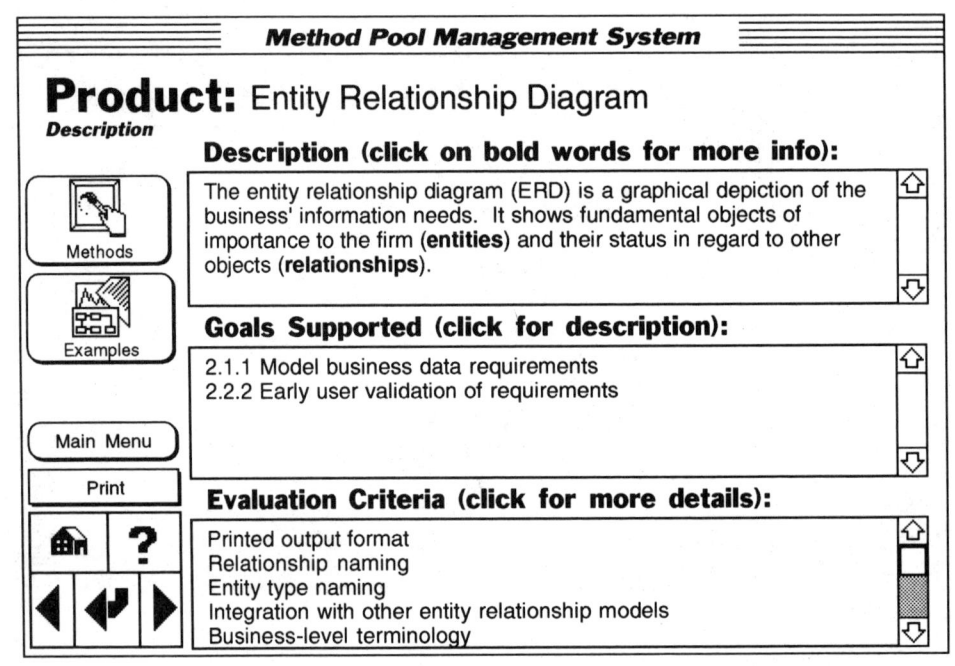

[Main Menu]

[Print]

Evaluation Criteria (click for more details):

Printed output format
Relationship naming
Entity type naming
Integration with other entity relationship models
Business-level terminology

Fig. A-5. Detailed product description screen

Method Pool Management System

Product: Entity Relationship Diagram

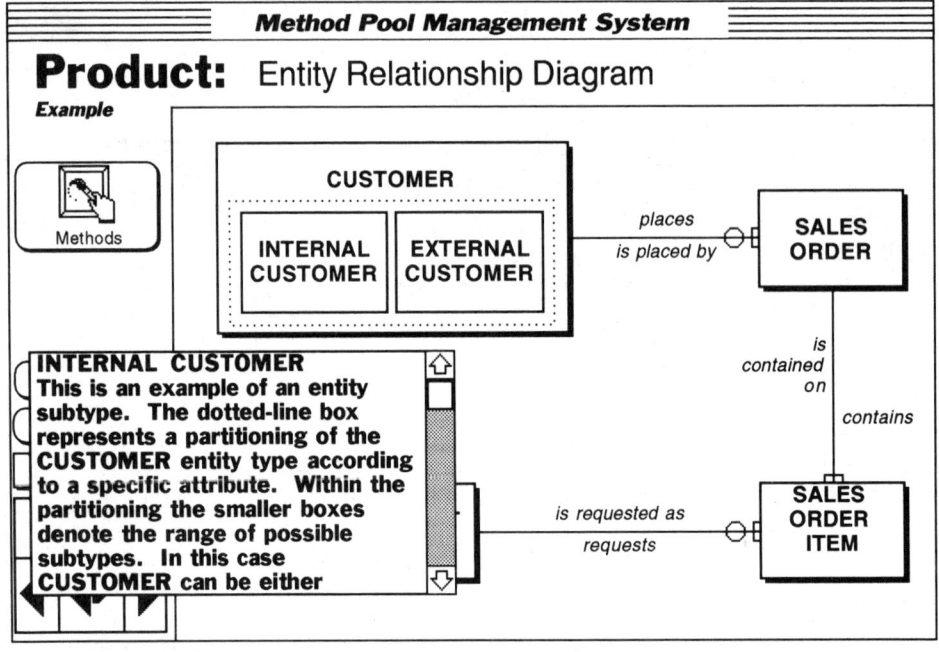

Example

[Methods]

CUSTOMER
 INTERNAL CUSTOMER | EXTERNAL CUSTOMER

places / is placed by → SALES ORDER

is contained on / contains

is requested as / requests → SALES ORDER ITEM

INTERNAL CUSTOMER
This is an example of an entity subtype. The dotted-line box represents a partitioning of the CUSTOMER entity type according to a specific attribute. Within the partitioning the smaller boxes denote the range of possible subtypes. In this case CUSTOMER can be either

Fig. A-6. Product example screen, with pop-up box explaining diagram details

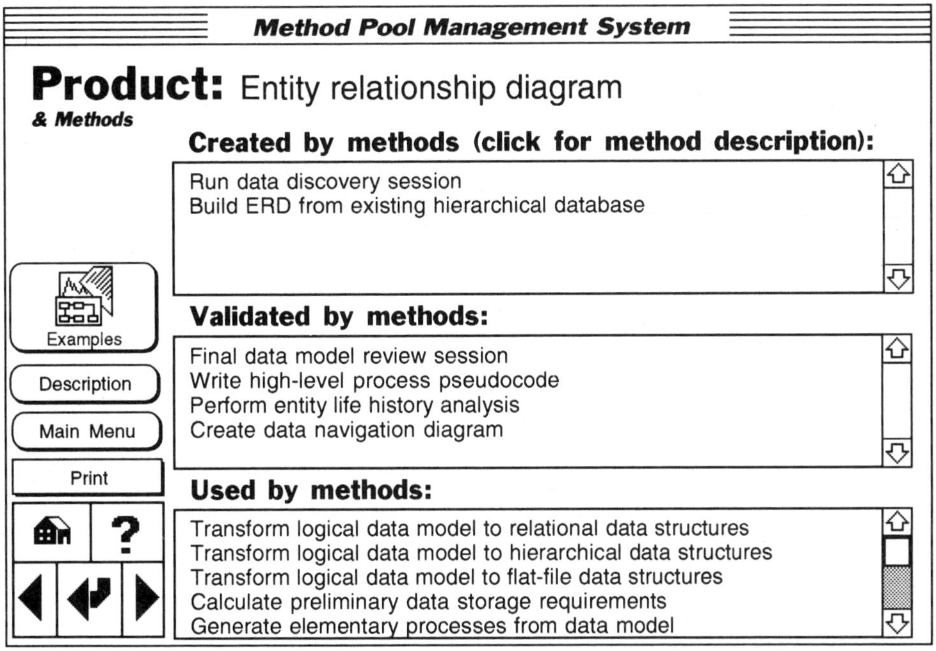

Method Pool Management System

Product: Entity relationship diagram
& Methods

Created by methods (click for method description):
- Run data discovery session
- Build ERD from existing hierarchical database

Validated by methods:
- Final data model review session
- Write high-level process pseudocode
- Perform entity life history analysis
- Create data navigation diagram

Used by methods:
- Transform logical data model to relational data structures
- Transform logical data model to hierarchical data structures
- Transform logical data model to flat-file data structures
- Calculate preliminary data storage requirements
- Generate elementary processes from data model

[Side buttons: Examples, Description, Main Menu, Print]

Fig. A-7. Screen showing all methods that use or affect a product

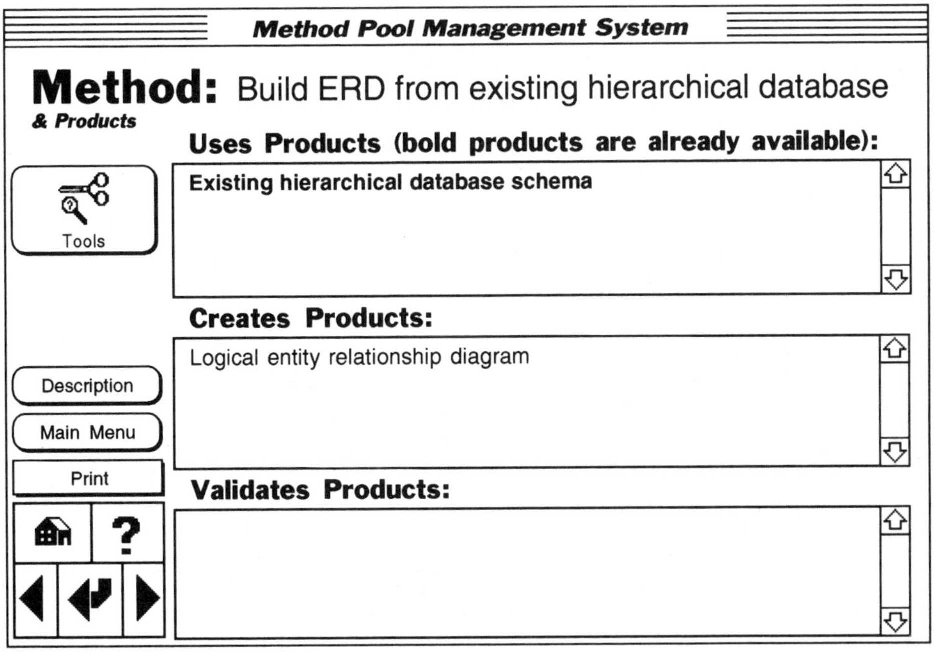

Method Pool Management System

Method: Build ERD from existing hierarchical database
& Products

Uses Products (bold products are already available):
- **Existing hierarchical database schema**

Creates Products:
- Logical entity relationship diagram

Validates Products:

[Side buttons: Tools, Description, Main Menu, Print]

Fig. A-8. Screen showing all products used or affected by a method

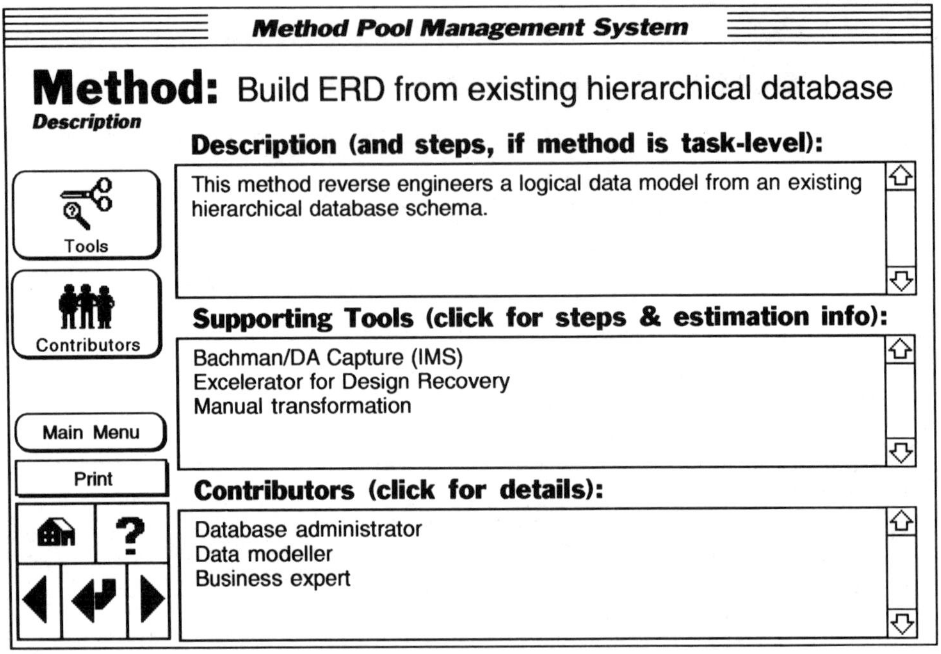

Method Pool Management System

Method: Build ERD from existing hierarchical database

Description

[Tools] [Contributors] [Main Menu] [Print] [home] [?] [◀] [↵] [▶]

Description (and steps, if method is task-level):

This method reverse engineers a logical data model from an existing hierarchical database schema.

Supporting Tools (click for steps & estimation info):

Bachman/DA Capture (IMS)
Excelerator for Design Recovery
Manual transformation

Contributors (click for details):

Database administrator
Data modeller
Business expert

Fig. A-9. General method description screen

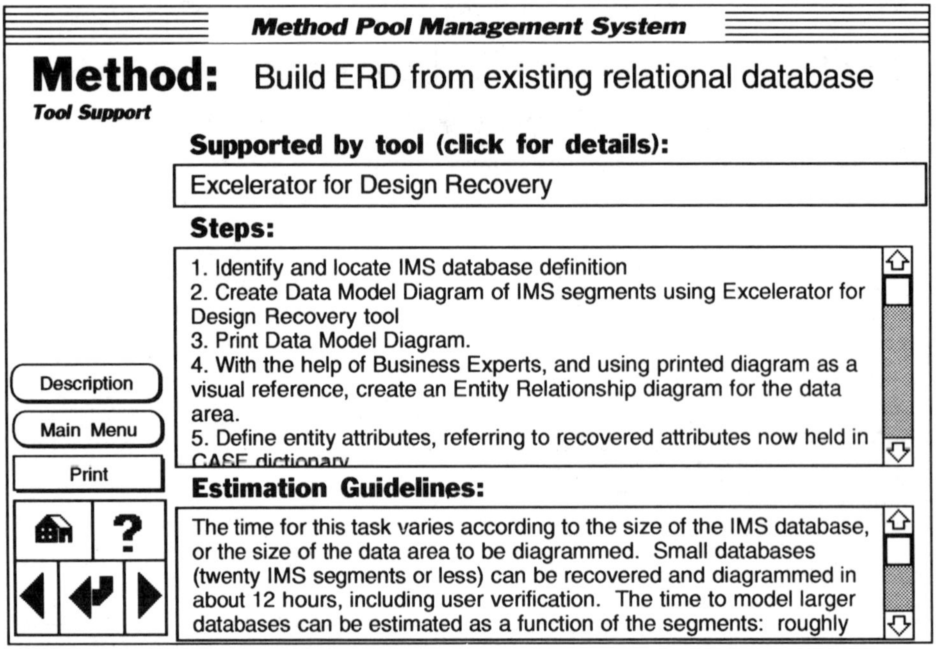

Method Pool Management System

Method: Build ERD from existing relational database

Tool Support

[Description] [Main Menu] [Print] [home] [?] [◀] [↵] [▶]

Supported by tool (click for details):

Excelerator for Design Recovery

Steps:

1. Identify and locate IMS database definition
2. Create Data Model Diagram of IMS segments using Excelerator for Design Recovery tool
3. Print Data Model Diagram.
4. With the help of Business Experts, and using printed diagram as a visual reference, create an Entity Relationship diagram for the data area.
5. Define entity attributes, referring to recovered attributes now held in CASE dictionary.

Estimation Guidelines:

The time for this task varies according to the size of the IMS database, or the size of the data area to be diagrammed. Small databases (twenty IMS segments or less) can be recovered and diagrammed in about 12 hours, including user verification. The time to model larger databases can be estimated as a function of the segments: roughly

Fig. A-10. Detailed description of a method as supported by a specific tool

Method Pool Management System

Method Path Listing

Path Name	Products Covered	Goals Covered
Path 1	100%	80%
Path 2	100%	63%
Path 3	100%	80%
Path 4	100%	55%
Path 5	100%	40%

Main Menu

Print List

Click on path name for method path details.

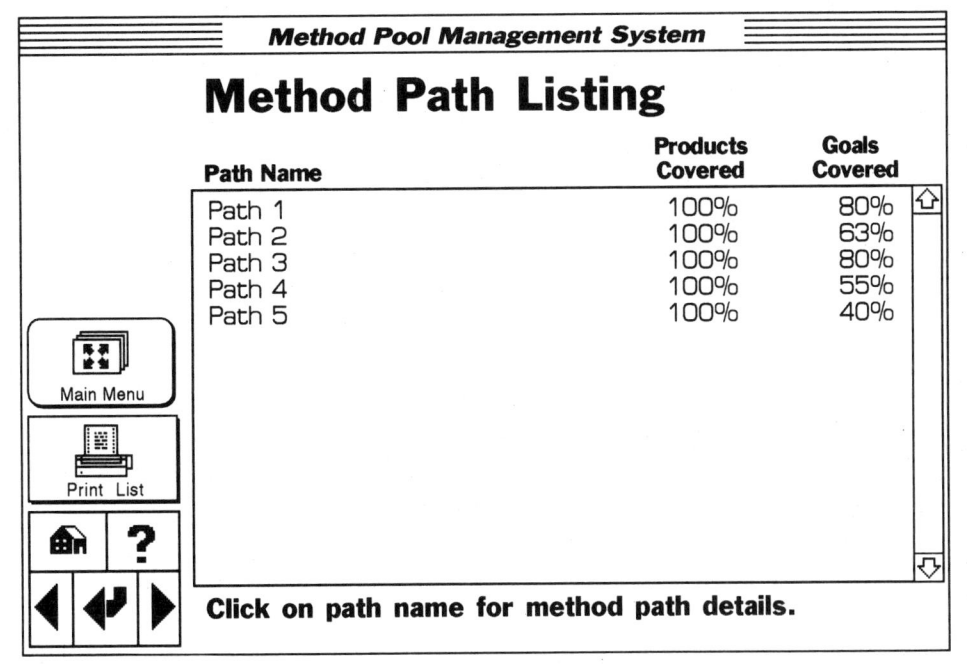

Fig. A-11. Screen showing all method paths being built and their support of goals and products

Appendix B
CASE evaluation criteria

The following outline shows an extensive set of criteria for classifying CASE tools. It attempts to cover the full range of features you can expect from CASE tools and identify additional factors that can affect CASE tool selection. I don't recommend that you use this outline as an actual evaluation checklist—it is far too detailed. However, you can use it as a source from which to draw a few important criteria for judging tools, using the process described in chapter 10.

In the outline, numbered items represent categories of tool features or selection criteria, while bulleted items indicate varying degrees of feature support.

1. **Tool features**
   1.1 **Development cycle coverage**
      1.1.1. Strategic planning
         1.1.1.1. Business goals and strategies
            - Business goal analysis
            - Critical success factors
            - Problems or issues
            - Information needs
            - Business segment profitability analysis
         1.1.1.2. Enterprise-level business modeling
            - Enterprise process modeling
            - Enterprise data modeling
            - Modeling information transfers to analysis phase
         1.1.1.3. Matrix processing features
            - Flip matrices
            - Sort rows and columns
            - Clustering or affinity analysis
            - Coherent, well presented matrix display
            - User-definable matrices

1.1.2. Process modeling
   1.1.2.1. Process identification
      - Process decomposition diagrams
      - Automatic process generation (from data model or input parameters)
      - Entity life cycle analysis
      - Business event analysis
   1.1.2.2. Process logic representation
      - Unstructured text (no standard syntax)
      - Structured text (e.g., bracketed, indented)
      - Generic procedural definition language (e.g., 4GL level)
      - Direct references to data and process model objects
      - Visual programming/graphical descriptions
   1.1.2.3. Process logic creation method
      - Prompt-driven (guided, multiple-choice)
      - Free form entry with syntax checking
      - Free form entry
   1.1.2.4. Process and data interaction
      - Data flow diagrams
      - Process dependency diagrams
      - Object flow diagrams
      - State-transition diagrams
1.1.3. Data modeling
   1.1.3.1. Data diagramming notation
      - Chen style
      - Bachman style
      - Other style
      - User-definable
   1.1.3.2. Object modeling notation (object-oriented analysis)
      - Booch style
      - Constantine, Page-Jones & Weiss style
      - Other style
      - User-definable
   1.1.3.3. Subtyping support
      - Entity heirarchy diagram
      - Class inheritance diagram
   1.1.3.4. Normalization aids
      - Automatic data normalization
      - Normalization reports
   1.1.3.5. Relational integrity
      - Process models cannot violate datamodel integrity
      - Integrity constraints limited to target DBMS capabilities
   1.1.3.6. Derived data
      - Distinguishes between static and derived data
      - Stores derived data in database

- Calculated
- User-defined algorithms

1.1.3.7. Data element domain types
- Numeric
- Character
- Date
- Time
- Other
- User-definable

1.1.3.8. Multiple data names, with traceability
- Business name
- Field name
- DBMS name
- Programming language name

1.1.3.9. Data naming standards
- Enforces predefined standards
- Enforces user-defined standards
- Generates standard data names according to predefined algorithms
- Generates standard data names according to user-defined algorithms
- Supports business name aliases

1.1.4. Database design
 1.1.4.1. Database types supported
 - Object-oriented database models
 - Relational database models
 - Hierarchical database models
 - Flat file data structure models

1.1.4.2. Data structure modeling features
- Can add additional indexes
- Calculates table sizes and volumes
- Can set technical parameters (e.g., tablespace, buffer pool)

1.1.4.3. Denormalization
- Allowed, with traceability back to logical model
- Allowed, without traceability

1.1.4.4. Transformation of logical to physical data model
- Automatic, with traceability
- Manual, with traceability
- Manual, no traceability

1.1.4.5. Database generation
- Generates complete database schema, and builds entire database
- Generates complete database schema
- Generates skeletal database schema
- Generates reports about data structures

1.1.5. System design
  1.1.5.1. Program structure design
    - Jackson structure charts, with data flows
    - Jackson structure charts, without data flows
    - Flowcharts
  1.1.5.2. System navigation design
    - Dialog design (shows navigation between screens or windows)
    - Menu hierarchy charts
  1.1.5.3. Data access design
    - Data access statements generated along with code
    - Reusable SQL through in-line macros
    - SQL statements embedded in diagrams or pseudocode
1.1.6. Interface design
  1.1.6.1. Report painting
    - Interactive report painter
    - Integrated fourth-generation reporting language
    - Reports must be written as programs
  1.1.6.2. Screen painting
    - Interactive screen painter
    - Text-based screen definition language
    - Function key definition
1.1.7. Prototyping and simulation
  1.1.7.1. Screen prototyping
    - Screen slide-show
    - Navigation enabled (function keys or mouse)
    - Able to use live data
    - Data edit routines enabled
  1.1.7.2. Report prototyping
    - Layout only
    - Able to use sample data
  1.1.7.3. Prototype integration level
    - Hard-coded screen prototypes, independent of structured models
    - Built from data and process models
    - Prototyped screen specs can generate live systems
  1.1.7.4. Simulation type
    - Time-based process simulation
    - Finite state machine
  1.1.7.5. Simulation integration level
    - Hard-coded simulation, independent of structured models
    - Interprets data and process models
    - Simulation models can generate live systems
1.1.8. Code generation
  1.1.8.1. Completeness of code generation
    - Full code, including data access
    - Full code except for data access

- Skeletal code
- Able to link in external object code

1.1.8.2. JCL generation
- Complete JCL generation for batch programs
- Skeletal JCL generation

1.1.8.3. Detail of pre-generation components
- Generates from purely graphic models and specifications
- Generates from high-level pseudocode (4GL-level)
- Generates from detailed pseudocode
- Generates from actual source code or source code macro language stored with CASE objects

1.1.8.4. Completeness of pre-generation components
- Everything needed for code generation is stored in the CASE tool repository
- Generates from a mix of CASE repository objects and additional code specifications

1.1.8.5. Number of platforms you own that the tool generates systems for
- Single hardware/OS platform
- Multiple hardware/OS platforms

1.1.8.6. Number of programming languages you're experienced in that the tool generates systems with
- Single language
- Multiple languages

1.1.8.7. Runtime environment
- Fully independent programs
- Requires CASE tool to run

1.1.8.8. Runtime performance
- Worse than most hand-coded programs
- Equivalent to most hand-coded programs
- Better than most hand-coded programs

1.1.8.9. Development performance
- Executable specifications; no generation necessary
- Local workstation code generation
- Seamless host code generation from workstation
- Code generation requires simple file transfer
- Code generation requires multiple file transfers

1.1.9. Maintenance

1.1.9.1. Code documentation
- Program maps (e.g., call structures, paragraph structures)
- Data maps (e.g., working storage, flat files)

1.1.9.2. Code restructuring
- Code restructuring
- Database restructuring

1.1.9.3. Program analysis
- Identifies unused code portions
- Identifies unreferenced data items

- Performance maps of code to identify bottlenecks
- File or database usage reports (input and output analysis)

1.1.9.4. Change impact analysis
- Extrapolates impacts of data item changes
- Extrapolates impacts of process logic changes

1.1.10. Reverse engineering

1.1.10.1. Existing system capture
- Import existing database definitions
- Import existing source code
- Import existing object code
- Import existing screen definitions

1.1.10.2. Integration level
- Reverse engineer back to business (analysis) model
- Reverse engineer back to technical (design) model
- Reverse engineer to cleaner program source code

1.2. Development services

1.2.1. Repository services

1.2.1.1. Usage mode
- Passive repository/dictionary
- Active repository during development
- Active repository during production

1.2.1.2. Standards followed
- AD/Cycle
- ATIS (A Tools Integration Standard)
- IRDS (Information Resource Dictionary System)
- PCTE (Portable Common Tools Environment)

1.2.1.3. Metamodel extensibility
- Can change fundamental schema
- Can add additional entity types to model, but can't change basic model

1.2.1.4. Tool interface customization
- Can build new interfaces to CASE tools
- Can alter existing interfaces to CASE tools

1.2.1.5. Metamodel reporting
- Public reporting interface
- Ad hoc inquiry capability using standard 4GL or user tools
- Predefined inquiries and/or reports

1.2.1.6. Object sharing scheme
- Multiple simultaneous readers and updaters
- Check-in/check-out with object-level locking
- Multiple simultaneous readers, single updater
- Single reader or updater

1.2.2. Reusability support

1.2.2.1. Predeveloped application model availability

- Models available for desired applications
- Application model market exists
- Design templates
- Data model templates

1.2.2.2. Object templates
- Manages screen templates
- Manages process templates, or supports process generation from data models
- Manages module structure templates
- Manages data model templates
- Manages data access statement library

1.2.2.3. Reusable library management
- Catalogs reusable code modules
- Catalogs reusable design modules
- Search aids for reusable modules
- Able to catalog existing (non-CASE) routines

1.2.3. Project management

1.2.3.1. Task estimation
- Aggregate phase and project estimates (parameter-driven)
- Detailed task estimation routines tied to methodology

1.2.3.2. Task tracking
- Can record actual time spent on task
- Can track costs applied to tasks
- Task dates shift according to predecessors

1.2.3.3. Resource management
- Resource allocation
- Resource leveling

1.2.3.4. Project diagramming
- Gantt charts
- PERT charts

1.2.4. Methodology support

1.2.4.1. Level of automated method enforcement
- Automated: applies methodology rules
- Coupled: a few methodology restrictions or suggestions
- No methodology enforcement

1.2.4.2. Method pool management
- Fully customizable method pool
- Customizable methodologies
- Multiple predefined methodologies
- Single predefined methodology

1.2.4.3. Method pool contents
- Objectives and subobjectives of the IS organization
- Software engineering products or deliverables
- Evaluation or quality assurance criteria for each product

- Method and task information
- Contributors or resource requirements for tasks
- Opportunities for CASE tool usage
- Estimation guidelines or other metrics
- Past experiences of previous methodology users (e.g., project journals)

1.2.4.4. Method path creation
- Active methodology advisor: suggests paths based on project parameters
- Allows you to interactively create custom method path for each project
- Lets you select from multiple predefined methodologies
- Lets you enable or disable optional methodology tasks from a standard methodology

1.2.4.5. Methodology presentation format
- Online methodology help while working in CASE tool
- Online methodology information outside of CASE tool
- Paper-based methodology

1.2.4.6. Generate project plans and schedules from method pool
- Export tasks and schedules to project management tools
- Generate task and schedule reports

1.2.5. Metrics support
1.2.5.1. Metrics gathering
- Pulls information from project management tools
- Pulls information from automated testing tools
- Directly analyzes repository objects

1.2.5.2. Standard metrics calculations
- Function point calculation
- Bang metric calculation
- Lines of code calculation

1.2.6. Quality assurance
1.2.6.1. Consistency/completeness checking range
- Diagram consistency checking
- Full model consistency checking

1.2.6.2. Consistency checking rule base
- Checks based on standard methodology rules
- Checks based on customizable methodology rules
- Checks based on technical tool criteria

1.2.6.3. Application debugging level
- Analysis model, for simulations or prototypes
- Design model, for simulations and prototypes
- Design model, for generated applications
- Generated application source code

1.2.6.4. Test plan creation
- From business requirements (including data model)
- Ties to system objects

- Manages test plan document creation
1.2.6.5. Automatic test case generation
- From business requirements (including data model)
- From test plan parameters
- From manual input parameters
1.2.6.6. Test data management
- Ties test data to test objectives
- Ties test data to programs or system components
1.2.6.7. Traceability to test cases
- To test plan
- To business requirements
- To specific programs or modules
1.2.6.8. Test run automation
- Automated online system testing
- Automated batch system testing
- Test run uses catalogues test data

1.3. Technical services
1.3.1. Version control/change management
1.3.1.1. Change propagation
- Dynamic propagation: all object references are affected when an object property changes
- Stakeholder notification when object changes
1.3.1.2. Change auditing
- Audit trail storage mechanism
- Recovery procedure
1.3.1.3. Change control level
- Repository level
- Object level
- Association level
1.3.1.4. Version control level
- Repository level
- Object level
- Association level
1.3.1.5. Type of version created
- Passive (archive for records)
- Active (object migration possible)
1.3.2. Security level
1.3.2.1. Security level
- Object level
- Installation level
1.3.2.2. User identification
- Single user
- User group membership
1.3.2.3. Capability
- Selective action per user or group
- All or nothing

1.3.2.4. Copy protection
- Physical key
- Disk-based
- Off disk
- None

1.3.3. Diagramming services
  1.3.3.1. Diagrams generated from text
  1.3.3.2. Can enhance diagrams with additional text and graphics
  1.3.3.3. Repository stores positioning of objects in diagrams
  1.3.3.4. Repository stores abstract CASE object information only
  1.3.3.5. Scalable diagrams
  1.3.3.6. Customizable icons/standards

1.3.4. Help
  1.3.4.1. Online tutorial companion
  1.3.4.2. Online help
  1.3.4.3. Real-time error-checking

1.3.5. Text editing
  1.3.5.1. Embedded text-editing capability
  1.3.5.2. Export to popular word processor

1.4. Physical characteristics

1.4.1. Integration
  1.4.1.1. Distribution mechanism
  - Mainframe or minicomputer repository, with satellite workstations
  - LAN-based central server with satellite workstations
  - No central repository; information spread across multiple workstations

  1.4.1.2. Method for passing objects between tools
  - Upload/download to central repository
  - Direct connection to same data files
  - One-way data export and import
  - One-way file transfer
  - No objects passed between tools

1.4.2. User interface
  1.4.2.1. Technical sophistication
  - End-user
  - Business analyst
  - Designer
  - Programmer

  1.4.2.2. Interface type
  - Graphical user interface
  - Mouse- or pointer-based interface
  - Character-based interface

  1.4.2.3. Complexity management
  - Hypertext links
  - Telescopic diagramming
  - Windowing: multiple views

1.4.3. Output quality
  1.4.3.1. Printing capacity
    - Printing
    - Plotting
  1.4.3.2. Manipulating graphics and diagrams
    - Allows full manipulation or annotation of graphics and text within tool
    - Exports popular graphics formats for external manipulation
  1.4.3.3. Printing large diagrams
    - Scale diagrams to fit pages
    - Print over multiple pages, forcing manual cut and paste
    - Print or plot on oversize paper
1.4.4. Tool compatibility
  1.4.4.1. CASE tool links
    - Exchange data with other unowned CASE tools
    - Exchanges data with owned CASE tools, one way
    - Exchanges data with owned CASE tools, both ways
  1.4.4.2. Other software links
    - Word processor
    - Graphics package
    - Project management software
  1.4.4.3. Common output file formats
    - CDIF (CASE Data Interchange Format) support
    - Graphics files usable by currently owned graphics programs

2. Development path criteria
2.1. Methodology support
  2.1.1. Paradigm
    2.1.1.1. Procedural
    2.1.1.2. Object-oriented
    2.1.1.3. Rule- or logic-based
    2.1.1.4. Neural network
    2.1.1.5. Fuzzy logic
  2.1.2. Standard methodologies supported
    2.1.2.1. Information engineering
    2.1.2.2. Yourdon-DeMarco
    2.1.2.3. Gane-Sarson
    2.1.2.4. Ward-Mellor
    2.1.2.5. Hatley-Pirbhai
    2.1.2.6. SADT
    2.1.2.7. Merise
  2.1.3. Development process model
    2.1.3.1. Sequential waterfall
    2.1.3.2. Spiral; risk management
    2.1.3.3. Iterative (e.g., rapid prototyping)
    2.1.3.4. Evolutionary delivery model

2.2. Development platform
  2.2.1. Hardware requirements (*List those particular to your environment*)
    2.2.1.1. Developer workstation hardware
      - _____
      - _____
    2.2.1.2. Repository hardware
      - _____
      - _____
    2.2.1.3. Communications equipment
      - _____
      - _____
    2.2.1.4. Range of development platforms
      - Single vendor for all components
      - Multiple vendors
  2.2.2. Operating system requirements
    2.2.2.1. Developer workstation database management system
      - _____
      - _____
    2.2.2.2. Developer workstation operating system
      - _____
      - _____
    2.2.2.3. Repository operating system
      - _____
      - _____
    2.2.2.4. Repository database management system
      - _____
      - _____
  2.2.3. Environment integration
    2.2.3.1. Links to other tools in use or under consideration
      - _____
      - _____

2.3. Characteristics of generated systems
  2.3.1. Types of systems
    2.3.1.1. Online screen-based systems
    2.3.1.2. Client/server or cooperative processing
    2.3.1.3. Batch
    2.3.1.4. Real-time
    2.3.1.5. Expert systems
    2.3.1.6. Neural networks
  2.3.2. System capabilities
    2.3.2.1. Windowing
    2.3.2.2. Repeating group fields on screens
    2.3.2.3. Mouse support
  2.3.3. Hardware requirements
    2.3.3.1. Host hardware
    2.3.3.2. Workstation hardware

2.3.3.3. Communications requirements
2.3.3.4. Peripherals
2.3.4. Software/OS requirements (*Particular to your environment*)
    2.3.4.1. Operating systems
        • _____
        • _____
    2.3.4.2. Programming languages
        • _____
        • _____
    2.3.4.3. Database management systems
        • _____
        • _____
    2.3.4.4. Communications software
        • _____
        • _____
2.3.5. Application content
    2.3.5.1. Template availability
        • Specific desired applications available in template form
        • Template market exists, but nothing you want is available yet
        • No template market
    2.3.5.2. Specialized industry capability
        • Scientific instrument control
        • Computer Integrated Manufacturing
        • _____

3. Vendor criteria
3.1. Cost
3.1.1. Product cost
    3.1.1.1. Software cost
        • Host repository components
        • Workstation components
        • Database management system components
        • Other required software costs
    3.1.1.2. Hardware costs
        • New hardware required
        • Upgrades to existing hardware
        • Usage costs of current hardware (e.g., additional load upon existing mainframe)
    3.1.1.3. Training cost
        • Methodology training
        • CASE tool training
    3.1.1.4. Consulting cost
        • Technical support costs
        • Methodology and tools consulting costs
    3.1.1.5. Maintenance cost
        • Upgrade cost for workstation software components
        • Upgrade cost for repository software components

- Upgrade cost for other software components
- Maintenance contract for repository software

3.1.2. Discounts
  3.1.2.1. Volume purchase discount
    - Volume discount available (discount at projected volume)
    - No volume discount
  3.1.2.2. Site license
    - Site license available
    - No site license available: pay for each copy

3.1.3. Availability
  3.1.3.1. Release schedule
    - Tool on market today
    - Available for alpha- or beta-testing
    - Still in development
    - Development not yet started
  3.1.3.2. Delivery
    - Immediate delivery possible
    - Significant delivery lead time

3.2. Support and training (vendor or third-party)

3.2.1. Documentation
  3.2.1.1. Quality
    - Excellent manuals and documentation
    - Average
    - Poor
  3.2.1.2. Availability
    - Online, while tool is running
    - Online, separate from tool
    - Paper-based

3.2.2. Training
  3.2.2.1. Tool usage
  3.2.2.2. Methodology usage
  3.2.2.3. Project management with tool

3.2.3. Consulting
  3.2.3.1. Tool usage only
  3.2.3.2. Development support
  3.2.3.3. Technical consulting

3.2.4. Technical support
  3.2.4.1. Support hotline available
  3.2.4.2. Technicians make house calls
  3.2.4.3. Electronic bullet board support

3.3. Vendor characteristics

3.3.1. Survivability
  3.3.1.1. Years in CASE business
  3.3.1.2. Market
  3.3.1.3. Financial status (debt/equity)

3.3.1.4. Strategic partnerships
- IBM business partner for AD/Cycle
- Member of ESPRIT consortium
- Member of SIGMA consortium
- Member of MCC consortium
- Member of other consortium

3.3.2. Vision
3.3.2.1. Symbolic vision (does it match yours?)
- Confederation of multivendor tools
- Full life cycle software factory
- So easy a child could do it (end-user CASE)
- Programmer's best friend

3.3.2.2. Architecture
- Open, customized interfaces
- Open, common file formats
- Single-vendor

3.3.2.3. Commitment to future industry developments
- AD/Cycle
- PCTE
- SIGMA
- Other

3.3.3. Purchase terms
3.3.3.1. Trial evaluation period
3.3.3.2. Lease option

3.3.4. Client base
3.3.4.1. Copies sold (not a great indicator of value, just marketing ability)
3.3.4.2. User groups
3.3.4.3. References available from other customers

Appendix C
CASE product directories

Prices are listed for informational purposes only.

The CASE Trends 1990 Product & Industry Guide, $179
Evaluation of Leading Information Engineering CASE Tools, $395
CASE/CASM Industry Survey Report, $195

CASE Trends
P.O. Box 294-MO
Shrewsbury, MA 01545-0294
(508) 842-4500

CASE Outlook's Guide to Products and Services, $195

CASE Consulting Group, Inc.
11830 Kerr Parkway, Suite 315
Lake Oswego, OR 97035
(503) 245-6880

CASE Evaluation Report, $210

Foresite Systems
(517) 349-4934

CASE Industry Directory, $195

CASE Research Corporation
Seattle, WA
(503) 226-0420

The CASE Locator, $100 each
CASE Associates
(503) 656-0986

The CASE Technical Report
Extended Intelligence
(617) 648-8700

Notes

Chapter 1. The CASE arms race

1. John Pallato, "Wary Developers Slow CASE's Advance, Survey Shows," *PC Week*, 6 August 1990, 55.

2. Norman Statland, "Payoffs Down the Pike: A CASE Study," Datamation, 1 April 1989, 32.

3. Mike Bucken, "MIS Backlog Lives On," *Software Magazine*, February 1990, 26

4. Statland, "Payoffs," 33.

5. Pallato, "Wary Developers," 55.

6. Mike Feuche, "CASE Tool Saves Firm $5 Million," *MIS Week*, 31 July 1989, 1.

7. Stuart M. Dambrot, "Japan Prepares for Software Crisis," *Datamation*, 1 May 1989, 31.

8. Michael Sullivan-Trainor and Joseph Maglitta, "Competitive Advantage Fleeting," *Computerworld*, 8 October 1990, 4.

9. Max D. Hopper, "Rattling SABRE—New Ways to Compete on Information," *Harvard Business Review*, May–June 1990, 118.

10. Peter F. Drucker, *The New Realities* (New York: Harper & Row, 1990), 207–220.

11. Shoshana Zuboff, *In the Age of the Smart Machine* (New York: Basic Books, 1988), 414

12. Christopher Lindquist, "Is Integration All It Seems?" *Computerworld*, 6 August 1990, 93

13. Noboru Akima and Fusatake Ooi, "Industrializing Software Development: A Japanese Approach," *IEEE Software*, March 1989, 13.

14. Joanne Connelly, "Study Sees Japan Software Challenge," *Electronic News Weekly*, 10 April 1989, 3.

Chapter 2. The faceless acronym

1. *CASE: The Potential and the Pitfalls* (Wellesley, MA: QED Information Sciences, Inc., 1989), 1.

2. B. Terry and D. Logee, "Terminology for Software Engineering Environment and Computer-Aided Software Engineering," *Software Engineering Notes*, April 1990, 85.

3. Carma McClure, "The CASE Experience," *Byte*, April 1989, 235.

4. CASE: The Potential and the Pitfalls, 54.

5. Girish Parikh, "Restructuring Your COBOL Programs," *Computer World Focus*, 19 February 1986, 39–42.

6. McClure, "The CASE Experience," 237.

7. See early texts on structured analysis and design such as Tom DeMarco's *Structured Analysis and Systems Specification* (New York: Yourdon, Inc., 1978).

8. Carma McClure, CASE is Software Automation (Englewood Cliffs, NJ: Prentice-Hall, 1989), 152.

9. Hans Brinkkemper et al., "Derivation of Method Companionship," *Software Engineering Notes*, January 1990, 49–58.

Chapter 3. Waiting for the revolution

1. Mike Bucken, "MIS Backlog Lives On," *Software Magazine*, February 1990, 26.

2. Marcus Loh and R. Ryan Nelson, "Reaping CASE Harvests," *Datamation*, 1 July 1989, 31.

3. "CASE is No Solution," *Computing Canada*, 16 March 1989, 16.

4. Greg Boone, "The Paradox of CASE," *Database Programming and Design*, May 1989, 70.

5. Charles R. Necco, Nancy W. Tsai, and Kreg W. Holgeson, "Current Usage of CASE Software," *Journal of Systems Management*, May 1989, 60–5.

6. Tom Gilb, *Principles of Software Engineering Management* (Wokingham, England: Addison-Wesley, 1988), 252.

7. Jeff Moad, citing a 1989 survey conducted by Software Productivity Research, Inc., in "The Software Revolution," *Datamation*, 15 February 1990, 22.

8. Caper Jones, "Using Function Point to Evaluate CASE Tools, Methodologies, Staff Experience, and Languages," *Case Trends Magazine*, January–February 1191, 8–16.

9. Edward J. Joyce, "Reusable Software: Passage to Productivity?" *Datamation*, 15 September 1988, 7.

Chapter 4. Forging an alliance

1. John E. Phipps and E. Ray Cotten, "The Integrated Apparel Company," *Apparel Industry Magazine*, January 1991, 55.

2. George P. Huber, "The Nature and Design of Post-Industrial Organizations," *Management Science*, August 1984, 939.

3. This challenge is analyzed in depth by Huber, 943–5.

4. William Durell, "Information Anarchy," in *Data Base Management*, (New York: Auerbach Publishers, 1990), Number 21–20–20.

5. Max Schindler, *Computer-Aided Software Design* (New York: John Wiley & Sons, 1990), 87 and 345.

6. The high-tech system used by George Moody, CEO of Security Pacific Corporation, is commonly used as an example of the quintessential DSS. See for example Stephen W. Quickel, "Management Joins the Computer Age," *Business Month*, May 1989, 46.

7. Shoshana Zuboff, *In the Age of the Smart Machine* (New York: Basic Books, 1988), 357.

8. William H. Inmon and Michael L. Loper, "Integrating Information Systems Using a Unified Data Architecture," *Data Resource Management*, Spring 1990, 44.

9. Cited by Eileen Carlson in "What Color is Your EIS?" *Computerworld*, 16 July 1990, 79.

10. Bertrand Meyer, "The New Culture of Software Development," *Journal of Object-Oriented Programming*, November/December 1990, 79.

Chapter 5. Diving into the method pool

1. Jeff Moad, "The Software Revolution," *Datamation*, 15 February 1990, 22.

2. From a presentation by Paul Price at the GUIDE Conference, San Francisco, CA, April 1990.

3. Harry C. Benham, R. Leon Price, and Jennifer L. Wagner, "Comparisons of Structured Development Methodologies," *Information Executive*, April 1989, 18

4. Carma McClure, "Software Automation," *Business Software Review*, September 1987

5. Albert F. Case, Jr., *Information Systems Development: Principles of Computer-Aided Software Engineering* (Englewood Ciffs, New Jersey: Prentice-Hall, 1986), 138.

6. Robert H. Wallace, John E. Stockenberg, and Robert N. Charette, *A Unified Methodology for Developing Systems* (New York: Intertext/McGraw-Hill, 1987), 247.

7. Sue Conger, "The Active Dictionary in a CASE Environment," *Data Base Management*, Number 25-01-20, 7.

8. S. Brinkkemper, M. de Lange, R. Looman, and F. H. G. C. van der Steen, "On the Derivation of Method Companionship by Meta-Modelling," *ACM SIGSOFT Software Engineering Notes*, January 1990, 49.

9. Ronald J. Norman, et al., "CASE Technology Transfer: A Case Study of Unsuccessful Change," *Journal of Systems Management*, May 1989, 42.

10. Walter Kiechel III, "The Organization That Learns," *Fortune*s, 12 March 1990, 133.

11. Watts S. Humphrey, "Characterizing the Software Process: A Maturity Framework," *IEEE Software*, March 1988, 73.

12. Howard Rubin, "Dashboards, Waterfalls and Spaghetti Code," *Computerworld*, 19 February 1990, 105.

13. See John Crawford's "Changing the Applications Development Life Cycle at The Hartford," in *CASE: The Potential and the Pitfalls* (Wellesley, MA: QED Information Sciences, Inc., 1989), 510–4, and L. J. B. Essink's, "A Conceptual Framework For Information Systems Development Methodologies," in *Information Technology for Organizational Systems*, ed. H.J. Bullinger et al. (Elsevier North-Holland, 1988), 354–62.

14. Ron A. Radice, et al., "A Programming Process Architecture," IBM Systems Journal, 24 (2), 1985, 79–90.

15. Charles C. Hayden, et al., "The Software Development Assistant," *AT&T Technical Journal*, March–April 1990, 76.

Chapter 6. Living in the neutral zone

1. Roger S. Pressman, *Making Software Engineering Happen* (Englewood Cliffs, New Jersey: Prentice-Hall, 1988), 21.

2. James Martin, "IS Executives Must Manage the Cultural Change to RAD," *PC Week*, 26 March 1990, 44.

3. Albert F. Case, Jr., *Information Systems Development: Principles of Computer-Aided Software Engineering* (Englewood Cliffs, New Jersey: Prentice-Hall, 1986), 212.

4. P. N. Le Quesne, "Individual and Organizational Factors and the Design of IPSE's", *The Computer Journal*, Vol. 35, #5, 393.

5. Quoted by Patricia Keefe, "The Art of Managing Programmers," *Computerworld*, 12 November 1990, 87.

6. Cyrus F. Gibson and Richard L. Nolan, "Managing the Four Stages of EDP Growth," *Harvard Business Review*, Jan–Feb 1974, 84.

7. See for example the Texas Instruments cost model described in QED Information Sciences' *CASE: The Potential and the Pitfalls* (Wellesley, Massachusetts: QED Information Sciences, Inc., 1988), 85–96.

8. James R. Johnson, *The Software Factory: Managing Software Development and Maintenance* (Wellesley, Massachusetts: QED Information Sciences, 1989), 116.

9. Le Quesne, 395.

10. Shoshana Zuboff, *In the Age of the Smart Machine* (New York: Basic Books, 1988), 9.

11. Adapted from models by Ross A. Webber, Management: *Basic Elements of Managing Organizations* (Homewood, Illinois: Richard D. Irwin, 672–675.

12. William Bridges, *Surviving Corporate Transitions* (New York: Doubleday, 1988), 17.

13. Samuel A. Culbert and John J. McDonough, *The Invisible War: Pursuing Self-Interests at Work* (New York, John Wiley & Sons, 1980), 60.

14. J. Daniel Cougar and Robert A. Zawacki, "What Motivates DP Professionals?" *Datamation*, September 1978, 116A23.

15. Culbert and McDonough, 67.

16. Michael Beer, Russell A. Eisenstadt and Bert Spector, "Why Change Programs Don't Produce Change," *Harvard Business Review*, November-December, 1990, 158–166.

17. As told to Jeff Moad, "The Software Revolution," *Datamation*, 15 February 1990, 22.

18. Le Quesne, 394.

19. Kuldeep Kumar and Neils Bjorn-Andersen, "A Cross-Cultural Comparison of IS Designer Values," *Communications of the ACM*, May 1990, 535.

20. Quoted by Robert Howard in "Values Make the Company: An Interview with Robert Haas," *Harvard Business Review*, September–October 1990, 143.

21. Bridges, 137.

22. Tom Peters and Nancy Austin, *A Passion for Excellence* (New York: Random House, 1985), 304.

23. Le Quesne, 396

24. Zuboff, 283.

25. Ramchandran Jaikumar, "Postindustrial Manufacturing," *Harvard Business Review*, November – December 1986, 69 – 76.

26. Le Quesne describes a firm whose attempt to use CASE "as a means of getting control over projects and as a means of getting a set of standards in place" failed miserably (p. 393).

27. David J. Osborne, *Computers at Work* (New York: John Wiley & Sons, 1985), 57, summarizing the findings of studies by D. K. Perry and W. M. Cannon, first published as "Vocational Interests of Computer Programmers," *Journal of Applied Psychology*, No. 51, 1967, 28 – 34.

28. Gibson and Nolan, 81.

29. Tom Peters, *Thriving on Chaos* (New York: Harper & Row, 1988), 479.

30. Ronald J. Norman, et al., "CASE Technology Transfer: A Case Study of Unsuccessful Change," *Journal of Systems Management*, May 1989, 55.

31. Culbert and McDonough, 80 – 5.

32. Bridges, 71.

33. Peters, 565.

34. Peter F. Drucker, *The New Realities* (New York: Harper & Row, 1990), 215.

35. Thomas J. Peters and Robert H. Waterman, Jr., In Search of Excellence (New York: Harper & Row, 1982), 132.

36. Zuboff, 360.

37. Tom Gilb, *Principles of Software Engineering Management* (Wokingham, England: Addison-Wesley, 1988), 170, citing data from Schneiderman, *Datamation*, January 1980.

38. Gerald M. Weinberg, *The Psychology of Computer Programming* (New York: Van Nostrand Reinhold, 1971).

Chapter 7. Planning for the software factory

1. A. Boynton and R.W. Zmud, "Information Technology Planning in the 1990's: Directions for Practice and Research," *MIS Quarterly*, Vol 11 #1, March 1987, 61.

2. Boynton and Zmud, 59.

3. Clinton Wilder, "Re-engineering is IS priority," *Computerworld*, 5 Feb. 1990, 6

4. Similar recommendations are offered by Ann Helmuth Allard and Tom Flecher, "A Structured Approach to CASE," *System Builder*, April/May 1990, 19 – 20; Cary T. Hughes and Jon D. Clark, "The Stages of CASE Usage", *Datamation*, 1 February 1990, 41 – 43; Lockwood Lyon, "CASE and the Database," *Database Programming and Design*, May 1989, 28 – 32.

5. J. A. Zachman, "A Framework for Information Systems Architecture," *IBM Systems Journal*, 26(3), 1987.

6. Examples include James M. Kerr, "A Blueprint for Information Systems Architecture," *Database Programming and Design*, September 1989, 60–67, and Jerry Kanter and Joe Miserendino, "Systems Architectures Link Business Goals and IS Strategies," *Data Management*, November 1987, 17–25.

7. W.R. King and T.S. Raghunathan, "How Strategic is Information Systems Planning?" *Datamation*, November 1987, 137.

8. A. L. Lederer and A. L. Mendelow, "Issues in Information Systems Planning," *Information and Management*, May 1986, 245–254.

9. From William R. Synnott, *The Information Weapon* (New York: John Wiley & Sons, 1987), 44.

10. A. L. Lederer and A. L. Mendelow, "Information Resource Planning: Overcoming Difficulties in Identifying Top Management's Objectives," *MIS Quarterly*, September 1987, 389–399.

11. Two authors who apply this model to the prioritization of software development projects are John G. Burch in "Planning And Building Strategic Information Systems," *Journal of Systems Management*, July 1990, 21–7, and Richard T. Dué in "Evaluating Systems Feasibility," in *Data Base Management* (New York: Auerbach, 1990), Number 22–01–05.

Chapter 8. Designing an IS architecture

1. James Martin, *Information Engineering, Book II: Planning and Analysis* (Englewood Cliffs, New Jersey: Prentice-Hall, 1989), 138.

2. As described by William R. Synnott in The Information Weapon (New York: John Wiley & Sons, 1987), 56–62 and John F. Barlow in "Putting Information Systems Planning Methodologies Into Perspective," Journal of Systems Management, July 1990, 8–9.

3. SISP is described in detail by John G. Burch, "Planning And Building Strategic Information Systems," *Journal of Systems Management*, July 1990, 21–7. David F. Dantzig describes Booz-Allen's "Fourth Wave" planning methodology in "Untangling Information Systems, Part II," *Journal of Systems Management*, July 1990, 20–1, 34–7.

4. A survey of research in this area is presented by A. Boynton and R.W. Zmud in "Information Technology Planning in the 1990's: Directions for Practice and Research," *MIS Quarterly*, March 1987, 62–67. The need to establish the context of strategic planning before beginning is described in depth in R.L. Nolan's "Managing the Crises in Data Processing," *Harvard Business Review*, March–April 1979, 115–126; and by J. I. Cash, et al, in Corporate Information Systems Management: Text and Cases (Homewood, Illinois: Richard D. Irwin, Inc., 1983).

5. Quoted by Robert Howard in "Values Make the Company: An Interview with Robert Haas," *Harvard Business Review*, September–October 1990, 134.

6. A. L. Lederer and A. L. Mendelow, "Information Resource Planning: Overcoming Difficulties in Identifying Top Management's Objectives," *MIS Quarterly*, September 1987, 397.

7. Martin, *Information Engineering*, Book II, 80.

8. Similar recommendations come from Samuel B. Holcman, "Preparing for AD/Cycle," *Computerworld*, November 26, 1990, 69–71; Carma McClure as quoted by

Gary Flood in "Order and Method Lead to CASE Success," *Computer Weekly*, 13 April 1989, 16; Barton Hodge, "A Blueprint for Software Development," *Information Center*, December 1988, 18–24.

    9. Edward Rivard and Kate Kaiser, "The Benefit of Quality IS," *Datamation*, 15 January 1989, 53–8.

    10. John G. Burch, "Planning And Building Strategic Information Systems," *Journal of Systems Management*, July 1990, 21–7.

Chapter 9. Reengineering the development process

    1. Peter Freeman, *Software Perspectives* (Reading, MA: Addison-Wesley, 1987), 225.

    2. Ronald Henkoff, "Make Your Office More Productive," *Fortune*, 25 Feb 1991, 72.

    3. Henkoff, 72.

    4. Stephen R. Rosenthal and Harold Salzman, "Hard Choices about Software: The Pitfalls of Procurement," *Sloan Management Review*, Summer 1990, 84.

    5. Freeman, 88.

    6. Richard Dawkins, *The Blind Watchmaker* (London: Penguin Books, 1988), 72.

Chapter 10. Retooling the software factory

    1. W.J. Fabrycky, P.M. Ghare, and P.E. Torgerson, *Applied Operations Research and Management Science* (Englewood Cliffs, New Jersey: Prentice-Hall, 1984) 208.

    2. Fabrycky, 208.

    3. Stephen R. Rosenthal and Harold Salzman, "Hard Choices about Software: The Pitfalls of Procurement," *Sloan Management Review*, Summer 1990, 88.

    4. Cited by Jud Breslin in *Selecting and Installing Software Packages* (New York: Quantum Books, Inc., 1986), 96.

    5. Based in part upon steps described by L. Zucconi in "Selecting a CASE Tool," *ACM Sigsoft Software Engineering Notes*, April 1989, 42–4.

    6. Rosenthal and Salzman, 84.

    7. Rosenthal and Salzman, 84.

    8. Barry Boehm, *Software Engineering Economics* (Englewood Cliffs, NJ: Prentice-Hall, 1984), 296.

    9. Rosenthal and Salzman, 82.

    10. Edward Rivard and Kate Kaiser, "The Benefit of Quality IS," *Datamation*, 15 January 1989, 53.

Chapter 11. Shaping the method pool

    1. Michael W. Evans, *The Software Factory* (New York: John Wiley & Sons, 1989), 58.

    2. Lynn Brooks and Stuart Levy, "Tailoring Information Engineering Methodology at the Library of Congress," presented at the GUIDE conference in San Francisco, 15 March 1990.

    3. Michael A. Jackson and Daniel D. McCracken, "Life Cycle Concept Considered Harmful," *ACM SIGSOFT Software Engineering Notes*, April 1982, 29–32.

    4. W.J. Fabrycky, et al., *Applied Operations Research and Management Science* (New York: North-Holland, 1985), 212.

5. John Crawford, "Changing the Applications Development Life Cycle at The Hartford," in *CASE: The Potential and the Pitfalls* (Wellesley, MA: QED Information Sciences, Inc.,1989), 511.

6. Ron A. Radice, et al., "A Programming Process Architecture," *IBM Systems Journal*, 24(2), 1985, 79

7. Roger S. Pressman, *Making Software Engineering Happen* (Englewood Cliffs, NJ: Prentice-Hall, 1988), 101.

8. Evans, 63.

Chapter 12. Measuring the splash

1. From a survey by American Management Systems, Inc. Quoted by Diane Sherman in, "COBOL Gold: Measuring the Productivity Ore," *Systems Builder*, June – July 1989, 35.

2. Sandhiprakash Bhide of Mentor Graphics makes an excellent case for this in, "Generalized Software Process-integrated Metrics Framework," *Journal of Systems Software*, December 1990, 249.

3. Howard Rubin, "Dashboards, Waterfalls and Spaghetti Code," *Computerworld*, 19 Feb 1990, 105

4. See for example Tom DeMarco, *Controlling Software Projects: Management, Measurement and Estimation* (New York: Yourdon/Prentice-Hall, 1982) and Tom Gilb, *Principles of Software Engineering Management* (Wokingham, England: Addison-Wesley, 1988).

5. Bhide, 250.

6. Watts S. Humphrey, "Characterizing the Software Process: A Maturity Framework," *IEEE Software*, March 1988, 73.

7. Capers Jones, "Using Function Points to Evaluate CASE Tools, Methodologies, Staff Experience, and Languages," *CASE Trends*, January/February 1991, 8.

8. See Tom DeMarco, *Controlling Software Projects: Management, Measurement and Estimation* (New York: Yourdon/Prentice-Hall, 1982)

9. See Richard Schonberger, World Class Manufacturing: The Lessons of Simplicity Applied (New York: The Free Press, 1986).

10. See Edward Rivard and Kate Kaiser, "The Benefit of Quality IS," *Datamation*, 15 January 1989, 53 – 8 for suggestions about quantifying intangible benefits of software.

Chapter 13. Stacking the deck

1. Watts Humphrey quoted by Jeff Moad in "The Software Revolution," *Datamation*, 15 February 1990, 22.

2. Tom Gilb, *Principles of Software Engineering Management* (Wokingham, England: Addison-Wesley, 1988), 11.

3. Robert H. Wallace, John E. Stockenberg, and Robert N. Charette, *A Unified Methodology for Developing Systems* (New York: Intertext/McGraw-Hill, 1987), 267.

4. Quoted by John Desmond in "Lab's CASE Experiment Considered a Business

Success," *Software Magazine*, March Special 1991, 24.

5. Alan S. Fisher, *CASE: Using Software Development Tools* (New York: John Wiley & Sons, 1988), 228.

6. Barry W. Boehm and Rony Ross, "Theory-W Software Project Management: Principles and Examples," *IEEE Transactions on Software Engineering*, July 1989, 903.

7. P. J. Plauger, "Heresies of Software Management," *Computer Language*, March 1991, 20.

8. Gilb, 96.

9. Evans, 241.

10. Tracy Kidder, *The Soul of a New Machine* (Boston, MA: Little, Brown and Co., 1981), 116.

11. Peters, 618.

12. A 1979 survey found that only four percent of project managers planned projects by defining specific tasks, estimating the duration of each, and adding them into a total estimate. See John H. Lehman, "How Software Projects Are Really Managed," *Datamation*, January 1979, 119–29. With the advent of automated project management tools, this percentage has certainly increased, but not as much as it should.

13. These findings are discussed at length by Gilb and also by Albert F. Case, Jr., *Information Systems Development: Principles of Computer-Aided Software Engineering* (Englewood Cliffs, New Jersey: Prentice-Hall, 1986).

14. Barry W. Boehm, "A Spiral Model of Software Development and Enhancement," *IEEE Computer*, May 1988, 71.

15. P. J. Plauger, "Heresies of Software Management," *Computer Language*, March 1991, 24.

16. Kuldeep Kumar, "Post Implementation Evaluation of Computer-Based Information Systems: Current Practices," *Communications of the ACM*, February 1990, 203–12.

Chapter 14. Spreading the word

1. Roger S. Pressman, *Making Software Engineering Happen* (Englewood Cliffs, NJ: Prentice-Hall, 1988), 83.

2. Cited by John Eckhouse in "How Training Produces Profit, *San Francisco Chronicle*, 18 March 1991, B9.

3. Brian Dickinson, *Developing Quality Systems* (New York: McGraw-Hill, 1988), 308.

4. J. Daniel Cougar and Robert A. Zawacki, "What Motivates DP Professionals?" *Datamation*, Sept 1978, 116–23.

5. Peter Freeman, *Software Perspectives* (Reading, MA: Addison-Wesley, 1987), 132.

6. Alan S. Fisher, *CASE: Using Software Development Tools* (New York: John Wiley & Sons, 1988), 235.

7. Pressman, 125.

8. Clive Finkelstein, *Introduction to Information Engineering*, (Reading, MA: Addison-Wesley, 1989), 11.

Index

A

action diagrams, 28
AICorp, 68
alternative method selection, 285-286
American Airlines, 4, 5
American Society for Training and Development, 331
analysis methods
  complementary data analysis, 28
  diagramming, 27-28, 43
  Gane-Sarson, 28
  Hatley-Pirbhai, 28
  reengineering IS processes, 218-220
  requirements analysis, 26-28
  structured analysis, 28-29, 43, 69
  Ward-Mellor, 28
  Warnier-Orr, 28
Andersen, 67
Apple, 30, 31
Application Development Cycle (AD/Cycle), IBM, x, 40-41, 234, 240, 276
application development workbench (ADW), 44
architecture development, 159-165, 177-210, 346-347
  benefits analysis, 205-208
  Booz-Allen Hamilton planning method, 178-179
  business strategy planning (BSP), 178-179
  context of strategic plan vs. architecture development, 180
  cost assessment, 205-208
  current development system analysis, 199
  data grouping identification, 192-197
  data types, data models, 199
  feasibility studies, 205-208
  goals and objectives, 187-192
  guidelines and principles development, 187
  Information Architecture, 162
  Information Resource Infrastructure, 162
  information strategy planning (ISP), 178-180
  needs assessment: how much planning do you need?, 163
  organizational structure issues, 182-185
  planning-method selection, 178-180
  project planning, 185, 199, 203, 199
  reengineering IS processes, 195, 198, 200-202, 211-227
  resource allocation, 210
  SISP methodology, 178-180
  subfunction identification, 192-197
  team/committee formation, 186-187
  Technology Architecture, 162
  top-down vs. bottom-up planning, 164
AT&T, 112
Austin, Nancy, 133
automated software development, 2-7, 16, 18, 21-22, 22-37
  business system design, 28-32
  code generators, 32
  fourth-generation languages, 49
  implementation of system, 34
  interface generators, 31
  maintenance tools, 35-36
  PC packages, 49
  prototyping tools, 30-31
  quality control, 33-34
  requirements analysis, 26-28
  simulators, 31-32
  strategic systems planning, 25-26
  systems construction, 32
  testing, 33-34
  top-down development, 22-24
automated transformations, code generation, 66
automation, methodology providing opportunities for, 104

B

Bachman, Charlie, 28
Bang calculations, 294-295
baseline method paths, 282-283
BASIC, 6
BDM International, 3
Beer, Michael, 129
benefits analysis
  architecture development, 205-208
  strategic planning, 171-172
Benetton, 4
best-fit analysis, CASE tool selection, 254-257
Bhide, Sandhiprakash, 293
Bjorn-Andersen, Neils, 131
Boehm, Barry, 250, 311

Boone, Greg, 57-58
Booz-Allen Hamilton planning method, 178-179
bottom-up planning, 164
Boynton, 152
Bridges, William, 126, 142
budgeting
    project management, 325-326
    strategic planning, 157
business strategy planning (BSP), 178-179
business system design, 28-32
    interface generators, 31
    prototyping tools, 30-31
    simulators, 31-32
"buzzwords," CASE tool selection, 243

C

Carnegie Mellon University, 108
CASE Research Corporation, 58
CASE technology overview, x-xii, 15-18
CASE tool selection (see also evaluation methodology), 229-265
    best-fit analysis, 254-257
    candidate CASE tool identification, 245-247
    cost analysis, 237-239, 258-264
    custom-requirements analysis, 248
    customer-reference check, 253
    delivery platform evaluation, 241
    demonstration software copies, 252
    development task coverage, 240
    documentation, 250-251
    evaluation-team formation, 237
    expanding requirements, meeting needs, 247-248
    extendability issues, 242
    feature matrix, comparing features, 246
    flexibility issues, 242
    hardware assessment, 238
    in-depth needs analysis, 252
    information search, gathering information, 242-245
    information search, scanning products, 252
    information search, scope of search, 236
    integrating CASE into existing system, 241-242
    make vs. buy decisions, 275-276
    management support, 250
    prioritizing requirements, 248, 251
    productivity assessment, 260
    project management, 318-320

purchasing CASE tools, 264-265
qualification criteria, 239-240
request for proposal (RFP) and request for quotation (RFQ), 236, 257
resource allocation, 237-239
roles and responsibilities, 238
sensitivity analysis, 263-264
skills assessment, 238-239
spreadsheet analysis, 255-257
strategic-planning goals re-assessment, 248-249
targeting system-characteristics, 240-241
tool vs. tool "dogfights," 236-237
vendor demonstrations, 253-254
vendor questionnaires, 252-253
Case, Albert F. Jr., 117
change-plan development, 155
Chen, E.R., 28
clustering technique, project management, 203
COBOL, 6
code generators, 32, 39, 64, 66, 69, 247
    cross-platform system generation, 67
Cohen, Richard, 335
communication skills and techniques, 59-60, 121, 157-159, 327
competitive advantage, CASE usage, 2, 53
    integration/data-sharing applications, 79-83
    research consortiums, 9-14
complementary data analysis, 28
computer-aided programming (CAP) tools, 16
computer integrated manufacturing (CIM), 18
conferences, CASE tool selection, 244
consortium-type research, 9-14
construction of systems, 32
consultants, CASE tool selection, 244
contributors, methodology development, 104
Controlling Software Projects, 284
cost analysis, 69-70
    architecture development, 205-208
    CASE tool selection, 237-239, 258-264
    strategic planning, 171-172
Cotten, Ray, 75
Cougar, 335
Crawford, John, 274
cross-platform system generation, 67

cross-system product (CSP), 41, 67
Culbert, Samuel A., 126, 138

D

data dictionaries, 38, 39, 43
    active, 39
    dedicated, 39
    intelligent-repository, 39
    open-repository, 39
data flow diagrams, 27, 43
data models, 199, 247
data navigation diagrams, 28
databases, 38, 39, 75-76
    method-pool storage and retrieval, 113
Dawkins, Richard, 225
decision support systems (DSS), 74-75, 152
    cross-functional, 80-81
    warehouses of decision-support data, 89-90
DeMarco's Bang calculations, measurement of processes, 294-295
DeMarco, Tom, 28, 284
Department of Defense (DoD), research consortium, 12, 13
design concepts, 17, 28-32
    gestalt visualization techniques, 52
    interface generators, 31
    project management, 272-281
    prototyping tools, 30-31
    simulators, 31-32
DevelopMate, IBM, 41
Dickinson, Brian, 335
dictionaries (*see* data dictionaries)
directories, CASE tool selection, 244
DMBS (*see* databases; integration/data-sharing)
documentation, 61-62, 250-251, 287-288
Drucker, Peter, 7
DuPont Corporation, 3

E

Easel, 31, 68
Eisenstadt, Russell A., 129
electronic research services, CASE tool selection, 245
engineering, 16
    reengineering IS processes, 167-168, 195, 198, 200-202, 211-227
    reverse engineering, 22, 69
entity-relationship diagrams, 27
error analysis, 60-61
ESPRIT European research consortium, 9-10, 13, 40, 276

estimation, methodology development, 104-105
Eureka Software Factory, research consortium, 14
evaluation criteria/methodology, 101-102, 231-265, 357-371
  best-fit analysis, 254-257
  candidate CASE tool identification, 245-247
  cost analysis, 237-239, 258-264
  custom tools and utilities, 235-236
  custom-requirements analysis, 248
  customer-reference check, 253
  delivery platform evaluation, 241
  demonstration software copies, 252
  development task coverage, 240
  documentation, 250-251
  evaluation methodology, 231-265
  evaluation-team formation, 237
  expanding requirements, meeting needs, 247-248
  extendability issues, 242
  feature matrix, comparing features, 246
  flexibility issues, 242
  hardware assessment, 238
  in-depth needs analysis, 252
  information search, gathering information, 242-245
  information search, scanning products, 252
  information search, scope of search, 236
  integrating CASE into existing system, 241-242
  interfacing various CASE products, 232-235
  management support, 250
  prioritizing requirements, 248, 251
  productivity assessment, 260
  purchasing CASE tools, 264-265
  qualification criteria, 239-240
  request for proposal (RFP) and request for quotation (RFQ), 236, 257
  resource allocation, 237-239
  roles and responsibilities, 238
  scope of projects, 232-235
  sensitivity analysis, 263-264
  skills assessment, 238-239
  spreadsheet analysis, 255-257
  strategic planning goals re-assessment, 248-249
  targeting system-characteristics, 240-241
  tool vs. tool "dogfights," 236-237
  vendor demonstrations, 253-254
  vendor questionnaires, 252-253
Evans, Michael, 268, 286
extendability issues, CASE tool selection, 242

F

Fabrycky, W.J., 229, 274
feasibility studies
  architecture development, 205-208
  strategic planning, 171-172
Finkelstein, Clive, 319
flexibility issues
  CASE tool selection, 242
  project management, 273-274
Ford Aerospace and Communications Corp., 3
Foundation, 67
Freeman, Peter, 211
functionality, CASE tools, 21-22

G

Gane-Sarson analysis, 28
gestalt visualization techniques, 52
Gibson, Cyrus, 123
Gilb, Tom, 62, 147, 280
goal setting, 187-192
  criticality ranking of goals, 192-193
  documentation of objectives, 281-282
  methodology/methodology support, 99-100, 111, 274-275
  project management, 312, 313-315, 317-318
  refining goals, reengineering IS processes, 222-223
  strategic planning of IS systems, 165-175
  unifying IS goals with corporate goals, 165-167
graphics, 6-7
"grassroots" change-transition-implementation of CASE, 129-130

H

Haas, Robert, 131, 187
hardware assessment, CASE tool selection, 238
Harley-Davidson Company, 4
Hartford Insurance Company, 274
Hatley-Pirbhai analysis, 28
Hector, 276
Henkoff, Ronald, 214
Hopper, Max, 5
Humphrey, Watts, 95, 305
HyperCard, 31, 68

I

IBM, 30, 67, 112, 234, 240, 276
implementation of CASE tools, 8-9, 34, 68, 117-149
  announcing CASE implementation plans, 138-141
  career-counseling for employees, 137-138
  "CASE-as-punishment" perceptions, 135
  change-plan development, 155
  changes faced by specific jobs/roles, 120
  communications, 121, 157-159
  contingency plans, 140
  current problem evaluations, 131
  disclosing possible problems during transition, 139-140
  easing into change: big plans, baby steps, 133-134
  employee-input and management support, 130-131, 132-133, 143
  empowerment concepts, 143
  expense, 69-70
  flexibility in transition/implementation planning, 133, 142-143
  incentives for use, 138
  information flow, 144-145
  installation of CASE tools, 339-341
  integrating disparate projects, 343-344
  JAD concepts, 147-148
  management support, 140
  middle management roles, 144
  nondirective, bottom-up changes, "grassroots" change, 129-130
  personal benefits of CASE use stressed, 134-138
  PERT chart representation, 156
  political skills changes, 121-122
  poor-fit to company/organization, 70-71
  principles and guideline development, 131-132
  quick-result CASE tools, 134
  realignment/reorientation of jobs and people, 126
  reorganization of corporate structure, 335-338
  research and development, 145-146
  risks/risk management, 157-159
  rollout plan development, 338-339
  sequencing and selecting CASE projects, 341-343
  shared-vision development for entire organization, 130-134
  short-term uncertainties, 71-72
  slow-downs in preliminary phase of use, 71

implementation of CASE tools (*cont.*)
  staff involvement in planning, 168-170
  strategic planning steps, 155-157, 341-343
  symbolic activities, 141
  task force formation, 146-148
  technical skill changes, 120-121
  technological advances, planning, 168
  training programs, 71, 136-138
  transitioning into CASE use, 125-130, 141-142, 157
In Search of Excellence, 146
information architectures (*see also* architecture development), 5-6, 162
information engineering facility (IEF), 64, 67, 135, 241, 294
information engineering methodology, 26
information management, 160-161
information resource infrastructures, 162
information strategy planning (ISP), 178-180
information systems (IS)
  architecture design, 5-6
  benefits analysis, 171-172
  challenges facing IS organizations, 50
  cost assessment, 171-172
  feasibility studies, 171-172
  information-based organizations, 7-8
  organizational structures:matrices, task forces, etc., 49
  poor-fit of CASE to organizational structure, 70-71
  prioritization of projects, 170-171
  reengineering processes, 167-168, 195, 198, 200-202, 211-227
  staff involvement in planning, 168-170
  strategic planning's importance, 153
  strategic systems, 4-5
  technological advances, implementation and plan, 168
  unifying corporate goals with IS goals, 165-167
information-based organizations, 7-8
Inmon, William, 89
inputs, methodology development, 103
installation of CASE tools, 339-341
integrated CASE (ICASE) tools, 19-20, 90-91

centralization/distribution of data, 54
integration/data-sharing applications, 79
repositories, 43
integrated computing environments (ICE), 20-21
integrated product support environments (IPSE), 20
integration/data-sharing, 49, 73
  administration/management of data and processes, 91
  barriers to full integration, 83-86
  bridge programs to provide connectivity, 74
  centralization/distribution of data, 54, 74-76, 152
  common or duplicated data, 81
  coordination of implementation processes, 87-89
  cost of developing integrated system, 82-83
  data connectivity level, 78
  DBMS software limitations, 86
  decision support systems (DSS), 74-75
  decision support systems, cross-functional, 80-81
  decision support systems, warehouses of information, 89
  end-user development, 85
  funding/financial resource distribution problems, 84-85
  greedy use/nonessential demand for data, 84
  hardware connectivity level, 78
  incentives for integration, 92
  integrated CASE (ICASE) tools, 79, 90-91, 241
  integration levels, 77-79
  integration of data and processes, 76-77
  integration using central database, 75-76
  ownership-of-data questions, 83-84
  process connectivity level, 78
  productivity enhancements, 79
  repository services, 38
  reusable software and processes, libraries, 81-82
  "ripple-effect" of changes to data in integrated system, 74
  stages of integration, 92-93
  strategic planning: data and processes, 87
  strategies for creating integrated systems, 86-92
  technological limitations of systems, 85-86
Intellect, 68

interface generators, 31
iterative methodology, 102-103

J

JAD concepts, 147-148
Johnson, James R., 124, 131

K

Kidder, Tracy, 323
Knowledgeware, 44
Kumar, Kuldeep, 131

L

language development, 6-7, 49
Le Quesne, P. N., 118, 134
Learmonth & Burchett Management Systems Inc. (LBMS), 43
learning curve for CASE usage, 65, 105
Lederer, Albert L., 165
Levi Strauss & Company, 4, 5, 44, 131, 187
LeviLink system, 4, 5
libraries, software and processes, 81-82, 65, 66-67, 69
life cycles, 22
Loper, Michael, 89

M

Macintosh, 30, 31
maintenance tools, 35-36, 64
Making Software Engineering Happen, 226
management support, 51, 53-57, 140, 152
  CASE tool selection, 250
  centralization/distribution of data, 54
  integrated systems: data and processes, 91
  managing CASE repositories, 344-346
  process control, 56
  project management, 56-57, 322
  project-boundary clarification, 55-56
  staff involvement in planning, 168-170
ManagerView, 41
Martin, James, 117, 160, 317, 319
materials requirements planning (MRP), 205-206
matrix organizations, 49
maturity framework, methodology development, 108
MCC Corporation, research consortium, 12-13
McDonnell Douglas, 235
McDonough, John J., 126, 138

measurement of processes, 46, 291-304
  analyzing results, 302-303
  collection processes, simplicity of collection, 297-300
  comparisons to current environment, 294-295
  current vs. past projects comparisons, 300-302
  DeMarco's Bang calculations, measurement of processes, 294
  determining processes for measurement, 294
  effectiveness measurements, 302
  goal-based measurements, 295-297
  metrics program development, 292-293
  reviewing measurement procedures, 303-304
  simplicity of measurement program, 297
  staffing, 293
  starting the measurement program, 293
Mendelow, Aubrey L., 165
metamodels, 38, 42-43
method companionship, 44
method pools (*see also* methodology/methodology support), 95, 109-116, 267-289
  consultants/external support, 114-115
  DBMS systems for storage and retrieval, 113
  gathering and storing information, 113
  management system prototype, 349-355
  method paths, 112
  objectives vs. deliverables, 111
  programming process architecture (PPA), 112
  publishing text-based methodologies, 113
  Software Development Assistant, AT&T, 112
  training for use, 114
methodology/methodology support
methodology/methodology support, 16, 21, 22, 43-45, 95-116, 267-289
  alternative method selection, 285-286
  approach to planning, 271
  automated method pools, 114
  automation opportunities, 104
  baseline method path identification, 282-283
  benefits of good methodology, 96
  building the method pool, 268
  CASE use complementary to methodology, 97
  comprehensiveness of planning, 275
  consultants/external support, 114-115
  contributors to planning, 104, 271
  customized vs. SDLC-based, 98
  database system for storage/retrieval, 113
  designing method pool, 272-281
  documentation of objectives, 281-282, 287-288
  estimation guidelines, 104-105
  evaluation criteria, 101-102
  fitting CASE tool to methodology, 98-99
  flexibility issues, 273-274
  functionality of method pool, 277, 279
  gathering and storing information, 113
  goal setting, 274-275
  incremental delivery of results, 277, 280-281
  inputs description, 103
  interaction of components in methodology, 106
  iterative vs. discrete methods, 102-103
  make vs. buy decisions, 275-276
  maturity frameworks, 108
  method companionship, 44
  method paths, finding, 283-285
  method pools (*see* method pools)
  objectives statement, 99-100, 111
  past-experience utilization, 105
  products description, 100-101
  project planning, 270-272
  publishing text-based methodologies, 113
  reviewing methods, 288-289
  scheduling, 272
  scope of project, 270-272
  selectors of methodology, 44-45
  simplicity of design, 272-273
  software development life cycle (SDLC), 56, 97-98
  structure of method pool, 276-277
  structured analysis, 43
  tasks and methods, 102-103
  techniques, importance, 106-109
  training for use of method pool, 114
  validation techniques, 103
metrics program development, 292-293
Microdynamics, 75

N
NEC Corporation, 18
Nolan, Richard, 123
Nomura Securities, 3
Norman, Ronald J., 137
NRI & NCC Company, 3

O
object-oriented programming, 64
objectives (*see* goals)
open repositories 40-41
organizational structure
  architecture development issues, 182-185
  reorganization for CASE implementation, 335-338
organizational structures
  guidelines and principles development, 187
  information-based organizations, 7-8
  matrix, task force, project teams, 49
  poor fit of CASE, 70-71
  productivity vs. change, 64
Osborne, David J., 135
outsourcing vs. quality control, 59

P
Pact standards, 41
Peters, Tom, 133, 146
Phipps, John, 75
pilot projects (*see* project management)
planning (*see* strategic planning)
Plauger, P.J., 329
Plott, Curtis, 331
portable common tool environment (PCTE), 40-41
Pressman, Roger, 117, 226, 285, 294, 331
Price, Paul, 96
principles and guidelines development
  architectural development, 187
  implementation stage, 131-132
Principles of Software Engineering Management, 280
prioritizing projects, 170-171, 208-209
Pro*Kit, 235
process control, 56
process decomposition diagrams, 27
process dependency diagrams, 27
process maturity framework, 226
process redesign, CASE usage, 5
product directories, 373-374
productivity, 2, 3, 18, 50-51, 58-59, 62-68, 96, 167

productivity (*cont.*)
  abstract specifications, 67-68
  automated transformations (code generation), 66
  CASE tool selection, 260
  changes to software environment vs., 63
  cross-platform system generation, 67
  effort redistribution using CASE, 64-65
  "housekeeping" chores of development, 67-68
  integration/data-sharing, impacts, 79
  larger developer base accessible, 68
  learning curve for CASE, 65
  motivation of employees, 68
  organizational-structure changes, 64
  reusable software, libraries, 65, 66-67
products, methodology development, 100-101
programmer workbenches, 20
programming process architecture (PPA), 112
progress monitoring, project management, 327
project management (*see also* management support), 21, 22, 45-46, 56-57, 69, 226-227, 305-330
  alternative method selection, 285-286
  approach selection, 271
  architecture development preliminaries, 199, 203
  baseline method path identification, 282-283
  benefits analysis, 205-208
  "Big Brother" syndrome, 124
  boundary of project, clarification, 55-56
  budgeting, 325-326
  business experts, 322
  CASE specialists, 321-322
  clustering techniques, 203
  communications, 327
  comprehensiveness of planning, 275
  contributors to planning, 271
  cost assessment, 205-208
  designing method pool, 272-281
  disparate-project integration, 343-344
  documentation of objectives, 281-282, 287-288
  enjoyable projects, utilizing characteristics of, 329
  feasibility pilots, 306
  feasibility studies, 205-208
  flexibility issues, 273-274
  full-cycle pilots, 306-307
  goal setting, 274-275, 312, 313-315, 317-318
  guidelines for analysis project, 203-205
  incremental delivery of results, 277, 280-281
  integrating pilot projects to ongoing projects, 309-311
  live pilots, 307-308
  make vs. buy decisions, 275-276
  management support, 322
  matching pilot project to situation, 308-309
  method paths, finding, 283-285
  methodology selection, 270-272, 318-320
  monitoring progress, 327
  prioritization, 170-171, 208-209
  process measurement, 46
  progressive monitoring of progress, 327
  project manager, 320-321
  project-plan drafting, 185
  publicizing successful projects, 329-330
  quality control, 327-328
  resource allocation, 210
  reviewing methods, 288-289
  risk management, 327-328
  scheduling, 272, 323-326
  scope of project, 232-235, 270-272, 312, 315-317, 318
  selecting and sequencing CASE-based projects, 341-343
  successful projects, defining success, 311, 328-329
  successful projects, publicizing success, 329-330
  task scheduling, 46
  team formation, 320-323
  tool selection, 318-320
  transition planning, 322-323
  workload distribution, 325
project manager roles, 320-321
project teams, 49
prototyping, 30-31, 64, 69, 102
pseudocode, 28, 102
PTD Consulting, 96
purchasing CASE tools, 264-265

Q

quality control, 22, 33-34, 51, 57-62, 96, 327-328
communications improvement between developer/user, 59-60
documentation, 61-62
error analysis and control, 60-61
outsourcing issues, 59

R

rationale development in strategic plans, 52
reengineering IS processes, 167-168, 195, 198, 200-202, 211-227
  analysis methods, 218-220
  CASE usage, 212-214
  charting processes for reengineering, 215-217
  current-methods assessment, 225-226
  essential-processes identification, 223-224
  evolving new methods, 225
  goals refinement, 222-223
  needs analysis, 211-212, 214-227
  project identification, 226-227
  requirements-analysis steps, 223-226
  researching new methods, 224-225
  strategic-plan development, 217-218
  structured analysis, 219
  team development, 220-222
repository services, 21-22, 38-42, 69
  code generators, 39
  data dictionaries, 38-39
  integrated CASE (ICASE) tools, 43
  management and utilization, 344-346
  open repositories, 40-41
  security control, 41-42
  version-control tools, 41
request for proposal (RFP)/request for quotation (RFQ), 236, 257-258
requirements analysis, 26-28
research and development, implementation, 145-146
research consortiums, 9-14
resistance to CASE implementation, 8-9, 68, 71, 117-149
  automation fears, 123-125
  "Big Brother" syndrome, 124
  career-counseling, 137-138
  "CASE-as-punishment" perception, 135
  changes faced by specific jobs/roles, 120
  competence questions, loss of abilities, 123
  cynics and careerists, 126

easing into change: big plans, baby steps, 133-134
employee-input to counteract resistance, 130-131
empowerment concepts to counteract resistance, 143
formalities, discomfort with conforming, 123
incentives, 138
information flow questions, 144-145
interpersonal communications changes, 121
letting employees choose roles, 132-133
loss-of-identity issues, 122
middle management roles, 144
nondirective, bottom-up changes, "grassroots" change, 129-130
perceived threat of CASE implementation, 140
political skills changes, 121-122
professional freedom issues, 135-136
realignment/reorientation of jobs and people, 126
stressing personal benefits of CASE, 134-138
technical skill changes, 120-121
training programs, 136-138, 143
transitional process to ease resistance, 125-126, 141-142
"victim-of-change" perceptions, 124-125
resource allocation
architecture development, 210
CASE tool selection, 237-239
strategic planning, 172-173
reusable software (*see* libraries, software)
reverse engineering, 22, 69
risk management, 157-159, 327-328
rollout plans, 338-339
Rosenthal, Stephen R., 242
Ross, Rony, 311
Rubin, Howard, 110, 291

S

SABRE system, 4, 5
Salzman, Harold, 242
scheduling, 155, 272, 323-326
security control, 41-42
selectors, methodology, 44-45
sensitivity analysis, CASE tool selection, 263-264
sharing data (*see* integration/data-sharing)
SIGMA Japanese research consortium, 11, 13
simulators, 31-32, 69

SISP planning, 178-180
skills assessment, CASE tool selection, 238-239
software development (*see* automated software development)
software development assistant, AT&T, 112
software development life cycle (SDLC), 56, 97-98
Software Engineering Institute, 108, 226, 305
Software Factory, The, 268
Soul of a New Machine, The, 323
Spector, Bert, 129
spreadsheet analysis, CASE tool selection, 255-257
StarSys Inc., 335
state-transition diagrams, 28
strategic planning, 4-5, 25-26, 51-53, 69, 151-175
architecture development, 159-165
benefits analysis, 171-172
Booz-Allen Hamilton planning method, 178-179
budgeting, 157
business strategy planning (BSP), 178-179
CASE tool selection, 248-249
change-plan development, 155
competitive advantage, 53
context of plan, importance of, 173-175, 180
cost assessment, 171-172
criticality ranking of goals, 192-193
feasibility studies, 171-172
framework of IS planning, 162-163
gestalt visualization techniques, 52
goal setting, 165-175, 187
guidelines and principles development, 187
implementation of CASE, 155-157, 341-343
information management, 160-161
information strategy planning (ISP), 178-180
information systems (IS), importance of planning, 153
integrated systems: data and processes, 87
levels of overall planning, pyramidical structure, 154
major steps for CASE planning, 155
needs assessment: how much planning do you need?, 163

PERT chart representing CASE-implementation plan, 156
planning-method selection, 178-180
prioritizing projects, 170-171
project plan drafting, 185
rationale development, 52
reengineering IS processes, 167-168, 195, 198, 200-202, 211-227
resource allocation, 172-173, 210
risk management, 157-159
scheduling, 155
SISP methodology, 178-180
staff involvement in planning, 168-170
team/committee formation, 186-187
technological advances, implementation and planning, 168
top-down vs. bottom-up, 164
transitioning into CASE use, 157, 173
unifying IS goals with corporate goals, 165-167
structured analysis, 28-29, 43, 64, 69, 219
structured informations strategy planning (SISP), 4-5
suppliers/manufacturers, 373-374
Synnott, William, 165
Systems Engineer tools, 43

T

task forces, 49, 146-148
task scheduling, 46
tasks, methodology development, 102-103
teams and committees, 186-187, 220-222, 320-323
technological advances, implementation and planning, 168
technology architecture, 162
testing tools, 22, 33-34, 64, 69
Texas Instruments, 64, 67, 134-135, 241, 294
toolkits, CASE, 19
top-down development concepts, 22-24
top-down planning, 164
training programs, 8-9, 68, 71, 136-138, 143, 331-346
ad hoc training, 334-335
developing training programs, 331-334
informal training programs, 334-335

training programs (*cont.*)
  internal vs. external training, 332-334
  knowledge-sharing groups, 335
  methodology/method pool use, 114
  organizing for CASE implementation, cooperative development, 335
  rollout plans, 338-339
  sequence of training steps, 335
  transitioning into CASE use, 125-120, 141-142, 157-159, 173, 322-323, 346-347

U

user manuals (*see* documentation)

V

validation techniques, methodology development, 103
vendor questionnaires, CASE tool selection, 252-253
vendors, CASE tool selection, 244
version-control tools, 41

W

Wallace, Robert H., 306
Ward-Mellor analysis, 28
warehouse concept, decision-support data, 89-90
Warnier-Orr analysis, 28
Waterman, Robert, 146
Weinberg, Gerald, 147

Y

Yourdon, Ed, 28

Z

Zachman, John, 159
Zawacki, 335
Zmud, 152
Zuboff, Shoshana, 7, 84, 124, 135, 147